Advanced Database Techniques

MIT Press Series in Information Systems
Michael Lesk, editor

*Nested Transactions: An Approach to Reliable Distributed
Computing*
J. Eliot B. Moss, 1985

Advanced Database Techniques
Daniel Martin, 1986

Peter Denning, consulting editor, computer science books

Advanced Database Techniques

Daniel Martin

The MIT Press
Cambridge, Massachusetts
London, England

This book was originally published as *Techniques avancées pour bases de données,* ©
1985 by BORDAS, Paris, France.

This book was set in Times Roman by Achorn Graphic Services and printed and
bound by Halliday Lithograph in the United States of America.

Library of Congress Cataloging-in-Publication Data

Martin, Daniel, ingénieur I.D.N.
  Advanced database techniques.

  (MIT Press series in information systems)
  1. Data base management.   I. Title.   II. Series.
  QA76.9.D3M349   1986   005.74   85-24019
  ISBN 0-262-13215-X

Contents

Series Foreword   xvii

How to Read This Book   xix

Acknowledgment   xxi

1   AN OVERVIEW OF DATABASE MANAGEMENT

1.1   Introduction   1

1.1.1   Purpose of a Database   1

    1.1.1.1   A Database Provides a Means for Answering All Questions   1

    1.1.1.2   A Database Provides a Means for Horizontal Integration   2

    1.1.1.3   A Database Provides a Means for Vertical Integration   3

    1.1.1.4   Using a DBMS Improves the Performance of the Data Processing (DP) Department   4

    1.1.1.5   A Data Dictionary Is a Benefit in Itself in Some Cases   5

1.1.2   Definition of a Database   5

1.1.3   When Is a Database Required? Subject Overview   7

    1.1.3.1   Application Development Ease and Speed   7

    1.1.3.2   Application Evolution Ease: Program-to-Data Independence   8

    1.1.3.3   Unpredictable Queries: Completeness   8

    1.1.3.4   Integrity, Backup, and Restore Capabilities (Multitasking)   9

    1.1.3.5   Security   9

    1.1.3.6   Improved Horizontal/Vertical Integration and Communication   10

1.1.4   Database Requirements by Application Area   10

    1.1.4.1   Business DP and Performance Considerations   10

    1.1.4.2   Management Information Systems (MISs)   11

    1.1.4.3   Personal Databases   12

    1.1.4.4   Industrial and Scientific Applications   12

1.2   Key Steps of a Database Project   13

1.2.1   Preliminary Functional Specifications   13

1.2.2   Detailed Functional Specifications   18

1.2.2.1	Contents of the Detailed Functional Specification	19
1.2.2.2	Appoint Members of a Functional Specifications Group	20
1.2.2.3	Obtain Future User Agreement	21
1.2.2.4	Comments	21
1.2.3	Documenting Acquisition Requirements for Hardware and DBMS	22
1.2.4	Choosing DBMS and Hardware	24
1.2.5	Documenting Project Plan, Costs, and Risks	25
1.2.6	Designing File Architecture	26
1.2.6.1	Derive the Conceptual Schema from the Data Dictionary	26
1.2.6.2	Derive File Access and Relationship Paths from Processing	27
1.2.6.3	Use AREA-Type Data Grouping When Available	27
1.2.6.4	Calculate DBMS Load at Peak Usage	27
1.2.7	Designing Program Architecture	27
1.2.8	Writing, Testing, and Documenting the Programs	28
1.2.9	Initial Database Loading, Parallel Running, and Testing	28
1.2.10	Writing the Documentation for Users and the DBA	29
1.2.11	Initiating the DBA Function and Starting Daily Use	29
1.3	**Database Fundamentals**	29
1.3.1	Views	29
1.3.1.1	Single-Level View	31
1.3.1.2	Multilevel View	31
1.3.2	The First Three Schemas of a Database	33
1.3.2.1	Data Fields and Data Groups	33
1.3.2.2	Data Existence Constraints	33
1.3.2.3	Conceptual Schema	35
1.3.2.4	Physical Schema	35
1.3.2.5	The External Schemas or Subschemas	36
1.3.3	Definition of a Relation (Static, Dynamic)	36
1.3.3.1	Relationships: 1-to-N, 1-to-1, N-to-P	39
1.3.3.2	Relational Model	40
1.3.3.3	Normal Forms of a Relation: Fourth and Other Normal Forms	41

	1.3.3.4	Physical Implementation of a Relational Database	44
1.3.4	Relational Algebra		45
	1.3.4.1	Defining a Relation in the Data Dictionary	45
	1.3.4.2	Evolution of a Database	45
	1.3.4.3	Adding, Deleting, and Modifying Tuples	45
	1.3.4.4	Selecting Tuples That Satisfy a Set of Constraints	46
	1.3.4.5	Projecting a Relation to Remove Unwanted Attributes	47
	1.3.4.6	Joining Two Relations, Associating Matching Tuples	48
	1.3.4.7	Joining Master and Event Files to Avoid the Connection Trap	50
	1.3.4.8	Building the Union of Two Relations	51
	1.3.4.9	Eliminating Duplicate Tuples in a Relation	51
	1.3.4.10	Building the Difference of Two Relations	51
	1.3.4.11	The Dynamic Model of Data	51
1.3.5	Nonrelational Models: Comparisons with Relational Models		54
	1.3.5.1	The Hierarchical Model	56
	1.3.5.2	The Network Model	58
	1.3.5.3	The Entity-Relation Model	62
	1.3.5.4	The Master-Event Model	64
	1.3.5.5	Example: Education Database	65

2	**DETAILED SPECIFICATION: RELATIONAL TECHNIQUES**	
2.1	**MSD: A New Approach to Specification and Design**	70
2.1.1	Requirements for the DFSs of an Interactive Application	70
	2.1.1.1 DFSs Must Be Sufficiently Detailed	70
	2.1.1.2 Implications of Sufficiently Detailed Specifications	72
	2.1.1.3 A User-Oriented Approach: Scenarios and Dictionary	73
	2.1.1.4 The Need for a Relational Model	76
2.1.2	Results of the MSD Detailed Functional Specification Phase	77

2.1.3   Database Design Phase   78
2.1.4   Program Module Design Phase   79
2.1.5   Objections to the Detailed Specification Approach of
         MSD   80
2.1.6   Organization Prerequisites   81
2.1.7   Scenarios   82
2.1.8   Scenario Description Rules   83
2.1.9   Sample Scenarios   86

2.2   MSD Dictionary   89

2.2.1   Computer-Supported Dictionaries   89
2.2.2   The MSD Data Dictionary   90
         2.2.2.1   Identification Rules for Relations and
                    Attributes   90
         2.2.2.2   Attribute Slip   91
         2.2.2.3   Relation Slip   95
2.2.3   Other MSD Descriptions   99
         2.2.3.1   Screen Form and Report Layout Slips   99
         2.2.3.2   Co-Routine Slips   104
         2.2.3.3   Notes to the Programmer   108
         2.2.3.4   Transaction Slip   109
         2.2.3.5   View and Access/Relationship Path Slips   116

**2.3   Conclusions on Detailed Functional Specification
           Methods**   122

2.3.1   Information Systems   123
2.3.2   Transforming an Information System into a DP
         Database   125

**3   DATA REPRESENTATION, PACKING, AND
           PROTECTION**

3.1   Data Representation and Packing   128

3.1.1   Full-Length Storage   128
3.1.2   Representing Data with Codes   128
3.1.3   Vocabulary and Alphabet   129
3.1.4   Base   130

3.1.5   Data Packing in Remote Communications   132

3.1.6   Packing Entire Records Using Multiple Bases   132

3.1.7   Packing Using Multiple Words   137

3.1.8   When Is Data Packing Worthwhile?   140

3.1.9   Reducing the Cost of Packing: Bases 2^n 142

3.1.10   Special Representation Methods for Technical Data 143
          3.1.10.1   Continuous Data Streams   143
          3.1.10.2   Slow-Evolution Processes   144
          3.1.10.3   Coding by Exception   145
          3.1.10.4   Coding by Dictionary Rank   145
          3.1.10.5   Using Functions   145
          3.1.10.6   Suitable Data Manipulation Technique   146

3.2   **Access Security Protection**   147

3.2.1   Secret Packing (Encryption)   147

3.2.2   Dynamic Password   148

3.3   **Keyboard Input Protection**   149

3.4   **Protection of Stored and Transmitted Data**   154

3.4.1   Preliminary Requirements   154

3.4.2   Design Specifications of the Verification Code (VC) 155

3.4.3   Verification Codes Form a Group   156

3.4.4   Implementation   158

3.4.5   Conclusion: Protection Quality   159

4   **SELECTION IN A DATABASE: A COMPLETE
          DISCUSSION**

4.1   **Problem Summary**   160

4.2   **Selection Constraints**   160

4.3   **Horizontal Constraints**   160

4.3.1   Existence Constraints   160

4.3.2   Nonexistence Constraint   161

4.3.3   Existence in a Discrete Set   161

4.3.4   Nonexistence in a Discrete Set   161
4.3.5   An Attribute Verifies a Strict Comparison Constraint   161
4.3.6   An Attribute Verifies a Soft Constraint   162
        4.3.6.1   A Function of Constraints: The Overall
                  Distance   163
        4.3.6.2   Strict Constraint   164
        4.3.6.3   Soft Constraint   164
4.3.7   Minimum Difference Constraint   171
4.3.8   Alphanumeric Inclusion   171
4.3.9   Alphanumeric Inclusion with "Wild Card Characters"   172
4.3.10 Constraints on Virtual Attributes   172
4.3.11 Constraints on Integer Attributes   173

4.4   Vertical Constraints   173

4.4.1   Vertical Functions   174
4.4.2   Position Constraints   175
4.4.3   Soft Vertical Constraints   176

4.5   Selection Using Relational Algebra   176

4.6   Pattern Recognition   178

4.6.1   Definition and Application Areas   178
4.6.2   Extended Database Structures   179
4.6.3   Search Constraints   180
4.6.4   Database Manipulation for Pattern Recognition   180
4.6.5   Structure Definition Language (SDL) Concepts   182
        4.6.5.1   Element   182
        4.6.5.2   Domain   183
        4.6.5.3   Structure   184
        4.6.5.4   Link   184
        4.6.5.5   Rule   185
        4.6.5.6   Law   187
4.6.6   Image Pattern Recognition   187
        4.6.6.1   Global Recognition   188
        4.6.6.2   Detailed Recognition   188
        4.6.6.3   Light Gradient Technique   188
        4.6.6.4   Pattern Recognition with Varying Positions   189

5   DBMS TECHNIQUES AND DATABASE
         ARCHITECTURES

5.1   Features and Functions of a DBMS   191

5.1.1   Disk Space Management   192
5.1.2   File Access Management   193
5.1.3   File Linking   195
         5.1.3.1   One-to-One (1-TO-1) Relationships   196
         5.1.3.2   One-to-Many (1-TO-N) Relationships   196
         5.1.3.3   Many-to-Many (N-TO-P) Relationships   200
5.1.4   Data Dictionary Management   200
5.1.5   Application Program Interface   202
         5.1.5.1   Application Development Language Interface   203
         5.1.5.2   Standard DBMS Operations   208
         5.1.5.3   Insertion: Also Called Record Creation or
                    Record Addition   208
         5.1.5.4   Modification: Also Called Field Update   209
         5.1.5.5   Deletion   213
         5.1.5.6   Link Creation and Suppression   214
5.1.6   Program/Data Independence through Mapping   215
5.1.7   Program/Structure Independence Using Multilevel
         Views   216
5.1.8   Access Conflict and Deadlock Protection   217
         5.1.8.1   Access Locking   217
         5.1.8.2   Deadlocks and Dynamic Backout   218
         5.1.8.3   Undoing Multiple Transactions: Committing   219
5.1.9   Backup and Recovery   222
         5.1.9.1   Cold Restart   223
         5.1.9.2   Warm Restart   223
5.1.10   Data Restructuring Capabilities   224
5.1.11   Security   226
5.1.12   Database Administration   227
         5.1.12.1   Job Description   227
         5.1.12.2   DBA Personal Profile   228
         5.1.12.3   Installing the DBA   229
         5.1.12.4   Administration Effort, Budget, and Reporting   229
5.1.13   Application Portability   230

5.1.14   Data Query   232
5.1.15   Evolution Capabilities   235

5.2   File Structures   236

5.2.1   Files, Records, and Fields   236
5.2.2   Segments, Blocks, Buffers, and Areas   238
5.2.3   DBMS-to-Operating System File Interface   239
5.2.4   Sequential File   240
5.2.5   Direct (Random) Access File   242
5.2.6   Index Structures   243
         5.2.6.1   Primary and Secondary Indexes   245
         5.2.6.2   Sequential Index: Implementation Issues   246
         5.2.6.3   Hierarchical Index: Optimizing Index Block
                    Size   247
         5.2.6.4   Structure Consequences of Index Updating   250
         5.2.6.5   Indexing Performance Problems   254
5.2.7   Hash-Coding   256
         5.2.7.1   Principle of Hash-Coding   256
         5.2.7.2   Synonyms   257
         5.2.7.3   Overcoming Collision Problems   258
5.2.8   Bit-Inverted Files   265
5.2.9   List Structures: One-Way, Two-Way Rings   268
5.2.10   Dichotomy (Binary Search)   272
         5.2.10.1   Binary Tree (B-Tree)   273

5.3   One-to-Many (1-TO-N) Relationships and Links   275

5.3.1   Pointer + List   276
5.3.2   Secondary Indexing   278
5.3.3   Pointer Arrays   280
5.3.4   Hash-Coded Links   281

5.4   Extended Databases: Unstructured, Open Content   282

5.4.1   Purpose of an Extended Database   282
5.4.2   Definition of an Extended Database   283
5.4.3   Topics Discussed in This Section   284

5.4.4   Definition and Physical Storage of Data, Links, and
         Rules   284
         5.4.4.1   File Space Allocation   284
         5.4.4.2   Record Management: File System Hierarchy   285
         5.4.4.3   Definition and Representation of Links:
                    Vector Function   287
         5.4.4.4   Definition and Representation of Rules and
                    Laws   288
         5.4.4.5   Storage of Structures   289

5.4.5   Access by Element Content   289

5.4.6   Access by Structure (File Level, Database Level)   290 ·

5.4.7   Access by Structure and Content   291

5.4.8   Access Structure for Links and Lists   292

5.4.9   Access Structure for Rules   292

5.4.10   Structure Definition Language (SDL)   293
         5.4.10.1   Preliminary Definitions   293
         5.4.10.2   Element   294
         5.4.10.3   First Conclusions   296
         5.4.10.4   Structure   296
         5.4.10.5   Link   298
         5.4.10.6   Key   298
         5.4.10.7   Rule   299

5.4.11   Principles of Unstructured Data Recognition and
         Manipulation   299

6   OPTIMAL DATABASE IMPLEMENTATION
         TECHNIQUES

6.1   Computer Load Evaluation   300

6.1.1   Purpose   300

6.1.2   Benchmarking DBMS Performance   300
         6.1.2.1   Average Path Length   300
         6.1.2.2   Load of Each Type of DBMS Call   301
         6.1.2.3   Estimating the Average DBMS Call
                    Execution Time   302

6.1.3   Evaluating Computer Load from Specifications   304
         6.1.3.1   Number of DBMS Calls per File at Peak
                    Usage Hour   304

6.1.3.2   Total DBMS Load at Peak Usage Hour   305
6.1.3.3   Simulating the DBMS Response Times   306
6.1.3.4   Simulation Using a Running Model of the
          Application   308

6.2   Optimizing Access and Linking Structures   314

6.2.1   The Dynamic Schema (the Fourth Schema) of a
        Database   314
6.2.2   Qualitative Architecture Decisions   314
        6.2.2.1   Deriving Physical Files from Logical Files
                  and Accesses   315
        6.2.2.2   Areas and Clusters   317
        6.2.2.3   Situations Where a Sequential Index Is
                  Required   318
        6.2.2.4   Situations Where Direct Access Is Possible   319
        6.2.2.5   Situations Where a Bit Index Is Required   319
        6.2.2.6   Direct and Indirect Hashing   319
        6.2.2.7   File Linking Decisions   320
6.2.3   Quantitative Architecture Decisions   320
        6.2.3.1   Principles   320
        6.2.3.2   Divide the Database into Subdatabases   321
        6.2.3.3   Decide Which Access and Link Paths Are
                  Explicit/Implicit   322
        6.2.3.4   Calculate the Impact of Various Alternatives   323

6.3   The Functional Interface   326

6.3.1   Principle   326
6.3.2   Architecture   326
        6.3.2.1   Modules of the FI   326
        6.3.2.2   Application Program Interface (API)   328
        6.3.2.3   The Sequencer   331
        6.3.2.4   Attribute-Level Co-Routines   336
        6.3.2.5   Relation-Level Co-Routines   337
        6.3.2.6   Database-Level Co-Routines   337
        6.3.2.7   Interpretive Relational DBMS Interface   338
        6.3.2.8   Interfacing with Nonrelational,
                  Noninterpretive DBMSs   339
        6.3.2.9   The Views Catalog   340
        6.3.2.10 Multitasking, Uninterruptibility   341

6.3.2.11   Functional Journaling   343
6.3.2.12   Data Representation, Packing, and
           Encryption   343
6.3.2.13   Temporary Work Files   344
6.3.2.14   Virtual Attributes   344
6.3.2.15   The Functional Interface as a Package   345

6.3.3   Performance Issues   345

6.3.4   Conclusion: Pros and Cons of the FI Technique   346

6.3.5   Limited Functional Interfaces   348

6.4   The Decision Machine   349

6.4.1   Purpose   349

6.4.2   Principle   349
6.4.2.1   Parameters and Consequences of a Program
          Starting Decision   349
6.4.2.2   Schematic Operation of a Decision Machine   350

6.4.3   Architecture   351
6.4.3.1   Processing History File   351
6.4.3.2   Authorization File   352
6.4.3.3   Startup Queue   353
6.4.3.4   Startup Rules File   353
6.4.3.5   Rules Language   354
6.4.3.6   Modules of the Decision Machine   357

**7   RELATIONAL DBMS ORACLE (Product Review of
         Version 4: April 1985)**

7.1   Product Description   358

7.1.1   Relational Model   358

7.1.2   The SEQUEL Language   359

7.1.3   Completeness   360

7.1.4   Physical Model   360

7.1.5   Data Dictionary   361

7.1.6   Programmer Workbench   362

7.1.7   Application Language Interface   362

7.1.8   Direct Keyboard Interface   363

7.1.9   Portability   363

7.1.10 Linking Two ORACLE Sites: IMPORT/EXPORT and
        ORALINK   364
7.1.11 Documentation and Learning   364

7.2   The Case Study   365

7.2.1   Functional Specifications of the Test Application   365
7.2.2   Processing Times   366
7.2.3   Problem Areas   367
7.2.4   Limitations   368
7.2.5   Program Development Speed   369

7.3   Software License Policy and Prices   369

7.4   Conclusion   369

        Index   371

Series Foreword

In *Advanced Database Techniques*, Daniel Martin provides an excellent overview of databases and their use. Researchers, practitioners, and students looking for a way to understand many kinds of databases using a few powerful concepts should read this book. The classification of relational and navigational databases is simpler and includes more kinds of databases than the traditional division into relational, hierarchical, and network databases. The book is remarkable for its specific information about timing, sizes, and other practical matters. Its many examples and analogies, plus the clear writing, make it easy to use. In addition, this book goes beyond the core of database technology to talk about specification, testing, and other areas essential to problem solving but ignored in more abstruse works. It will repay both quick reading and longer study.

Michael Lesk

How to Read This Book

Readers with *considerable background* in database management and data processing (DP) in general may want to read this book in its natural order, starting with chapter 1. They will find useful information and valuable ideas and techniques in all chapters.

Readers with *some DP experience* but no database experience and those who wish to consider this as *a course in database management* can read section 1.1.2, next chapters 3, 4, and 5 (except section 5.4), and then chapters 1, 2, 6, and 7.

Readers mainly interested in *new ideas* can concentrate on section 1.3 and chapters 2, 3, 4, and 6, which contain many new, far-reaching concepts.

References to chapter, section, and subsection always begin with the chapter number: subsection 3 of section 2 of chapter 1 is numbered 1.2.3.

Acknowledgment

I would like to thank my friend Malcolm Stiefel for the superb proof-reading task he performed on this book. He corrected many language and spelling mistakes and suggested improvements to the readability of some complex technical paragraphs.

Malcolm is a Group Leader with the MITRE Corporation of Bedford, Massachusetts, with considerable background in DP. He contributes to a number of DP magazines and lectures in the United States and overseas. He also teaches a public course that I wrote based on this book at Integrated Computer Systems, an educational institution.

Advanced Database Techniques

1 An Overview of Database Management

1.1 Introduction

1.1.1 Purpose of a Database

Most computer users purchase a database management system (DBMS) to manage the disk files on their computers. They also call the collection of files a "database," because this name sounds better and more modern than just "files." In fact, the DBMS was not invented to replace the disk file management software of the computer's operating system.

All operating systems feature at least two file access modes: sequential and direct (file access methods are covered in detail in chapter 5). But many provide no other types of access and ignore such services as data dictionary management, use of query languages, access conflict protection, and backup-recovery. The DBMS is intended to solve those problems.

In addition, few programmers know how to design and implement the software required for such functions, and most companies would not provide the budget for such software developments, so the DBMS is a standard software solution purchased to replace the shortage of programmers or development funds.

In short, the DBMS is a necessary complement for management of files by people who are not satisfied with what the operating system provides. And because this complement is called a database management system, people feel free to call their files a database.

From a company's standpoint, a database is not the consequence of the use of a DBMS; it is an information and communication tool.

1.1.1.1 A Database Provides a Means for Answering All Questions

Many years ago companies had enough time, when a competitor came out with a new product that could threaten the company's own sales, to formulate an adequate response. Communications were slow enough to ensure slow market penetration, thus leaving time for an appropriate reaction. Generally, companies reacted slowly. Today reactions must be fast because communications are fast and powerful. Modern decisionmaking requires complete, accurate, and timely information for most people with responsibilities in such areas as finance, personnel, production, and marketing.

Activities such as international banking and transportation demand high-quality data. The daily work of physicians and scientists benefits from knowledge databases. The decisions of engineers rely on technical databases about spare parts. Historical data are needed for accurate prediction of future trends.

The value of the decisions that rely on facts from a database is often strategic; the entire future of a company may depend on a good product marketing decision. This is a far more important goal to a general manager than the management of files by some piece of software in the computer room. He is prepared to pay for a tool that will help him obtain the information to deal with big issues. He is not prepared to pay much for a tool to help his programmers supplement the capabilities of his computer, if the only result of such an investment is in the area of administrative data processing (invoicing, accounting, etc.).

For managers who have the power to decide, the primary motivation for installing a database is to facilitate decisionmaking. This implies *few* queries, perhaps one per week or per month for a general manager. It implies *unexpected* queries; no one can predict what exactly will be asked or when it will be asked. In general, however, the answer will not be required within a few seconds but within a few hours, and will probably bring about more questions. Giving a decisionmaker information makes him think, and then ask for more.

An operating system's file management capabilities do not include query facilities for managers, so a DBMS is required. But the database itself needs to abide by certain rules:

• To contain the answers to *all* potential questions, it must be exhaustive—that is, know everything about the subject.

• To contain accurate information, it must be *consistent;* no contradiction between two pieces of information can be accepted.

• To allow for the retrieval of vast amounts of data, it must be *structured*. The data must be organized in categories and groups with clearly defined meanings and interrelationships.

We shall use these necessary properties of a database to define it in section 1.1.2.

1.1.1.2   A Database Provides a Means for Horizontal Integration
In the old days, when computers ran exclusively in batch mode, each department of a company was an isolated user, sending data for key-

punching and processing to the computer and receiving thick listings in return. Whenever something was wrong or late, it was the computer's fault.

Blaming the computer was a way of life for large organizations, a way for each individual to protest against the sheer size, tyranny, and inhuman behavior of the working and living environment. Of course, people knew that the computer itself did not make mistakes, that human errors in programming, processing, or data supply were the origin of the defects; nevertheless, since each department interacted with the computer alone, all errors seemed to come from it.

Today large organizations access a database using terminals. The central database is common to all departments and updated permanently. As data are fed into it by a user, all other users can perceive the change of the information if they care to look at what is in the machine. Each user has a feeling for the progress of the work of other users, and associates each data element with the name of the person who supplies it; the impression of interacting with the computer alone has been replaced with the perception of participation in the daily work of an organization of people. *A shared database accessed via terminals provides horizontal integration.* People tend to communicate with other people more frequently and better, understand their problems, and participate in their efforts toward the common goals of the organization. Improving communication has become an issue for many organizations, and today this implies a shared database accessed via terminals.

Horizontal integration is not initially well accepted by all employees. Many people dislike others seeing what they are doing, when and how they are doing it, and what errors they make. Many people regard the association of some information with their name as an intrusion, an invasion of privacy. Even the possibility of viewing the work of others is not enough to offset the disadvantages of integration. Nevertheless, because decisions today must be made quickly, since improving the effectiveness of organizations demands integration, managers support it.

1.1.1.3 A Database Provides a Means for Vertical Integration

In a large organization, management cannot have a clear perception of daily small events. A general manager learns facts from reports made by another manager, who in turn receives reports from subordinates. This hierarchy is necessary, but it has an obvious drawback: managers tend to receive and use only abstract information, ignoring the human reality of problems. In turn, people in lower levels of the hierarchy perceive management as a distant deity, whose decisions are difficult to understand or even erroneous because the managers do not know the hard facts. Managers are afraid of receiving biased information from their subordinates, who are afraid of receiving poorly justified orders from upper management.

The presence of a database changes the picture to a certain extent. Whenever they need to verify small facts or compute a statistic based on all available information, managers can do the work via the database. They can access information directly if they wish, thus developing a better understanding of details and the corresponding work of their subordinates. If the accounting department is always late, a manager can better understand why by looking at the volume of postings and perceiving how fast they are entered into the computer; this information provides an understanding of the accountants' efforts.

In addition, everybody shares the same database, thus using the same information. This decreases the possibility of biased reports. Finally, whether the various levels of the hierarchy expect it or not, better vertical integration of the organization is achieved.

1.1.1.4   Using a DBMS Improves the Performance of the Data Processing (DP) Department
Because organizations today must respond quickly, the computer department must be able to provide results such as the following:

• Software development and maintenance must be fast, so that software availability does not impede the evolution of the company. Data dictionaries, programmers' workbenches, fourth-generation languages, prototyping tools, and other tools based on DBMSs will help achieve software development and maintenance speed.

• Data consistency must be ensured, no matter what failures occur in hardware, electric power, or humans; DBMS facilities and database administration will provide for that.

• Answering an unexpected question of a manager must be a matter of minutes or hours using the DBMS query language, not a matter of weeks writing a special program, if the DP department wants to appear useful to top management. Otherwise it appears as a necessary evil that helps with low-level administrative work.

• Protecting sensitive data against unauthorized access using DBMS features such as subschemas and encryption.

1.1.1.5   A Data Dictionary Is a Benefit in Itself in Some Cases

When many different types of data exist, two issues arise: knowing what information exists on a given subject and knowing the precise meaning, origin, and format of a given field.

For example, a personnel database may comprise as many as 1000 different fields for a given employee, to describe level of education, professional background, skills, and other qualities. Knowing what information is available is valuable. In addition, knowing what the exact meaning of *social benefits* is (definition, cost elements, eligibility rules) is important in order to make good use of the information, or simply to permit all people to mean the same thing when using the same words. All these definitions are part of the data dictionary.

1.1.2   Definition of a Database

The following definition satisfies the requirements and objectives that have just been described.

A database is a collection of information on a well-defined subject that is exhaustive, nonredundant, and structured.

Exhaustivity implies that the database contains all data about the subject. For example, a customer database contains all the customers and all the information on each individual customer. Exhaustivity is required to answer all potential questions about the subject.

Nonredundancy implies that no data element is stored twice: the database contains 100% of the information, but not 101%. This is required to ensure consistency. If the information is stored only once, it is correct or incorrect, but it cannot contradict itself. If it is stored more than once, chances are that one occurrence of a field will be updated, while another occurrence is not updated yet; queries can then yield contradictory results, possibly undermining the confidence of users. In addition, nonredundancy saves disk storage space.

Note that nonredundancy is not always easy to achieve and must sometimes be compromised. For example, a manufacturing database contains an item file and an order file. When a user queries the database to find the total value of the orders for a given item, he can access the order file, read the order value field for each order line of that item, and add up to make a total. This process can take time if the item has many outstanding order lines. If this type of query is likely to be frequent, a better approach is to maintain a total value field in each item record. Answering the query is then much faster, but the new field is redundant.

So, the first exception to the nonredundancy rule is made to satisfy speed or response time requirements.

In the previous manufacturing database, an order line does not logically need to have an item number field. Since the order lines of a given item are accessed after accessing the item's record and since the DBMS maintains interfile pointers to link each item with its order lines, an item number field is not required in each order line, because it would be redundant and unnecessary to the processing.

It is good practice, however, to have an item number field in each order line in case the pointers are lost and item-to-order relationships have to be reconstructed. DBMSs do lose pointers due to software errors, hardware malfunctions, or faulty user programming or processing.

Thus, the second exception to the nonredundancy rule is made to satisfy data recovery requirements.

In addition, some file accessing techniques do not use pointers. Hash-coding (discussed in chapter 5) can be a means of implementing an item-to-its-order-lines relationship using an item number field in each order line, without pointers. In this case, the presence of that field is not redundant; it is the means used for implementing the relationship.

Structuring the data implies storing them in such a manner as to make processing efficient. This statement has many implications; optimizing database architecture will be discussed in great detail in this book.

A *well-defined subject* is a set of data elements described in a data dictionary. By definition, a query is valid if (and only if) it relates to data described in the dictionary.

Potentially any question about a well-defined subject can be answered using the DBMS. From a database standpoint, such questions are *good* questions; questions requiring information outside the data dictionary are *bad* questions. We shall see in the section covering selection that a relational DBMS can answer any good question *without programming*, if the question does not imply pattern recognition.

It is good practice not to mix different unrelated subjects in the same database. Inventory control and payroll, for example, must reside in different databases. Otherwise the user and the computer may have difficulty retrieving the information in this artificially complex base. The user may have problems finding the fields he is interested in if the data dictionary is too big. This is why, in addition to separating subjects in different databases, it is good practice to use subschemas that restrict the data available to a specific user. The fewer the fields, the better the user's understanding.

1.1.3 When Is a Database Required? Subject Overview

A database is required when one of the following advantages counts.

1.1.3.1 Application Development Ease and Speed
The data dictionary helps document the specifications of the application, avoiding inconsistent and duplicated data definitions in programs.

Programs do not have to perform data management. Instead they use the DBMS as a sort of secretary, to store and retrieve information in a transparent mode. This reduces their size considerably while making their structure simpler. As a result, programming speed is considerably increased.

Complex technical problems are eliminated:

• *File access management.* In addition to single-file accessing, modern and relational DBMSs provide *views*, which are a means of accessing in a single operation fields located in several interrelated files. The structure of the database, as the program sees it, appears to be single-file and seems to contain only those fields required by the program, which makes programming logic much simpler.

• *Powerful data retrieval with multiple search criteria.*

• *Access conflict and deadlock protection.* This prevents two programs from causing trouble when accessing the same record(s).

• *Undoing multiple transactions.* When a program has performed a succession of database updates, this feature makes it possible to confirm them all or to "undo" them, restoring the database as it was before the updates.

• *Journaling for backup, recovery, and restructuring.*

• *Access security.*

• *Disk storage space economy* through the elimination of trailing blanks in alphabetic fields and data packing.

1.1.3.2   Application Evolution Ease: Program-to-Data Independence

Over time, organizations change, their processing requirements change, and their data change. Program adjustments are required to cope with the changes or simply to fix errors.

When an application is complex, featuring many data fields used in many programs, adding a new field to an existing file or changing a field may cause unexpected damage in some programs if each program sees the complete contents and layout of each file it accesses. As a minimum, the program has to be recompiled and relinked.

Using a DBMS, each program sees only its own *subschema* of the database, only the fields it needs. Thus when a file layout is changed, only the programs that use the new or altered fields are concerned. This minimizes the consequences of the change, making evolution easier, faster, and less error prone.

Indeed program-to-data independence was considered so important a few years ago that it was one of the main reasons for using a DBMS. For instance, a database containing test results of a research process can never have a fixed structure and contents. Each week new types of fields are added to existing files or new types of files or new interfile relationships are created, linking related results. In this case, ease of evolution is the most important software purchasing criterion, and a truly relational DBMS would be chosen regardless of its processing performance.

1.1.3.3   Unpredictable Queries: Completeness

Managers and scientists using research information databases need to be able to ask questions for which no specific program has been prepared. The modern tools available for that purpose are relational DBMSs, featuring sophisticated query capabilities, using a special language or a fill-in-the-blanks approach to describe the question and output requirements.

Programmers can also benefit from the possibility of querying the database to check the effect of a program suspected of malfunction.

The minimum requirements for a relational DBMS to achieve *completeness* (the ability to answer any good question without programming) is the following set of "relational algebra" verbs: Select, Join, Project, Union, and Difference. These verbs are defined in section 1.3.4. In practice the ability to eliminate duplicate tuples (if any) is also necessary.

1.1.3.4   Integrity, Backup, and Restore Capabilities (Multitasking)
When a computer configuration features true multitasking, with several batch and interactive programs running concurrently, excellent protection is required in case of power failure, hardware breakdown, or software error. In practice, the whole configuration must be able to restart execution in a few minutes, without losing the data that were entered or updated that day. The DBMS has an important role to play in that respect because the software required to ensure adequate protection and quick restart is very complex indeed, too complex (or too expensive) for a user to develop.

1.1.3.5   Security
When confidential data are stored, access must be granted only with caution, to protect it in three ways:

1. Make sure that each user or program gains access only to the authorized files and fields. That is achieved through the use of subschemas managed by the DBMS and passwords managed by the database administrator (DBA).

2. Make sure that each user's execution rights are limited to well-defined operations within his subschema: Read, Write, and Append, for example, may be restricted to certain data.

3. Make sure that unauthorized access to the physical data by a programmer (directly on disk, during a data transfer operation or telecommunication, or by removing a storage medium such as a magnetic tape) will still not allow the user to decipher truly sensitive parts of it; that is achieved with encryption, described in chapter 3.

1.1.3.6 Improved Horizontal/Vertical Integration and Communication
This subject was discussed in 1.1.1.2 and 1.1.1.3.

1.1.4 Database Requirements by Application Area

1.1.4.1 Business DP and Performance Considerations
Business data processing is still the most important computer usage
area today. The reasons for using database management are those
covered in the previous section.

One important application area cannot even be considered today
without database management: production scheduling and control. The
innumerable files required for production scheduling, with their dozens
of interfile relationships, the files required for the bill of materials, and
the history files required to monitor the various shop activities, make
up too complex a structure to be handled without a DBMS.

Databases have been in use since 1965; the technique is just about as
old as the COBOL language itself. Unfortunately, early DBMSs have
gained a reputation for inefficiency in terms of processor load, memory
size, and disk storage space.

Indeed, using a DBMS instead of the operating system's file access
capabilities costs more resources. For example, on IBM mainframes
under DOS/VS, a file access using VSAM/RRDS (a relative record
access) requires about 2500 assembly language instructions to be processed. The path length is said to be 2500. In the same environment,
using DL/1 (IBM's DBMS) to do the same thing will require a path
length of 9800, almost four times as much. In terms of memory size
requirements, DL/1 requires about 400KB of virtual memory space
during the process of opening a file under DOS/VS and about 700KB
under IMS in an MVS system. Version 4 of ORACLE, released in
September 1984, on an IBM/PC, requires at least 512KB of main memory and a 10MB Winchester disk to run and runs faster with more main
memory.

Much progress has been made in eliminating software inefficiencies
since 1965, yet database management will continue to require more
hardware resources than the use of standard files, for three reasons.

First, many users design poor architectures for their databases, due
to their complete ignorance of many important rules of efficient database design. Generally they learn to design a database from the database software vendor, who teaches how to describe the structure of the

data by data dictionary utility and how to access it from a high-level language. No teaching of efficient design is available, and no benchmark information concerning structure and processing alternatives is provided. Learning database management from the software vendor is like learning data processing from a COBOL manual; no efficiency information is provided; indeed, no actual understanding of what is going on in the black box is documented.

Second, although good language compilers have an optimization postprocessor, very few DBMSs have something similar: trajectory optimization for multifile accesses (among recent DBMSs, IBM's SQL/DS and DB2, ORACLE Corporation's ORACLE, and RTI's INGRES have that). And no efficient DBMS buffer-pool management algorithms are implemented, using query-look-ahead, for example.

Third, the most important reason for the apparently poor performance of DBMSs when compared to standard file management is that the services provided cannot be compared! A DBMS does so much more for a user that it makes no sense comparing it to a standard file processor.

If the same 15 services (listed in chapter 5) were to be implemented by a user using his own code, the performance results would be the same, if not worse (who can still program in assembly language at system level today in a user's organization, how much does that person cost, how long would it take, etc.).

In spite of the increased resources required, all computers are starting to use DBMSs today in business applications. This is similar to what happened with high-level languages: they are less efficient than assemblers, but they are used universally.

1.1.4.2 Management Information Systems (MISs)

MISs provide better justification for the increased cost of database management than business data processing because strategic questions are worth more than administrative documents. Today MISs are spreading rapidly at both ends of the hardware spectrum: on micros and large mainframes.

A micro MIS is very simple. It generally comprises a personal database (a notebook or a few table files), a spreadsheet, and a few communication utilities such as word processing and graphics.

Micro databases can be built by connecting a micro to a mainframe and accessing its database in a user-transparent fashion. Using Cullinet's DBMSs IDMS/R and GOLDENGATE, an IBM PC/XT user can access local or remote information without difficulty. If the local PC database does not contain the information needed, the PC will obtain it from the mainframe.

Micro databases can also be built using a local area network where individual micros access a file server, which can be another micro under a special version of MS-DOS or a dedicated database machine such as Britton Lee's IDM500.

Mainframe MISs are built using such powerful software as Cincom's TIS-SUPRA (THE INFORMATION SYSTEM-SUPRA), Dun and Bradstreet's NOMAD2, or Cullinet's IDMS/R, often to support corporate databases.

MISs are also built by commercial organizations, which make them available on service computers, for access in time-sharing mode (General Electric, Tymshare). And some are built for large national or international economic databases—for economic modeling, for example.

1.1.4.3 Personal Databases

A personal database is in fact a file (sometimes several) managed by a very simple DBMS. The DBMS generally comprises

• a screen formatting utility, to build key-in forms for loading the database and displaying its contents, on a record-by-record basis,

• a file-management and storage utility, to store and retrieve the records,

• a report-generator, to produce a printed output of selected database records.

The software is end-user oriented, as many DBMSs do not feature any high-level language interface. They are intended more for non-EDP users than for programming professionals, as they do not feature data dictionaries (some have rudimentary files called dictionaries), backup-recovery, program-to-data independence, undoing multiple transactions, and so forth.

1.1.4.4 Industrial and Scientific Applications

This is the fastest-growing area of use for DBMSs. It concerns both minicomputers and microcomputers. The information stored can be data (in the classical sense) but also images (pixels) and sounds.

In computer-aided design (CAD) applications, the database stores geometrical elements of parts, from which the graphic representations are recalculated on demand. It also stores a catalog of standard shapes used to design actual parts as simple variations of the standard shapes. The standard shapes can be as simple as a screw or a bearing or as complex as a fully equipped kitchen. The CDS 5000 system of Computervision uses a combination of minicomputer and IBM 4341 mainframe (with the SQL/DS DBMS) to yield one of the most advanced CAD systems in existence.

Artificial Intelligence (AI) applications use *knowledge* databases combining text and data. The operations on the database include retrieval and storage, but also inference to deduce more knowledge from the existing knowledge. The database builds up as the AI machine is used; it gains experience.

This book contains some information on database management techniques suitable for CAD, AI, and some scientific applications such as signal processing databases.

1.2   Key Steps of a Database Project

This overview of a database project is intended to help the reader understand where the various methods and techniques described in the rest of the book fit in. The intent is not to describe software project management completely; this would require a book in itself. However, a number of approaches and actions specific to projects involving databases are covered in sufficient detail as to be of immediate practical use.

1.2.1   Preliminary Functional Specifications

The purpose of the preliminary functional specifications document is to describe the goals of the application and the results expected, and to obtain a consensus on these objectives.

The document is written by an organizer or a person who acts in that capacity, whether an employee of the organization or an outside consultant. The process of developing these preliminary specifications is a classical initial step of application development projects.

The following points should be covered:

1. What is the *current situation:* How are things done, and what is wrong with this situation?

2. *What* should be obtained:

• *functions* (such as "keep inventory up to date," or "invoice new services"),
• *printouts, results of queries* (such as "on demand, the turnover and credit status of each customer must be available"),
• *data* to be stored for future reference (such as an invoice history file, to be used for market analysis and statistics that cannot be defined yet),
• *improvements:* operational costs, timeliness of information, reliability, amount of information, level of service to customers, reduction of errors or returns of merchandise.

3. *Who* should benefit from the new application or use it to supply data?

4. *How much* can the organization afford to pay for it? What is required here is an approximate budget, or an order of magnitude of what the results would be worth if achieved. In general, when an application is developed without a budget, it turns out to be too expensive when it is finished, if it ever is. The budget must comprise two elements: the initial investment and the daily (or monthly or yearly) usage costs.

5. *When* are the results required, or what approximate schedule is considered? (A breakdown into project phases is recommended.) How important is it to adhere exactly to the schedule, or how serious would unexpected delays be?

An internal project leader must be appointed to follow the development and completion of these specifications if the organizer is an outside consultant.

The implications and consequences of these specifications for the organization must be documented to provide good criteria for evaluation:

• What will the *information flow* be when the new application is operational (that is, what document or data will go from what person or department to what person or department)?

• What will the *user activities* be (the implications for each user impacted by the project must be evaluated)?

• What volumes of transactions are considered (example: how many orders must be keyed in and processed daily?) and what volumes of data are anticipated for the database (an order of magnitude will suffice)? These volumes will be used to configure the hardware, of course, but also to decide how many employees and hours are required every day.

The following example will help clarify the notions of preliminary functional specifications, preliminary budget, and information flow.

Sample Preliminary Functional Requirements Document

The Steelbolt case

1. *Objectives*   A manufacturing company, Steelbolt, produces small mechanical parts. Its managers wish to run new applications on their existing minicomputer to improve the administration of the following departments: warehouse, purchasing, and vendor accounting. They need

• to improve their inventory control and replenishment procedures to avoid costly out-of-stock situations,
• to implement a better control of the quality of the supplies they purchase, by monitoring the returns to the suppliers,
• to decrease the administrative workload of purchasing and vendor accounting.

2. *Current solutions*   Today the mini supports invoicing, payroll, and order processing. It has enough power to support several additional user terminals. The areas of purchasing, vendor accounting, and warehouse are not computerized.

• Purchases are initiated by the warehouse employees when they fear that an item may run out of stock.
• Warehouse movements are written on slips of paper—supplier deliveries, output to shop, returns from shop, returns to suppliers (bad quality). The slips are filed and used at year end when a reconciliation with the physical inventory counts is performed.
• Verification of the supplier invoices is performed by an accountant who comes to the warehouse twice monthly to check them against the delivery slips.
• There is no follow-up procedure to compute the cost of purchased supplies.

Benefits expected from computerization

1. *Warehouse*

• Transaction slips will be suppressed.
• Each of the two employees will enter the transactions on a terminal as the transactions are performed.
• The quantities in stock, on order, and the past transactions of a given item will be queried, to replace the existing Cardex system.
• Two terminals will be installed in the warehouse.

2. *Supplier invoice verification* Will be accelerated using two new printouts containing the day's transactions, and every evening will be printed

• a listing of supplier deliveries, by item,
• a listing of item orders, by supplier.

3. *Vendor accounting*

• Vendor invoice verification will be performed by comparison with the daily listings of deliveries and orders.
• All reconciled vendor invoice lines will be entered on a terminal located in the accounting office, for the computer to calculate the WAC (weighted average cost) of each purchased item.

The expected improvement concerns

• speeding up the accountant's work,
• the availability of the WAC,
• avoiding the reconciliation errors in the checking of vendor invoices.

Limits and phases of projected application During an initial phase, the application described above will be installed. A subsequent phase will feature design of an economic purchasing strategy and optimal management of the inventory. Finally, after a certain amount of history has been accumulated about the returns to suppliers, better negotiation of supplier contracts will be possible to improve the cost/performance ratio.

1. *Preliminary budget checklist* For each project phase, budget must be prepared for these items:
• preliminary functional requirements,
• detailed functional specifications,
• system design,

• program development and testing,
• documentation,
• initial load and testing,
• DBA installation.

Other costs:
• hardware and software purchases and installation,
• hardware and software maintenance,
• daily run,
• data acquisition,
• telecommunications,
• outside services.

2. *Sample information flow diagram (figure 1.1)*

3. *Information flow*   Each column in figure 1.1 describes the activities
in that department related to the project.

• In the Warehouse there are two activities:
  • a screen dialog to key in transactions that reflect the local activity,
  • another screen dialog to query the inventory file and the inventory
  movements file.

• In the data processing department, there are also two activities *related to the key-in activity of the warehouse* (their descriptions are
aligned to show the connection): print two daily listings of the supplier
deliveries and returns to supplier, sorted by item number and supplier
number, respectively. Every day, after all warehouse activity is
finished, the computer will print those two listings in batch mode for
use by the accounting department the next day. Information flows from
the warehouse (key-in operation) to the computer and from there to the
accounting department. Information flows are from left to right in this
case. In cases where the flow is less obvious, the chart can contain
arrows to show the origin and destination of data or documents.

• In the accounting department, manual verification of the invoices
received from the suppliers is performed. The prices are checked
against the prices that had been agreed on when the supplies were
ordered, and the quantities actually delivered are compared with the
quantities invoiced (after subtracting the returns, if any). The listings
are used for the verifications.

After the verifications are finished, the supplier invoices are sent to

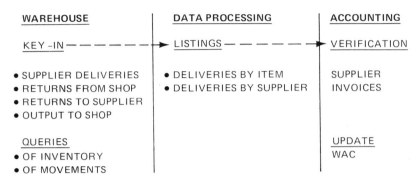

Figure 1.1
Sample information flow diagram.

the manager, who writes the checks, stamped for approval. This document transfer is not shown in figure 1.1 because it is not relevant in the application. The update operation, which is shown, concerns the WAC field of each item supplied. The cost is updated after each delivery to reflect any changes in price, delivery charges, etc., as they impact one item. This is an interactive key-in operation, so it is described in the chart. It is performed *after* the verification, so it is located below it.

Information flow diagrams are required to represent the main activities of the organization, as they relate to each other and to the computer. The example presented here is very simple. Nevertheless, we have seen that it is not self-explanatory; text is always required to supplement the preliminary specifications and the detailed specifications if actual programs are to be written.

1.2.2   Detailed Functional Specifications

The purpose of the detailed functional specifications is to provide

· complete and accurate information to programmers for subsequent development and implementation,
· a basis for purchasing hardware, software, and outside services.

The approach presented here is recommended as part of the Method of Scenarios and Dictionary (MSD) and will be covered in more detail in chapter 2.

1.2.2.1 Contents of the Detailed Functional Specification

For *each activity of each user* or each visible result, the following must be described (note that "each activity of each user" means that the description must be very detailed, covering all functional details in such a manner that the programmer is left with technical decisions only):

• The *screen dialog,* called "scenario" because two actors, human and computer, "speak" in turn. The scenario is not a flowchart because the computer does not work alone with data; the user can interact and interrupt as desired. The dialog is described using a hierarchy of scenarios, often limited to two levels: high-level (or general) and low-level (or detailed) scenarios.

• The *screen and printout contents* and layouts to show *what* the user will see and *in what format.*

• The *data dictionary,* containing
• logical data groups or files with all their fields,
• data integrity and consistency constraints,
• processing constraints (example: the balance sheet may not be printed as long as the journals have not been confirmed),
• lists and cross-references showing in what scenarios, screens, or printouts a given field or group of fields is used.

• *Test data*
• *To illustrate general and particular cases of data and logic.* The programmer is not supposed to have the complete functional competence required to guess what special cases may exist besides the general case; he is not necessarily an expert accountant, well aware of all the sales tariffs, the economic order quantity (EOQ) calculation technique for inventory resupply, and the social and legal rules involved in payroll!

It is the functional specifier's duty to describe the general case and illustrate it with test data, and then to describe each situation that could cause functional problems and illustrate it with appropriate test data for clarity. No such statement as "There are too many cases to be explained" can be accepted. How can a person program a computer for cases that have not been described? How can a program be verified without a list of cases to be checked, supported by actual test data?

• *To check that the specifications described actually work* with sample data in all cases (a protection against the specifier's own mistakes).
• *To provide acceptance criteria for the future software.* The definition of a working, acceptable software is "software that passes all predefined tests." This definition can be used in a contract between the purchaser and supplier of the software, to eliminate such criteria as user satisfaction, which are not always objective.
• *To provide complete training cases for future end users.* Since good training implies knowledge about both the general case and all the special situations, the test data are excellent training material. Using them will also test the software during the users' training, thus saving time.

1.2.2.2   Appoint Members of a Functional Specifications Group

The above approach obviously requires a lot of work during the specification phase, which will no longer be necessary during program writing. This is not *more* work or *less* work than with other methods, since the number of decisions to document and program is the same. But the work is done earlier in the project, and most of it is done by end users instead of software professionals. This eliminates the problem of communicating functional knowledge to programmers, which is difficult, subject to misunderstanding, and uninteresting to many.

In many cases the approach has another substantial advantage: lower cost. The users do not always charge their time to a new project, as software houses do, and since the programming load is reduced, the apparent cost is less. In fact, the *real* cost is less, since the learning of functional details by programmers is greatly reduced. It is also reduced because programmers' time tends to be more expensive than end users' time, and the approach replaces programmer time with end user time.

Chapter 2 will show how end users can achieve excellent functional specification with the method of scenarios and dictionary (MSD). But we can already note that we will need to appoint a group of functionally competent future users to describe how they want to work. When a person is competent, he or she can easily imagine how to interact with the computer: what the dialog must be, what must be displayed on the screen or printed in a report.

The technical knowledge required will be supplied by the project leader, who must have previous experience in MSD and, if possible, in the development of computerized applications. The project leader will explain such things as screen size (80 by 25), keyboard function keys, and menus. He will explain that the scenario implies that the computer waits until the user has finished entering data or a command to take over and work, and that the user must then wait for an invitation to enter more data. This is so simple that no formal training is required; the specifier and project leader must simply start working together for a few hours. After a while, the project leader may leave the specifier alone for some time, and then come back to answer questions and verify the technical quality of the documents. Such meetings can take place once a week, bringing the ratio of project leader time to specifier time to less than 20%.

Besides the leader and specifiers, the group must comprise a project secretary, preferably the future database administrator (DBA), whose role and work are described in section 1.2.11. For now, let us simply keep in mind that he will keep the data dictionary up to date and check the completeness and validity of the test data supplied.

1.2.2.3 Obtain Future User Agreement

When the functional specifications are complete, they must be "signed" by the future users. Each must agree (preferably in writing) that

• his requirements are fully and correctly described,

• he will receive the results as specified and supply the data as requested (both in the manner covered by the scenarios and with the required volumes),

• the data and processing integrity and consistency constraints are complete and accurate,

• the time frame and project phases are acceptable,

• he will pay for his share of the project costs.

1.2.2.4 Comments

Development of detailed functional specification can consume as much as 50% of the total application development elapsed time. The quality of such specifications can be so good that subsequent programming time and maintenance costs are greatly reduced.

If an otherwise competent user does not want to participate in the specifications group ("I don't have time for that stuff!"), the project leader should inform him that the project will describe how *he* is going to do his daily work in the future, and then ask, "May I (or others) decide how *you* should work, and if so will you accept our decisions?"

Indeed, the group members will have to find time somehow: working overtime, doing away for a while with some of their current responsibilities, etc. But if they cannot find the time to say what they want, someone else will have to do it for them and will definitely not define something that meets their approval.

The gathering and description of test data can cost as much as 30% of the total specification time, and program testing by programmers (the so-called alpha test) as much as 20% of development time. That is the price of good quality, reduced subsequent maintenance, and peace with the end users.

All data dictionary development can be done by specifiers, who are end users, under the supervision of the DBA (or the project leader if there is no DBA). This process will also use up quite a percentage of the total specification load, perhaps 40%. Orders of magnitude of the numbers of fields to be described are

· 100 for a simple order entry and invoicing application,
· 500 for a production scheduling application,
· 1000 for a complete personnel management system.

The detailed functional specifications make up about 50% of the total user documentation of the application. No other functional documentation is required, and this stands true even for standard packages to be sold to many customers.

Functional documentation that follows the MSD rules comprises more than 50% of the technical documentation usually required from a programmer; this will become apparent in chapter 2.

1.2.3 Documenting Acquisition Requirements for Hardware and DBMS

The following procedure can be used for database applications.

From the functional specifications, derive

• the disk storage volumes for the *permanent* data that will make up the database,

• the input/output (I/O) traffic volumes and duration that will be used to define the number of VDTs and printers.

Note that I/O volume is not a sufficient criterion to determine the number of terminals and printers; the location of the terminals in the building (for convenience) counts also.

Check the number of VDTs and printers with organization decisions. Is there a discrepancy between what was originally planned in the preliminary functional requirements and what was decided by the future users in the detailed specification? Are there enough terminals to take the whole workload? If this verification was not performed before deciding that the detail functional specification was complete, it should be done now. Perhaps some iteration will be required.

Obtain price and performance information about suitable hardware. Before the project receives final approval to start, the budget has to be verified now that the detailed functional specifications are available. We shall assume here that the cost of hardware is greater than the cost of software. This is true for micros used with standard packages and generally true for minis, even when some custom programming is performed, but not true if little hardware is purchased (to upgrade the computer) and a lot of software is developed. The assumption will lead us to consider hardware cost first, and then software cost, but if software cost is more important, we shall have to consider that first.

The hardware price information does not have to be accurate at this time because we are not in a position to order it yet. Generally, comparable hardware power (including processor, disks, and terminals) sells for comparable prices, no matter what manufacturer is selected; at least, that assumption will provide sufficient accuracy at this stage.

Qualifying the performance may be quite difficult. We need to know, besides obvious capacity information (memory, disks, printer speed), *how many DBMS calls per second* can be processed on an average. For large mainframes, IBM publishes the processor speed (in millions of instructions per second, or MIPS) and DBMS requirements (an average DL/1 call requires 9800 instructions). This implies that a machine with a speed of 0.98 MIPS can process 100 DL/1 calls per second . . . in theory.

Unfortunately most computer manufacturers do not publish that sort of information. Some have it but keep it secret, but most do not even have it, and configure systems "by experience."

The reason for wanting to qualify the performance is that the DBMS is in general the biggest power consumer of all software, often requiring half the processor power and 90% of the disk access power.

If the performance information is not readily available, a benchmark is necessary unless a truly comparable application can be used for reference. Chapter 6 describes DBMS benchmarking techniques.

Check adequacy of the budget; iterate if required. If the hardware cost alone is more than the allocated budget, something must be changed. If not, whatever is left when the hardware cost has been subtracted from the budget must suffice for the software and other expenses.

Specify DBMS characteristics in writing. Whether a request for proposal is issued, or if a number of candidate DBMSs will simply be compared, the following list of required features is a minimum:

• hardware and operating systems that support it,
• the number of simultaneous users,
• file volumes and the maximum number of records,
• throughput (DBMS calls per second) and memory space for DBMS, backup and recovery capabilities,
• availability and quality of data dictionary,
• ease of use for programming and evolution (adding new fields),
• program-to-data independence (subschemas),
• utilities: screen forms management, query language, sorting, restructuring, interfaces to other packages,
• high-level language interfaces (COBOL, BASIC, PASCAL, C, etc.),
• security (passwords, encryption, Read/Write/Append),
• support by vendor (education, quality of documentation, assistance).

1.2.4 Choosing DBMS and Hardware

The choice of the DBMS is more difficult than the choice of the hardware and must be performed first; the selection of the hardware and associated operating system must be based on the qualities of the DBMS.

For micro DBMSs, evaluation diskettes are often available and can be used to run simple benchmarks and develop an idea of the package quality.

For mini DBMSs, benchmarking is even more important, but so is support. Does the vendor offer an assistance contract and guaranteed 8 A.M. to 5 P.M. telephone support? Can he perform on-line remote diagnostics, by connecting to the customer mini to find out what a problem is? How long ago was his DBMS first installed? (DBMSs are so complex that it often takes two or three years after the initial release to have them reasonably bug free and correctly documented.)

Buying a DBMS license for a mini or a mainframe is not like buying another piece of software. Many programs, some of them of strategic importance to the organization, will have to run with that DBMS for a number of years. Therefore the reliability of the vendor is of paramount importance.

Buying the hardware and DBMS from the same supplier implies that the organization agrees to keep that same supplier for a long time. A computer without a DBMS can be changed since the programs are not integrated via the database and can be converted one by one to a new computer or operating system. But a computer with a DBMS is accessed by many users, who are accustomed to it. And since all applications are integrated via the database, replacing the computer or DBMS implies replacing the entire application *at one time*—for example, over a weekend. Perhaps several hundred programs may have to be converted, tested, and installed; the whole database may have to be loaded and the whole system made ready to run at the same time. This task is impossible in practice, so many users have discovered that they are stuck with their hardware-plus-DBMS supplier and have to buy one system and software version after the other because they are compatible. Thus it is sound practice to choose a *portable* DBMS, which runs on several types of computers. Such DBMSs are not often, for obvious reasons, sold by hardware manufacturers.

1.2.5 Documenting Project Plan, Costs, and Risks

From what has been described, readers can easily guess that database projects have quite a number of risks associated with them. Because of those risks, they do not often run as planned. They can be delayed, some developments can turn out to be impractical, or response times can be so bad as to make the computerized application unacceptable.

Therefore careful planning is necessary for a sound management decision. The project must be broken down into phases, with each phase carefully considered and its risks well evaluated.

For each foreseeable event of the project, management needs the following information:

• event name,

• person in charge,

• start and completion dates (earliest and latest),

• starting prerequisites (completion of previous phase),

• cost,

• risks of noncompletion, delay, or bad performance (describe each risk and what can be done to prevent it from becoming a serious problem, or what fallback actions exist),

• profit if the project is completed up to this event but not further.

Sometimes even the first phase of a project, if completed, can be valuable. For example, a good data dictionary can be useful in a large organization to clarify the concepts used by various people and the information about the subject available throughout the organization. A large 28,000 employee group with 17 companies benefited from a one-year project devoted to building the data dictionary of personnel management. About 2000 different concepts were identified and documented, leading the way for a unified employee policy, which was undreamed of before. A group-wide employee database subsequently installed opened the door to improved use of human resources.

At this point, final project approval can be obtained, and development may start.

1.2.6 Designing File Architecture

This step is covered in detail in the rest of the book. The following text provides only an overview, consistent with the MSD approach.

1.2.6.1 Derive the Conceptual Schema from the Data Dictionary

The conceptual schema is the set of all logical files of the database, each file defined with all its fields. The schema concept is discussed in section 1.3. This schema will be derived from the relations (logical data groups) of the data dictionary. The conceptual schema is *optional*, as discussed in 1.3.2.3.

1.2.6.2 Derive File Access and Relationship Paths from Processing

One of the main differences between MSD and other database architecture methods is that MSD does not consider that file access paths (indexes, hash-coding, etc.) and interfile links (1-to-N, N-to-P) exist a priori. Rather MSD derives all file accesses and links from processing requirements to obtain an optimal architecture. This is done using a qualitative and quantitative approach and the concept of *dynamic schema* (see section 6.2.1).

1.2.6.3 Use AREA-Type Data Grouping When Available

The processing requirements often use a number of files *always* simultaneously. For example, a customer file is *always* used when an order file is. In addition, processing *always* requires the program to read a customer record, and then read or create its orders; the customer-to-orders relationship is *always* "traversed" (followed). When the *area concept* is available, a customer and all its orders will share the same physical disk space (called a block), to minimize disk accessing when going from a customer record to its order records and establishing the associated pointer structure.

When areas have been chosen, the file block and buffer sizes must be chosen.

1.2.6.4 Calculate DBMS Load at Peak Usage

To check whether the architecture will yield a correct throughput and response time, the load and response time will be evaluated using a three-step approach. If the performance is not acceptable, the hardware power or the specifications may have to be changed. Note that this will happen *before* actual development has taken place.

1.2.7 Designing Program Architecture

The hierarchy of actual program modules will be derived from the hierarchy of MSD scenarios and from the technique of standardizing screen and database access operations using *co-routines*. Co-routines, a concept somewhat similar to MODULA-2's co-routines, stands for both "control routines" (to control the quality of data before they reach the database, or the correct sequence of program module execution) and "associated routines" (since each co-routine is a watchdog associated with a subdatabase or a subapplication).

1.2.8 Writing, Testing, and Documenting the Programs

Actual program development will be performed in a modular fashion, following the architecture established. Co-routines and data input programs will be developed first, and the DBMS's query facilities will be used to check their correctness. Then the other application programs will be written. The data dictionary will play a major role in the documentation phase. The test data documented in the functional specifications will be used for the programmers' test (called the alpha test).

1.2.9 Initial Database Loading, Parallel Running, and Testing

Loading the database with data can be quite a task. The volumes can be a problem, of course, but the main difficulty is having *synchronous* data. The database being a photograph of the reality, all of it has to reflect *the same point in time,* from which actual usage can proceed.

Because many things can go wrong, it is advisable to run the new database application in parallel with the old one or with the previous manual procedures for some time. If the volume of work is too much for the staff, running with part of the volume is still far better than nothing, though it implies reloading a synchronous database at the end of the test. This is the *beta test,* performed with a few selected users and lesser volumes.

Before the application is turned over to the computer room staff for normal daily processing, the corresponding processing procedures and documentation must be written *and tested,* with emphasis on backup and recovery. If recovery procedures are not ready, accurate, and truly operational, users are likely to get discouraged after the first few losses of data.

Initial testing includes verifying the performance level of big batch programs and selected response times. It also includes testing the error resistance of the application programs. It is difficult to persuade programmers to test their programs extensively. Unfortunately even the exhaustive tests documented in the functional specifications do not suffice, since they test situations that are normal even if they are infrequent. It is also necessary to verify what happens when users make

mistakes; will erroneous data reach the database? To find out, it is best
is to ask "innocent" users to start working. It is likely that, in a few
hours, they will have done more faulty manipulations than programmers would have in a year. The error-resistance problems will
then be known, and useful advice can be added to the user
documentation.

1.2.10   Writing the Documentation for Users and the DBA

An application development cannot be considered complete without its
documentation. A database project requires additional documentation
for the DBA, mainly an up-to-date data dictionary and administration
procedures for the database schemas, access permissions, and integ-
rity-consistency verifications.

1.2.11   Initiating the DBA Function and Starting Daily Use

The DBA function being mostly routine, it is necessary to make sure
that the person understands the daily work he is expected to perform.
The various routine administrative procedures documented in the DBA
guide must be followed by the project leader for a few weeks until the
DBA can continue on his own. The difficulty comes not from the
technical nature of the procedures; they are not so difficult, after the
database query and definition languages have been mastered. It comes
from the perfection required to ensure the quality of the data.

1.3   Database Fundamentals

1.3.1   Views

A call to the DBMS, made by an application program, the DBMS's
own query facility, or one of the DBMS utility programs, *accesses one
or several files at the same time*. The files accessed simultaneously are
logically related.

   For example, a call can retrieve the "customer-name" field in the
customer file, for a given "customer-number," then follow the 1-to-N
relationship between the customer and his N orders, and retrieve the
"order-number" and "order-date" fields from each of the N associated records of the order file. The call will return these three fields to
the calling program as if they had been found in the same file. With

nonrelational DBMSs, N calls in succession may be required to obtain the N triplets.

If this call must be executed often, it can be cataloged in the data dictionary. It is termed a VIEW because the program views the database through it in a special way. To use it, the program obtains it from the data dictionary using its identification code, adds the required "customer-number" value, and sends it to the DBMS. Alternatively the program sends to the DBMS the code of the view and the "customer-number" value, and the DBMS retrieves the view in the data dictionary and executes it. A view can contain search criteria and retrieve more than one record, but if the DBMS is not relational, only the first record will be delivered to the program, and the others will be delivered after a "NEXT" request. If the DBMS is relational, the result of the view is a file with N records called a *relation*.

Views have a *dynamic* nature. A search view will only pass to a program the data it has retrieved, or store the resulting file as a *temporary* file that does not belong to the database. Views provide subsets of databases that exist only after a view is executed.

Views can also perform update operations, not only searches. In that case, all the fields located in records that match the search criteria are updated in the database. (See the example in section 2.1.8.)

A view completely defines a single-file or multifile access to a database. It always implies a search operation:

• because it is a *selection,* which is a retrieval operation,

• or because it is a *deletion,* which must first retrieve the records to be deleted,

• or because it is a *modification,* which must alter the values of a field in all the records it has first retrieved,

• or because it is an *insertion,* which must perform a retrieval operation before it adds new records to the file.

The retrieval operation is used to try to find a record with the same key value if *uniqueness* must be verified (that is, if the DBMS must guarantee that there is only one record with that specific key value). The retrieval operation may also be required to find *where* to insert the new record if a collating sequence of records is specified.

The definitions below, intended for advanced readers, use relational algebra notions such as selection, projection, and join. These notions are defined in 1.3.4.4, 1.3.4.5, and 1.3.4.6.

1.3.1.1 Single-Level View
A single-level view is derived from a relation using

• *A selection* that retains a subset of the tuples.

• *Virtual attributes* (attributes that are not stored but calculated in each tuple combining other attributes of the tuple with constants and arithmetic operators to form an arithmetic expression). These attributes are called *horizontal* virtual attributes, because they are calculated from other attributes of the same "horizontal" tuple.

• *A projection* that retains a subset of the attributes.

Example
From the relation CUSTOMER (c#, name, type, total-debit, total-credit) a view defines:

• a selection that retains customers of type 2 (international),

• a virtual attribute called *balance* = total-debit − total-credit,

• a projection that retains only c#, name, and balance.

Through the view, the relation is seen as

INTERNATIONAL-CUSTOMER (c#, name, balance).

Since a single-level view is defined using both a projection and virtual attributes, it can perform more than a mere selection. It can actually modify the values of some attributes, replacing the old attributes and their values with new attributes with calculated values. And the dynamic capabilities of a view can be further expanded to include the deletion of the tuples selected. In short, a single-level view can select tuples, then (optionally) modify some of their attributes or delete the selected tuples.

1.3.1.2 Multilevel View
A multilevel view is derived from N relations $R_1, R_2, \ldots, R_N$ linked by $N-1$ joins $J_{12}, J_{23}, \ldots, J_{N-1N}$. At each level L a selection S_L retains only some of the tuples before they are joined with tuples of the next level, a projection P_L retains only some of the attributes, and some virtual attributes are added using horizontal arithmetic expressions.

• Selection S_1 retains some of the tuples of R_1, projection P_1 restricts the set of attributes of R_1, horizontal virtual attributes are added to R_1. Then

• Each (retained) tuple T_i of R_1 is joined to $N_1(T_i)$ tuples of R_2 using the join rule J_{12}.

• Selection S_2 retains some of the tuples of R_2 reached by the previous operation, projection P_2 restricts the set of attributes of R_2, and a new set of horizontal virtual attributes is added to the resulting relation. Then

• Each tuple T_j of R_2 thus joined to a tuple of R_1 and retained by S_2 is joined to $N_2(T_j)$ tuples of R_3 using the join rule J_{23}.

• And so on.

This hierarchy of linked tuples can be seen through the multilevel view as a single-level relation R that contains all the attributes of R_1, R_2, . . . , R_N remaining from the projections P_1, P_2, . . . , P_N, and all the added horizontal virtual attributes. The key of each tuple of R is made up of the various keys of the component relations R_1, R_2, . . . , R_N that have survived the projections. All attributes, real or virtual, of the component relations are eligible for existence in the multilevel view, but they may or may not be retained. In addition, virtual nonhorizontal attributes calculated using attributes of several component relations R_i, R_j, etc., can be part of the resulting view.

Example
This example features a two-level view used to modify attribute values. In the following relations the keys are italicized:

R_1 is the order-header relation (*order#*, date, discount).
R_2 is the order-line relation (*order#, item#*, quantity, price).

For a given order#, item#, and item unit price, the view adds a given quantity Q to the existing quantity and changes the price in the appropriate order line.

  The operations performed by this two-level view are

• select the order-header tuple where the order# matches the given order#,

• join the order-header tuple with the corresponding order-line tuples in the order-line relation for matching order#,

• select the tuple where the item# matches the given item#,

• add Q to the quantity attribute in that tuple,

• add (item-unit-price ∗ Q) ∗ (1 − discount) to the price attribute (this calculation uses attributes from several tuples of several relations).

This example demonstrates the fact that multilevel views always include selections and joins, but sometimes also update operations on the *last level* reached by the selection: attribute value modifications or tuple deletions.

1.3.2   The First Three Schemas of a Database

The information in a database can be seen in three different ways, called its *schemas*. In order to define the schemas, let us first define the "information" of the database.

1.3.2.1   Data Fields and Data Groups

The DBA sees all the data: all files, all fields in each file, all *artificial* fields obtained through views. For example, the database contains in each customer record the "total-debit" and "total-credit" fields. Through a particular view, the DBMS computes and delivers to the requesting program their difference, called "customer-balance." It is delivered as a field, yet it is not a stored field; it is recalculated each time the view is processed, and it can never be updated by a program. For this reason, it is also called a *virtual field*. The DBA also sees all artificial field *groups* delivered by views. Such groups, as seen from a program, appear to belong to a single file, yet they come from several files that have been accessed in a single view execution. These groups, like everything else the DBA sees, are described in the data dictionary.

1.3.2.2   Data Existence Constraints

In addition to data elements or groups, the DBA also finds in the data dictionary *existence constraints:* conditions that must be verified in order for the data to be valid. There are 3 levels of existence constraints: field level, file level, and subdatabase level.

• *Field-level* constraints apply to one field, to describe such things as
type (numeric, alpha, date, logical, city name, color, etc.),
size (number of digits before and after the decimal point, etc.),
syntax (example: first two digits are a family name, last two digits are
an item name),
value (example: a state number must be in the range between 1 and 50;
a color must belong to the table of valid colors).

• *File-level* constraints apply to 1 file to describe conditions to be met
by the various fields that make up the file, such as

horizontal constraints (example: in an accounting file, when an accounting operation is posted to a bank account, the field "date-value"
must be filled in, in addition to the field "date-posted")—these constraints are defined within a given record,
vertical constraints (example: in an accounting file the total of debits
must be equal to the total of credits)—vertical constraints are defined
across some or all of the file's records.

• *Subdatabase-level* constraints apply to a relationship between two or
more files of a given portion of the database called a subdatabase. A
subdatabase is often a set of related files such as a commercial subdatabase (customers, items, orders) or an inventory control subdatabase (items, history of events).

The most common type of interfile relationship is the 1-to-N relationship, introduced in section 1.3.1. When such a relationship exists, the
record on the "1" side must exist in order for any given record on the
"N" side to exist. For example, an order record cannot exist if the
customer record does not.

This type of relationship and existence constraint is also called *multivalued functional dependence*, since the N (multiple) orders exist for
1 customer.

Existence constraints can also be subdivided into integrity, consistency, cardinality, and syntax constraints.

• An *integrity* constraint describes a condition that must be met so that
the data are *complete, but not overabundant*. If it is not met, something
is missing or something extra is in the database; the exhaustivity or
nonredundancy conditions are not met. Examples: a customer record
must have a customer name. There can be only 1 customer with a given

number. Integrity constraints are verified in co-routines (MSD approach).

• A *consistency* constraint is a *noncontradiction* constraint. Examples: if a customer record contains a "total-turnover" field, it must be equal to the sum of the "invoice-total" fields of each invoice. The total amount invoiced each day must be equal to the total amount posted to "customer-debit" in accounting. Consistency constraints are verified in DBA procedures, in addition to other verification possibilities.

• A *cardinality* constraint is a constraint on the volume-limit or a number of occurrences. Examples: the number of states cannot exceed 50, or the number of customers 12,000. Cardinality constraints are verified by the DBMS using data dictionary and installation parameters.

• A *syntax* constraint is a rule for writing a field. Example: a state name may only contain letters and spaces. Syntax constraints are verified by co-routines for screen and database.

1.3.2.3 Conceptual Schema

The conceptual schema is a complete, logical picture of the database, as seen by the DBA. It contains *all* the data definitions of the data dictionary and *all* the associated existence constraints.

Some authors consider that, with the exception of the subdatabase-level constraints, the existence constraints are *not* part of the conceptual schema. However, this point of view tends to minimize the role played by the constraints in the understanding and the definition of the data and to maximize the role of the functional dependences; we shall not agree to that. Considering only multivalued functional dependences (subdatabase-level existence constraints) as part of the conceptual schema is in fact a modern way of defining a database as "files and pointers"; the DBMS used to be a file and pointer handler many years ago, and such constraints are an abstract way of calling pointers. (See 2.3 for a more in-depth discussion.)

1.3.2.4 Physical Schema

The physical schema is a complete technical picture of the database as seen by the operating system. It contains all physical file descriptions, with field layouts and sizes. It defines the area-to-file mappings, the implementation of file accesses (hashing, indexing, etc.), and interfile relationships (pointers, pointer-arrays, secondary indexes, etc). See chapter 5 for definitions and discussions.

1.3.2.5   The External Schemas or Subschemas

Each user or each program sees only part of the database called its *subschema* or *external schema*. These subschemas are defined in the data dictionary by the DBA, and the DBMS will use them to check that a call can be granted access. Note the two dimensions of this external schema notion:

• the *static* aspect of the data and functional dependences, which can be defined regardless of processing,
• the *dynamic* aspect of the access type permissions (Read, Write, Append), which can be granted to each user/subschema combination. Subschemas are further described in section 5.1.4.

1.3.3   Definition of a Relation (Static, Dynamic)

So far we have used the notions of file, group of fields, and artificial group of fields without discussing the grouping conditions. Fields can be grouped when they have something in common, either in their very definition or in their processing.

For example, all the fields that make up the identification of a customer can be retrieved knowing the customer-number: customer-name, street-address, city, etc. There is an obvious single-valued dependence among all those fields. To be exact, there are two classes of fields: the *key* fields, such as the customer-number, which determine the other fields, called *attributes*.

Static and dynamic relations   A key and its attributes are linked by a 1-to-1 relationship. If we know the value of the key, we know the value of each attribute of that key; this is a 1-to-1 (also called *single-valued*) functional dependence. Grouping a key and its attributes is natural because of the way they are defined. Since such a group can exist *for semantic reasons* regardless of how it will be used, it is called a *static* group.

It is possible to define an N-to-P functional dependence. The values of a group of N record keys determine those of another group of P record keys. In practice, however, we shall not use functional dependences: we shall use existence constraints instead, and implement them using co-routines, described in chapter 2.

An example of grouping *for processing reasons* is provided by the contents of a screen that displays a customer account. The top of the screen contains the customer identification: fields coming from the customer file. The rest of the screen contains postings: invoice dates and amounts, and payment amounts and dates coming from an accounting file. The screen groups fields from two files, plus an artificial (virtual) field (the balance) displayed on the bottom line of the screen, which was calculated from all debit and credit amounts, and is not stored in any file.

Such a group has a *dynamic* nature since it is recalculated each time but never stored on disk. However, using a view (as defined in section 1.3.1), the entire screen contents can be retrieved from the disk in one DBMS call for the two files, plus one calculation for the balance field.

A group (static or dynamic) is defined using precise *rules:*

• a 1-to-1 relationship between a key and its attributes for a static group, or

• one or several views and additional calculations for a dynamic group.

When the key of a static group varies, a *set* is defined: its elements are the various group occurrences, one for each key value. This set is finite because the number of keys is limited by a cardinality constraint, such as the maximum number of customers.

When the parameters of a dynamic group vary in such a manner that the database access and arithmetic calculation *rules* do not change, the occurrences of the groups make up another set.

In both cases, the variations generate sets because unique generation conditions induce unique, well-identified group occurrences, which are the elements of the set. Such a set is called a *relation*. Its elements are data groups. The name *relation* comes from the fact that the attributes of a group are related, statically in the database or dynamically for input/output.

The tricky notion is that of "unique generation conditions." In practice, fortunately, it often amounts to something simple: a small collection of fields, making up the KEY. Examples:

• A customer-number value defines one customer, and only one.

• A customer-number value defines a customer account statement because the 1-to-N relationship between the customer and its postings defines the latter unambiguously.

• An item-number value and a date-of-shipment condition define all items that have to be manufactured by a certain date. In this case, the key comprises two fields: item-number and date-of-shipment.

Absence of key—"event" files   In some instances, no key value exists. This may happen when each record of a static (stored) relation represents an event of history. Since two events may yield identical records, no key uniqueness may be guaranteed, and the resulting relation will not be a set in the mathematical sense. Similarly dynamic (I/O) relations may contain duplicate records. Such nonset relations are sometimes called "bags."

Dynamic relations do not define data to be stored, of course. This notion will be used in the method of scenarios and dictionary (MSD) described in chapter 2. Relations that can be either static or dynamic are an easy way to describe data, particularly well suited for non-DP specialists who write the detailed functional specifications. Both static and dynamic relations are protected using co-routines.

Static co-routines check the data existence constraints, while *dynamic co-routines* check the start and stop conditions of the transactions that produce the dynamic relations.

Internal structure of a relation   The contents of a relation can be considered vertically or horizontally.

• Vertically, a relation is a set of groups of data, where each group is defined by a unique value of a key (single-field or multiple-field key). A trivial example is a customer file, where each group is a record.

• Horizontally, a relation is a set of fields; some fields, considered together, make up the key; the others are the attributes of this key.

Notations   From now on, we shall use the following terminology:

• A *field* is the *physical* space that contains a data element.

• An *attribute* is a former key, or a former attribute of a former key.

• A *tuple* is what we have thus far called a group.

• Vertically, the number of elements (tuples) of the set (relation) is its *cardinal*.

• Horizontally, the number of attributes of the relation (remember: that includes the key) is its *dimension*.

Example (related to the Steelbolt case—table 1.1)

Table 1.1
Relation parts[a]

| TUPLE # | KEY | ATTRIBUTE | | | |
	ITEM	ITEM-NAME	SUPPLIER	WAC	UNIT
1	1320	BOLT B5/2	GEN. BOLT	2.04	100
2	1366	BOLT B6/3	GEN. BOLT	2.30	100
3	1530	NUT H 5	MECANUT CY	6.81	1000

a. Notation: PARTS (*ITEM*, ITEM-NAME, SUPPLIER, WAC, UNIT); attributes are enclosed in parentheses; the key is italicized.

1.3.3.1   Relationships: 1-to-N, 1-to-1, N-to-P

When two relations have an attribute in common, they are linked by a relationship, which implies a functional dependence. Consider the following examples.

Example 1
CUSTOMER (*customer-number*, name, city, state),
ORDER (*order-number*, date, customer-number).

These are two relations that have the customer-number attribute in common; they are linked by a 1-to-N relationship called "HAS" (1 customer HAS N orders). *Rule:* A relationship is designated by a verb.

Example 2
CUSTOMER (*customer-number*, name, city, state),
CUSTOMER-ACCOUNT (*customer-number*, account-number, balance).

These are two relations linked by a 1-to-1 relationship: "same customer." In reality there is only one relation:

CUSTOMER (*customer-number*, name, city, state, account-number, balance).

Rule: Each time two relations have the key in common, they make up one relation only.

Example 3
PART (*part-number*, part-name, . . .),

MACHINE-TOOL (*tool-number*, tool-name, maximum-dimension, . . .).

These are two relations linked by two relationships:

• 1 part *is made on* N machine-tools,
• 1 machine-tool *makes* P parts.

These two relationships between two relations make up a global N-to-P relationship. This notion of N-to-P relationship is confusing, however, because it covers two (or sometimes more) 1-to-N relationships. Using it, with some DBMSs, may be the source of errors. In practice, to represent the components of such an N-to-P relationship, one can use one or more additional relations: for example,

PARTS-MADE-BY-A-TOOL (*tool-number, part-number, . . .*),   (1)
TOOLS-TO-MAKE-A-PART (*part-number, tool-number, . . .*).   (2)

The . . . represent additional attributes, which are uniquely defined by the two-field keys. Examples:

• minimum-number-of-parts-in-a-batch, for an additional attribute in (1),
• time-to-make-the-part-on-that-tool, for an additional attribute in (2).

The notion of existence constraint applies to relationships as it does to attributes, relations, and subdatabases. Such a constraint describes the conditions under which the functional dependence implied by the relationship exists.

Consider the following example: If a machine-tool in (1) above can only make parts with a maximum dimension of X, relationships (1) and (2) exist only between a tool and parts that fit on that tool.

1.3.3.2   Relational Model

The relational model is an approach used to describe a database. Static (nondynamic) groups of data are represented as relations. Relationships are not explicitly represented, except that some attributes exist in several relations. The meaning of the attributes or the relationships is not represented in the model; this is a *formal*, not a semantic, model. The existence constraints and dynamic relations are not represented either. It is assumed that a text is available to describe the semantics and constraints: the detailed functional specifications. Since only one notion exists, the nondynamic relation, the representation of the database comprises only two parts:

• the list of relations, with their attributes,

• the description of existence constraints.

This representation is 100% text; no map of the database is usually drawn or required. And since some people need a map to "see" the database, they tend to prefer other (nonrelational) models, where the relationships (but none of the existence constraints) are represented with arrows and the files with boxes. We shall see the drawbacks of these nonrelational models.

1.3.3.3   Normal Forms of a Relation: Fourth and Other Normal Forms

Historically it took many years to study the implications of relations of functional dependence between attributes, which is the opposite of independence. Both within a given relation and between different relations, the semantics of functional dependence interfered with the representation of the relation's data. We shall see that semantic problems occur when manipulating relations with relational algebra and show an example: the connection trap. Today a consensus has been reached: the use of the Fourth Normal Form. Therefore, we shall describe the rules of this form only, and assume thereafter that *all the relations we will manipulate are in Fourth Normal Form.*

Rules of the Fourth Normal Form

1. One key value determines one tuple with all its attributes.

2. The existence of the relation implies a functional dependence between each key and its attributes.

3. The relation is represented as a flat table, where each tuple is a row and each type of attribute occupies a given column. The flatness of the table means that

there is only one element per (row, column) box.

Consider the following example: If such a box is called "customer-address," only one address can fit into it. If the customer has several addresses, another solution will have to be found; for example, if the customer can have N delivery addresses (N = 1,2,3, . . .), a second relation can be

DELIVERY-ADDRESSES (*customer-number, address-number,* address), where a given customer-number value can be associated with address-numbers 1,2,3, and 4 if the customer has 4 delivery addresses. It will then take 4 tuples to describe these 4 addresses. There is an obvious 1-to-N relationship between the CUSTOMER relation and the DELIVERY-ADDRESS relation; the customer-number, which is the key of CUSTOMER, is also the first attribute of the two-attribute key of DELIVERY-ADDRESS.

4. All tuples have the same contents: the same attributes in the same order. This rule justifies the notation

RELATION-NAME (*KEY,* ATTRIBUTE-1, ATTRIBUTE-2, . . . , ATTRIBUTE-N).

In every tuple, the ith attribute is the same. This is identical to the record-layout of physical files. Another way of expressing this is, The flat table is *rectangular.*

However, this does not mean that the memory or disk physical size of each tuple of the relation is the same. Sizes of alphanumeric attributes may vary depending on the length of the string, especially if the DBMS permits suppression of trailing blanks. The table is rectangular because each tuple row has the same number of attribute columns.

5. Each key (therefore each tuple) *is unique;* the relation is a *set.* Making the key unique is not always technically simple. Sometimes this requires that the key be made of several attributes, some of which may be artificial counters like the address-number in DELIVERY-ADDRESS above.

The requirement for the uniqueness of the key has a theoretical origin in set theory and a historical origin. Relations were designed to be *accessed by contents* ("Tell the DBMS *what* you want retrieved, not *where* to look for it"). With access by contents, duplicate tuples are not acceptable, because the DBMS would not know which one to process, how many different tuples there are, etc. But this theoretical requirement is not acceptable in practice, because sometimes relations describe *events,* and two or more identical events can occur. For example, a history relation that stores inventory control movements can contain several movements of the same item, the same type (delivery to shop, for instance), the same quantity, on the same date. This limitation is bypassed by adding an extra attribute to the key, such as a counter (1,2,3, etc.) or a time stamp (hh:mn:sec). And relational DBMSs are equipped to handle duplicates; they can be allowed or not or eliminated when they have appeared after a projection operation (described in section 1.3.4).

6. When the key is made of several attributes, a given nonkey attribute is determined by the entire key. That implies that the entire key is necessary in order to determine attributes; a subkey comprising some of its attributes will not suffice. That also implies that there is no subrelation comprising part of the key within the relation. The only functional dependence in existence links the full key with each isolated attribute.

7. An attribute is determined by no other attribute but the key. That implies that there is no subrelation within the relation, even among nonkey attributes, and, again, that the only functional dependence in existence links the full key with each isolated attribute.

8. In a given tuple, all attributes have a value (none is "empty"). If necessary, values meaning "not defined" must be supplied.

9. A relation comprises at least one key attribute and one other attribute. If it comprises only one attribute (the key) it is degenerate. This requirement for at least two attributes results from the meaning of the concept of relation, which is a functional dependence between a key and something else.

10. When the key of a relation comprises several attributes, these attributes are mutually independent. Each may be assigned an arbitrary value.

How DBMSs follow the rules of the Fourth Normal Form   In practice, DBMSs do not follow the rules of the Fourth Normal Form, because these rules are not acceptable in many data processing situations. In addition, MSD defines dynamic relations, which are unheard of in any normal form; it also encourages the use of *sorted* relations, which are required in the real world.

1. The first and fifth rules are not respected whenever the relation contains duplicate keys; one key value may determine more than one tuple.

2. The eighth rule is not respected, as DBMSs feature optional attributes.

Other normal forms   Other normal forms have been defined, besides the Fourth Normal Form, to describe the implications of the concept of functional dependence. They will not be described in this book. The author considers such theoretical developments to be of modest practical use, since DBMSs do not respect the rules of the normal forms, and the modern database design techniques now replace the concepts of functional dependence and normalization with more powerful concepts, such as existence constraints and the *dynamic schema* (the fourth schema of a database).

1.3.3.4   Physical Implementation of a Relational Database

Physically a relational database is implemented as a set of isolated relations, each of which occupies one file. Isolated means that there are no interfile pointers and that the relationships that may exist appear through attributes that are common to two or more relations. Access by contents is implemented using a classical access by key technique: index sequential in general, sometimes hashing or hashing with an index. The obvious advantage of this design, besides simplicity, is resistance to loss of pointers, the worst thing that may happen to other types of databases. If a relation-file is damaged, the damage does not spread to other relations.

Depending on the capabilities of the DBMS and supporting operating system, the tuples (records of the relation-files) may have fixed or variable length to save disk storage space for alpha strings and may incorporate end-of-field space compression (elimination of trailing blanks).

Relational DBMSs also feature *multiple indexes*. A given relation can have an access by contents based not only on its key, but also on any other attribute or group of adjacent attributes. The relation

CUSTOMER (*customer-number*, name, street-address, state, city, . . .)

may have an index by key (called *primary index*) and two more indexes: by name and by state + city (called *secondary indexes*). The primary index features only one key of a given value, describing only one associated tuple; the secondary indexes may comprise several keys with a given value: there may be more than one customer called Smith, and more than one in Miami, Florida.

(For details on indexes and hashing and how they work, see chapter 5. For now, it is sufficient to know that both are file structures that will allow us to retrieve a record if we know its key.)

1.3.4   Relational Algebra

Relational algebra is a list of operators for the manipulation of relations. In the following development, we shall not attempt to describe the theory completely. Instead we shall describe the capabilities required for a practical use of a relational database.

1.3.4.1   Defining a Relation in the Data Dictionary

Before we manipulate relations, we must be able to define them. In practice, this is done using a DBMS utility, which helps the user describe the name of a relation and the attributes it contains and some additional information such as primary and secondary indexes, cardinality, and the description of each attribute. Examples of how this is done are provided in chapter 2 (MSD). Some DBMSs, such as ORACLE, store these definitions in a data dictionary, which is a database in itself. Others, such as dBASE II and dBASE III, store them in a nondatabase way.

1.3.4.2   Evolution of a Database

Because the world changes and because design errors appear and have to be fixed, the definition of a database must vary from time to time. Secondary indexes may have to be added (frequently) or removed (less frequently); attributes may have to be added to existing relations (frequently), removed, or have their length changed (infrequently); and entire relations may have to be added or removed. These are *database evolutions*.

Real (professional) DBMSs have utilities to make all types of evolution possible and easy. This is one way to judge the quality, called *flexibility*.

1.3.4.3   Adding, Deleting, and Modifying Tuples

When a relation has been defined, it remains empty until actual tuples have been *added* to it (some people say "*inserted* into it"), with all their attributes defined. The tuples may be keyed in or created by a program. From the DBMS's point of view, it is always a program that calls it to give it the order to create a tuple, with the values it supplies in the same call.

When a tuple exists, it can always be removed (*deleted*), using an appropriate call to the DBMS. However, care must be taken, since the relations are isolated, not to make the database lose its integrity. For example, removing an item tuple because the item will no longer be sold is dangerous if there still exist in the relation ORDERS tuples that make up order lines for that item. The MSD approach recommends using co-routines to check whether that danger exists and not relying on a programmer to remember to do it.

When a tuple exists, after a retrieval operation has been performed based on some given search criteria, any attribute value that is not part of the key can be *modified*. This is done by a call to the DBMS, which defines the operation (modification of an attribute value), the selection criteria (how to find the tuple(s), where this attribute is to be modified), and the new value to be given to the attribute. The same precautions concerning the consistency of the database must be taken as those used to preserve integrity while deleting a tuple. MSD recommends that the safe modification rules be enforced using co-routines.

1.3.4.4   Selecting Tuples That Satisfy a Set of Constraints
A complete discussion of selection is provided in chapter 4. The text here defines its purpose and principles.

The selection is a retrieval operation performed by a relational DBMS. It results in an output relation, which can be empty if no satisfactory tuple has been found. It can comprise a single tuple—for example, when the unique search constraint defines the value of the key of the relation—or many tuples.

It can scan a single relation or several relations at the same time when these relations are linked by a relationship. For example:

CUSTOMER (*customer-number*, name, state, . . .),
ORDER-HEADER (*order-number*, customer-number, delivery-date-promised),
ORDER-LINE (*order-number, item-number*, quantity).

These are linked by

1. customer HAS order-headers, using a secondary index on ORDER-HEADER based on customer-number, and

2. order HAS order-lines, using a secondary index on ORDER-LINE based on order-number (the index is secondary because this attribute is not the key, it is part of the key).

A selection can define the following criteria:

• the customer address must be in New York, and
• the delivery-date-promised must be January 5.

In addition it will have to define the attributes of the requested output relation—for example, customer-number, order-number, item-number, and quantity, in that sequence.

The output will look like this:

DELIVERY (*customer-number, order-number, item-number,* quantity).

1.3.4.5   Projecting a Relation to Remove Unwanted Attributes

In the relation DELIVERY above, assuming that the order-number is not necessary in a picking slip printed for the warehouse, we can perform a projection to get rid of it. We shall obtain

PICKING-SLIP-LINE (*customer-number, item-number,* quantity)

if we assume that each customer had only one order that included a given item.

The word projection must be understood with a mathematical image in mind: if the relation had a dimension of D attributes, after the projection its dimension is d<D: one or several attributes have been dropped.

Dropping attributes can cause problems. If our assumption that each customer has only one order that includes a given time is not true, the relation PICKING-LINE-SLIP can have several tuples with the same key: it is no longer a set!

Even if we decide that the key comprises all the attributes of the relation, uniqueness cannot be guaranteed, if, for example, a customer has two orders for the same item-number with identical quantities.

If uniqueness cannot be guaranteed, tuples cannot be uniquely retrieved based on their contents. If the DBMS eliminates duplicate tuples, we shall actually lose information. This problem is part of a general problem of integrity violation called *the connection trap*. It does not prevent the use of relational database management; it simply requires understanding and caution in the data manipulation.

1.3.4.6 Joining Two Relations, Associating Matching Tuples
Consider the two relations

CUSTOMER (*customer-number*, name, state, . . .),
ORDER-HEADER (*order-number*, customer-number, delivery-date-promised).

The operation that associates each customer with his orders is the JOIN. The association process uses the 1-to-N relationship "customer-HAS-orders," implemented using the secondary index of ORDER-HEADER based on customer-number. The resulting relation is

CUSTOMER-ORDER (*customer-number, order-number*, name, state, . . . , delivery-date-promised).

It includes all the attributes of both relations, each attribute existing only once. Order-number has been placed exactly after customer-number because it is part of the new key.

  This form of join, based on equal values of two attributes, one in each relation, is called *equi-join*. When one of the equi-join attributes is the key of one of the two relations, a 1-to-N matching is performed, as was the case in this example: each tuple of the relation R1 is associated with N tuples of R2.

  When none of the attributes of R1 and R2 is a key or if one or both are only parts of their respective keys, the resulting relation contains, for each tuple of R1, all the tuples resulting from associations with matching tuples of R2.

  The notion of matching can be extended to criteria other than just the equal value of two attributes:

• by using a superattribute made of several component attributes for R1, and perhaps for R2, or

• by defining a horizontal function F(R1), evaluating it for each tuple of R1, and finding what tuple(s) of R2 satisfy a comparison between a given horizontal function G(R2) and F(R1).

Example

R1 (*customer-number*, total-debit, total-credit),
R2 (*ratio*, bonus-value),

F(R1) = |total-debit − total-credit|/total-debit (the customer's relative balance), where |. . .| is the absolute value,

G(R2) = ratio.

Comparison criterion: |F(R1) − G(R2)|/G(R2) < 10%, where |. . .| is the absolute value.

What this attempts to do is find the customers who have a negative or positive balance and a relative balance within 10% of one of the ratios defined in R2, in order to give them a bonus. The matching is between N tuples of R1 and 1 tuple of R2 (or 0).

Note the following: In general, join operations are followed by projections because the user does not need all attributes of both original relations in the resulting relation. In addition, a join operation can be obtained by performing a cartesian product followed by a selection that restricts the resulting relation to "matching" tuples.

Example

A software company has programmers who know computers, as described in

MAN-MACHINE (*programmer-name, machine-name*),

and customers who use machines, as described in

CUSTOMER-MACHINE (*customer-name, machine-name*).

We can consider finding which programmer has worked for a given customer by performing a join on machine-name, with the assumption that the only programmers who will work for a customer are those who know his machine(s). The DBMS will perform the join if asked to do so, but the result may be wrong. The result describes which programmers *could* work for a customer, not which programmers *have* worked for him.

This is another form of the *connection trap*. But this time, instead of losing information, the DBMS creates false information: all the programmers who could have worked for a customer but have not. Again the relational algebra performs formal operations on the relations, without checking the semantics. If intelligent operations are required, an Artificial Intelligence (AI) machine must be used, with a well-adapted DBMS.

1.3.4.7 Joining Master and Event Files to Avoid the Connection Trap
The connection trap is not dangerous when joining two relations with
equi-join, using the key of at least one of the relations.

This happens in the very common case where the architecture of the
database features a Master file linked to an Event file by a 1-to-N
relationship.

The Master-Event model is explained in detail in 1.3.5.4, but a short
explanation will now be given.

The *Master file* is a relation that has the following properties:

1. *Tuples are not related to time.* They do not describe events that
have happened and may or may not happen again; they describe objects that exist for some length of time, such as customers, items, and
account numbers.

2. There is *no problem with the uniqueness of the key* of the relation.
No artificial time stamp needs to be added to make it unique.

3. The *relation is stable.* There are very few tuple insertions and deletions, perhaps a few more attribute modifications, and many selections
over a period of time.

The *Event file* is a relation that has the following properties:

1. *Tuples are related to time.* They describe events that happened
once and may or may not happen again. Examples are orders, postings,
bank transactions, and inventory movements.

2. *There may be a problem with the uniqueness of the key,* as two
identical events may occur. A time stamp or an artificial counter field is
necessary as the last part of the key, to keep it unique.

3. The relation is *not stable.* Many insertions occur, and perhaps deletions and modifications as well.

Two well-known, similar, top-selling DBMSs feature this architecture:
Cincom's TOTAL and Hewlett-Packard's IMAGE. The Master +
Event architecture was chosen because it is simple to understand and
use and because many actual situations can be described using this
two-level hierarchy. However, both TOTAL and IMAGE severely restrict the possibility of relating two Master files or two Event files.
Joining a tuple of the Master file with the corresponding tuples of the

event file, using an equi-join on the Master file's key, cannot cause connection trap problems. Example: A Customer joined to his Orders.

1.3.4.8 Building the Union of Two Relations

This is the equivalent of the union of two sets, applied to two relations *that have the same attributes*. The resulting relation contains all the tuples of both relations. Some DBMSs eliminate duplicate tuples automatically, but most do not. Note that duplication can be based on keys alone, in which case other attributes are ignored.

1.3.4.9 Eliminating Duplicate Tuples in a Relation

In the resulting relation, no two tuples have the same key. Only keys, not the other attributes, are considered.

1.3.4.10 Building the Difference of Two Relations

D = A − B contains all the tuples of A that do not exist in B. The relations A and B do not need to have identical attributes, as long as they have identical keys; D will have the same attributes as A. Note that D′ = B − A yields a different result, keywise and attributewise.

Example

PAINTER (*name,* date-of-birth, date-of-death, . . .),   (A)

IMPRESSIONIST-PAINTER (*name,* . . .).   (B)

D = A − B = (*name,* date-of-birth, date-of-death, . . .) contains the names of painters who were not impressionists. D′ = B − A = (*name, . . .*) contains the names of impressionist painters not listed in A (if any).

1.3.4.11 The Dynamic Model of Data

These paragraphs, intended for advanced readers, are rather abstract. To appreciate the concepts developed here one must first understand the issues involved in data modeling. Ideally, the reader should read sections 4.6 and 5.4 before proceeding to this text. The only reason for inserting this text after the description of the relational model (and before the description of nonrelational models) is that it can most easily be seen as a generalization of the relational model. The dynamic model of data is a superset of all other data models, so this text can also be considered an introduction to the theoretical model used in MSD, and one of the conclusions of this book.

Classical data models   Classical data models, navigational and relational, are all based on two notions: attributes and functional dependence. Functional dependence relates two elements X and Y. (The notion of element is defined in 4.6.5.1 and 5.4.10.2; an element can comprise one or more fields.) There exists a single-valued (1-to-1) dependence from X to Y if a value of X determines one value of Y: X is a key and Y is a nonkey element determined by X. Single-valued dependence is used to define records and relations. There exists a multivalued (1-to-N) dependence from X to Y when a value of X determines a set of values of Y. Multivalued dependence is used to define relationships between different relations.

The notion of functional dependence, however simple, has drawbacks. It does not describe the semantics, properties, and behavior of the data with enough accuracy for the purpose of designing a database and the associated application programs. For example, the multivalued dependence "account *HAS* postings" implies that a posting may not be defined for an account that does not exist. But it does not imply that the postings of an account must respect the constraint "debit = credit." It does not describe all the existence constraints (defined in 1.3.2.2). It prioritizes one type of constraint, functional dependence.

A drawback of classical models is that they describe the data independently of processing, as if data could be defined, understood, and used for purposes other than processing. The use of these models leads to the design of databases starting with a conceptual model that disregards the technical aspect of the data, then optimizing that model to make up a physical model suitable for processing. Ideally it should be possible to design a database without ever undoing any of the previous design work, and the MSD approach is one way of achieving that goal. MSD achieves that smoothness because it does not use functional dependence for modeling.

Another drawback of classical models is that they are only suitable for simple, well-defined, stable data types as used in business applications. They are not suitable for databases containing images, signals, or knowledge (in the AI sense); those data simply cannot be defined in any useful manner with such modest concepts as functional dependence and flat tables, hierarchies, or networks. Such concepts do not apply to variable-length strings of bits or words, variable-content records, and unstable definition domains. Yet processing such data becomes more and more important every day.

I suggest a different approach to data modeling based on a simple idea: **replacing functional dependence with existence constrainsts.**

The dynamic model of data   In this new model the two key notions are the element and the existence constraint. The element can be defined using semantics and simple descriptive properties, as an attribute is. But it can also be defined by a set of physical properties and existence constraints, as it is in sections 4.6 and 5.4 (in industrial applications, for example).

Existence constraints are a superset of functional dependence. They can apply to elements and to the other concepts of the dynamic model: links and structures. **The dynamic model is a superset of the navigational and relational models.**

Operations on Data

Data structuring   Elements may be combined into simple structures, such as records and tables, or into more complex structures, such as the source code of a program. Single-valued functional dependence is one particular instance of a linking operation. Its effects can be built into the database from the time it is created, as is the case with file records, or occur at execution time. Structures may be defined from the beginning or be constructed and broken down during execution. Linking elements to make up structures, and substructures to make up superstructures, is performed while observing existence constraints.

Selecting   The process of selection attempts to retrieve and recognize elements and structures. It may break down a structure into its elements or substructures. It may recognize a structure in the strict or soft sense, as defined in chapter 4. Selection operates on the database and returns a subset of the data. It can also return a logical variable meaning "recognized" or "not recognized," or a distance variable that evaluates the quality of recognition in the soft sense.

Updating   The classical operations of insertion, modification, and suppression can be defined and performed on elements and structures so long as they observe the existence constraints. They imply a preliminary selection operation.

Linking Links may be set and broken between origins and destinations observing linking constraints. The new structures or substructures thus defined may become permanent only if no existence constraint is violated.

Evaluating vector functions A vector function operates on a structure to produce a vector, which is a record-type structure. The function evaluates all the fields of the record. Example: calculate the sum of two numeric attributes for all the records of a file.

1.3.5 Nonrelational Models: Comparisons with Relational Models

There is a fundamental difference between a relational DBMS and a navigational (nonrelational) DBMS. The latter manipulates *one record at a time,* whereas a relational DBMS manipulates *one relation at a time*. For example, a relational DBMS can (using a single relational algebra instruction) modify the value of an attribute in *all* tuples that satisfy a given set of selection criteria, while a navigational DBMS requires a small program to do the same.

The presentation of database fundamentals has emphasized the relational model. Although the concepts of view and schema exist in some nonrelational DBMSs, the entire presentation has been oriented toward relational database management approaches. The reasons are that today the best DBMSs are relational, and relational thinking can be used as a general way to present database issues. Most important, the functional specification techniques described in chapter 2, and the software architecture concepts described in the rest of the book, use the relational concepts. And although the methods described are applicable to nonrelational DBMSs, they apply more readily, allowing faster development and maintenance with relational DBMSs.

The reasons for describing nonrelational models and database architectures in this section are primarily historical. The first DBMSs were not relational but *navigational*. They were built around 1963 by programmers for programmers. Their thinking reflects the thinking of programmers; *navigational* means "what describes which path to use to find the data in the database." Following such a path, a program "navigates" in the database among the file-islands, using interfile 1-to-

N or N-to-P relationships as bridges that run from island to island. By contrast, the relational DBMSs do not require a description of *how* to navigate but a description of *what* to obtain.

The difference between relational algebra, used with a relational DBMS, and the data manipulation language of a navigational DBMS is a difference in nature, not just details. The user does not have to be concerned with the technicalities of navigation, but only with the logical expression of his requirements. This amounts to very complex navigational languages (CODASYL/network-oriented languages for database definition and manipulation have well over 200 reserved words), whereas relational languages are quite simple (IBM's SQL uses only 24). However, the use of relational algebra requires some understanding of the relational operators: join, project, select, and so on. This in turn requires a logical turn of mind, which some people do not have, because it is the kind of abstract logic used in set theory. Therefore the main drawback of relational DBMSs is that users may tend to ask questions that do not mean what they wanted them to mean. An example of this is the *connection trap* (1.3.4.5 and 1.3.4.6.).

Another reason for describing nonrelational data models, such as the entity-relation model, is to show their major defect: promoting an approach that tends to consider data while ignoring their dynamic usage aspect.

Most database specialists still make that mistake; they give priority to *static* (processing-independent) data relationships in their database architectures, which leads to poor performance, and even in their functional specifications, which leads to errors of omission. Describing data as if relationships existed intrinsically, because of the semantics, or 1-to-N existence constraints, encourages the analyst to neglect other constraints, such as vertical constraints. *In the relational MSD approach, data and relationships cannot be defined or separated from their processing because their existence constraints appear only for processing.*

In addition, nonrelational conceptual data models are difficult to map onto physical data files, using the modern possibilities of area or clustering. The way to do this remains an art in many respects. Some specification and design methods, such as MERISE, based on the entity-relation model, use quantitative techniques for physical architecture optimization but in a slightly unconvincing way. The same techniques, used with a relational (or dynamic) conceptual model, as in MSD, are far easier to understand and apply. This will be shown in chapters 2 and 6.

1.3.5.1 The Hierarchical Model

This is one of the oldest data representation models and somewhat obsolete today. Nevertheless, some DBMSs, such as IBM's DL/1, use it, and millions of programs throughout existing large DP centers access their files through DL/1. It is mainly because of the sheer number of programs that use hierarchical DBMSs that such file managers are still being used. IBM now promotes SQL/DS and DB2, which are 100% relational, more vigorously than it promotes DL/1, which is, however, still available and supported.

Principle

The hierarchical model represents files and their 1-to-N relationships. Note that N-to-P (dual or multiple 1-to-N) relationships are *not* represented. If required, each N-to-P relationship must be broken down into several 1-to-N relationships, usually two.

The model represents record types (called *segments*) and their 1-to-N relationships with other segments. The database is made of several hierarchies (also called *trees*). Each tree has a *root segment,* which is the top of the hierarchy, and *dependent segments.* The usual representation features a tree placed upside-down, with 1-to-N relationships represented as branches and segments represented as nodes. See figure 1.2.

There are five 1-to-N relationships (vertical lines) in this example. The physical and conceptual representations are identical. The root segment is accessed using any keyed access technique: indexed, index-sequential, hash-coding.

After finding the correct root segment (also called *parent* segment), the DBMS can retrieve the appropriate dependent (also called *child*) segment. To do that, it follows the appropriate 1-to-N relationship (example: customer ---) invoice), and then the various "child" invoices of that customer until it finds the right invoice. It can then continue and retrieve a given invoice line, a child of its parent invoice.

The physical implementation of relationships uses a pointer in the parent segment, which points to the first child segment, and then a list

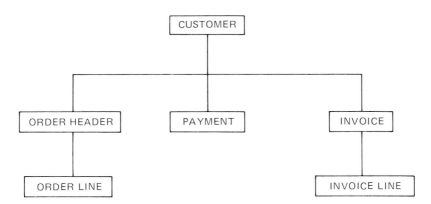

Figure 1.2
Example: commercial database.

structure, with pointers in each child segment pointing to the next child segment.

This implementation causes performance problems if the number of segments linked in a list of children is long. Many disk accesses may result. (This and other structures will be discussed in chapter 5.)

Let us simply note here that hierarchical DBMSs often exhibit poor performance, especially if retrieval is to be performed at level 3 or below (level 1, the Customer here, permits fast keyed access; level 2, the invoice, exhibits slow list access; and level 3, the invoice line, also exhibits slow list access). See figure 1.3.

Since the physical and conceptual models are identical, analysts who design a database for implementation with a hierarchical DBMS tend to use the same model in the functional specification and database design phases. This is very restrictive. DL/1, for example, limits the number of structures going through a given segment to two. See figure 1.4.

In figure 1.4

• in the *physical* hierarchy, C is the child of B and parent of D,
• in the *logical* hierarchy, C is the child of A and parent of E.

When these structures have been defined, the limits have been reached, so no other (third) structure can be defined; C cannot be part of more than two paths.

Because of such limitations, hierarchical DBMSs impose constraints on the database structure, often implying a breakdown into many sepa-

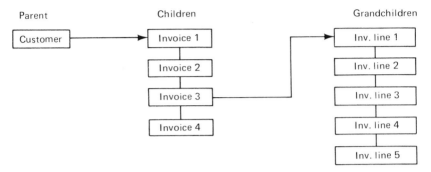

Figure 1.3
Sample physical structure (DL/1).

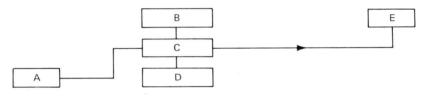

Figure 1.4

rate smaller hierarchies or the creation of artificial files. This is not only
a problem in physical database design; it is even a greater problem
when one designs the logical relationship structure of the database.
The analyst is compelled to think with restricted mental patterns.

Note that in a hierarchy, there is only one path from the top (root
segment) to any given lower-level segment. This brings forth logical
design difficulties in complex databases, such as the ones used for
manufacturing applications, where several paths are necessary. From a
logical standpoint, the difficulty can be offset using secondary indexes,
which provide direct access to any node segment. But regarding updating performance, the degradation associated with the use of many such
indexes is considerable.

1.3.5.2 The Network Model

The network model features N-to-P relationships. Each N-to-P relationship usually consists of two 1-to-N relationships in opposite directions linking the same pair of records. This was claimed to be a definite
advantage over the hierarchical model, but it is not. The analyst must

distinguish between the 1-to-N components of an N-to-P relationship if he wants to achieve good performance, because the two components are generally not traversed the same number of times.

The real advantage of the network model over the hierarchical model is that it does not restrict the number of relationships that can arrive at or depart from a given node:

Anything can be linked with anything.

This is a real advantage during the functional specification and database conceptual design phases, and during the physical implementation phase.

In addition, modern network databases can let the user specify direct (indexed or hashed) access to any file. The use of such secondary accessing may carry performance penalties as it does with hierarchical databases, but it is used nevertheless.

The third major advantage is the *area* concept (see 1.2.6.3 and 1.3.2.4). The clustering effect provided by judicious use of areas is very beneficial in terms of performance, though it does require more memory and disk space.

Example 1 (N-to-P relationship)

PART (*part-number,* part-name, . . .),
MACHINE-TOOL (*tool-number,* tool-name, function . . .).

These are linked with the following 1-to-N relationships:

1 part *IS MADE ON* N machine-tools,	(1)
1 machine-tool *IS USED IN THE MAKING OF* P parts,	(2)
1 part *IS A COMPONENT OF* C machine-tools.	(3)

Example 2 (N-to-P relationship)

1 part *IS AN ASSEMBLY OF* (or *COMPRISES*) N parts (of the same part file),
1 part *IS A COMPONENT OF* P parts (in fact: assemblies) of the same part file.

In this second case, the same "part" file contains both individual parts and assemblies of parts. One assembly can comprise subassemblies, which in turn can comprise subsubassemblies, and so on, which finally comprise parts. Network DBMSs generally allow the user to define such reflexive relationships; however, since the mere lists of components or assemblies where a part is used do not suffice in general, an auxiliary file is used, as in the following examples:

• COMPONENT (*assembly-part-number, component-part-number,* quantity),

• USAGE (*component-part-number, assembly-where-used-number,* quantity).

In a network, there may be more than one path between two nodes. This is very useful for complex databases, such as those used in manufacturing, which sometimes require three or even four paths, each representing a different relationship. See figures 1.5 and 1.6.

A hierarchy is a network, but a network is not a hierarchy in general.

The notion of "top" or "root" of the network does not exist in practice, since access using a key can be defined for any record. However, priority-ordered high-performance access using hash-coding can be defined for some records and associated areas.

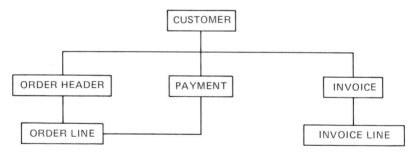

Figure 1.5
Sample network structure.

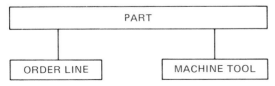

Figure 1.6
1-to-N and N-to-P relationships.

The nodes linked by a many-to-many (N-to-P) relationship make up a *set*. Several interrelated sets can be stored in the same area.

The best and most widely used network model is the CODASYL model. CODASYL (COmittee for DAta SYstems Languages) recommends using *two* languages: one to describe the database itself and one to describe how it is processed. The Data Definition Language (DDL) describes the sets, files, fields, and so on, and the Data Manipulation Language (DML) describes the navigation used by a program that accesses the database.

These languages have a syntax that resembles COBOL; they are very wordy and comprise a huge vocabulary (well over 200 reserved words). DDL and DML statements can be written with COBOL programs, and are processed by a compiler-preprocessor, which replaces them with calls before the COBOL compilation proper can begin.

The overall philosophy of this model is clearly one of tools for professional programmers. The separation between DDL and DML encourages working in two phases: design, and then programming. It also encourages (through the conceptual schema approach) the initial design of database architectures without regard to future usage, which is a mistake.

Since 1983, some of the major DBMS vendors, Cullinet (which sells IDMS/R), Cincom (which sells TIS), and Software AG (which sells ADABAS), have recognized the superiority of relational systems. They now provide DBMSs with the advantages of both fully relational and navigational systems. In IDMS/R, the relational capabilities have been designed as a superstructure of the navigational file manager, which still exists and remains compatible with previous releases. The user can freely combine relational algebra and views with navigational DDL-DML on the same database.

The dynamic dictionary (Cincom calls this the Directory) capabilities provide improved evolution possibilities. A few new fields, paths, and relationships can be added to an existing database without recompiling, relinking the programs, or reloading the database. All three DBMSs provide extensive programmers' workbench capabilities for such work as screen management, report generation, documentation, and even coding. All three provide excellent manager-oriented access capabilities, and some distributed-database and micro-to-host synergy possibilities. Today state-of-the-art production DBMSs combine relational and navigational DBMSs.

Note the relationship between a payment and one or several order lines, to represent prepayments. Because an order line can be accessed using two different paths, the structure is no longer a tree.

Relationships

PART ---⟩ ORDER LINE (IS ORDERED BY: 1-to-N),
PART ⟨--⟩ MACHINE-TOOL (IS MADE BY, MAKES: N-to-P).

1.3.5.3 The Entity-Relation Model

Also called the entity-relation*ship* model, or the entity-association model, this model represents the data in a database using two concepts: entity and relationship.

An *entity* is what we have previously defined as a relation: a group of attributes identified by its key.

A *relationship* is defined by two functions, D and R. These two functions are sometimes single-valued (that is, their result is a unique value for each value of their variable), but in general they are multivalued (that is, their result is made of several values). For example, D, the direct function, associates one element of entity Machine-Tool with all the parts for which it is used; R, the reverse function, associates one element of entity Part with all the tools used to manufacture it. Relationships are generally given names, such as verbs:

Tool *MAKES* parts.
Part *IS MADE ON* tool.

Multivalued functions represent 1-to-N relationships, whereas single-valued functions represent 1-to-1 relationships.

A relationship is *partial* if, for at least one of its functions, some elements of the origin entity have no corresponding element in the destination entity; some relationships may be of type 1-to-0 for some elements (example: a Customer may have no Orders).

The entity-relation model generally represents a database using rectangles for entities and lozenges ("diamonds") for relations. The entities and relations are linked by lines representing the association functions. It is a habit not to represent *all* functions but only the most "interesting" ones. Figure 1.7 presents an example.

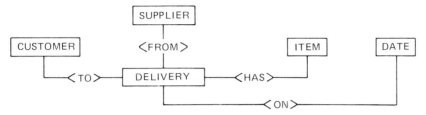

Figure 1.7
Entity-relation model.

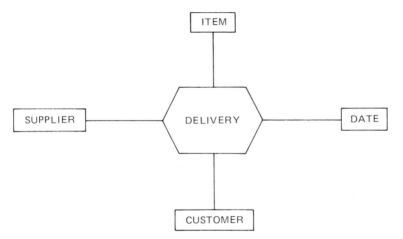

Figure 1.8

In it, the entity DELIVERY is linked to the other entities:

- Delivery *TO* 1 customer.
- Delivery *FROM* 1 supplier.
- Delivery *HAS* N items.
- Delivery *ON* 1 date.

The previous presentation of the notion of relation, as used in the entity-relation model, involved binary relations—that is, relations that link two entities. This is a fairly common case. However, there exist cases when a relation links more than two entities. The previous example of delivery can be considered nonbinary (N-ary) if a delivery is considered to be a relation instead of an entity; the relation then links four entities as in figure 1.8.

Comparison with the Relational Model
The drawbacks of the entity-relation model are

• There is no DBMS that uses it directly, so it is used only for the conceptual schema of databases and during the functional specification phase, by those analysts who know it.

• The model does not clearly specify which relations (in fact, relationships) must be described and which can be omitted. The confusion extends to the fact that most relationships also are (or imply) existence constraints. Analysts using this model tend to describe some existence constraints but not others, such as vertical constraints. In addition, this model admits the existence of 1-to-1 relationships between entities; therefore, it tends to specify more than one file (or entity, or relation in the relational theory sense) with the same key. It does not have the uncompromising quality of the relational model, which clearly separates relations and relationships.

In a graphic representation of the relational model, relations are drawn (if the user insists on drawing his conceptual schema), but constraints and relationships are not. Instead, they are listed and documented in the data dictionary.

In the "DELIVERY" example, the relational model would list the five relations, the four relationships, and whatever existence constraints are required in addition to those implied by the relationships (such as customer existence and date validity). The list of constraints could also include such conditions as "type B customers only accept deliveries Monday through Friday," which cannot be taken into account by the entity-relation model.

Note that, in all models, a 1-to-N relationship generally implies a 1-to-1 relationship in the opposite direction. For example, if a customer may have N orders (N = 0,1,2,. . .), each order must have 1 customer.

1.3.5.4 The Master-Event Model
This model was briefly described in 1.3.4.7. It is an old model, obsolete today and without interest from a theoretical standpoint. Nevertheless, because it is so simple to understand, and so widely used (TOTAL and IMAGE were so successfully sold!), it is described here and compared with other models.

Master records are accessed by key using a hashing technique (hashing is described in chapter 5). Each master record can be linked with many different kinds of event records. For instance, a Customer master record can be linked with Order records, Invoice records, Payment records, and others. In a given kind of event related to a master, the records are placed in sequence, using a two-way list structure (described in chapter 5). The master record has a pointer that points to the first event record; this event record has a pointer that points to the second event record of the same kind, etc. This is a two-level hierarchy. See figure 1.9.

Several types of masters can point to a given type of event, which is impossible in a hierarchical structure. For example, if orders are manufactured in batches, a given batch master record can point to its list of order-events; each order-event also belongs to a customer-master: several list structures can run through an event file.

In addition, each event can point to several types of masters. The only impossibilities concern master-to-master and event-to-event relationships, and the need to access event records through a master record but not directly.

1.3.5.5   Example: Education Database

The training department of a large corporation runs a number of different courses. The text below describes the various relations involved. Keys are italicized, and all attributes are replaced with "etc." The details of the database are as follows:

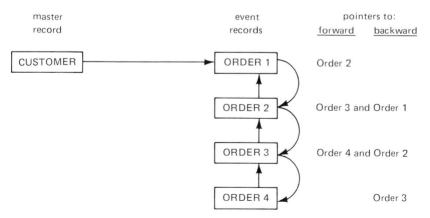

Figure 1.9
Master-Event model.

1. For each course: *course-number,* prerequisite courses, details of all offerings (past and planned), teachers qualified to teach it, etc.

2. For each offering: *course-number, date,* teacher, students, etc.

3. For each teacher: *teacher-number* (which is an employee-number), courses he or she is qualified to teach, etc.

4. For each student: *student-number* (which is also an employee-number); note that a teacher can be a student of courses that he or she is not qualified to teach.

We assume that it is necessary to retrieve quickly

1. a course, with its qualified teachers, prerequisites, offerings,

2. a teacher, with his course qualifications, offerings where involved,

3. an offering, with its students,

4. an employee, using his employee-number.

The text below shows how this database can be designed using the various models: relational, hierarchical, network, entity-relation, and master-event.

Relational model   Using this model, the database contains isolated relations:

• COURSE (*course-number,* etc.).

• PREREQUISITE (*course-number, course-number*), where the second course is a prerequisite for the first course. Note that there may be several prerequisites for a given course.

• OFFERING (*course-number, date,* teacher-number, etc.).

• COURSE-TEACHER (*course-number, teacher-number*). There may be several teachers qualified to teach a given course.

• OFFERING-STUDENT (*course-number, date, student-number*).

• EMPLOYEE (*employee-number,* etc.), where the employee-number can be a student-number, a teacher-number, and some employees can be teachers and students at the same time (but not on the same date).

These relations are implemented as independent indexed files. Each file has a primary index (index-sequential) built on its key and sometimes one or several secondary indexes on other attributes or attribute groups. Index-sequential files feature the ability to retrieve records based on the *beginning* of the key. For example, accessing an OFFER-ING by course-number alone (the first part of the key) will retrieve all offerings (dates, past and planned) of that course.

The secondary indexes are

• on OFFERING, by teacher-number (to retrieve the offerings of a teacher),

• on COURSE-TEACHER, by teacher-number (to retrieve the qualifications of a teacher).

Hierarchical model   Using this model, the database has the COURSE as its root segment, accessed by course-number (index-sequential or hash-code). Three types of children of a COURSE exist: PREREQUI-SITES, TEACHERS, and OFFERINGS. All three are accessed after accessing their parent course. The TEACHER segment is a parent of its course-QUALIFICATIONS, and the OFFERING segment is a parent of its STUDENTS. The QUALIFICATION segment is not neces-sary if the "logical parenthood" notion is used: the COURSE segment can then be the logical child of TEACHER.

An additional file, separated from the previous course hierarchy, contains the employee segments, accessible by employee number.

Secondary indexes are

• on OFFERING by teacher-number,

• on TEACHER by teacher-number.

See figure 1.10.

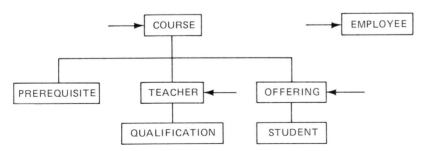

Figure 1.10
Hierarchical design of the education database. The indexes (primary and secondary) are represented by arrows.

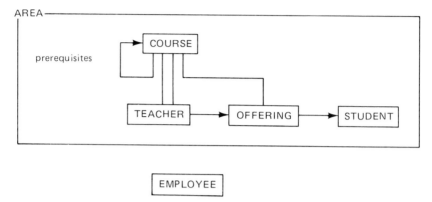

Figure 1.11
Network design of the education database.

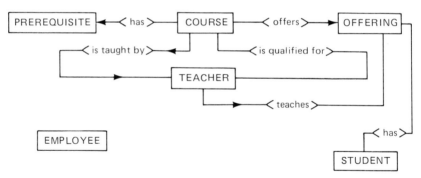

Figure 1.12
Entity-relation design of the education database.

Network model   The network model permits linking any record with any other record and allows grouping by area. In the schema shown in figure 1.11, COURSE and TEACHER are linked by 2 vertical 1-to-N relationship lines, representing an N-to-P relationship: which courses can be taught by a given teacher and which teachers can teach a given course.

Access by key is hash-coded on COURSE by course-number, and on EMPLOYEE by employee-number. Secondary (index-sequential) access is provided by teacher-number on TEACHER and OFFERING.

Entity-relation model   Since there is no DBMS featuring this model, no keyed access will be discussed; we shall assume in figure 1.12 that

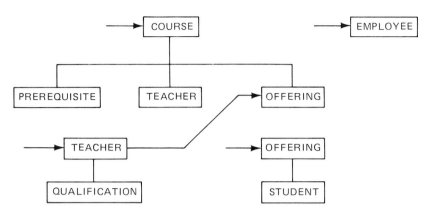

Figure 1.13
Master-Event design of the education database.

"the accesses required can be provided." The relationships are represented by arrows and verbs.

Master-Event model   Because of the two-level limitation, and without using a variable record size capability that exists for event files, the structure is as shown in figure 1.13:

• Two artificial master files have been created, to provide keyed access (hashed): TEACHER and OFFERING.

• The OFFERING events may be accessed through two different kinds of masters: COURSE and TEACHER.

2 Detailed Specification: Relational Techniques

2.1 MSD: A New Approach to Specification and Design

Creating functional specifications comprises two steps:

1. The first step, called definition of *preliminary* functional requirements (or specifications), involves *strategic decisions* about a new project: general objectives, manpower and budget for development and subsequent daily use, target schedule, etc.

This specification work is generally performed by an organizer, a person who specializes in the preparation and documentation of such strategic decisions. The organizer interviews managers and future application users, in an effort to understand their requirements. Then he documents these requirements as a proposal submitted to the decision-makers. After a few iterations, the requirements are approved, and the human, financial, and other impacts on the organization are documented too. Finally, these preliminary requirements are approved and budgeted.

2. The second step, called development of *detailed* functional specification (DFS), involves detail decisions, as required for program development, hardware, and standard software acquisition.

2.1.1 Requirements for the DFSs of an Interactive Application

2.1.1.1 DFSs Must Be Sufficiently Detailed

In general, DFSs are not sufficiently detailed. The specifier in charge of this document often leaves it to programmers to decide the contents and formats of screen forms, printouts, and keyboard conversations. The reasons often given are

• This is technical stuff, so it's his job, not mine.

• I don't know how to specify a conversation.

• It takes too long already to describe the functionalities that really count, so if I had to take more time to describe user conversation trivia, the specifications would never be finished on time.

• Management told me to hurry. They want to see running programs, not English text.

A number of consequences result from too concise DFSs:

• Programmer *decisions that do not satisfy the future users* because the user interface is not user oriented. Screen or printout layouts are hard to use and understand; they do not contain the right information; the conversations do not follow a natural order; and so on.

• Programmer *misunderstandings*: Lack of detail in the specifications causes programmers to make big (not-too-successful) efforts to understand the logic or algorithms of the application. And since a programmer is not an accountant when he develops an accounting application or a production engineer when he develops a manufacturing application, he makes a number of mistakes. Some of these mistakes are discovered by a user in the first minutes at a keyboard, but some come up years later.

• *Contract interpretation problems*: Since the specifications require programmer initiatives, some of the application is in fact undefined. When rare cases appear, they seem obvious to the user and not obvious at all to the programmer. The user claims that the programmer has to implement the solution of these cases as part of the contract and with no extra charge, but the programmer claims that these are additions to the specifications. How can one decide what had to be developed as part of the contract for cases that are not described? Do programmers have to be knowledgeable in the application area to the extent that they can spot unwritten specifications?

• Projects that start with incomplete specifications always end up requiring *extra development time and costs* because

• unspecified features were obviously not taken into account when manpower and financial resources were planned,

• discovering the need for program alterations when the programs are already written causes more damage than discovering a specification error, and correcting it in English.

• The *quality of software developed is necessarily poor* if the specifications do not include *a complete list of acceptance criteria and tests*. This is so important that the certification process of an ADA compiler involves running about 5000 predefined test programs! Every software development manager knows that programmers do not like to test programs and that they do not have the patience to do it carefully unless a predefined list of tests is given to them and adequate time is allocated.

Therefore DFSs without complete test data, covering the general and all special cases, are not sufficient.

2.1.1.2 Implications of Sufficiently Detailed Specifications

If we assume that specifications have to be detailed enough not to require an in-depth understanding by the programmer of the end user's business, it follows that a large percentage of the application development costs will be incurred during the DFS phase. The issue is *minimizing the overall development cost*, including the DFS.

To achieve that, it is necessary to follow five guidelines.

1. *Avoid redundant effort.* Since the user (by definition) knows and understands his business, any DFS method that requires the programmer to understand and learn that business too is redundant. Ideally the user should describe 100% of the functionalities of the application, so that the programmer only has to make technical design and implementation decisions, and write code.

• In addition, whatever the user describes must be in such a format as to make up final documentation; any copying task is redundant. For example, the output of the DFS process must comprise the structure of the functional (nontechnical) code to be written; since the code must be the exact image of the keyboard interaction, the DFS must produce the program structure, without requiring additional flowcharting. MSD scenarios will thus be written in a pseudocode language.

• Last but not least, the end result of the DFS process must be a *database* of the specifications: exhaustive (containing 100% of the specifications), nonredundant, and structured. This implies the use of dictionaries to describe attributes, relations (attribute groups), and user-interaction processes (called *scenarios* in MSD).

2. *Reduce the technical knowledge required for each task.* Making a programmer understand and write the DFSs of an application such as payroll is as unnatural and costly as making a personnel manager understand programming and write programs! Ideally each person should have to do only what he or she does best. Therefore *functional* specifications will be written by knowledgeable end users in a format suitable for a programmer to use without problems. Providing such a format is one of the main objectives of MSD.

It is less expensive to use programmers for programming only and end users for the description of their requirements because this minimizes the communication costs between them.

3. *Maximize the quality of the DFSs to minimize risks.* The DFS technique must make omissions and contradictions impossible or very unlikely so as to minimize program errors. In addition, it must contain self-checking information to minimize programmer misunderstandings. This will be achieved with *test data* to help both specifier and programmer verify their own understanding of what the specifications mean and the correct performance of the program from a contract standpoint.

MSD contains procedures for the verification of DFSs, to avoid omissions and contradictions, and test data description recommendations.

4. *Separate functional constraints from technical constraints.* Since the users will have to do most of the DFS work, the specification method must not depend on a priori DP knowledge. The user must be able to describe his future interaction with the computer very freely; the interaction model and the data model must be very simple.

This will be achieved by

• *making the functional description nontechnical,* independent of the computer and of its software;

• *allowing the user to follow his natural train of thought*: starting with whichever part of the application he wishes; jumping from one description to another and coming back if he likes it; yet making his work nonredundant and directly usable by a programmer;

• making the technical design and implementation decisions *after* the functional requirements have been completed, yet verifying the feasibility of these requirements (from the point of view of computer power requirements) *before* programs are written.

5. *Tolerate all personal styles.* The DFS method must accommodate most of the personal habits of both specifiers and programmers. It must seem very free-form to the specifier while still protecting him from errors and omissions. It must work with all DBMSs, all languages, all operating systems, all programming techniques.

2.1.1.3 A User-Oriented Approach: Scenarios and Dictionary
To be a good specifier, a user needs to master the following concepts:

• *fields*: numbers, alphanumerics, dates, keys, and nonkey fields,
• *groups of fields*, as they appear when the machine displays them on a screen, prints them on a report, or stores them in a disk file,
• *scenarios* describing the conversation at the keyboard (the user types a response to a computer prompt, then the computer answers, etc.).

The word *scenario*, coming from theater vocabulary, is used to describe this interactive process, the conversation between a man and his machine, because each of these two parties "speaks" in turn. The words *flow* and *flowchart* cannot be used, because they have already been defined as the logic of computer processing when the machine has data and works on it; these words apply to a batch or algorithmic process.

The elementary functions of a computer are these: store on disk, retrieve, display, print, compute, and make logical decisions (if. . .else. . .). These functions are easy to understand, and learning their existence does not really require a course, although a quick introduction to computers cannot hurt. These functions can be explained during the first day of MSD specification work, when the project leader and specifier work together.

Basically the principle behind MSD—and the main reason why it has gained end user acceptance since 1977—is that the user specifies his dialog with the computer *as he imagines it*. In the process of imagining the dialog—the scenario—he discovers the data required, field by field or group by group. In that case the data are not specified a priori; in MSD, they have no meaning, no existence if separated from the scenarios. The only data that exist a priori are user-visible results, and these are meaningful only if supported by a scenario or algorithm. As an example, specifying an order entry application could be done as follows:

1. The user/specifier has in front of him a filled-out order form. He must describe how to key the contents of the form in (scenario) and what data are involved (dictionary). He begins with a *high-level* scenario, deciding that, for each order, there will be three steps in the dialog:

• identify the customer and his special shipping address, if any; this scenario covers the order-header information,
• key in an order line, and repeat until there are no more lines,

• depending on the total value of the order, as calculated by the computer, grant (or do not grant) an additional volume discount, and finish.

2. Break down each of the three steps above into a *low-level* scenario, which describes all the details of the conversation for the step.

3. While he describes the scenarios, the user discovers the data required. He first discovers an entire group: the order itself. Then he discovers three subgroups: the header, the order line, and the order footer. Each time a piece of data (group or elementary field) is discovered, it is documented in the data dictionary, with all the descriptive information that comes to the mind of the user at that time. Detailed scenarios reference individual fields, which are described in turn in the dictionary, when they appear in the user's reasoning. Each time a dictionary entry is made, the user checks to see whether that field or group has not already been described, with either the same name or the same meaning. This ensures nonredundancy.

4. To support his own thinking, the user describes the screen contents for each scenario. High-level scenarios are often described as menus, and low-level scenarios as a succession of screen forms, computer prompts, and user answers. This description is first done in free-form, simply listing what will be on the screen. Then, when the scenario has taken shape, the data elements are laid out on the screen in their exact final position. A special form (called a "slip") featuring an 80 by 25 screen is used for that description. The data dictionary is updated each time a new field or group appears.

5. In the process of describing the scenarios and dictionary contents, the user thinks of the *existence conditions* for the data and describes them in the dictionary too. Similarly he thinks of processing requirements or precautions and makes note of them also. All of these conditions, requirements, and precautions are described on special slips called "co-routine" slips.

6. When he believes that he has described the entire order-entry process, the user verifies the accuracy of his description by adding *test data* that document the general case of each scenario, and all the special cases, such as special discount policies.

A casual end user, even if he knows his business thoroughly, cannot be expected to be able to do all of the above alone from the beginning. The project leader begins to do it with him, writing the scenarios and filling in the data dictionary slips each time new decisions have been made. After a few hours, the user realizes how simple most of the work is. The scenarios are described in plain English, the dictionary slips are filled in with information he can easily supply, and the screen forms and printouts are described as they have to appear; the project leader's inputs become less and less frequent, concentrating on technical aspects, such as the explanation of the "if. . .then. . .else. . ." style to be used in the scenarios or the role of keyboard function keys.

The user starts doing the actual writing himself, pausing to ask for advice from the project leader when necessary. By the end of the second day, the project leader's inputs have become so infrequent that the user can work alone for several hours without help. Subsequently one four-hour meeting per week may well suffice to proofread the specifications, and make required changes.

MSD has been used for nine years, and the accuracy of the DFSs developed has been such that in most cases less than 1% dictionary errors or omissions have been discovered at implementation time, and a comparably small proportion of scenario inconsistencies.

All this will be shown in more detail in the rest of this chapter. The sole purpose of the remarks in this subsection was to show how DFSs can be built by end users with the MSD scenario and dictionary approach.

2.1.1.4   The Need for a Relational Model

Since 80–90% of the work of DFS is done by end users, the method followed must be nontechnical. The user must view the database and its DBMS as a black box. The data must be described as fields and groups of fields, which abide by existence constraints. Some groups of fields will be stored permanently, making up the database. Others will only exist while they are displayed on a screen, or used within a program. The specifier needs the ability to describe all groups in the same way, and simply point out which groups are permanent. No relationships will be described by the specifiers, other than those that appear with the existence constraints.

All of this implies the use of the relational or dynamic models. The groups will be relations, permanently stored or made up with views. All relations will be in fourth normal form, as described in 1.3.3.3. The project leader, who has sufficient technical background, will help the user understand and apply the rules of the fourth normal form. He himself, or the DBA, will verify adherence to the normal form rules.

To access a group for retrieval purpose, the user will only specify that he uses the group's data. No specific Read, Find, or Get operation will be required as far as he is concerned. The actual database access operations will be specified during the technical design phase that follows the DFS—by the project leader, the DBA, an analyst, or a programmer.

To update the database, the user will only write something similar to "update relation X" in a scenario, and this will be translated into actual database access operations during the technical design phase.

The relationships will be derived from the existence contraints and processing requirements during the technical design.

Finally, the MSD data dictionary will comprise a set of attributes grouped by relation, and supplemented with existence and processing constraints described in co-routine slips. The relations will be isolated. All of this follows the representation of the relational data model—extended as the dynamic model.

However, the actual DBMS does not need to be relational. We shall see, when we discuss the physical database implementation approach, that any DBMS can be used following an MSD DFS, especially if the implementation uses the *functional interface* technique, described in chapter 6.

2.1.2 Results of the MSD Detailed Functional Specification Phase

When the DFS phase is complete, the following documentation has been produced:

1. *Scenarios* (all levels, in general, two or three) with their algorithms, and processing constraints described in co-routine slips (defined below in this chapter).

2. *Data dictionary* (relations and attributes).

3. *Existence constraints* (including integrity, consistency, cardinality, syntax) at all three levels: attribute, relation, subdatabase. These constraints are also described using co-routine slips.

4. *Screen forms* and *report layouts*.

5. *Test data*, for the general and all special cases, described using the

actual screen forms, report layouts, and data dictionary entries. Input screens are described, with their impact on the database, and the output screens and reports, with their exact future layout and user-visible aspects.

6. *Lists* and *cross-references* of all of the above for easy retrieval of the dictionary contents, and lists showing where a given data element is used.

7. (After the technical design phase) the *dynamic* and *external* schemas of the database. The conceptual schema is optional.

8. "*Notes* to the Programmer," written in free form, with any recommendations the specifiers wish to make.

All of this documentation can benefit from the use of a computerized data dictionary, but that is not so important during the DFS, when user creativity must be given free rein with minimal constraints. The computerized data dictionary will be built during the technical design phase by the programmers or the DBA.

After the preliminary functional requirements have been included, this application documentation makes up an excellent functional description, which does not need to be rewritten after the programs are ready. Each main function of the application is described using a top-down approach (the hierarchy of scenarios), with examples to illustrate all cases (the test data). Each attribute and relation is clearly defined in the data dictionary. The limitations, logical existence constraints, and processing requirements are described in co-routine slips. And, in spite of the existence of screen and report layouts, the document does not concern itself with the actual processing manipulations. It is purely functional and thus easier to read and understand.

Note, however, that although this documentation technique is adequate for in-house users, it is not intended for definition of standard software packages to be sold commercially. The latter requires some additional wording to explain features, functions, and benefits better, and an easy-to-read and commercial style.

2.1.3 Database Design Phase

The technical design phase of MSD is divided into two parts:

· database design,
· program module design.

Both phases are quite technical, and will be undertaken by DP specialists. From this point on, the user/specifier's role will be limited to learning how to use the final implemented application, testing it, and using it daily.

While the technical design is in progress, the investigations required for the strategic decision steps covered in sections 1.2.3, 1.2.4, and 1.2.5 must be conducted.

The database design phase comprises the following steps:

1. Completing the data dictionary: documentation of the (optional) conceptual schema and external schemas.

2. Documenting the *transactions*, using the transaction slips of MSD. This process translates the scenarios into pseudocode, which is very close to the final high-level language code. The transaction slips of MSD are described in 2.2.3.4.

3. Documenting the file accesses and relationships required by the transactions: key-indexed accesses and 1-to-N relationships, with such technical details as the number of keys of each index and the average number of children of each parent of a relationship. The appropriate MSD file access and relationship path slip is discussed in 2.2.3.5.

4. Deciding when to use the area or clustering concept, using the access paths defined previously with their frequency of use and the capabilities of the DBMS, and defining the *dynamic* and *physical schemas* of the database.

5. Calculating the DBMS load, as implied by the functional processing requirements of the transactions and the proposed physical schema of the database.

6. If the load is high, calculating the response time at peak usage hour, and even building a benchmark model to verify the performance and choose the best hardware and software parameters. This will be described in chapter 6.

7. Iterating as required, changing the database architecture, DBMS, or hardware choices, or making the application requirements less ambitious when necessary.

2.1.4 Program Module Design Phase

The hierarchy of scenarios (high level, lower levels) translates into a hierarchy of transactions. Each transaction description consists of the corresponding scenario together with minor additions: volume (per day, for example), I/O (database, screen, printer), begin-end constraints to be implemented in the program proper or in co-routines, and names of possible follow-on transactions (see the transaction slip in figure 2.9). If the specifiers have good practical experience in using MSD, they will write the scenarios in transaction form directly; if not, the analyst or project leader will have to rewrite them in a stricter pseudocode form, the future module flow diagram.

When the design phase is over, the lower-level modules are written and tested using artificial programs, which supply the input data and receive the output data. Then they are assembled into higher-level modules, which are tested too; this is a standard procedure in modular programming.

Co-routines are low-level modules, but they may be grouped in a special program called the *Functional Interface*, described in chapter 6. For now, let us think of the functional interface as a module that interfaces the application programs with the DBMS, performing the verifications specified in the co-routine slips, and translating the relational views received from the application programs into DBMS calls.

2.1.5   Objections to the Detailed Specification Approach of MSD

MSD has been in use since 1977. In each organization where it was used for the first time, there was always somebody who had objections. The technical design phase appealed to DP specialists, but the DFS phase sometimes frightened them.

Nothing gets done without motivation. So it is important to know what objections are usually made to MSD (in fact to future users' participation as specifiers) so that a negative attitude does not spread throughout an organization.

No time   A computer specialist said, "My users don't have the time to work on DFSs." He finally realized that even when *he* does the writing of the DFSs, the users spend a lot of time explaining to him what they want, and then proofreading what he wrote. Asking a nonuser to write detailed specifications takes more time and costs more than having a user do the job. It is true that users who participate in a DFS team ten hours a week may have to work overtime to get the rest of their everyday work accomplished, but that happens with every new project: it requires an investment of time.

No motivation A prospective user, asked by his manager to participate in the writing of the DFSs, said that he did not care what was written there. His manager asked him then if he agreed to let someone else decide how he was going to work every day, what the computer would ask him to enter, and what information would be available to him. Since the would-be specifier could not agree to have others decide how he would have to work in the future, he agreed to participate in the DFS team.

Lack of imagination A purchasing manager was against computers and computerization. When asked what sort of statistics the new replenishment application should print for him, he said he did not know. His boss then asked him if he made his decisions based on intuition alone or using figures. Obviously his boss thought that a purchasing manager who does not know what information is required for inventory replenishment is not qualified for his job. By the next day, the purchasing manager had found, and was showing the boss, the statistics he would need "because he was already using something similar compiled manually."

Lack of intelligence A project leader working for a software company said that he did not think that his users could actually participate in the DFS work, MSD or not MSD, "because in my area people aren't smart enough." He lost the contract to another software company, which offered to develop the software required for less since the DFS costs were almost negligible using MSD . . . and a lot of unbilled user effort. In reality, the level of intelligence required to participate in an MSD DFS team is the same as that needed to use a terminal in a responsible way. Over the years, all sorts of employees have done MSD specification work successfully: secretaries, accounting clerks, middle managers, a retired army colonel, engineers, etc.

2.1.6 Organization Prerequisites

Describing in detail the functional specifications of an application obviously requires that *the specifier know what he wants*.

We must assume that the user/specifier is competent enough to make the decisions needed during the DFS phase or that he can call on his manager for help. The specification work will not stop merely because nobody knows what to decide about some nonstrategic issues of the

DFS phase. Computer specialists will avoid making functional decisions that should be the privilege of an end user because the user must be able to express *his* thoughts. Indeed, if nobody in an organization has an opinion about a given issue, then it is not an issue; it is unimportant or entirely a technical matter.

2.1.7 Scenarios

By definition a scenario is the description of an interactive process, involving a person and his VDT (video display terminal, or keyboard and screen). This description is written in the person's natural language: English, Spanish, French, etc. The purpose of the description is to explain to other people, future users or programmers, how the man-machine conversation can be conducted.

• what actions are permitted to the user,

• what response the computer must give, or what execution it must initiate after a user's command.

Scenarios are used to describe conversational applications, not batch programs. A batch program receives data without user interaction, and then processes them without requiring further user action. Batch programs can be described with algorithms and flowcharts.

A scenario usually describes one phase of a process, which can repeat this phase as many times as necessary. For example, it will describe the keyboard entry of one order, which can be repeated 82 times if there are 82 orders to key in that day.

Scenarios are derived from the preliminary functional requirements, which describe the flow of information among the various employees and the overall task performed by each employee at his workstation. This overall task is broken down into more specialized workstation activities.

For example, a given workstation's activities may be the following:

1. key in all orders arrived so far;

2. examine back orders generated on the previous day, convert some into new orders, and cancel all others;

3. key in invoicing information for orders shipped so far.

The highest-level scenario will let the employee choose which of the three activities he wants to perform; it will be a simple three-choice menu.

The next level of scenario will describe the steps of each specific activity. For example, the scenario of the order-entry activity listed as activity 1 will be (for one order)

1. display customer information on screen in response to the entry of the customer number and change any parameters required;

2. type in order header information: delivery date and place, etc.;

3. type in order lines;

4. if the next order is for the same customer, go to activity 2;

5. if there is a next order, go to activity 1 or else return to menu.

Note the "if. . ." constructs and the use of activity line numbers. The next level of scenario will describe the details of one of the lines of this level. For example, activity 1 (display customer information. . .) will be detailed as follows:

1. Display customer information form (empty) for the user to key in the customer-number.

2. Find the customer information and display it for the user to key in any changes.

3. If changes were entered, validate them using the appropriate co-routine. If OK, go to order-header scenario, else display error message and wait for user changes.

The highest-level scenario deals with the workstation activity description of the preliminary functional requirements, and the lowest-level scenario covers the detailed conversation: this is a *hierarchy*. In general, this hierarchy has only two or three levels in simple minicomputer or microcomputer business applications.

2.1.8 Scenario Description Rules

Rule 1 *There are no more than 10 lines per level.*

To keep the interactive process simple to define, understand, and use, the number of activity lines per level must not exceed ten. The description of one level must always fit on one page.

Rule 2   *One page of level N + 1 describes one line of level N.*

The various levels must reside on different pages. Each page must have a title announcing what it describes and what higher-level scenario it describes.

Rule 3   *Programmer-obvious actions are not described.*

A scenario is not a program; it is a document needed by a programmer to write a program. Many technical actions are quite obvious to a programmer, so the specifier need not describe them:

Database accesses required to retrieve information. If the specifier writes: "Display customer information" after having asked for a keyboard entry of customer-number, the programmer will obviously know that a database selection operation is needed.

Constraints to be verified: syntax, existence, integrity, consistency, cardinality—all of these constraints are described in the data dictionary because they must be respected no matter what scenario updates the data. Since these constraints do not depend on the scenario, they are not described in any scenario and must be respected in all scenarios. The programmer is supposed to read the data dictionary to interpret the scenarios fully. Section 2.2 describes how to build the data dictionary.

Note that *scenario constraints exist* and must be specified. They are not *data* constraints but *processing* constraints, such as "Do not start keying in today's orders if yesterday's invoices aren't finished." Both types of constraints will be verified using the same type of software module—a co-routine—and similar types of software architectures—functional interfaces and decision machines (described in chapter 6).

The Purpose, Meaning, or Use of Standard Function Keys
Keyboards have function keys. It is good practice to make the meaning of these keys standard throughout all applications for the simplest actions. For example, the following meanings can be used:

• F1: confirm, yes, OK to update, I am done: next please.
• F2: no, give me another choice, I want to modify this.
• F3: quit this transaction, return to higher level of menu, or chain to next transaction if mandatory.

The user will then understand better and develop instinctive keyboard manipulation habits. When it is safe, it is better to encourage instinctive reactions and habits than to force the user to consider the situation and then make a decision; it is also faster and less tiring.

All database accesses, implied or described, are supposed to be multilevel. They can access several interrelated files at the same time, with the same view. Views are described in section 1.3.1.

A multilevel update should affect only the last level accessed.

Example: Multilevel Update

Three relations make up the database of an order processing system:

CUSTOMER (*customer-number,* name, etc.),
ORDER-HEADER (*order-number,* customer-number, order-date, etc.)
ORDER-LINE (*order-number, item-number,* quantity, etc.).

A customer calls and asks, "Please add two dozen more of item 5289 to my order of November 14."
The view that will perform the desired modification will

1. Access the CUSTOMER relation using a secondary index on the customer-name to find (the word used is "select") the customer-number.

2. Access the ORDER-HEADER relation using a secondary index on the customer-number and find the header tuple of November 14 (in fact this is a Join operation involving 1 CUSTOMER tuple and the ORDER-HEADER relation, followed by a selection to restrict ORDER-HEADER tuples to the one of November 14); in that tuple, find the order-number.

3. Access the ORDER-LINE relation, selecting the tuple that matches the key order-number + item-number 5289.

4. Compute new-quantity = old-quantity + 24, replace old-quantity with new-quantity, then rewrite the tuple.
The last level alone (the ORDER-LINE level here) was altered.

Notes

· The specifier does not need to know this relational mechanism. He can describe the operation as the customer did; the programmer will translate it into relational algebra expressions.

• The exact relational algebra expressions will depend on the capabilities of the DBMS used. Some DBMSs may require more than one view to perform the necessary retrieval and update. The MSD approach calls for disregarding this during the DFS phase and implementing a functional interface that will give any DBMS a fully relational aspect. This issue is discussed in chapter 6.

Rule 4 *Data dictionary entries are made on the fly.*

While the specifier describes his scenarios, he discovers data. Some data are groups, such as the set of attributes of a complete invoice. Others are subgroups, such as the set of attributes of an invoice header. And many are individual attributes.

All the data discovered, individuals or groups, are written in the data dictionary as soon as they are discovered: see section 2.2 for more details.

2.1.9 Sample Scenarios

The rules discussed in section 2.1.8 are now demonstrated.

Example: High-Level Scenario

ORDER PROCESSING

1. ORDER ENTRY AND MODIFICATION
2. PRINT ORDER ACKNOWLEDGMENTS
3. PRINT PACKING SLIPS
4. ORDER PREPARATION FOR DELIVERY (MANUAL)
5. ENTRY OF MISSING AND SUBSTITUTED ITEMS
   COMPLETED ORDERS: GO TO 7; INCOMPLETE ORDERS: GO TO 6.
6. BACK ORDER GENERATION, GO TO 1.
7. PRINT DELIVERY SLIPS AND INVOICES

At this level, it may be necessary to include in a scenario the manual operations, though they are not performed with a computer. Line 4 in this example is listed only to help the programmers and other readers of the DFS document understand better.

The various operations are listed in vertical sequence in the order they must be performed. Whenever a change in sequence is required or an iteration, a GO TO or ITERATE UNTIL must be used.

The first activity of this high-level scenario is now further detailed.

ORDER-ENTRY: Detail-Level Scenario (F1, F2, etc., are function keys)

1. INPUT CUSTOMER DATA USING FORM 1.   (1)*

(STANDARD) IF END = F1: GO TO 2.   (2)
(STANDARD) IF END = F2: MODIFICATION, CURSOR HOME GO TO 1.
(STANDARD) IF ONLY INPUT IS F3: RETURN TO MENU

2. INPUT ORDER HEADER USING FORM 2.

(STANDARD) F1: GO TO 3
(STANDARD) F2: GO TO 2
(STANDARD) F3: CANCEL ORDER, GO TO 1

3. INPUT ORDER LINE USING FORM 3.

4. DEPENDING ON FINAL FUNCTION KEY OF FORM 3:   (3)

F1. LINE IS OK: STORE IT AND CONTINUE INPUT, GO TO 3.
F2. MODIFICATION: CURSOR HOME, GO TO 3.
F3. CANCEL LINE, GO TO 3.
F4. BROWSE THRU PREVIOUS LINES (NEXT LINE = F4), GO TO 4   (4)
F5. DISPLAY ORDER HEADER, GO TO 5.   (5)
F6. DISPLAY CUSTOMER DATA, GO TO 6.
F7. END OF ORDER. START NEXT ORDER AT 1.

5. ORDER HEADER IS DISPLAYED AND CAN BE MODIFIED

F1. IF HEADER WAS ALTERED, STORE IT. GO TO 3.
F2. CURSOR HOME, GO TO 5.
F3. CANCEL ORDER: ASK "ARE YOU SURE? Y/N"
       IF "Y" DO IT THEN GO TO 1, ELSE GO TO 5.
F6. DISPLAY CUSTOMER DATA, GO TO 6.

6. CUSTOMER DATA IS DISPLAYED AND CAN BE MODIFIED

F1. IF CUSTOMER DATA WAS MODIFIED, STORE IT. GO TO 3.

---

* See notes (1)–(5), following this list.

F2. CURSOR HOME, GO TO 6.

F3. CANCEL ORDER: ASK "ARE YOU SURE? Y/N"
    IF "Y" DO IT THEN GO TO 1, ELSE GO TO 6.

Notes

1. Form 1 is a screen entry and display form, drawn on an MSD 80 ×
25 screen-form design slip. This slip and the instructions for filling it in
are described in this chapter. Each slip of a given kind ("form" here) is
numbered and stored in a screen-form dictionary.

2. The word STANDARD means that "IF END = F1: GO TO 2" is the
standard interpretation of the action of function key F1. If at the end of
form 1, the user terminates and returns control to the application program by hitting F1, he considers his input (or the display as it was
without modification) to be correct and asks the system to continue at
action line number 2.

Standard lines such as this one need not be written since they are
obvious to the programmer. The usage of function keys must be a
standard, agreed on by both specifiers and programmers. Then when a
key is used with its standard meaning, nothing is written. The specifier
will indicate only exceptions: INHIBIT F2, for example, if he wants
the user to be unable to modify the data displayed.

3. Seven possible function key assignments are listed here. The use of
F1 and F2 is standard, and the corresponding lines could have been
omitted. The use of F3 is not standard. This line is written to allow the
user to abort an order line and obtain a fresh empty form by returning
to 3.

4. After the user hits F4, the system displays the first line of the order
and lets the user do what he wishes with it, as if it had just been entered
with action line 3. If the user wants to see the next line, he hits F4
again. When he is back in the last entered line, if he hits F4 again he
returns to the first line, and so on. If he alters the line, he must confirm
his alteration with F1, and is then returned to the line he left. If he
cancels it with F3, the deletion is performed, a message "canceled" is
displayed (this is a programmer initiative), and then he is returned to
the line he left when he started browsing.

5. When the user hits F5, the order header is displayed, and available
for changing, as specified in action line 5.

This scenario demonstrates the flexibility that modern interactive applications must provide to the end user. He must be able to change his mind, go back to the beginning of his work, delete or modify his entries, or abort a transaction.

2.2 MSD Dictionary

MSD has a data dictionary to record the descriptions of the various attributes and relations on the appropriate slips. This dictionary also stores the other slips used to describe the DFSs of an application:

- screen forms (80 columns × 25 lines),
- report layouts (132 columns × 66 lines),
- co-routines,
- transactions,
- notes to the programmer,
- multilevel views,
- access or relationship paths.

The dictionary also contains lists, designed for quick retrieval of any given slip. In addition, the data dictionary also contains two cross-references: one for attributes and one for relations. These cross-references indicate where a given data element is used or mentioned: screens, reports, co-routines, transactions, etc.

2.2.1 Computer-Supported Dictionaries

The various subdictionaries may or may not be computerized. If the DBMS that will be used in the end has a data dictionary, that will help; if an index-sequential filing system is available for the various lists and cross-references, that will help greatly. However, the number of free-form comments that must be entered into an MSD set of dictionaries to help future programming is such that existing data dictionary utilities do not generally provide the required capabilities. Even if a real DBMS, featuring variable-length alpha strings, is available, screen and report layouts will not be easy to manage. Some DBMSs available are quite close to the ideal dictionary capabilities: IDMS/R, TIS, ORACLE, STENO (of CIG), and MULTIPRO (of CAP GEMINI SOGETI).

The ideal computer tool is an integrated programmer's workbench. But such a tool has its own set of constraints. It requires a lot of

computer power to run efficiently and demands a screen for each specifier. In the future, such tools will become more and more available and
affordable and will be capable of supporting a development from early
preliminary requirements phase to the DFS phase, to programming,
testing, and documenting.

Today a good specification method such as MSD can be used with
profit *without* a computerized set of dictionaries. Specifiers will write
the scenarios and fill in the dictionary slips by hand, in pencil.

2.2.2 The MSD Data Dictionary

During the process of writing DFSs, the specifier discovers data. User-
visible results may be identified first, followed by the data required as
input, and then the data that need to be stored permanently in the
database. Whatever the type of data, groups (relations) appear before
attributes. For example, when specifying an invoicing system, the relation INVOICE appears first, then its details—the relations INVOICE-
HEADER and INVOICE-LINE, then finally the attributes.

2.2.2.1 Identification Rules for Relations and Attributes

In the MSD approach, each relation or attribute is documented in the
data dictionary as soon as it is *identified*.

Identifying a relation (static or dynamic) is possible when

1. there is at least one scenario that needs it,

2. there is a uniqueness key, or unique, well-defined tuple generation
conditions,

3. the specifier can quote at least one sample occurrence of the relation, and make it part of the test data,

4. at least one user needs this relation in this scenario.

For example, an invoice is identified when

• a scenario that participates in the invoicing procedure needs it—for
example, the key-in of invoicing parameters,

• a uniqueness key is known (the invoice-number in this case),

• a sample invoice is available, to be included in the test data,

• a specific person or department, such as sales administration, needs
the scenario and the relation.

Identifying an attribute is possible when

1. There is at least one relation that includes it, with a key such that the attribute is unambiguously known when this key is known. This means that the relation must embody a single-valued dependence between its key and the attribute. Alternatively, the attribute may be assigned arbitrary values; it is then a key. If the relation is a keyless event file or dynamic relation, there exists a well-defined generation procedure that creates the tuples.

2. The specifier can quote at least one sample value of the attribute, and this value is part of the test data.

3. At least one user needs or supplies this attribute value.

When a relation or an attribute is identified, the specifier can start filling in a slip to describe it and insert it in the data dictionary. However, the data element will be *completely defined* only when all the information required to program its processing has been documented. That implies filling in the MSD slip completely, but also defining the existence constraints, the test data, and the use of this element in all other scenarios.

2.2.2.2 Attribute Slip
The attribute slip is a form that describes the attribute. See figure 2.1.

The A___ field in the upper right-hand corner is for the *attribute-number*. Each attribute has a unique number. Numbers are assigned to attributes in the order in which they are discovered. No relationship between the attribute-number and the relation is implied. The attribute-number is used to designate the attribute in a concise way. For example, let attribute A582 be the item-type and A504 the discount value. To write "If the item-type is 8, then the discount must be 10%," the specifier writes: "If A582 = 8 then A504 = 10%."

The *NAME* field allows plenty of space to write the name of the attribute. This is a symbolic name, meaningful to the specifier, which has no special syntax rules. It can comprise several words. It will be used in all cross-references to designate the attribute and wherever needed in the DFS. It is not meant for use within programs as a variable name or as a prompt text on the screen; such names are defined below.

The *PROMPT TEXT* field is used for a unique prompt definition. It is

MSD

ATTRIBUTE   A___

NAME

PROMPT TEXT	COLUMN HEADER
VARIABLE NAME	IMAGE
MEANING	

DEF. DOMAIN AND INTERVAL

EXISTENCE CONSTRAINTS

CALCULATION METHOD

USED IN RELATIONS

R___   R___   R___   R___   R___   R___   R___   R___   R___

COMMENTS

Figure 2.1
Sample attribute slip.

quite confusing for a user to get used to varying prompts. If the customer-name is called CUST-NAME in order entry, CUSTOMER in
accounting, and NAME in sales analysis, the user has to learn three
different notations. To avoid this, the MSD approach uses unique text
for prompting and naming the attribute column (*COLUMN HEADER*),
when a query is answered by a formatted screen display.

It is good practice to limit the length of the column header to the
usual length of the attribute. This is not a problem with 25-character
alphabetic names, but it may be with 2-digit codes. Nevertheless, even
if a header page may be required in each printout to define short column headers, this uniqueness discipline must be enforced.

The *VARIABLE NAME* field is used to define a unique variable
name, for use within all programs. This name can be concise since the
meaning of the variable is well defined in the data dictionary. Long
COBOL names are no longer indispensable for that reason. This field
will be filled in by the programmer, not the DFS specifier.

The best name for an attribute, when a user has to enter it using a
keyboard during a query operation, is the most concise name. Users
are not always expert typists. The name can be chosen from among a
list of NAMEs (in the attribute NAME sense defined above) using a
mouse to point to it on a screen. Or it can be the concise A____
attribute number, after the user has looked it up in the data dictionary
to make sure of its meaning. But long names such as CUSTOMER-
ADDRESS should be avoided.

The *MEANING* field is quite long. It is intended for a complete
description of the meaning of the attribute. If the space provided in the
slip is not sufficient for long explanations, a separate free-format paper
may be attached to the slip.

The *DEF. DOMAIN AND INTERVAL* field is used to specify the
type of variable: integer, alpha (character), date, real, logical, etc.
These are technical DP terms. The user needs to know only three
types: number, name, and date. For a number, he will specify the
length in digits in the *IMAGE* field or the number of digits before and
after the decimal point. The sign, if any, can be noted there too. Any
convention can be used as long as it is clear to both the specifier and
the programmer.

For example, the "999" COBOL convention can be used for a three-
digit integer, as well as the trivial "3 digits." For a decimal number, the

"S9(13).99" of COBOL is as good as " – 13.2 digits" to specify a signed decimal number that may have a maximum of 13 digits before the decimal point and 2 after. For a real number, only the precision class needs to be specified: "real 1" for simple precision, "real 2" for double precision, etc. For an alpha string, "A25" or "25 char" is just as good. The project leader, DBA, or programmer will review this definition of IMAGE and correct it if necessary.

The notion of *DOMAIN* is more powerful than the computer representation of the variable described above. A domain is a semantic notion; it defines a class of values. For example, the first name of a person and a city name are both alphabetics. But the first name domain comprises only names that can be the first name of a person, and the city name domain comprises only names of cities. Another domain can be color, and can comprise the values White, Green, Black, Yellow, and Blue. A color variable can have only one of these five values. If the specifier understands this notion, if he needs it and wants to use it, it is available and could be valuable with modern languages such as PAS-CAL, ADA, and MODULA-2 in the subsequent programming phase, particularly for the data co-routines.

The notion of *INTERVAL* specifies the range of the variable's values. Sometimes specifying the physical type (decimal, 5.2 digits) will suffice because no precise boundaries can be given. Sometimes an interval, open or closed, can be given: > (greater than) 1000, or – 999 to +999 for example. But MSD's interval can also designate a set of values. For example, a sales representative code, IMAGE 2 digits, must be one of these 17 values: 00, 01, 02, 04, 05, 07, 08, 09, 10, 11, 15, 16, 21, 25, 41, 70, 99. The "interval" specified is the name given to this finite set or the above list of values. If the set contains many elements and must be stored in a table, this is indicated.

The *EXISTENCE CONSTRAINTS* field is the location available for the rules to be respected by the attribute, no matter how its value is generated. This notion was defined in 1.3.2.2.

The *CALCULATION METHOD* field is the place where the algorithm or calculation formula used to obtain the value of this attribute is written. If the space provided is not sufficient, a separate paper may be attached to the attribute slip. The specifier may also use a NOTE slip, described in this section.

The *USED IN RELATIONS* field is for cross-reference purposes.

The *COMMENTS* field is provided for any additional free-format information the specifier may choose to document, for his own benefit or the information of the programmer.

The slip shown in figure 2.2 is a sample attribute slip for the key of R1 = PARTS.

2.2.2.3 Relation Slip

The relation slip holds the description of a relation. See figure 2.3.

The R____ field in the upper right-hand corner is for the *relation-number*. Numbering relations follows the same rules as numbering attributes; however, a relation in the MSD sense used for DFS can compromise both attributes and other relations.

If it is a STORED relation—that is, if it will be stored in the data-

---

MSD

	ATTRIBUTE	**A1**

NAME   ITEM NUMBER

PROMPT TEXT ITEM #	**COLUMN HEADER** ITEM
VARIABLE NAME ITEMNR	**IMAGE** 4 DIGITS

MEANING   FIRST 2 DIGITS = FAMILY CODE
              LAST 2 DIGITS = ITEM IN FAMILY
      EXCEPTIONS: SEE Paul PRESTWITCH

DEF. DOMAIN AND INTERVAL
              1001 TO 9999

EXISTENCE CONSTRAINTS
IF FAMILY CODE IS 99 THE LAST 2 DIGITS MUST BE 03, 04, OR 05

CALCULATION METHOD

USED IN RELATIONS
R1__   R2__   R__   R__   R__   R__   R__   R__   R__

COMMENTS THIS IS THE KEY OF R1 = PARTS
A NEW ITEM IS CREATED USING THE FORM FOR R1=PARTS.
IT IS UPDATED WHEN INVENTORY MOVEMENTS OCCUR

Figure 2.2
Attribute slip for R1 = PARTS.

MSD

RELATION   R___

NAME   _/_

KEY ATTRIBUTES   VOLUME

A___ + A___ + A___ + A___
                                              STORED   I/O   WORK

CONSTRAINTS: EXISTENCE, INTEGRITY, ETC...   CO-ROUTINE
                                                        C___

LIST OF ATTRIBUTES (NUMBER, NAME)

Nr	Name	rqd	Nr	Name	rqd
A___			A___		
A___	— — — — — — —	A___	— — — — —
A___	— — — — — — —	A___	— — — — —
A___	— — — — — — —	A___	— — — — —
A___	— — — — — — —	A___	— — — — —
A___	— — — — — — —	A___	— — — — —
A___	— — — — — — —	A___	— — — — —
A___	— — — — — — —	A___	— — — — —
A___	— — — — — — —	A___	— — — — —
A___	— — — — — — —	A___	— — — — —
A___	— — — — — — —	A___	— — — — —
A___	— — — — — — —	A___	— — — — —
A___	— — — — — — —	A___	— — — — —
A___	— — — — — — —	A___	— — — — —

COMMENTS

Figure 2.3
Sample relation slip.

base—it must be in fourth normal form, and follow all the rules described in 1.3.3.2. It can then comprise only attributes.

If it is a relation used for I/O (a screen form, for example) or for temporary WORK (in memory or variable-record length sequential disk files, for example), it can comprise subrelations mixed with attributes.

Example

The relation INVOICE has to be created and documented in the data dictionary when the specifier describes the invoicing procedure. This relation will comprise all the data elements of an invoice:

· 1 HEADER (*invoice-number,* inv-date, customer-number, invoice-amount, etc.),

· N INVOICE-LINEs (*invoice-number, item-number,* quantity, etc.).

Since the number of INVOICE-LINEs can be *variable*, the relation INVOICE, which comprises the HEADER and INVOICE-LINEs, is not in fourth normal form. It cannot be stored in a single relation-file by any existing relational DBMS, except perhaps if its contents are considered mere text and can therefore have a variable length.

But the reason for describing INVOICE in MSD is because *each group of data that appears as a group during an I/O operation or in memory for some calculation process must be documented as a group.* The specifier will in fact use three relation slips to document an invoice:

· the HEADER (static) relation slip,

· the INVOICE-LINE (static) relation slip,

· the INVOICE (dynamic) relation slip, where the list of "attributes" at the bottom will comprise only Rxxx and Ryyy, where the xxx designates the HEADER relation and the yyy the INVOICE-LINE relation.

The INVOICE slip must exist because a group of data appearing together on a printout called "invoice" exists. The INVOICE slip will describe the VOLUME (number of invoices per day), the CONSTRAINTS (conditions that must be respected in order for an invoice to be printed), and the uniqueness KEY—the invoice-number in this case—when there is one. When the programmer finds a report-layout slip describing the invoice, he must find an INVOICE relation slip in the data dictionary, even if that refers him to two other slips.

When two relations are very similar—differing in only three attributes, for example—the specifier may write in the LIST of ATTRI-
BUTES: "same as Rxxx except. . ." and describe only the exceptions.

When a relation contains subrelations, it may still have a key, made
of one or several attributes. The key of an INVOICE is obviously the
invoice-number; this is written in the KEY ATTRIBUTES field of the
slip.

When the key of the relation comprises several attributes, all the
attributes are written in the A____ + A____ etc. field in the decreasing
order of their importance. For example, the key of INVOICE-LINE
that comprises invoice-number (A32) and item-number (A7) will be
written "A32 + A7," in that order.

The —/— sign on the right side of the NAME line is for the number
of pages (slips) of the relation description. A relation may have too
many attributes to fit on one slip in the LIST OF ATTRIBUTES part.
When this happens, the first (full) slip is numbered 1/2 and the second
(and last) slip 2/2. If necessary, a third slip can be used. The numbers
are then 1/3, 2/3, 3/3.

The VOLUME field describes the number of tuples of the relation. If
the relation is stored, this will be the maximum number of records in
the future relaton file, the *cardinal* of the relation. If the relation is
described for I/O, it will be the number of such operations per day,
hour, or month, whichever is most significant. The information will be
used to dimension the disk or the I/O device(s): printer(s), VDT(s), and
so on. In chapter 6, it will also be a basis for evaluating the processor
power required to handle the load.

The CONSTRAINTS: EXISTENCE, . . . field describes the existence constraints of the entire relation, assuming that a preliminary
check has been performed on its attributes (see 1.3.2.2). The CO-
ROUTINE field C____ describes the number of the associated control-
routine, which implements the required existence controls for both
static and dynamic relations.

In the LIST OF ATTRIBUTES section, the A____ stands for an
attribute number, "Name" for the attribute name, and "rqd" for "required": when the existence of the attribute is mandatory for the existence of the relation, the specifier writes "Y" (for "yes"); when the
existence of the attribute is not mandatory, he writes nothing or "N."
Naturally, A____s can be replaced with R____s to indicate subrelations.

Figure 2.4 shows a filled-in relation slip.

Note that the specifier has checked both the STORED and I/O fields. When this happens, the programmer must then find a screen form slip or a report layout slip or both using this relation to describe its contents, in addition to implementing the relation in the database.

2.2.3 Other MSD Descriptions

Besides the data dictionary that describes the attributes and relations, MSD has other descriptions generated during the DFS phase and the subsequent technical design phase.

2.2.3.1 Screen Form and Report Layout Slips

In the process of describing his DFS, the specifier describes the exact outputs he wishes to obtain. Sometimes one of the important functions of the application is to produce such an output, not to engage in a conversational process. The user interaction is then limited to a simple request for output: a query or the selection of a report in a menu, for example.

Such a simple request is not described in the DFS using a scenario because this technique is specifically intended for interactive processes. The specifier draws the layout of what he wishes to see on his CRT or report, and the project manager or an analyst will subsequently (during the technical design phase) convert that layout slip (into a chain of programs, for example).

The screen form slip and report layout slip are identical, except perhaps in size.

A screen form needs to be large enough to accommodate the entire contents of a screen. In some cases (DEC hardware, for example), the screen can display as many as 132 columns and 25 rows. But in most cases, it can display only 80 columns by 25 rows. We shall not concern ourselves with the graphics capabilities; the specifier will not attempt to draw what he wishes with an accuracy of 1 pixel! The rule is, As long as the programmer can understand accurately what the specifier wishes, the slip is correct. A DFS is a means of communication, not a work of art.

A report may be as wide as 132 columns or sometimes even wider. It can contain as many as 72 lines per page. Whatever its size, the identical description technique is used for screen and report slips, so we shall describe only screen form slips.

MSD

RELATION   R2__

NAME   STOCK   1_/1

KEY ATTRIBUTES				VOLUME
A1__ + A___ + A___ + A___				2500 ITEMS

STORED X   I/O X   **WORK**

CONSTRAINTS: EXISTENCE, INTEGRITY, ETC...   **CO-ROUTINE**
                                                      C2

THIS RELATION CAN ONLY BE CREATED AFTER R1 WAS (SAME ITEM)
C2 WILL CHECK NON-NEGATIVE QUANTITIES AND REQUIRED
ATTRIBUTES

LIST OF ATTRIBUTES (NUMBER, NAME)

Nr	Name	rqd	Nr	Name	rqd
A1	ITEM #	Y	A___		
A6	QTY ON HAND	Y	A___		
A7	QTY USED	N	A___		
A8	QTY ON ORDER	N	A___		
A9	QTY RESERVED	N	A___		
A10	QTY RETURNED TO VENDOR	N	A___		
A18	LAST PURCHASE PRICE	Y	A___		
A___			A___		
A___			A___		
A___			A___		
A___			A___		
A___			A___		
A___			A___		

COMMENTS

Figure 2.4
Completed relation slip.

The sample slip shown in figure 2.5 should be interpreted as follows:

• Lines 1 and 9 contain titles: INVENTORY CONTROL and MOVE-MENT HISTORY, respectively. The specifier simply writes the titles he wants in the location where he wants them.

• Lines 3, 5, and 7 contain PROMPT TEXTS: ITEM, PRICE, SUP-PLIER, IN STOCK, and so on.

• Line 11 contains column titles, which are also PROMPT TEXTS, as defined in the attribute slips.

• Near the values announced by the prompt texts, the specifier has written attribute numbers A____ in small ovals. Each attribute number tells the programmer what attribute should be displayed or keyed in after its PROMPT TEXT. The values are examples. The whole slip may actually be part of the test data supplied with the DFSs.

Note that the titles and PROMPT TEXTs do not have attribute numbers. They would if they were attributes of the data dictionary. They do not need any if they are titles and prompts.

• The screen is divided into two parts by a horizontal line. The upper part displays selected attributes from the ITEM relation: A85, A86, A116, A95, A90, etc. The lower part displays selected attributes from tuples (remember: tuples are logical records) of the MOVEMENT-HISTORY relation. Five tuples are featured here as examples, each with five attributes: A8, A88, A89, A12, and A50.

• The last line displays a menu of commands (function keys) available to the user:

• F1 will display more movement history lines if the screen is full,
• F2 will ask for another item to be queried, then display it,
• F3 will return the user to the MENU, thus exiting from this query,
• F4 will let the user browse through the various history lines: it will redisplay the first screenful of history lines; the user may then move to the next screen by depressing F1, etc.

The cursor is normally located near the YOUR CHOICE: prompt, to indicate that the system expects the user to choose one of the 4 function keys.

Figure 2.6 presents the relation slip associated with this screen form. Note the simple way of filling it in used by the specifier; he listed the

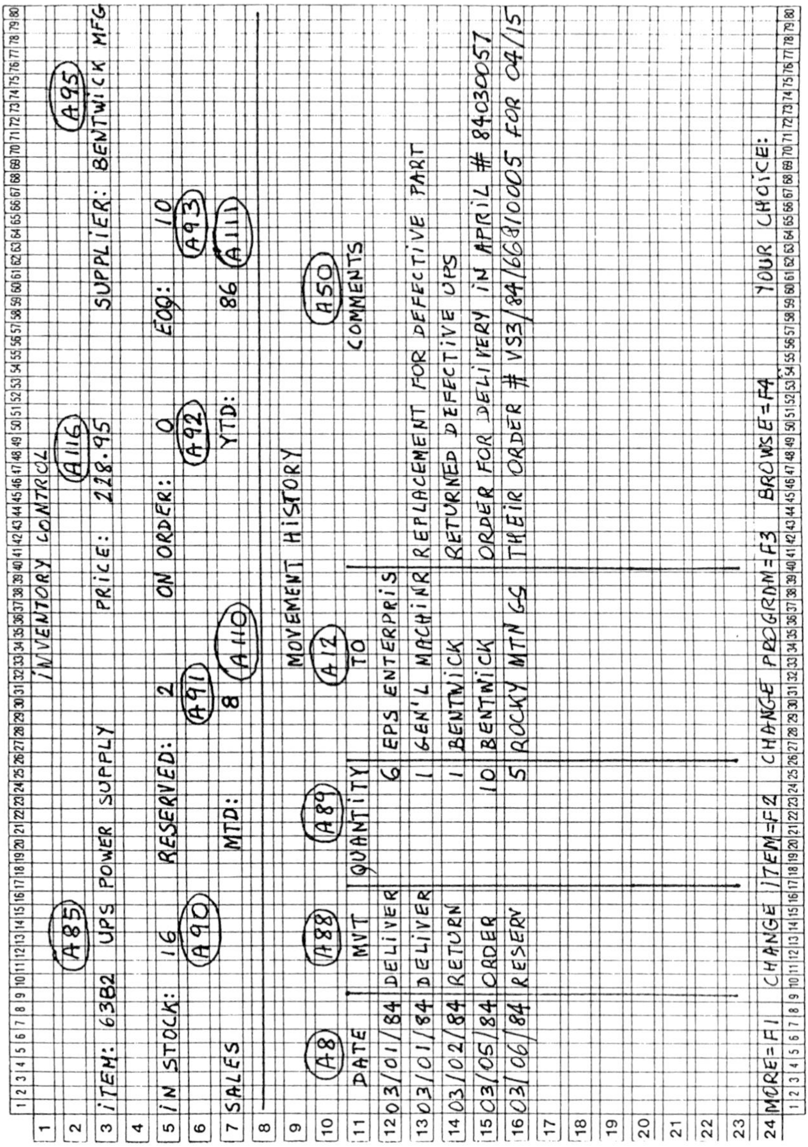

INVENTORY CONTROL

```
   1 (A85)
   2
   3 ITEM: 6382  UPS POWER SUPPLY      PRICE: 228.95      SUPPLIER: BENTWICK MFG
                                        (A116)                      (A95)
   4
   5 IN STOCK: 16      RESERVED: 2      ON ORDER: 0      EOQ: 10
   6  (A90)             (A91)            (A92)            (A93)
   7 SALES   MTD: 8                      YTD: 86
   8        (A88)  (A110)                     (A111)
   9              MOVEMENT HISTORY
  10                                    (A50)
  11 DATE       MVT     QUANTITY   TO            COMMENTS
       (A89)            (A12)
  12 03/01/84  DELIVER     6   EPS ENTERPRIS
  13 03/01/84  DELIVER     1   GEN'L MACHINR  REPLACEMENT FOR DEFECTIVE PART
  14 03/02/84  RETURN      1   BENTWICK       RETURNED DEFECTIVE UPS
  15 03/05/84  ORDER      10   BENTWICK       ORDER FOR DELIVERY IN APRIL # 84030057
  16 03/06/84  RESERV      5   ROCKY MTN GS   THEIR ORDER # VS3/84/66810005 FOR 04/15
  17
  18
  19
  20
  21
  22
  23
  24 MORE=F1   CHANGE ITEM=F2   CHANGE PROGRAM=F3   BROWSE=F4      YOUR CHOICE:
```

Figure 2.5
Sample screen layout slip.

MSD

RELATION   R237

NAME   QUERY OF INVENTORY MOVEMENT HISTORY   1/1

KEY ATTRIBUTES   **VOLUME**

A85_   + A___   + A___   + A___   250 / day

                                     STORED   I/O x   **WORK**

CONSTRAINTS: EXISTENCE, INTEGRITY, ETC...   **CO-ROUTINE**

                                                        C___

LIST OF ATTRIBUTES (NUMBER, NAME)

Nr	Name	rqd	Nr	Name	rqd
A85	ITEM-NUMBER (INPUT)		A8__	MOVEMENT-DATE	
A86	ITEM-NAME _ _ _ _		A88_	MOVEMENT-NAME	_
A116	SALE-PRICE		A89_	MOVEMENT-QUANTITY	
A95	SUPPLIER-NAME _ _		A12_	MOVEMENT-DESTINATION	
A90	QUANTITY-IN-STOCK		A50_	MOVEMENT-EXPLANATION	
A91	QUANTITY-RESERVED-BY-CUSTR		A___	_ _ _ _ _ _	
A92	QUANTITY-ON-ORDER		A___		
A93	ECONOMIC-ORDER-QUANTITY		A___	_ _ _ _ _	
A110	TOTAL-SALES-MTD		A___		
A111	TOTAL-SALES-YTD _ _		A___	_ _ _ _ _ _	
A___			A___		
A___	(ALL ABOVE ATTRIBUTES_		A___	(ALL ABOVE ATTRIBUTES	
A___	FROM R26=INVENTORY CONTROL)		A___	FROM R31=MVT HISTORY)	
A___	_ _ _ _ _ _		A___	_ _ _ _ _	

COMMENTS   BROWSING THROUGH MOVEMENTS

FUNCTION KEY USE:

    F1--->NEXT SCREEN OF MOVEMENTS FOR THIS ITEM
    F4--->FIRST SCREEN OF MOVEMENTS FOR THIS ITEM

Figure 2.6

Relation slip associated with the screen slip in figure 2.5.

attributes of both relations that make up the screen contents, feeling certain that the programmer would understand without requiring three relation slips: one for the entire screen, one for the upper part, and one for the lower part. This attitude is still acceptable when only *some* of the attributes of a given subrelation are used: the attributes of both the lower and upper parts are only a subset of the sets of attributes of the INVENTORY CONTROL and MOVEMENT-HISTORY relations. They can be extracted using project operations, quite familiar to programmers.

Note that the specifier does not describe the scrolling technique to be used for the movement history. He simply indicates the MORE = F1 and BROWSE = F4 keys and explains these keys in the COMMENTS field of the relation slip.

2.2.3.2   Co-Routine Slips

A co-routine is a program module that verifies that a database update can be performed safely or that a program can be started or terminated safely. There are two types of co-routines: data verification co-routines and program protection co-routines. Both are described using the same type of MSD slip. (See 1.2.7, 1.2.8, 1.3.2.2, and 1.3.4.3 in chapter 1 and 2.1.1.3, 2.1.1.4, 2.1.2, 2.1.3, and 2.1.4 in chapter 2 for an introduction to the co-routine concept.)

A *data verification co-routine* is specific to a certain part of a database: a relation or a subdatabase. It is inserted as an interface between all application programs that access that part of the database and the DBMS itself. (See section 6.3 for a discussion of the appropriate software architecture.) The principle of the co-routine is simple; it is interesting only because it is unique.

All three existence constraint levels of a given relation (attribute, relation, and subdatabase levels) are verified in the same functional interface. All types of constraints—integrity, cardinality, interval (value) or domain, consistency, and syntax are also verified there. The consequences are as follows:

• The verification software is written only once. Even if many different programs can update the database, their programmers do not have to concern themselves with verifying the quality of the data sent to the database for insertion, deletion, or modification. A program's raw data (for example, as after key-in) are sent to the functional interface (FI). If they are correct, the FI passes them to the DBMS for update. If they are not, the program receives an error message and must resubmit corrected data. Thus, only one programmer writes the co-routine verifications; the others simply use the co-routine. *The co-routine concept implies less coding.*

• The uniqueness of the co-routine implies that no matter what program sends data to the database, the tests performed are the same. So if the DBA discovers after some time that the database contains errors, it is not necessary to try to find which programmer forgot to implement a validation test. The co-routine will be improved, and the next time a program sends the same erroneous data, the update request will be denied. *The co-routine concept implies easier maintenance and more consistency.*

• The number of checks performed by a co-routine is the minimum required for the protection of the data. This concept does not imply fewer or more numerous verifications than careful programming of the necessary verifications in each update program. The only overhead induced by the user of the FI technique is due to the passing of data through one more module.

Tests have shown that even on slow micros, the processor time overhead (about 1 msec) is less than 10% of the processor load induced by one disk READ instruction. *The co-routine concept does not degrade the performance.*

• Each relation or each subdatabase such as inventory control (which comprises the relations INVENTORY-ITEMS and INVENTORY-MOVEMENTS) has its own co-routine. However, the FI architecture avoids redundant attribute verification code. *The co-routine concept conserves memory space.*

Example

An inventory management subdatabase comprises the relations

ITEM (*item-number,* item-name, price, supplier-name, quantity-in-stock, quantity-on-order, quantity-reserved, economic-order-quantity, sales-mtd, sales-ytd),
MOVEMENT (*item-number, mvt-date, mvt-code, mvt-number,* mvt-quantity, mvt-destination, mvt-comments),
MVT-TABLE (*mvt-code,* mvt-name).

The "mvt" abbreviation stands for "movement." The mvt-number attribute, which terminates the key of MOVEMENT, designates the number of the slip used to generate the movement; it also makes the key unique.

The verifications performed by the data co-routines of this subdatabase are as follows:

Attribute level

• syntax checks on all attributes: numeric attributes are numbers; the date is valid; the length of each attribute is corect;

• interval checks on numeric attributes (example: mvt-quantity > 0).

Relation level

• All required attributes exist: the keys, item-name, mvt-name, and mvt-quantity. Missing attributes are automatically assigned the value "not-defined."

• The keys of ITEM or MOVEMENT are not duplicated.

• Sales-mtd cannot be greater than sales-ytd.

• When X is added to sales-mtd, it is automatically added to sales-ytd.

Subdatabase level

• The item-number attribute of the MOVEMENT key exists in the ITEM relation.

• The mvt-code of a MOVEMENT exists in the MVT-TABLE.

• The mvt-quantity does not induce a negative quantity-in-stock.

• A DELIVERY movement automatically increases sales-mtd and sales-ytd.

• An item cannot be deleted if its movements still exist.

For another example, see figure 2.7.

Some of these existence constraints are described in the data dictionary. Example: attribute syntax and interval.

The others must be written during the DFS phase in the co-routine slip of the relation or the subdatabase. It is best to use one co-routine slip for each relation when there are too many verifications to be written in the CONSTRAINTS field of the relation slip. This slip will describe the relation-level constraints.

In addition, it is necessary to fill in one co-routine slip for each subdatabase, to describe the subdatabase level checks.

MSD

CO - ROUTINE   C6

NAME   VERIFICATION OF THE INPUT OF WAREHOUSE MOVEMENTS

CONTROLS   R4   OR   T

CONSTRAINTS

EXISTENCE (DD AND AUTOMATIC)
    A1=ITEM #, A14=QTY, A15=DATE, A11=MVT #, A16=SLIP #

DATE VALID IF AFTER PRINTING THE LAST LIST OF SUPPLIER DELIV
    BUT NO LATER THAN THE COMPUTER DATE A17

EXISTENCE OF ORDER
    IF A11=1 (DEL FROM SUPPLIER) CHECK THAT A16 IS
    AN ORDER #

COMMENTS

Figure 2.7
Sample co-routine slip. Note that the CONTROLS field designates the relation (static
or dynamic), or the transaction protected by this co-routine.

A program should not be started recklessly; *program protection co-routines* are needed. A number of context parameters must be checked:

• Functional context: if the execution of other programs before this one can be started is a prerequisite, have they been executed? Was their execution successful? If certain data elements must have precise values, do they have these values?

• Environment context: is the configuration correct for this program? Is there enough disk and memory space?

• User context: is the user who starts the program authorized to do so? Is there a time-of-day constraint on execution (start time must be after a given hour, for example)?

Similarly, when the execution of a program is finished, are there other programs that must execute immediately and automatically?

These verifications can be *static* (they are not expected to change) or *dynamic* (they may have to evolve). In both cases, it is good practice to separate them from the functional programs and include them in co-routines.

The specifier must describe his constraints in the co-routine slips, as he does for relations. The project leader or analyst will take the necessary technical steps to ensure that these constraints are enforced. A software architecture for program protection is discussed in section 6.4.

2.2.3.3 Notes to the Programmer

From time to time, a situation arises that cannot be conveniently described using the slips we have covered. The specifier may need to communicate to the programmer requirements, words of caution, or information that does not fit correctly under any of the previous slip headings. He will then make a note on an ordinary piece of paper, adding a subject title and a note number of future reference.

He may also make a note to himself. If he suddenly has an idea while he is working on a different subject, he will write a short note to remember to explore this idea later. At the end of the DFS phase, he will verify that he has covered all the subjects of his own notes. Figure 2.8 presents a sample note slip.

MSD

                           N O T E   N1__

SUBJECT   SUPPLIER INVOICE VERIFICATION (MANUAL)

NOTE THAT:
THIS OPERATION COMPARES THE INVOICES RECEIVED WITH THE DAY'S
MOVEMENTS, USING THE LISTINGS OF ORDERS AND DELIVERIES. THE
PRICES ON THE INVOICES ARE COMPARED WITH THE PRICES QUOTED
ON THE ORDERS.

IN CASE PRICES DISAGREE, THE INVOICE IS SET ASIDE UNTIL THE
CORRECT PRICE IS DETERMINED.

WHEN PRICES AGREE, THE INVOICE IS STAMPED "OK" AND PASSED
OVER TO THE PERSON WHO KEYS IN THE PRICES AND QUANTITIES FOR
THE COMPUTER TO CALCULATE THE WEIGHTED AVERAGE COST (WAC)

Figure 2.8
Sample note slip.

Comment on Note Slips

MSD has not reinvented the notepad! Of course, there is no need for a
preprinted MSD slip for writing notes. Actually none of the other preprinted slips is indispensable. During its first three years of existence,
MSD did not include preprinted slips. This relational method of DFS,
database, and program module design worked quite well with dictionaries written on individual pieces of paper, generally of a harder,
glossy quality. But as time went by and experience was gained, project
leaders noticed that it was easier to read pieces of paper with a standard format and standard contents, so preprinted slips were developed.

2.2.3.4 Transaction Slip

Before reading this subsection, the reader should review sections 2.1.3
and 2.1.4, which describe the steps of the technical design phase of
MSD.

The T____ field in the upper right-hand corner of figure 2.9 is used for
defining the transaction number. This number can be arbitrary.

The NAME field is used for defining the transaction name, which can be any title meaningful to the analyst. The NAME describes in one *short* sentence what this transaction will do. The transaction can implement a high- or low-level scenario, so the title can be a general function, such as "Order Entry," or a detail function, such as "Order Line key-in dialog."

The FUNCTIONAL PURPOSE field describes in more detail what the NAME suggests.

The VOLUME field designates the number of transactions to be performed per unit of time. Examples: 10/hour, 220/day, 5/month.

The SCENARIO column contains the scenario. The rules of writing the scenario in a transaction slip are the same as in a scenario paper (MSD has no special scenario slip because, after some practice, many specifiers write their scenarios directly on the transaction slips, under the control of the project leader):

• describe the various action steps of the dialog using a pseudocode style: use IF, GO TO, UNTIL, DO, and similar words,

• number the action steps, making sure that the number does not exceed 10,

• use function key symbols for processing selections,

• etc., as described in sections 2.1.7 and 2.1.8.

In addition to the scenario, this column contains the database I/O operations, described as relational multilevel views (defined in section 1.3.1). Each view is inserted at the action step line where it belongs, with full title and number. In fact, some views are not described by the specifier: the single-level selections, which are obvious to a programmer. The view itself is documented while the transaction slip is written or shortly after, using a View slip. This is done by the project leader, because it is a more technical step. *All* views are documented, including single-level selections, in order to count accurately all required DBMS calls for the physical database optimization phase.

The transaction will finally become a real program, large and freestanding, or a small module embedded in a larger program. To prepare the transformation, MSD requires that the analyst fill in the I/O data column. This will provide the basis for declaring in the to-be-written software module the external data elements to be used.

MSD

TRANSACTION   T___

NAME _____

FUNCTIONAL PURPOSE   VOLUME

SCENARIO	I/O	RELATIONS ATTRIBUTES	
	R/A Nr	Name	I/O
	START CONSTRAINTS		
	END CONSTRAINTS		
COMMENTS	**FOLLOWED BY**		
	T___ T___ T___		
	T___ T___ T___		

Figure 2.9
Sample transaction slip.

The R/A Nr column is for the relation or attribute numbers.

This well-defined data definition process, external to the actual scenario-processing code, is exactly in line with the approach of modern languages, such as MODULA-2 and ADA. It is also recommended for use with powerful programmer workbenches, such as the IDMS/R utilities. With such an approach, the software can easily be developed as *independent* modules, which communicate with the outside world using well-defined data.

MSD considers all data elements exchanged between one module and others, or real disk, CRT, or printer I/O, as I/O. This notion is sufficiently accurate at this stage, but it may be refined during the actual programming to take advantage of the environment: MODULA 2's IMPORT-EXPORT capabilities are not identical to the information exchange mechanism of ADA, which are not the same as those of the IDMS/R workbench.

The START and END CONSTRAINTS fields define the rules to be enforced by the program protection co-routine, if one is required. Writing these rules in the transaction slip is like writing the data existence constraints directly in the CONSTRAINTS field of a relation slip: a short form of a co-routine slip.

Quite often, when the entire transaction concerns itself with the dialog associated with a screen form, the start constraints govern the display of the form on the screen, and the end constraints dictate the chaining of the form with the next processing phase.

Whatever the start/end constraints require, it is good practice to implement the associated software as independent co-routines, as described in 2.2.3.2.

The FOLLOWED BY field lists the transactions that can follow the one described on the current slip. See the Decision Machine discussion in chapter 6 for modern implementation techniques of the dynamic chaining concept.

Example

The transaction slip in figure 2.10 describes a low-level key-in dialog. Figures 2.11 and 2.12 provide the descriptions of one of the view slips and one of the access/relationship path slips.

Notice the way in which the R/A Nr column in figure 2.10 is filled in. In addition to attribute numbers, it contains PP and Q, two names used

MSD

TRANSACTION   T15

NAME	KEY-IN DIALOG FOR WEIGHTED AVERAGE COST

FUNCTIONAL PURPOSE   **VOLUME**
KEY-IN OF PURCHASE PRICE "PP" AND QUANTITY "Q"   210 / DAY
THE COMPUTER CALCULATES THE NEW WAC
RELATIONS R1 AND R2 ARE UPDATED

SCENARIO	**I/O RELATIONS**

SCENARIO	I/O RELATIONS ATTRIBUTES		
1. DISPLAY FORM S1 TO KEY-IN A1=ITEM #	**R/A Nr**	**Name**	**I/O**
2. ANSWER: DISPLAY REST OF S1,	A1	ITEM #	I
ASK FOR PP AND Q USING FORM S3 WITH	A6	QTY ON HAND	I/O
"PUSH F2 IF WRONG ITEM", RETURN TO 1	A18	LAST PP	I/O
3. KEY-IN PP, Q	A4	WAC	I/O
4. DB: SELECT A6 IN STOCK R2 FOR GIVEN	PP	KEYED-IN PP	I
ITEM A1 (VIEW V41)	Q	KEYED-IN QTY	I

5. COMPUTE A4 = WAC:

$$A4 = \frac{A4 \times A6 + PP}{A6 + Q}$$

6. COMPUTE NEW UNIT COST $U = \frac{PP}{Q}$

7. IF $(U - A18) > 10\% \times A18$:
   DISPLAY FORM S4 AND OBTAIN ANSWER
   IF OK GO TO 8 ELSE GO TO 3

8. DISPLAY NEW A6 AND A4

9. DB: UPDATE R1 AND R2 (VIEWS V42, V43)

START CONSTRAINTS
USER NUMBER MUST
BE WAC ACCOUNTING

END CONSTRAINTS
OFFER ANOTHER WAC
TRANSACTION (F1)
OR RETURN TO MENU
(F3)

COMMENTS
THE QTY ON HAND A6 MUST BE RETAINED AS
IT WAS BEFORE THE DELIVERY, IN ADDITION
TO BEING UPDATED IN THE WAREHOUSE WHEN
THE DELIVERY OCCURS

FOLLOWED BY

T____   MENU   T____

T____   T____   T____

Figure 2.10
Transaction slip for low-level key-in dialog.

MSD

VIEW   **V**4̲1̲

NAME SELECT TUPLE OF R2 FOR GIVEN Al   **TYPE** S̲ M + -

SELECTION

RELATION ACCES/RELATN CONSTRAINT CONSTRAINT CONSTRAINT CONSTRAINT

R2̲___   P56̲   Al = INPUT

R___   P___

R___   P___

R___   P___

R___   P___

LIST OF ATTRIBUTES SELECTED, MODIFIED OR INSERTED

R2̲___ ALL   A___   A___

A___   A___   A___

A___   A___   A___

A___   A___   A___

A___   A___   A___

A___   A___   A___

A___   A___   A___

A___   A___   A___

A___   A___   A___

A___   A___   A___

A___   A___   A___

TRANSACTIONS WHERE USED

N A M E	Int/Batch	VOLUME	Per Day,Month
T15̲ KEY-IN DIALOG FOR WAC	INTERACT	210	Day
T___			
T___			
T___			
T___			
T___			
T___			

Figure 2.11
Sample view slip for transaction T15.

MSD

ACCESS OR RELATIONSHIP PATH   P56

FROM R___ TO R2___   1/1

ACCESS BY ITEM-NUMBER A1 **OR RELATION VERB** _____

UNIQUE	KEY ATTRIBUTES	VOLUME
Y/N	A1___ + A___ + A___ + A___	(KEYS)
YES		2500

VIEWS WHERE USED

N A M E	Int/Batch	VOLUME	Per Day,Mth
V41 SELECT TUPLE OF R2 (KEY=A1)	INTERAC	210	DAY
V82 INVENTORY QUERY BY ITEM A1	INTERAC	50	HOUR
V117DISPLAY INVENT MOVEMENTS A1	INTERAC	30	HOUR
T___			
T___			
T___			
T___			
T___			
T___			
T___			
T___			
T___			
T___			
T___			
T___			

COMMENTS

Figure 2.12
Access/relationship path P56 to relation R2.

to designate input fields. If an entire relation is used as input or output, its number appears in an Rxxx form. If an entire relation *minus a few attributes* is used, it is necessary to create a special relation slip, where the attribute list is "same as Rxxx minus Aaaa, Abbb, Accc, etc."

The I/O column carries an I for those attributes or relations used only for Input to the transaction, an O for the output-only elements, and I/O (or I + O) for elements that appear both as input and output.

The END CONSTRAINTS and FOLLOWED BY fields are related.

Being implicit, restarting the same transaction is not described in the FOLLOWED BY list, but the MENU is.

2.2.3.5 View and Access/Relationship Path Slips

The purpose of the access slip is to document a single-level file (or relation) access or a 1-to-N interfile relationship.

It does not document a single-level view completely, because a view also defines the data exchanged by the application program and DBMS. It documents only one access (primary or secondary) to a file required by a view.

Alternatively, it documents an interfile relationship when a navigational DBMS will be used.

Both access and relationship descriptions concern themselves with *functional* requirements. The actual physical implementation technique (if the access or relationship is actually physically implemented) will be decided later, during the physical architecture optimization phase, described in chapter 6.

Access operations reach one record (in navigational DBMSs) or many tuples (in relational DBMSs) that match given key value constraints.

Example

Find a customer record in the CUSTOMER file given the customer-number. The file is accessed using a navigational (nonrelational) DBMS through its keyed-access technique: indexed, hash-coding, and so on. The file is accessed *directly*; no preliminary access to another file is required in this single-level operation.

Second Example

Find an order header record given the order number; then find the first item line for that order. The ORDER HEADER file is accessed first, using an index-sequential technique, for example, and in the order header record a pointer is found that points to the first order line record. The DBMS follows this pointer, accessing the first order line of that order as requested. This is a two-level view. It uses a direct access for the first level (the order header) file, and then it follows the 1-to-N relationship pointer to the first order line record. It comprises one access and one relationship.

Three-level, four-level, and other views are also used, but most views involve single-level accesses. The access or relationship path slip is used to specify single-level accesses. The specification will be used in turn to define the physical access technique to be implemented: hashing, indexing, and so on.

Describing 1-to-N *relationships* is the second purpose of the access/ relationship path slip. Relationships can be described only one level at a time—that is, between two files or relations.

Both access and relationship paths are used to reflect one level of the database manipulations described in the view slips. One of the main assumptions of MSD is that they should not be defined a priori, using static processing-independent considerations, such as those that appear in the nonrelational models to describe functional dependence. MSD defines them as a consequence of processing needs that are identified.

Are access paths and relationship paths different? An access path describes a direct access to a file, whereas a relationship path describes an access to a file by a key that belongs at least partly to a previous file.

For example, a Customer *Has* Orders relationship can be specified with a two-field key: customer-number + order-delivery-date. The first attribute of the key is an attribute of the Customer (previous) file; the second attribute implements a collating sequence among the orders of a given customer. MSD uses *sorted* relations whenever required by the transactions.

The difference between an access path and a relationship path lies in the *previous* relation. In practice, MSD considers the two notions as identical in effect, and employs the notion of relationship path only when the use of a DBMS featuring AREAs or CLUSTERS is planned; the traversing volume specified in the relationship path slip is then used in the *dynamic schema* (described in section 6.2.1). Too often, relationships are a modern way of describing old-fashioned pointers, multi-valued dependences, or subdatabase-level existence constraints. MSD ignores the nonrelational pointer concept, and uses co-routines to specify *all* types of existence constraints including the practical impact of functional dependences.

Access/Relationship Path Slip

1. The P___ field in the upper right-hand corner of figure 2.12 is for the slip number.

2. The FROM R___ TO R___ field describes

a single-level access: To Rxxx,
a relationship: FROM Rxxx TO Ryyy.

Example 1 (1-to-N relationship)
A manufacturing database contains 2 relations, ITEM and ORDER, linked by a 1-to-N relationship ITEM *HAS* ORDERs:

R1 = ITEM (*item-number*, etc.),
R2 = ORDER (*item-number*, *order-number*, quantity),

Assuming that

A1 = *item number*,
A2 = *order-number*,
A3 = *item-number*, *order-number*,
the relationship path between an item and its orders is described:
FROM R1 to R2.

Example 2 (N-to-P relationship)
The database now contains R1 and

R3 = ORDER-LINE (*order-number*, *item-number*, quantity),

linked by ITEM *HAS* ORDERs, which gives all the order-numbers for one item-number, and ORDER *CONTAINS* ITEMs, which gives all the item-numbers for one order-number. To access the order lines of a given item, the type of notation is the same as before: FROM R1 TO R3 is sufficient and unambiguous.

To access the item tuples for all the order lines of a given order, FROM R3 TO R1 will be used. Two access/relationship path slips are required.

Example 3 (several 1-to-N relationships)

Assume that to example 2 we add a third relationship, which gives, for one item, all order-lines that are already manufactured: ITEM *HAS-READY* ORDER-LINEs. This relationship also links an R1 parent with R3 children, but the set of children of a given R1 tuple is not the same as in example 2. This time, to access order-lines knowing an item, one must specify: FROM R1 TO R3 USING ITEM *HAS* ORDER-LINEs, or USING ITEM *HAS-READY* ORDER-LINEs. Three slips are required.

3. The ACCESS BY field describes the number of the key attribute used for single-attribute access or the numbers of all the key attributes that make up a multiattribute access key.

4. The RELATION VERB field describes the verb associated with the relation*ship*, if the slip describes a 1-to-N relationship. Example: customer *HAS* orders.

5. The UNIQUE Y/N field is used to indicate that an access method should check the uniqueness of the key. The analyst will write YES to indicate that there should be only one key for each value. This will be the case only for the primary access of a master-type file or relation. Note that this type of file, defined in 1.3.4.7 by functional criteria only, can be implemented with any type of DBMS, relational, for example, and not only master-event DBMSs.

If the analyst writes NO, he implies that this access method should not check the uniqueness of the key; this will be the case for a secondary access, on any type of event-type file or relation.

6. The KEY ATTRIBUTES field is used for a single-level access or a relationship. If the key comprises several attributes, the analyst will use several of the A____ boxes.

7. The VOLUME (KEYS) field specifies

the *maximum* number of keys of a primary or secondary index, or

the *average* number of children for one parent in a relationship.

8. The VIEWS WHERE USED list is a cross-reference to all the views that need this access or relationship path. In addition to being helpful as a cross-reference, it is the basis for the optimal implementation techniques described in chapter 6.

Each view is described on a separate line.

The INT/BATCH column describes the type of transaction: interactive or batch. The VOLUME column contains the number of times the view uses this path per unit of time, described in the last column.

View Slip

Example 4 (multilevel view)
In example 3, let us specify a two-level view that accesses an already manufactured order-line of an item. We should write

"ACCESS BY item-number A1 to R1 then by A1 to R3 using ITEM *HAS-READY* ORDER-LINES."

This two-level view describes one DBMS call line of a transaction slip. A view can be single-level or multilevel.

The V____ field holds the view number.

The SELECTION field describes the hierarchy of relations of the view. Each RELATION name is followed by its ACCESS/RELATIONSHIP PATH Pxxx number and by the list of constraints to be respected by the selected tuples.

The field TYPE S M + − describes the type of DBMS call as follows:

• S stands for a *Selection* (search or retrieval) operation. This is the most frequently encountered operation. The result of a selection in the MSD sense is a relation that comprises several tuples; a single tuple may be selected depending on the search criteria. Since a navigational DBMS can retrieve only one record with one call, we shall use a functional interface (described in chapter 6) to make it behave in a relational way.

   Another difference with the behavior of a navigational DBMS is that the view can be multilevel, as explained in 1.3.1. The view accesses the various levels in succession in a hierarchical manner; levels L and L + 1 of this hierarchy are linked with JOIN operations, each tuple of level L being joined with N tuples of level L + 1. At each level, a tuple reached by the join operation is selected only if it matches the selection criteria. If it is, the view can reach the attributes described in the Attribute List part of the slip.

• M stands for a *Modification* operation. This operation changes the value of the specified attributes. Each attribute is replaced with the value supplied in the slip or by the application program; alternatively, the new value can result from the evaluation of an arithmetic expression, which comprises constants and attribute values retrieved by the selection part of the view. Alternatively, values resulting from the evaluation of vertical functions during the selection can also be used.

Sometimes a modification operation is used to supply the initial value of an optional attribute of a previously created tuple. The modification operation comprises a single- or multilevel selection. In the latter case, the modified attributes must all belong to the last level of the hierarchical selection.

This restriction is not a technical requirement—it is a sound programming practice; since the various levels of a hierarchy usually correspond to embedded loops within a program, it is not recommended to alter within an inner loop an attribute that belongs to a level associated with an outer loop.

• + (the addition sign) stands for an addition operation, where the word *addition* is a synonym of "insertion": an operation that adds one or several tuples to an existing relation.

1. When the addition inserts *one* additional tuple to the relation, the selection part of the operation is used to define either
• the *uniqueness* condition to be respected by the new tuple, or
• the *position* of the new tuple in the relation, when a collating sequence condition must be respected.
(Although the usual relational approach ignores the notion of collating sequence, MSD defines sorted relations when the transactions require them. The sequence of the tuples is physically implemented in a relational database using a secondary index; in a navigational database, the DBMS maintains a specified FIFO, LIFO, or ORDER BY FIELD sequence using a chain, an index, or a pointer array.) Sorted relations are required to implement the databases of applications such as production scheduling, where the order of manufacturing operations must sometimes be maintained by the DBMS without using the operation number.

2. When the addition inserts *several* tuples into the relation, the selection part of the operation is used to retrieve the tuples to be selected using a single-level or multilevel view. Depending on the uniqueness

condition specified for the primary access path, the DBMS will verify this condition for each added tuple.

Inserting several tuples in one operation is typically a relational capability: navigational DBMSs cannot do that, in general. The collating sequence of the relation, if any is required, will be maintained using an appropriate secondary index.

The attributes of the tuples added by the operation are defined in the LIST OF ATTRIBUTES part of the slip. The value of each attribute follows the same rules as for the modification operation: it can be a constant supplied by the slip definition or the application program, or it can be computed using vertical functions or attributes retrieved in the selection phase.

• − (the minus sign) stands for the subtraction of tuples from a relation, which deletes the tuples retrieved by the selection.

The relation where subtraction is performed is the last level of the specified selection, if a multilevel selection is used.

The list of attributes is *not* used for subtraction: all the attributes of all the tuples retrieved by the selection are deleted.

The three update operations M, + , and − are protected by the data existence co-routines, which check the integrity, consistency, and syntax constraints at all 3 levels: attribute, relation, and database.

The three types of slips (transaction, view, and access path) are filled in as follows: first the transaction slip, then the views described in it, then the access or relationship paths required by the views.

The transaction slip can be filled in at least in part by a specifier without special DP knowledge; he can describe the scenario and begin-end conditions.

Then the project leader or a person with DP knowledge can fill in the blank fields of the transaction slips, and then the corresponding view and access slips. The view and access slips are typically database architecture design documents, created when the project leader proof-reads the transaction slips created by the specifiers.

2.3 Conclusions on Detailed Functional Specification Methods

The method of scenarios and dictionary described in this chapter is intended for the description of detailed functional specifications

(DFSs) of business application programs. Today most programs are interactive, though some batch programs are (and will remain) necessary.

MSD specifies a *batch* process by describing its algorithm in the scenario part of a transaction slip. The algorithm is described using a traditional approach, such as tree-structured programming. MSD recommends in addition that the rest of the slip be filled in correctly, as it would be for an interactive transaction.

MSD requires an organization study and the resulting preliminary functional requirements before the detailed specification is conducted. This study decides what *functions* are to be computerized and what *data results* must be produced. Just as the DFS phase does, this phase simultaneously takes into account functions and data.

MSD is not intended for process control applications, where the notion of man-machine conversation is replaced with the notions of real-time monitoring and control of mechanisms and measuring devices. In such applications, the very notion of database is different, as will be seen in chapter 5.

2.3.1 Information Systems

There is, however, a class of applications that require a database: *information systems*. In such a system, the main purpose of the application is not the computerized processing of preprogrammed applications; there are no (or there are but few) repetitive procedures.

The primary goal of the system is the storage of information to be made available for queries, consolidations, decision simulations, and communication.

MSD is not applicable to such systems, which do not imply the frequent use of stable scenarios, processed with known volumes. No specifier can describe the future queries, consolidations, or simulations with sufficient precision. However, a conceptual schema of the information database can be described, without attempting subsequently to optimize the physical architecture; optimization would be meaningless for an unpredictable use.

Describing the conceptual schema of the database then becomes an end in itself. The DFS must describe the semantics of the information elements to be stored in a manner suitable for accurate understanding.

The requirement to understand static, nonquantified information re-placed the need to describe dynamic, quantified usage scenarios.

The representation of the information of the conceptual schema of an information system comprises the representation of the *data* and the representation of the *semantic links* among the data.

A data element is an isolated field or a group of fields that contains a key and its attributes.

A semantic link is an existence constraint or multivalued depen-dence (example 1), or a procedure that transforms input data into out-put data (example 2).

Example 1 (Customer ---⟩ Order)
The link ---⟩ means "Customer *SENDS* Order" and also "The exis-tence of the Order requires the existence of its Customer."

Example 2 (Sales History ---⟩ Sales Forecast)
The link ---⟩ means "is used to calculate" and "comes from": this is a transformation procedure even if no exact algorithm can be described because human appreciation is used.

In general, it is difficult to describe clearly data elements and seman-tic links without describing transformation procedures. In order to understand abstract definitions, we need to understand and describe their practical impact in a number of concrete situations.

Example
To understand the existence (consistency) constraints that link inven-tory control and accounting, we need to describe the various cases of inventory movements. For instance, when an inventory item record is deleted or when the quantity-in-stock field is modified, an accounting posting is required to reflect the operation if we want the accounts to reflect the actual inventory situation.

When the usage procedures are unknown and the practical effect of data values is unpredictable, it is very difficult to obtain an in-depth understanding of the semantics of the information system. We may even omit some data elements or links in the description of the concep-tual schema until we discover them using their impact: who generates them, who uses them, how they impact other data elements or process-ing conditions. *A conceptual schema alone cannot describe an infor-*

mation system accurately; additional descriptions are required, such as data transformation procedures or information flow diagrams.

Conclusions

1. When the objective of the application is to computerize predictable usage scenarios, as is the case in business applications, the DFSs are intended for the description of the programs to be written, as well as for the data they will process. The data dictionary contains the descriptions of the data elements and existence constraints.

The conceptual schema is not an end in itself; it is a representation of data and links intended for the design and use of programs. It is not indispensable when a good data dictionary is available, but it is an overview that can help human understanding.

2. When the objective is the description of an information system, we shall build a conceptual schema to represent the data elements and semantic links. The main difficulty will be the in-depth understanding of the information semantics, since no data impact or usage procedure is available. The schema will be independent of a future physical database architecture. The scenario part of MSD will not be applicable.

2.3.2 Transforming an Information System into a DP Database

Some DFS methods do not describe scenarios and data simultaneously, as MSD does. They first describe the conceptual schema of the information system, without considering the usage procedures. In a second phase, they consider the processing requirements and volumes to optimize the physical database architecture. The conceptual schema phase takes place during (or immediately after) the organization and preliminary functional requirements phase.

MSD can be used for the DFS phase even after an initial conceptual schema phase. The data dictionary building process will simply verify that the existing data descriptions are consistent with the scenarios and results. In that sense, MSD is compatible with other approaches.

Specialists who prefer the two-phase approach, which begins with the conceptual schema, generally cite three reasons:

1. *During the organization and preliminary requirements phase, the usage scenarios are not known.*
This is a false statement if it applies to business data processing

applications. During that phase, the activity of the organization is known, even if its *details* have not yet been described; it is represented by an information flow diagram showing who handles what data, and who communicates what data with whom.

Sometimes it is more convenient to represent the results expected from the application using *data* (example: the application is expected to provide sales statistics); sometimes it is more convenient to represent the results using *functions* (example: the application must monitor the manufacturing process).

No matter what approach we use during this strategic decision phase, we need details both to understand and to program; and the details comprise both data and usage scenarios.

If the reason given applies to an information system, the statement is true . . . as long as accuracy is not required in the specification or conceptual schema documents.

2. *The need for processing/data independence*

This objective was important in the bygone days when compilation and linking loads were a problem and data dictionaries of DBMSs were static, thus requiring unloading and reloading of the database at each evolution.

But today computer power and dynamic DBMS dictionaries are such that this objective is no longer important. In addition, it is achieved no matter what specification and design approach we use, simply because DBMSs provide a mapping feature. The need for independence cannot justify an approach that first ignores the use of the data, then integrates them to redesign the technically erroneous theoretical database architecture described in the conceptual schema.

I have discussed this issue with many specialists, and have never found any convincing reason why the two-phase approach is necessary or even preferable. I suspect that the true reason of the approach is the inability of those specialists to question principles they learned when they first started in database management.

3. *The stability of the conceptual schema*

This reason is another form of the previous reason: since a conceptual schema only describes information semantics, it is independent of usage procedures, and therefore it is stable when the application evolves.

Indeed an information system, which only describes the data elements and their "natural" links (functional dependences), is stable. But the reason is deceptive because it is superficial; stability can be achieved and maintained only at the expense of accuracy of understanding and representation. As soon as we need enough accuracy to design programs, we need to integrate usage scenarios. The semantics of the links, such as the existence constraints, cannot be described using data without the associated transformation procedures. And the details of the data appear only when their future use is defined.

So when the application evolves, the stable conceptual schema varies in many of its details; the only way to achieve conceptual schema stability is to keep it at a level high enough to avoid seeing the details.

Finally, *data never exist without usage procedures*. The two notions cannot be separated; they are two aspects of the same reality.

Any method used to represent the information world, whether its purpose is building an information system or computerizing a business application, must use both data and procedures from beginning to end.

3 Data Representation, Packing, and Protection

3.1 Data Representation and Packing

The database approach requires the presence of all data on line, both to retrieve and to update. As a result, the amount of disk storage required may be considerable, the volume of data transferred between the processor and the disks may be high, and the processor time required to search through the database may be costly.

This section describes a few cost-saving methods, oriented toward volume minimization. First we briefly describe the straightforward techniques known as *full-length* and *code* representations, and then we proceed with a detailed description of techniques particularly suited to databases.

3.1.1 Full-Length Storage

This is the simplest data representation and storage method. A word or text (series of words) or one or several numbers are simply written using the letters, digits, and signs required. Although this is a very simple operation, it uniformly leads to cumbersome storage and lends itself poorly to retrieval operations. The comparison of character strings is not easy to program (except with specific languages and correctly justified strings). The spacing and spelling of words and the use of abbreviations may result in unpredictable data search results.

All keypunch operators know that copying or verifying alphanumeric data is slower and less reliable than copying numeric codes.

3.1.2 Representing Data with Codes

This method consists of representing a concept with a numeric code, such as customer numbers, item numbers, and record-type codes. Codes have the disadvantage of all symbols: they are not self-explanatory. But they also have many advantages:

· they are not cumbersome—a two-digit code can represent a 40-character legend string;
· they are easy to compare during retrieval operations;
· they are easy to enter and verify.

All the techniques discussed in this chapter are in fact coding techniques.

3.1.3 Vocabulary and Alphabet

Consider the following example: the ITEM file of a manufacturer of gear boxes. A preliminary evaluation of the volume of the file produced the following results:

- number of items: 10,000;
- ITEM record size: numeric fields (part number, price, size, etc.), 30 characters; alpha field (part name), 30 characters;
- total file size: 10,000 × (30 + 30) = 600,000 characters.

A survey of actual part names led to the conclusion that some names or qualifiers appeared more frequently than others: wheel, pinion, sprocket, gear, case, bearing, shaft, etc. A list of these names was made: there were only 25, and they represented all the important words used in the part names. It was then decided to code each important word using one letter:

wheel = A;   pinion = B;   sprocket = C;   etc.

The part name was thus reduced from 30 to 5 characters, and each five-character name could accommodate up to five important words. The file size was thus reduced by 10,000 × (30 − 5) = 250,000 characters: a little over 40%.

The file could now reside on a single disk cylinder, thus reducing the number of arm movements and accelerating the accesses. A conversion subprogram was developed and included in the programs that print part names.

This example introduces the following concepts: 10,000 part names can be built up using only 25 words. The *vocabulary* is said to comprise 25 words. Storage economy can be achieved associating one code with each word.

The previous example contains 25 such letter codes, which shows how small the vocabularies used in many files are. Often they make up a set of 100 words or fewer. It is then convenient to code the various words using a two- or three-digit code, which can be used as an actual address in a conversion table. For example, if

16 = Lownoise   (16th table entry),
08 = Gearbox   (8th table entry),

21 = Light alloy   (21st table entry),
05 = Case   (5th table entry),

then

1608210500 = lownoise gearbox light alloy case.

It is often found that conversions are not required for all the processing operations. The internal, nonvisible, computer data handling may be performed using codes. Only the external representations (data entry, printout) need be converted.

We can state the following definitions:

• The *vocabulary* is the set of all the words required to build up the descriptions of the concepts to be handled.

• The *alphabet* is the set of codes used to represent the vocabulary, with the rule that 1 word is associated with 1 code and vice versa.

Notes

1. The "words" can be actual words, sequences of symbols such as phonemes, or short sentences. The only constraint is that they may not be split.

2. The codes of an alphabet can be letters, groups of digits, etc.

3. Associating one word with one code is an important source of savings in disk storage space, disk channel transfer load, and processor time (compare and move instructions, sorting operations).

4. The notions of vocabulary and alphabet imply the nonredundancy and exhaustivity of the set of words used to build up concepts.

5. Caution: the above definitions of vocabulary and alphabet apply to the realm of databases; different definitions are used in other data processing-related domains, such as the theory of languages.

3.1.4 Base

The data representation method described above is suitable for vocabularies limited to a few hundred words. But it can be generalized and extended to vocabularies that are arbitrarily large while still remaining practical.

Example

The prices of the items in a file are expressed in dollars and cents; the number of cents is always a multiple of 25 cents. Prices range from 50 cents to 80 dollars.

First storage technique: use 4 digits to store the price field.

Second storage technique: let us associate with each price P an integer x such that

$$x = (P - 0.50/0.25 \qquad \text{or} \qquad P = 0.25x + 0.50, \qquad (T)$$

which means that

$$x = 0 \text{ if } P = 0.50,$$
$$x = 1 \text{ if } P = 0.75,$$
$$x = 2 \text{ if } P = 1.00,$$
$$\vdots$$
$$x = 318 \text{ if } P = 80.00$$

This storage technique uses a three-digit field to store the price P; if we store x instead of P it saves 25% of the space. In this example, the vocabulary comprises 319 words, so the alphabet has 319 codes.

We can use a special numbering system to represent this set of codes: a numbering system *in base 319*. In this system, each number x is represented by a single digit. We shall not (of course) invent new and strange signs to represent the digits beyond 9. We can use the natural representation of numbers available in our computer, three-digit values of x, and convert x to P or P to x using formulas (T), where T stands for Transform. We shall note that *the base B of a vocabulary is the number of its words*. In this base, each word is coded with a one-digit number ranging from 0 to (B − 1). To calculate B and establish the (T) formulas, the following steps are necessary:

1. Obtain the maximum M and minimum m values of the numbers N to be represented.

2. Obtain the "step" S of the Ns: the Ns form an arithmetic progression.

3. Calculate $B = (M - m)/S + 1$.

4. The (T) formulas are

coding and packing: $x = (N - m)/S$ to find the x of each N; decoding and unpacking: $N = Sx + m$ to find the N of each x.

3.1.5 Data Packing in Remote Communications

Generally, the use of compact codes to represent data is called *data packing*. It is particularly useful for data transmission. A data transmission line has a maximum throughput. The ratio

$$\frac{\text{number of useful characters transmitted}}{\text{total number of characters transmitted}}$$

measures how efficiently the line is used. Thus, the transmission of many space characters in succession should be replaced by the transmission of TAB characters or of a special character followed by a two-digit number representing the number of spaces. There are special hardware devices that automatically pack identical consecutive characters. These devices are inserted between the modem (also called "data set") and the user's computer or terminal (figure 3.1). If both the computer and terminal have enough processor power available, the packing/unpacking can be performed within the computer and terminal, thus avoiding the need for a special device.

Interest in data packing is not limited to data transmission; we have seen above that it can also reduce storage costs and the load of disk channels.

3.1.6 Packing Entire Records Using Multiple Bases

The method of 3.1.4 was suitable for a single field. It can now be extended to an entire record. A record is an ordered set of fields. Each field is associated with a specific vocabulary, which in turn is associated with all the different concepts that can be represented in that field.

To a given field we know how to associate a base B, the number of different vocabulary words. The first word will be coded "zero," the second "one," the last "B − 1." That is easy for numeric fields, but not for alphanumeric fields, because the number of words of such a field is not always known. Fortunately, in most cases a *large* percentage of the words encountered build up a *small* vocabulary.

We know that a small vocabulary can be coded. We can then add a special code-character to our alphabet and use it as a beginning delimiter (prefix) and ending delimiter (suffix) around the strings of charac-

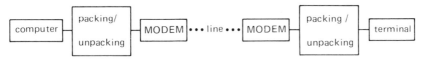

Figure 3.1

ters that represent the rare words. Those rare words can be stored with their natural full-length representation, a technique that will prove useful in some databases. It is the last step of the vocabulary definition process:

1. Build a file of all the words.

2. Count the number of occurrences of each word.

3. Code the words that are the most frequently used, the rest being represented in full length.

There is an alternative to the prefix + suffix technique: replacing the suffix with a one-byte string-length counter, which stores the length of the string that begins immediately after it. The advantage of this technique is that it can also be used to represent strings of duplicated characters, such as spaces or dashes. Assuming, for example, that the acceptable maximum for the length of a string is 127 characters, normal strings will have a positive character count, and repeated strings a negative count.

In the following examples, the prefix characters are noted P and S, respectively, and the length byte is represented using the number it contains.

Example 1
P very rare string of characters, unknown length S.

Example 2
P 11 exceptional (the word *exceptional* has 11 "chars").

Example 3
P -12- (this represents 12 dashes "-").

Throughout the rest of this section, we shall assume that the coding process has been performed for each field, numeric or alphanumeric, of the record in question; the remaining discussion pertains only to the packing of coded words.

Let us consider a record with p fields. Each field (i) has been converted using formulas (T) and contains an integer n_i, ranging from 0 to $(B_i - 1)$, where B_i is the base of field (i). We can pack the record field integers n_1, n_2, . . . , n_p into a single integer N. Unpacking will subsequently convert N into n_1, n_2, . . . , n_p.

1. *Packing* Packing will use the *multiple-base formula*:

$$N = n_1 + (B_1 * n_2) + (B_1 * B_2 * n_3) +$$
$$\cdots + (B_1 * B_2 * \cdots * B_i * n_{i+1}) + \cdots$$
$$+ (B_1 * B_2 * \cdots * B_{p-1} * n_p),$$

where * is the multiplication sign.

Interpretation of the packing formula: example Assume that the record contains 3 fields and that each field contains a word that belongs to a set of 10 words. The first field will be called "units," the second "tens," and the third "hundreds." We have:

$$p = 3; \quad B_1 = B_2 = B_3 = 10.$$

To pack $n_1 = 2$ units, $n_2 = 4$ tens, $n_3 = 6$ hundreds, we shall calculate

$$N = 2 + 10 * 4 + 10 * 10 * 6 = 642.$$

N is a three-digit integer:
- the first digit, in base $B_1 = 10$, is $n_1 = 2$ (rightmost digit);
- the second digit, in base $B_2 = 10$, is $n_2 = 4$, shifted one position toward the left of n_1;
- the third digit, in base $B_3 = 10$, is $n_3 = 6$, shifted one position (in base B_1) to the left of n_1, and then one position (in base B_2) to the left of n_2.

Comments

1. Using the multiple-base formula amounts to creating a p-digit integer N. The rightmost (low-order) digit is written in base B_1, the next digit is written in base B_2, etc. The representation of N using this multiple-base approach builds a number N with digits written in *different* bases. The value of the single integer N represents the values of *all* the fields of the original record. N exists independently of the multiple-base representation; it ranges from 0 to $(B_1 * B_2 * \cdots * B_p - 1)$. (In the previous example, N ranged from 0 to 999.)

2. The length of a physical record is the sum of the lengths of its fields, independent of their order. Similarly, no matter how the record repre-

sentation N is stored in the computer, the space it requires *is the same:* it is the space required to store

$$N_{max} = B_1 * B_2 * \cdots * B_p - 1$$

(the product of the bases $B_1 \cdots B_p$ is commutative).

3. The value N requires a record storage base $B = B_1 * \cdots * B_p$. This means that the number of possible different records is B, the product of the numbers of different individual field values. Therefore *the compactness of this packing technique is at a maximum.* No matter how the actual computer works (with bits, bytes, or words), it is impossible to achieve tighter packing.

2. *Unpacking* Unpacking is performed using a technique called *successive remainders:*

1. n_1 is the remainder when N is divided by B_1 (for example, in the usual decimal representation, the rightmost digit of a number is the remainder of the division of the number by 10). Using the *modulus* function of FORTRAN: $n_1 = MOD(N,B_1)$.

Let Q_1 be the quotient of the division $N = Q_1 * B_1 + n_1$.

2. Divide Q_1 by B_2: the quotient is Q_2 and the remainder n_2.
3. Divide Q_2 by B_3: the quotient is Q_3 and the remainder n_3, etc.

By way of example, the table shown here describes a five-field record, with maximum (Max) and minimum (min) values, steps (S), and actual field values (AFV).

Field	min	Max	S	AFV
1	-2	16	2	4
2	0	20.5	0.1	8.3
3	0	39	1	16
4	0	39	1	0
5	1000	1999	1	1500

Comments

Numbers: $-2, 0, 2, 4, 6, \ldots, 16$
Numbers: $0, 0.1, 0.2, \ldots, 20.5$
2 characters of an alphabet of 40 symbols (letters, digits, signs)
Numbers: $1000, 1001, \ldots, 1999$

Let us first calculate the bases, using the formula of 3.1.4:

$$B_i = (M_i - m_i)/S_i + 1.$$

Then the n_i digits using the (T) formula of 3.1.4 are

$n_i = (x_i - m_i)/S_i$.

Field	B_i	n_i
1	10	3
2	206	83
3	40	16
4	40	0
5	1000	500

We can now compute N using the multiple-base formula:

$N = 3 + 10*83 + 10*206*16 + 10*206*40*0 + 10*206*40*40*500$,

$N = 3 + 830 + 32960 + 1648000000$,

$N = 1648033793$.

Let us verify and unpack:

- Divide 1648033793 by 10: the quotient is $Q_1 = 164803379$ and $n_1 = 3$.
- Divide 164803379 by 206: the quotient is $Q_2 = 800016$ and $n_2 = 83$.
- Divide 800016 by 40: the quotient is $Q_3 = 20000$ and $n_3 = 16$.
- Divide 20000 by 40: the quotient is $Q_4 = 500$ and $n_4 = 0$.
- Divide 500 by 1000: the quotient is $Q_5 = 0$ and $n_5 = 500$.

It is now easy to apply the (T) formula $x_i = n_i * S_i + m_i$ and find the original x_i.

Comments

1. The last division was superfluous, since the last base was not used for multiplication (shifting by 1 digit): $n_5 = Q_4$. In general, we shall have $n_p = Q_{p-1}$: this saves one division.

2. We can verify that the packing achieved storage economy. Assume that the computer is byte oriented and stores two digits to one byte or one signed digit to one byte:

Field number	COBOL picture	Field size (bytes)
1	S99	1.5 (or 2)
2	99V9	1.5 (or 2)
3 and 4	X	1 (2 times)
5	9999	2
Total unpacked record size:		7 (or 8)

Then the maximum value of N is $B_1 * B_2 * B_3 * B_4 * B_5 - 1$:

$N = 10 * 206 * 40 * 40 * 1000 - 1 = 3,295,999,999.$

This ten-digit number requires 5 bytes, 29% less than 7 bytes.

3.1.7 Packing Using Multiple Words

The N numbers are generally big; they may have 100 digits or even more, depending on the contents of the record. Some computers can handle such integers; others cannot. This section describes the technique to use when a record to be packed results in an integer N greater than the largest permitted integer, M. The notion of an M integer is often associated with that of 1 computer word. Sometimes, integers can be as long as 2, 3, or 4 words. The name *multiple-word* packing comes from the need to use several words to store N.

Example

A computer such as the IBM 43XX has 32-bit words. When it stores an integer in one word, one bit is used for the sign and 31 bits for the integer value. The base is then 2^{31}:

$M = 2^{31} - 1 = 2,147,483,647.$

Method

In the following discussion, we shall define a "word" as the memory required to store M, regardless of the computer's actual memory-access technique (word, byte, double word, etc.).

Let $B_1, B_2, \ldots, B_p$ be the p bases associated with the fields of the records to be packed. Let us multiply $B_1 * B_2 * B_3 * \cdots$ until this product is the largest such product that still "fits" within $M + 1$: let B_h be the last base of this product. By definition:

$$B_1 * B_2 * \cdots * B_h \leq M + 1.$$

1. If $h = p$, the entire record fits within one word: multiple-word packing is not required.
2. If $h < p$, let $R = (M + 1)/(B_1 * B_2 \cdots * B_h)$, where R is an integer quotient.

   2.1. If $R = 1$, the word must be considered "full": start packing into another word with base B_{h+1}, etc.
   2.2. If $R > 1$, R is the greatest additional base that can be packed into one word together with $B_1, B_2, \ldots, B_h$.

2.2.1. If R belongs to the remaining set of bases $B_{h+1}, \ldots B_p$, R is a base B_r of that set. Exchange B_r and B_{h+1} and pack B_r with the first h bases into the first word. Then

$(M + 1)/(B_1 * \cdots * B_h * B_r) = 1$ (integer division).

This is case 2.1.

2.2.2. If there is a remaining base B_x such that $B_x < R$, B_x can be packed in the same word as $B_1, B_2, \ldots B_h$; then a new R can be calculated, etc.

2.2.3. If all remaining bases are greater than R, since $R > 1$, any remaining base B_x can be subdivided into two new bases B_a and R such that $(B_a * R) \geq B_x$. In other words, we can store one part (with a base R) of the field associated with B_x in the first word (with B_1, $\ldots$, B_h) and the other part (with base B_a) in the second word. The field with base B_x is then written using two digits: one in base R in the first word and one in base B_a in the second.

2.2.4. Continue packing bases into the second word, and so on.

We can now describe the method used to write the number n_x (in base B_x) with two digits in bases R and B_a:

• the first (high-order) digit, in base R, will be called C_1;
• the other digit will be called C_2.

Since we must have $n_x = C_2 + B_a * C_1$, C_1 and C_2 are, respectively, the quotient and the remainder in the integer division of n_x by B_a.

Example

Assume that our computer has words that can store integers in 31 bits: $M = 2^{31} - 1$. Further assume that, following the conversion of fields using formula (T), the four fields of the record to be packed have bases such as

Field number	Base
1	2^{20}
2	2^{10}
3	2^5
4	2^{24}

$B_1 < 2^{31}$, so B_1 fits in word 1.
$B_1 * B_2 = 2^{30} < 2^{31}$, so B_1 and B_2 fit in word 1.
$B_1 * B_2 * B_3 = 2^{35} > 2^{31}$, so B^3 does not fit in word 1.

Then $R = 2^{31}/2^{30} = 2$, and B_3 can be subdivided into

$R = 2$ and $B_a = 2^5/2 = 2^4 = 16$.

A number of the third field can be written with 2 digits: the high-order digit, in base 2, will be stored in the first word together with fields 1 and 2; the low-order digit, in base $2^4 = 16$, will be in the second word, where $B_a * B_4 = 2^4 * 2^{24} < 2^{31}$, so B_4 fits in the second word, and the record can be packed into 2 words.

A number in field 3 will be subdivided into its 2 digits using a division by 16: $n_3 = C_2 + C_1 * 16$. For example, if we want to store $n_1 = 8$, $n_2 = 70$, $n_3 = 10$, $n_4 = 49$, and if we want the fields packed in that order, we calculate the values N_1 and N_2 of the two words like this:

$N_1 = C_1 + R * n_2 + R * B_2 * n_1$ and $N_2 = n_4 + B_4 * C_2$.

That is,

$C_1 = 0$ and $C_2 = 10$ $(n_3 = 10 = 16 * 0 + 10)$,
$N_1 = 0 + 2 * 70 + 2 * 2^{10} * 8$ and $N_2 = 49 + 2^{24} * 10$,
$N_1 = 16524$, $N_2 = 167772209$.

To unpack, we calculate n_1, n_2, C_1, C_2, n_4, and n_3 in the following way:

Divide N_1 by R, giving Q_1 and C_1: $Q_1 = 8262$, $C_1 = 0$.
Divide Q_1 by B_2, giving Q_2 and n_2: $Q_2 = 8$, $n_2 = 70$.
Take $n_3 = Q_2 = 8$.
Divide N_2 by B_4, giving Q_1 and n_4: $Q_1 = 10$, $n_4 = 49$.
Take $C_2 = Q_1 = 10$.
$n_3 = 0 * 16 + 10 = 10$.

Comments

1. In this example, the same storage efficiency (the record packed into 2 words) can be achieved by packing B_1 and B_2 only in word 1, and B_3 and B_4 in word 2. This would result in fewer, faster computations; we must therefore use the multiple-word packing intelligently.

2. The sign bit of each word can also be used (why waste anything?). To use this bit, replace R with $2R - 1$, and map the last base of word 1 onto the set of integers

$-(R - 1), -(R - 2), \ldots, -1, 0, 1, \ldots, (R - 1)$: $(2R - 1$ numbers).

The reason that only $2R - 1$ numbers are available, instead of the $2R$ one would expect to find, is that zero has no sign, in general. On the rare computers that have $+0$ and -0, $2R$ numbers are available.

3. The reason for packing the fields of a record from left to right, instead of from right to left, may be the need to make the leftmost field the first, high-order digit of the p-digit N, the next field the second digit of N, etc. This need may arise for sorting.

3.1.8 When Is Data Packing Worthwhile?

Data packing saves disk and memory space. It also requires processor resources to pack and unpack. The following discussion is intended to help analysts decide when and how to use data packing.

Cost of packing   The cost elements of packing are

1. processor resources to pack and unpack (for the most part for integer addition, multiplication, and division),

2. memory space required by the packing/unpacking routines.

The orders of magnitude of the execution times (in microseconds, or millionths of a second) of the arithmetic instructions are as follows:

OPERATION	MICROCOMPUTER	MAINFRAME	SCIENTIFIC COMPUTER
Addition	30	1	0.1
Multiplication	35	1.8	0.2
Division	60	4.5	0.5

The values for a microcomputer are for 16-bit machines, using a compiled language and a mathematical co-processor such as the INTEL 8087. Using interpreted BASIC, typical execution times are 40 times slower. Including the time spent executing the packing-unpacking subroutine instructions, the order of magnitude of the time required to pack or unpack a character varies between 4 *milli*seconds on a slow microcomputer to 30 *micro*seconds on a mainframe. The differences are considerable. Not only do computations cost much less on a large computer, but large computers often store large databases. The conclusions are therefore

1. The larger the computer, the more worthwhile it is to pack.

2. It is in the interest of the user to find out the cost of packing and unpacking on his actual machine. This can be done easily with a few experiments.

Processing time economies when sorting or searching The time required to access a disk is generally about 20 to 60 milliseconds (sometimes 400 milliseconds on a microcomputer using diskettes). In a monoprogramming (single-tasking) environment, this time is wasted. In a multiprogramming environment, only a part of it is wasted. But whatever the environment, the computations associated with a disk access are relatively expensive, averaging from 1 to 10 milliseconds. In addition, the execution of a READ or WRITE statement in memory costs 0.2 to 5 milliseconds. The savings that can be achieved through the use of packing include

• the number of disk accesses (since each access can bring in more data);

• the memory space, if packed tables are used;

• the amounts of data transferred between the disks and processor (packed data are less cumbersome);

• the processing time (packed data require less time to compare or move than longer, unpacked data).

Sorting time savings The multiple-base formula yields an N that requires a space independent of the order of the packed fields. N has p digits; no matter how the computer actually stores and handles the integers, we can store the sort-key fields as the high-order digits.

Comparing two records amounts to comparing their associated Ns, and in fact the high-order digits of these Ns. These require less space, therefore making comparisons faster. And when it is necessary to exchange two Ns, packed Ns are exchanged faster than unpacked Ns.

Retrieval time savings In a memory table, comparing packed data is faster than comparing longer, unpacked data. Therefore, in a search for a given piece of data, the input data can first be packed before they are compared with the data in the table.

In fact, packing is much more worthwhile for *stable* databases. When few insertions, modifications, or deletions are performed, compared with the many selections that are required, packing actually generates processor time economies. This is the case with most master files, described in 1.3.4.7.

What fields should be packed?   The theory of packing does not apply only to arithmetic progressions.

• It also applies to *geometric progressions,* where each element n_i can be computed knowing n_{i-1} by

$n_i = a * n_{i-1}$ (where a is a constant).

• Generally packing applies to any finite, enumerable set of data, for which each element can be associated with an integer: 0, 1, 2, 3, etc. Such sets are "tabular"; they can be stored in tables.

For example, an item number has 8 digits. The first two digits are the family code: 11, 12, 18, 31, 42, 55, 56, 59, 61, 63 and 99. The next two digits are the color code: 00 to 18. The last four digits are the item code, for which only 300 codes exist. Using 3 tables for the 3 types of codes, with respective dimensions of 11, 19, and 300, the total length of a code may not exceed $11 * 19 * 300 - 1 = 62699$, which requires 5 digits, not 8.

• Packing does not apply to real numbers used in scientific applications if their precision exceeds a few digits. This is also true for large decimal numbers, used in business applications.

Packing should first be considered for data that are not frequently accessed because the processor overhead costs for packing-unpacking will be small compared with the storage costs.

The groups of fields that make up sort or search keys should be packed separately (in separate words) to avoid packing or unpacking an entire record to process a few keys.

3.1.9   Reducing the Cost of Packing: Bases 2^n

A method called *bit packing* is aimed at reducing the processing cost associated with the packing technique (which by contrast can be called numeric packing). Bit packing is a form of numeric packing that uses only bases of the form 2^n: 2, 4, 8, etc. The method is not applicable if the computer does not have a bit-access capability.

Choosing the bases   The method is the same as above, except that each base B_i must be replaced with a base $C_i \geq B_i$, where C_i is the smallest power of 2 that is at least as great as B_i. *Each field is packed into a series of adjacent bits.*

Packing and unpacking   Packing and unpacking can be performed field by field instead of packing and unpacking an entire record. A field value can be written into or read from the appropriate bit positions using fast bit manipulation instructions instead of slower arithmetic operations. Sample appropriate languages are C and Assembler.

Advantages and disadvantages   Bit packing appeared to be about five times faster than numeric packing in a number of benchmarks conducted on mainframe computers. However, the experiments involved packing and unpacking entire records. When only the appropriate fields of a given record are packed or unpacked, an additional (and substantial) economy can be achieved. The only information available in that respect from a microcomputer user is that batch processing times were "noticeably reduced" and response times "improved."

Section 3.2.1 describes another aspect of the multiple-base packing technique discussed above: *secrecy through data encryption.*

Bit packing does not preserve data security; it is far less difficult to build a translation table for each field of a record with bit packing than it is with numeric packing. The level of secrecy achieved may discourage only nonspecialist users.

3.1.10   Special Representation Methods for Technical Data

This section describes some techniques intended for working with engineering, technical, and scientific data. The purpose is to minimize the volume of the data that will be stored in the database.

3.1.10.1   Continuous Data Streams

When a computer receives data from different connected instruments, the data often make up a *continuous stream*. The computer must analyze, process, and store information while more information keeps coming in. The volume of data to be stored in the database can be large; in addition, the data may be not very informative, as will be seen below.

Continuous data streams are broken down into *time-sliced* data. In each time interval, only a few well-chosen data elements are used to represent the entire interval. For example, the *average* value of an input signal, sampled once a minute, may be used to represent all the signal values received during that minute. In other cases, *two* numbers, such as the mean and standard deviation of the input, can be used during each time interval to represent the incoming data. This sampling process replaces continuous data streams with discrete series of numbers. Even so, the numbers obtained for each interval may contain not-too-useful information.

For example, if we number the intervals and obtain

Interval number	551	552	553	554	555	556
Data	7.25	7.25	7.25	7.25	7.25	7.25

we shall think that very little has changed during those intervals, so a more concise representation should exist. So a first rule emerges from this discussion:

*Store in the database only the **minimum** data required to represent the information, even if processing is required to reconstruct the **useful** information contained in the original data.*

3.1.10.2 Slow-Evolution Processes

Some input signals can be known to vary quite slowly. By slowly, we mean that a lot of consecutive data may arrive with the same values or with values that have varied very little. The technique shown here using table 3.1 stores the initial data value, and then only the deviations and the times when these deviations occurred. At 8:00 (table 3.1), the value was 98.47: this initial information was stored in a type 0 record.

Then until 8:11, the value did not change; this stability is reflected in a type 1 record, using two small integers: 11 for the duration in minutes of the stable period, and 0 for the difference from the initial 98.47.

Then the value changed to 98.40 and remained stable (or was not sampled again) for 1 minute: this was represented using a type 1 record, with values 1 and −7, etc.

Table 3.1

TIME INTERVAL	DATA VALUE	REC. TYPE	TIME	VALUE
		0	8:00	98.47
8:01–8:11	98.47	1	11	0
8:12–8:12	98.40	1	1	−7
8:13–8:27	98.42	1	15	−5
8:28–8:30	98.47	1	3	0

In this representation technique, the computer stores the previous value each time. Using the differences (0, -7, -5, . . .) instead of the values themselves is obviously less cumbersome.

This technique lends itself quite well to data packing.

3.1.10.3 Coding by Exception
Sometimes the data almost always have the same value. The rule we shall use then is,

Represent only those instances where the data differ from the standard value.

Example
Small mechanical parts are machined on an automatic lathe. When the machining operation is complete, each part is measured. If the dimensions fall within accepted limits (the usual situation), no dimension is recorded. But when one dimension is outside the limits, the difference between the closest limit of the acceptable interval and the actual dimension is recorded. Thus if the acceptable interval is 0.24 to 0.26 inch and the actual measure is 0.27, the recorded difference is 0.27 $-$ 0.26 $=$ 0.01; if the actual measure is 0.22, the recorded difference is 0.22 $-$ 0.24 $=$ -0.02.

3.1.10.4 Coding by Dictionary Rank
When a certain field has a limited set of values (usually less than 1000) but must be stored in many records, it is possible to

• store the table of values separately,
• store in each record a field that represents the position of the value in the table.

This table position may be less cumbersome than the actual value and lends itself more readily to packing.

3.1.10.5 Using Functions
Often it is possible to represent a succession of numbers that result from a time-sampling technique using a function of time.

Example
Between 21:54:03 and 21:54:49, the 47 measured values can be represented by $X(t) = 8.5 + 0.42*t$, where t is measured in seconds, with an

accuracy better than 5%, which is acceptable. Instead of storing the 47 measures, we shall store

· the interval duration: 21:54:03 to 21:54:49,
· the parameters of the linear approximation: 8.5 and 0.42.

This technique is quite general. We shall attempt to represent a sequence of values using a simple function—polynomial, sine, or exponential, for example—and a curve-fitting technique to find the parameters. If the accuracy of the representation is acceptable, we shall use the same function until a value arrives that is not represented accurately; we shall then start evaluating another function, etc. The usable techniques for curve fitting are well known: least squares, spline, exponential smoothing, etc.

3.1.10.6 Suitable Data Manipulation Technique

The functional interface (FI) technique, discussed in chapter 6, is well suited as an intelligent software interface between the raw arriving data and the database for storage and retrieval operations.

Example

Let us suppose that the data are the same as in table 3.1:

TIME INTERVAL	DATA VALUE	REC. TYPE	TIME	VALUE
		0	8:00	98.47
8:01–8:11	98.47	1	11	0
8:12–8:12	98.40	1	1	−7
8:13–8:27	98.42	1	15	−5
8:28–8:30	98.47	1	3	0

The operations are

1. The input values are (8:15, 98.42); convert them to database format and store them. The effect will be: *nothing,* because the value has not changed since 8:13.

2. The input values are (8:31, 98.50); convert them to database values and store them. The data sent to the DBMS for storage are (3, 0) because this terminates the previous stable interval. The value $+3$ will be sent to the DBMS only when a new value has terminated the interval that began at 8:31.

3. Query: when was value 98.42 recorded? The FI converts this to -5,

sends the question to the DBMS, and receives the answer: third record of type 1. It then asks the DBMS to read the first record of type 0, then the first two records of type 1, adds the values $(11 + 1) + 1$ to 8:00, and answers: 8:13 to 8:27 (15 minutes).

The FI has interfaced the user-visible and database-visible formats intelligently.

3.2 Access Security Protection

3.2.1 Secret Packing (Encryption)

When multiple-base packing is used, a given field cannot be associated with a group of bits, but an individual bit can belong to several fields at the same time! For example, the low-order bit of each word changes from 0 to 1 each time the parity of the resulting N of that word changes from even to odd. This may happen when any one of several fields vary because

• the bases are not in general powers of 2, which alone would yield independent bit groups,

• packing uses the n bits of a word jointly, in order to store the maximum (2^n) possible data combinations.

This characteristic can be used to achieve data secrecy. When the disk is read, no matter how the bits are interpreted (in decimal, binary, hexadecimal, or octal form), one cannot set up a translation table. In each word, the value of N results from the values of *all* the fields. As a result, the field values seem to conceal each other: efficient encryption is achieved. The only conceivable deciphering technique is the unpacking technique itself. This implies knowing the succession of bases and the approach. In practice, no code-breaking method for numeric encryption is known today.

To protect the data effectively, the packing-unpacking subroutines must also be protected:

• The source code must not be available.

• The object code must be interspersed with absurd unused data to make understanding by unauthorized individuals more difficult. Dynamic (changing) addresses must be used to make a listing of the code incomprehensible, although the program will execute correctly.

• Access and use must require a feature such as the dynamic password, described below.

The combination of packing and dynamic password techniques results in very effective protection. It is used for databases *and communications* by the armed forces of at least two countries. It is also used by banks in a European country where banking secrets are considered *very* important.

I have seen the *total loss* of a database that had become unreadable following a sabotage; the DBA, who alone could assign new passwords and change the packing routines, left the organization after making undocumented changes.

3.2.2 Dynamic Password

The technique below uses a routine controlled by the protected program. It is not a substitute for the log-on password procedure.

The computer displays on the screen a long *random* number. The user *calculates* a password response to this display, such as: multiply the third digit by the fifth, add the eighth digit, and then add 0120 (the month and day).

Example

1 428 572 136   (a 10-digit random number):
$(2 \times 5) + 1 = 11$; $11 + 0120 = 0131$.

The user types in his dynamic password response (0131 above). The computer analyzes this response and decides whether to accept it. If it is acceptable, no approval message is displayed. Instead a second (different, by definition) random number is displayed, and the user must calculate mentally another password. After two good answers in succession the probability of unauthorized access is very small.

After two errors in succession, the computer denies access and locks the database until the DBA unlocks it. If a "spy" sees the two answers entered by a user and tries to give the same answers, he fails; the only way to know the dynamic password formula is to read a person's mind. Naturally, the password routine is protected with code that varies dynamically during execution to prevent reverse engineering.

This technique is reasonably simple and safe. It also features the possibility of a *hierarchy of passwords:* If several correct responses are acceptable, the computer can determine what type of access it should grant following a given set of responses. One DBA-level access can be designed to permit changes in the other users' passwords.

3.3 Keyboard Input Protection

This and the following section describe two techniques for data protection. The first technique is intended for the protection of keyboard input data. It is quite efficient and simple to understand. The second technique is intended for the protection of stored data and transmitted data. It will provide excellent data error detection capabilities at moderate computational and storage overhead costs.

To understand both techniques requires some mathematical background, but the second is more difficult to follow.

Both techniques provide error detection without the capability to correct an error automatically. Automatic correction requires some form of redundancy. Some auto-correcting techniques are

- double (horizontal and vertical) parity bits,
- Cyclic Redundancy Check (CRC),
- Hamming codes,
- Reed-Solomon codes.

The reader may refer to the book by W. Wesley Peterson and E. J. Weldon, Jr., *Error-Correcting Codes,* published by MIT Press. Warning: the mathematics of error correction are rather difficult!

This section describes some *check-digit* techniques for use with data input. The mathematical theory is explained first because it is quite simple; then the practical rules are covered.

Assumptions and notation The following theory applies to *integer* numbers. If we divide a number N by D and find a quotient Q and a remainder R: $N = QD + R$, we shall refer to the remainder R as MOD(N,D). MOD is the FORTRAN notation for the modulus intrinsic function, which finds the remainder in the integer division of N by D. When the notation is not ambiguous, however, we shall refer to the remainder as R(N) because this notation is shorter than MOD(N,D). For example, $N = 47$ $D = 6$; $R(N) = MOD(N,D) = 5$ since $N = 7 \times 6 + 5$.

(1) *Remainder of a sum*   Let N and P be two integers, and $A = MOD(N,D)$ and $B = MOD(P,D)$, where D is the same in the two divisions. Then, two integers Q and T exist such that $N = QD + A$ and $P = TD + B$. Sum: let $S = N + P$. Then $S = (Q + T)D + A + B$ and $MOD(S,D) = MOD[(A + B),D]$:

The remainder of the sum of two numbers is the remainder of the sum of their remainders.

For example, $N = 54$ $P = 27$ $D = 11$; then $A = 10$ $B = 5$ $S = 81$ $R(S) = 4 = R(A + B)$.

(2) *Remainder of a product*   Let $M = XD + A$, $N = QD + B$ (same D), and the product $P = MN$. Then $P = (XQD + XB + AQ)D + AB$, which means that $R(P) = R(AB)$:

The remainder of the product of two numbers is the remainder of the product of their remainders.

For example, $M = 54$ $N = 27$ $D = 11$; then $A = 10$ $B = 5$ $P = 1458$ $R(P) = 6 = R(AB)$.

Proof by 9   Let $D = 9$. Any integer number may be written using decimal notation (in base 10) as $N = A_0 \times 10^n + A_1 \times 10^{n-1} + \cdots + A_n$, where $A_0, A_1, \ldots, A_n$ are the digits of N. From (1) above, it follows that $R(N) = MOD(N,D) = R(P_0 + P_1 + \cdots + P_n)$, where the product $P_i = A_i \times 10^{n-i}$. From (2) above, it follows that $R(P_i) = R[R(A_i)R(10^{n-i})]$. Since $R(10^{n-i}) = 1$, $R(P_i) = R(A_i)$, and since $D = 9$: $R(A_i) = 0$ when $A_i = 9$ and $R(A_i) = A_i$ when A_i is any other digit:

The remainder in the division of a number by 9 is the remainder of the sum of its digits.

For example, $N = 12345$ $R(N) = R(1 + 2 + 3 + 4 + 5) = 6$, and $N = 294$ $R(N) = R(2 + 9 + 4) = 6$.

Some time ago, when calculations were done without the help of a calculator, some people used the following technique to verify multiplications and divisions.

1. *Verifying multiplications*   Let $P = MN$ be the product of M and N, and $R(P) = MOD(P,9)$.

To verify if the manual calculation of P can be correct, calculate R(M)
and R(N), then R[R(M)R(N)]. The last R should be equal to R(P).

For example, $M = 46$ $N = 321$ $MN = 14766$ $R(M) = 1$ $R(N) = 6$
$R(1 \times 6) = 6$ $R(P) = R(1 + 4 + 7 + 6 + 6) = 6$.

2. *Verifying divisions* Assume that we have divided X by D and
found a quotient Q and remainder B: $X = QD + B$.

To verify the result, calculate R(Q) and R(D) and multiply them:
P = R(Q)R(D); replace P with R(P); then add R(B): S = R(P) + R(B).
Now replace S with R(S) and compare with R(X): if these numbers are
equal, the division may be right.

For example, check if $1458 = 11 \times 132 + 6$. $R(Q) = R(11) = 2$, $R(D) = 6$,
$P = 2 \times 6 = 12$, $R(P) = 3$, $R(B) = R(6) = 6$, $S = 3 + 6 = 9$, $R(S) = 0$.
$R(X) = R(1458) = R(1 + 4 + 5 + 8) = R(18) = 0$: the division of 1458 is
probably correct.

3. *The "proof by 9" is not a proof* Consider the division
$1458 = 11 \times 123 + 6$, which is wrong since 132 is replaced by 123. However, the proof by 9 technique cannot detect the error because
$R(132) = R(1 + 3 + 2) = R(123)$ (the addition is commutative).

The implication is that the proof by 9 is a necessary but not a
sufficient condition. In practice, the level of safety provided by such a
verification technique is good, and quite worthwhile considering the
effort required to use it. No safety or security technique is perfect;
each technique must be evaluated using a cost/performance ratio.

4. *Using the proof by 9 as a check-digit technique* When a number is
typed by a keyboard operator, the technique above can be used to
check the accuracy of codes such as an item number, or a customer
number, or an account number. Each code will have to include a check
digit, usually the last digit, which is the remainder in the division by 9
of the rest of the code.

For example, an item code with a value of 3880 will be written 38801,
since $MOD(3880,9) = MOD(3 + 8 + 8 + 0,9) = 1$.

In general, if a digit was mistyped or omitted, the computer will find
a check-digit value that differs from the one entered and know that the
code must be wrong. It can perform this verification without going to
the database to retrieve the code and without displaying an associated

name on the screen for the operator to verify. Both the operator and the computer save time. In addition, the risk that a mistyped code is another *valid* code is substantially decreased. Finally, the operator is not disrupted by computer displays of names associated with codes, which are correct 99% of the time but still require verification; data entry is much faster.

This technique lends itself easily to the cerification of *alphanumeric* codes by replacing letters with two- or three-digit values such as their ASCII representation. The check digit can be a real digit or a letter that has an equivalent value to the computer.

Proof by 11   Let $D = 11$, and let us go through the same exercise as for the proof by 9. In addition, instead of writing numbers in base 10, we shall write them in base 100 by considering their base 100-digits: pairs of digits of the number taken from right to left. Since $MOD(100^i, 11)) = 1$,

To find the remainder $R(N)$ in the division of a number N by 11, consider the pairs of digits beginning at the right-hand side of the number, and the various remainders in the divisions of each pair by 11. Add these, take the remainder, and you have $R(N)$.

For example, $R(1458) = R[R(58) + R(14)] = 6$, and $R(876) = R[R(8) + R(76)] = R(8 + 10) = 7$.

1. The proof by 11 detects transposed adjacent digits. The problem with the proof by 9 is that if two consecutive digits are swapped (typed in the wrong order), this error could not be detected. The problem is serious, because swapping consecutive digits is a frequent typing mistake.

Let us see how the proof by 11 performs in that respect:

Case 1   The two swapped digits belong to the same pair, when counting the pairs from right to left. The pair can be written $A \times 10 + B$, where A and B are different. $A \times 10 + B = A \times 11 + B - A$: the remainder of the pair is

$B - A$ if $B > A$ or $11 + B - A$ if $B < A$.

If the two digits were swapped, the value of the pair is $B \times 10 + A$, and the remainder is

$A - B$ if $A > B$ or $11 + A - B$ if $A < B$.

So if $B - A$ was the correct remainder, reflected in the check digit, the computer will calculate $11 + B - A$ after the swap. And if the correct answer was $11 + B - A$, the computer will calculate $B - A$: in both cases, the error is detected.

Case 2 The two swapped digits belong to successive pairs. In this case, the proof is more complex because the number of cases to be considered in a proof similar to that of case 1 is quite high due to the many relative values the four digits involved in the two pairs may have. We shall use a different method.

Suppose that the four digit values A,B,C,D of the pairs $A \times 10 + B$ and $C \times 10 + D$ are plotted on an axis using points a,b,c,d, respectively. Values such as $B - A$ or $11 + B - A$ are the algebraic (signed) measures of the segment ab, oriented from a to b, depending on which of the two digits A or B is greater (or 0 if $A = B$).

If the correct value ABCD was mistyped as ACBD, the remainders to consider are, respectively, the lengths of the segments $S1 = ab + cd$ and $S2 = ac + bd$, adding 0, 11, or 22 as required. Let us show that $S1$ and $S2$ cannot be equal, or their difference be 11 or 22.

$S2 = ac + bd = ab + bc + bd$. If $S2 = S1$, $ab + cd = ab + bc + bd = ab + bc + bc + cd$, and $2 \times bc$ is equal to 0, 11, or 22, or $bc = 0$, 5.5, or 11:

• $bc = 0$ means that $B = C$: the proof does not detect the swapping of two identical digits, which is obvious and harmless;

• $bc = 5.5$ or 11 means that the difference between the one-digit integers B and C is 5.5 or 11, which is impossible: the theorem is proved.

2. Using the proof by 11 as a check-digit technique. Ideally, since the remainders in a division by 11 can be 0,1,. . .,10, two digits are required to describe the check-digit. The second digit, however, is used in only one of the eleven cases, which makes its use expensive in the cost/performance sense. For example, an item number 7562 would be written 756205 (75---)9, 62---)7, $9 + 7 = 16$---)5).

To improve the cost/performance ratio, it is possible to write the remainder (the check-digit) using a single digit: the digit itself, when its value is 0,1,2, . . .,9, and 5 (for example) when its value is 10. For example, 7562 would be written 75625, and 7567 would be written 75675 (75---)9, 67---)1, $9 + 1 = 10$---)5 not 10).

Conclusions This check-digit technique can prove useful to

- improve key-in performance,
- decrease operator fatigue,
- improve the accuracy of entries,
- decrease computer load, thus improving its response time.

It requires some preparation: adding a check digit to all codes.

3.4 Protection of Stored and Transmitted Data

The technique described here was developed by a French mathematician, Jean Bosset, and described in a paper published in February 1977 in 01 *Informatique Mensuel*. I obtained permission to extract the main ideas of the text below.

When information is transferred from a disk or a telecommunication line, it is important to know with a high degree of certainty whether it is correct. Communication devices and software cannot detect and correct *all* errors. Even disk management may produce one undetected error in 10 million disk accesses or so. If a computer performs an average of 10,000 disk accesses per hour, one undetected error may occur every 1000 hours. It is sometimes important to detect potential errors with a good probability of success.

The following text is a generalization of the check-digit technique. It shows that an intrinsic proof of correctness can be obtained and how to develop the necessary software.

3.4.1 Preliminary Requirements

A. The verification code (VC) we need must be usable for any input text or file, no matter how long or short.

B. The VC must be a function of *all* this input.

C. The VC must allow the usual update operations on the input and vary accordingly:
- new data may be appended to old data;
- parts of the data may be deleted;
- data elements may be modified.

D. The VC must protect against misplaced or swapped characters, fields, or records.

E. The VC must be very safe. All errors must be detected with a probability better than 99.999999999%.

3.4.2 Design Specifications of the Verification Code (VC)

We can translate the requirements above into an algebraic structure.

a. *The VC must vary progressively when data is appended.* The new VC must be a function of the old VC and of the appended data element. In other words, the VC of a text must be obtained progressively: character after character, word after word.

b. *Stability.* No matter how an input and the associated VC were constructed, the result must be the same. If the input is a succession of 1000 characters, for which the VC is calculated character by character 1000 times until the final code was obtained, or a concatenation of two texts of 600 and 400 characters, respectively, for which the code is derived from two codes, the result must be the same. In other words, the result is a function of the input, not of the history of the input.

c. *Associativity.* The stability property may also be termed *associativity.* If an input is a concatenation of three parts, A, B, and C, the same VC must be obtained by associating first A and B, which yields a code K_{AB}, to C, or by associating A to the association of B and C, which yields a code K_{BC}. The final key must be the same. If we represent the operation that transforms a part X into its VC by K_X, and the association of codes that is performed to reflect data concatenation by "+" ("addition"), we want

$$K_{AB} + K_C = K_A + K_{BC}.$$

d. *The VC must not be commutative.* To protect the input against unwanted swaps, the VC must not be commutative. When an input is made from parts A and B in that order, the key must not be the same as the one obtained from B followed by A.

e. *The set of VC must have a null element.* It may be useful in many instances to leave some nonsignificant input elements unnoticed. For example, spaces in texts may be considered unimportant and may be dropped when a code is calculated. The code associated to such input elements must be a null code. If we designate it by "0," that means

$$K_A + 0 = 0 + K_A = K_A.$$

f. *Subtraction, the opposite of addition, must exist.* When an input C results from the concatenation of parts A and B, we have $K_C = K_A + K_B$. If we now delete B from C, we have A again. This must be possible as well with the codes. Noting by " $-$ " the opposite of addition, $K_C - K_B \dashrightarrow K_A$. Obviously, $K_A - K_A = 0$.

g. *Closure.* Obviously, whenever addition and subtraction are performed, the operation must yield a VC that is part of the same set: the operations must be *internal* to the set.

3.4.3 Verification Codes Form a Group

The VCs form a noncommutative group. The elements of such a group cannot be numbers because the operations on numbers are commutative. We shall use square matrices with 2 rows and 2 columns and represent the addition defined above with the multiplication of matrices, which is noncommutative.

Our matrices will contain integer numbers belonging to a finite field. This field will be generated in modulus arithmetic, where the divisor is a prime number p.

To demonstrate what such modulus arithmetic is, let us use p = 5. The addition table is

+	0	1	2	3	4
0	0	1	2	3	4
1	1	2	3	4	0
2	2	3	4	0	1
3	3	4	0	1	2
4	4	0	1	2	3

The table is read like this: $3 + 2 = 0$, $3 + 4 = 2$, etc. Each row-column box contains the remainder of the division by 5 of the sum of the numbers that make up the head of the row or column.
The multiplication table is

×	0	1	2	3	4
0	0	0	0	0	0
1	0	1	2	3	4
2	0	2	4	1	3
3	0	3	1	4	2
4	0	4	3	2	1

The product of 3 by 4 is 2, etc.

The powers of 2 are $2^0 = 1$; $2^1 = 2$; $2^2 = 4$; $2^3 = 3$; $2^4 = 1$; $2^5 = 2$; etc. All the elements of the field except 0 can be generated by 2. For each element X there is a power N of 2 such that $2^N = X$. 2 is called a *generator* of the field.

The numeral 3 is also a generator, the only other generator for a modulus 5 field: $3^0 = 1$; $3^1 = 3$; $3^2 = 4$; $3^3 = 2$; $3^4 = 1$; $3^5 = 3$; etc. A matrix is written

$$\begin{vmatrix} a & b \\ c & d \end{vmatrix},$$

where a, b, c, d are four integers belonging to the finite field.

The four integer numbers that make up the matrix of each alphabet character must be chosen among the elements of the field in such a manner as to make the matrix a generator of its group. In practice, three numbers out of four may be chosen arbitrarily in the field, and the fourth will be calculated so that the determinant (ad − bc) of the matrix is a generator of the field.

Two cautions are in order:

· The same generator number will be used only once.

· It is necessary to check that the matrix thus obtained cannot form a commutative product with any other matrix already obtained.

Example

Consider the table of the elements of 64 matrices for p = 997:

Rank	a	b	c	d	Det	Rank	a	b	c	d	Det
1	67	397	903	455	7	33	372	173	101	58	115
2	177	808	873	155	11	34	150	380	929	440	116
3	677	437	982	413	17	35	188	847	285	49	118
4	514	439	791	567	21	36	787	945	796	89	123
5	313	748	281	197	26	37	486	767	22	275	127
6	267	124	880	771	28	38	432	601	739	853	129
7	785	9	238	888	29	39	810	539	673	464	132
8	238	927	937	89	33	40	459	179	269	90	138
9	445	402	568	912	38	41	157	754	867	37	141
10	333	897	734	130	41	42	892	341	551	621	142
11	856	367	897	960	43	43	350	959	211	476	143
12	350	557	12	663	44	44	103	283	953	984	146
13	65	494	222	967	46	45	751	376	596	53	152

14	960	252	881	681	47	46	255	433	250	820	153
15	539	620	929	425	51	47	197	39	594	918	154
16	211	645	891	248	61	48	77	10	783	285	157
17	772	418	84	176	63	49	304	946	566	286	158
18	697	858	79	608	65	50	886	163	401	245	163
19	36	473	625	210	68	51	458	18	353	36	164
20	420	630	725	423	70	52	576	125	800	392	170
21	911	370	298	711	78	53	488	610	815	492	172
22	705	275	28	984	84	54	273	456	730	800	175
23	613	90	406	629	87	55	764	568	769	953	176
24	112	75	820	274	95	56	352	294	906	423	178
25	95	177	94	512	98	57	907	818	69	955	179
26	530	569	108	957	99	58	790	751	216	15	181
27	68	378	585	541	103	59	493	936	310	142	183
28	393	409	355	286	104	60	226	832	833	447	184
29	445	228	144	782	106	61	969	735	803	172	188
30	857	630	703	254	110	62	537	600	516	187	189
31	195	955	358	854	112	63	18	208	824	504	191
32	893	26	469	917	114	64	975	461	931	785	195

3.4.4 Implementation

The steps of implementation are as follows:

1. Choose an alphabet and count the number of symbols it contains.

2. Choose a prime number p sufficiently large to generate enough matrices for this alphabet.

3. Determine the generators of the field of the arithmetic modulus p.

4. Build the table of matrices to represent the alphabet.

5. Store these matrices in a table such that a character value is the address of a matrix, so that the elements of the matrix can be read directly.

6. When using this system to calculate the VC for a text, start with the unit matrix and multiply by each character matrix in succession, always on the right-hand side.

7. The final matrix is the VC for the entire text.

It is recommended that one VC be used and stored for each record of a file and one special VC for the entire file. This will save time when computing VCs during a file update and when trying to pinpoint an error.

3.4.5   Conclusion: Protection Quality

There is no known mathematical solution to the problem of trying to find a text that matches a given key. A computed solution, by trial and error, cannot converge in a reasonable amount of time.

The probability of finding a given matrix using the wrong text is also extremely small. The total number of matrices that can be built with a given value of p is p^4. The number of singular matrices (which are useless, since their determinant is zero) is $p^3 + p^2 - p$. The number of usable matrices for a given p is then $p^4 - p^3 - p^2 + p$. This number increases very quickly with p.

The largest two-digit prime number is 97, and over 87 million different usable matrices can be built with the generators of the field of modulus 97.

If p = 997, over 987 billion usable matrices can be built. This means that a $4 \times 3 = 12$-digit key gives a probability of 1/987,000,000,000 of finding two different texts that yield the same matrix.

Note that after the alphabet representation matrices have been built, the algorithm that calculates a VC is quite simple. It is possible to implement it in microcode and use a dedicated microprocessor to save CPU time.

4 Selection in a Database: A Complete Discussion

4.1 Problem Summary

In recent years there has been a considerable increase in the number of DBMSs and associated query systems. This chapter describes the state of the art on an important issue in the area of information retrieval in a database: selection criteria.

A computer can perform comparisons of numbers and character strings. We shall see here how appropriate software can make it answer many types of questions about a database. Each time we shall consider a group of data elements called *candidate*, for which we shall evaluate a number of constraints called *selection criteria*. If the candidate satisfies the criteria, we shall call it *selected*, which means accepted. Sample candidates are

- a tuple of a relation,
- a customer record in the customer file and its associated order records in the order file; or
- the first 100 records of the item file,
- a complete relation, which is the result of a previous selection.

4.2 Selection Constraints

A selection constraint is a boolean (logical) function, which takes the value TRUE when it is satisfied and FALSE when it is not.

The constraint is called *horizontal* when it concerns one or several data elements of the same candidate and *vertical* when it concerns elements with the same meaning in a succession of candidates.

4.3 Horizontal Constraints

These are by far the most frequent constraints. The list here includes on the order of a dozen different types, beginning with the easiest to understand.

4.3.1 Existence Constraints

The constraint is that the candidate element simply *exists*.

Example 1
The record of Customer Number 61854 must exist in the customer file.

Example 2
The "comments" attribute of the Item Movement History tuple must contain a (nonblank) comment string.

Example 3
After data entry, the Special Delivery Address field must have an address in it.

Example 4
The customer must have orders.

In some instances, there will be nonexistence because a search for the data fails or because the value found means "not defined." For example, before the Special Delivery Address is keyed in, its field is filled with binary zeros, a value that cannot be keyed in. So if after data entry the field still contains these zeros, it was omitted. This is a well-known technique.

4.3.2   Nonexistence Constraint

This type of constraint is the opposite of the previous one. To satisfy it, the candidate must have no data in the element where it is sought.

4.3.3   Existence in a Discrete Set

The value of the candidate element must belong to the given set. For example, the attribute Sales-Rep-Code must contain a value that belongs to the set of existing sales representative codes. This case is the same as in 4.3.1, except that the existence search must be conducted in a table (set), not in an attribute of a tuple.

4.3.4   Nonexistence in a Discrete Set

This is the opposite of existence in a discrete set.

4.3.5   An Attribute Verifies a Strict Comparison Constraint

The value z of the candidate attribute verifies a constraint of one of the six types below, in the comparison with a constant v:

· z is less than or equal to v (written $z \leq v$),

- z is less than v (written z < v),
- z is equal to v (written z = v),
- z is greater than v (written z > v),
- z is greater than or equal to v (written z ≥ v),
- z is different from v (written z <> v).

This type of constraint can be applied to the following types of attributes:

- numbers,
- alphanumerics: > means "located after in the alphabetical collating sequence,"
- complex numbers: > means "which has a greater magnitude than,"
- dates or hours: > means "later than."

For logical variables, only = and <> have a meaning.

Generally, = and <> always have a meaning, but the other four criteria have a meaning only if the definition domain of the candidate element is an ordered set.

Thus, in PASCAL a variable can be of type COLOR and take one of the five values: white, green, red, black, and yellow. Unless we have defined an order of the colors, z > blue is meaningless.

Note that the opposite constraint of a comparison constraint is another comparison constraint. For example, the opposite of z < 3 is z ≥ 3.

4.3.6   An Attribute Verifies a Soft Constraint

Many query problems cannot be solved by today's DBMSs. Hierarchical, network, or relational DBMSs have the same rigid binary restriction: a constraint is satisfied or it is not. An employee is older than 65 or he is not. When a DBMS scans an employee file, the Age field of each employee record is compared against the value 65. At the age of 64 years 11 months and 26 days, the employee is less than 65, and the corresponding record will not be retrieved if the question is, "Select all employees aged 65 or more." This rigidity of the DBMS forces the user to adapt questions, thus making the usage of the computer more difficult and the computer itself rigidly unintelligent.

Sometimes, and even worse, the user cannot specify a precise limit of the difference between the ideal limit (age = 65) and the ages that are still worthy of interest. Perhaps in a search involving four simultaneous constraints, the user is ready to live with "two small differences" or "one slightly bigger difference" . . . without being able to specify what "a small difference" or a "slightly bigger one" really is. Indeed the user does not know in advance what precise acceptance criteria he can use. He would like the computer to suggest to him potentially acceptable candidates and leave the decision to him. And his decision may well be based on subjective, varying criteria. The rigidity, the binary nature of the selection criteria, of a DBMS is quite a problem for many users.

To demonstrate the nature of the problem, let us consider a couple trying to find an apartment to rent. They would like it to have three rooms and cost less than $500 per month. The realtor shows them several, and they finally rent a four-room suite for $620 "because it is such a beauty!" This case shows how a DBMS with *soft* constraints can help find the $620 suite when an ordinary DBMS cannot.

The main idea behind soft constraints is replacing the "equal to" limit with the "minimum of a difference function."

The realtor, an experienced professional, knows that in addition to the two constraints (number of rooms = 3 and monthly rental ≤ $500) a third constraint can be added: "as pleasant as possible." He knows that the couple is not looking for any apartment (a *feasible* solution) but for the best compromise among (in fact) three criteria. In operations research, this is known as an *optimal* solution. He also knows that the function to be maximized (a sort of optimality) cannot be formulated in his field. It is by seeing various solutions (apartments) that the customers finally choose one.

4.3.6.1   A Function of Constraints: The Overall Distance
A search constraint can be satisfied *strictly* (a 4-room apartment cannot be found when the DBMS looks for a 3-room unit) or *softly* (a 4-room is acceptable but not as good as a 3-room, a 5-room is also acceptable but not as good as a 4-room, etc.).

For a multiconstraint search, an overall constraint dissatisfaction function F can be defined as a positive number that measures the distance between conditions that satisfy the ideal and any compromise.

When F=0, all constraints are strictly satisfied. The DBMS will calculate F for all the candidates scanned, and then sort the candidates in order of increasing F; the candidates that adhere to the criteria best will come out first.

Definitions

4.3.6.2 Strict Constraint

A strict constraint can be defined as a couple (O, Z_0), where the letter O represents a comparison Operator and Z_0 the ideal value.

1. If the constraint applies to a number attribute, O can be one of the six operators of 4.3.5: $<$, $\leq$, $=$, $\geq$, $>$, $<>$, and Z_0 is also a number. This is a *numeric* constraint.

2. If the constraint applies to an alphanumeric attribute, O can be the same as above, and Z_0 is a string. This is a *string* constraint.

3. If the constraint applies to a number attribute, O can also be the set operator "belongs to" or "does not belong to," and Z_0 is a numeric set, as in 4.3.3. This is a *numeric set* constraint.

4. If the constraint applies to an alphanumeric attribute, O can also be the set operator "belongs to" or "does not belong to," and Z_0 is a set of strings. This is a *string set* constraint.

4.3.6.3 Soft Constraint

A. *Linear numeric difference.*   Consider a numeric constraint. When an attribute value Z is compared with the ideal value Z_0 we shall define the linear numeric difference as

• $e = |Z - Z_0|$ (the absolute value of $Z - Z_0$) when $Z \, O \, Z_0$ is false,
• $e = 0$ when $Z \, O \, Z_0$ is true.

In other words, the linear numeric difference is zero when the numeric constraint is strictly satisfied, and equal to the distance between Z and Z_0 when it is not.

For example, an appartment has 4 rooms instead of 3.
$Z=4$, $Z_0=3$, $e = |4 - 3| = 1$.
We can see here the existence of two types of soft constraints:

a. the soft constraint $Z_0 = 3$:

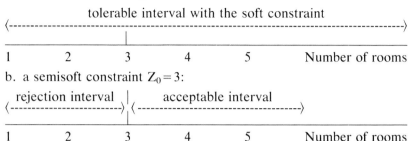

b. a semisoft constraint $Z_0 = 3$:

In the first case, the ideal number of rooms is 3, but any other number of rooms is acceptable. In the second case the ideal number of rooms is still 3, but more can be accepted: the constraint is *semisoft*. Note that this is not equivalent to the strict constraint $Z \geq 3$, which has $e = 0$ for any $Z > 3$, and rejects any $Z < 3$.

B. *Quadratic numeric difference.* Using the same theory as the linear numeric difference, we can define the quadratic difference as $e = (Z - Z_0)^2$. The distance between the ideal and the candidate values now varies as the square of the difference. In this manner, differences larger than 1 can be magnified more than with a linear measure.

In the following text, we assume that the user has chosen a way (linear or quadratic) to calculate the difference e. The same name, e, will be used no matter what method is used to measure the difference.

C. *Relative linear difference.* Let Z_0 be an ideal comparison value and e the difference between a candidate Z and Z_0. If $Z_0 <> 0$, we shall define the relative difference r as $r = e/|Z_0|$ (where the $/$ is the division sign).

If $Z_0 = 0$, let M and m be the Maximum and minimum values of Z obtained when the DBMS scans the entire database, and let N be the number of Z candidates found in that scanning process. We then define an average Z_0 as $Z_0 = |M - m|/N$. If Z_0 is now different from zero, we can use the definition $r = e/|Z_0|$. If not, all values of Z are in fact equal, we shall not be able to define a relative difference, and we shall not use the relative difference theory.

D. *Relative quadratic difference.* Similarly, we can define $r = e/(Z_0)^2$ or $r = ((M - m)/N)^2$ with the above hypotheses.

The notion of *relative* difference will be necessary for set constraints, defined below, and the evaluation of overall dissatisfaction functions F. The value of the notion of relative difference comes from the fact that it is a pure, dimensionless number.

For example (apartment with 4 rooms),

$e = |4 - 3| = (4 - 3)^2 = 1$,

linear relative difference: $r = 1/3$,

quadratic relative difference: $r = 1/9$.

E. *Relative distance from a set.* The definitions we just covered under (A), (B), (C), and (D) apply to numeric attributes compared with operators that are not $<>$ ("different from"). The following definition applies to an attribute subject to the constraint "must belong to."

If Z belongs to the set Z_0, the constraint is satisfied strictly, and $e = 0$.

If Z does not belong to Z_0, let N be the cardinal (the number of elements) of Z_0. Find the element Z_n of Z_0 that is the closest to Z—that is, such that $e = |Z_i - Z|$ is minimum when i varies between 1 and N. Calculate the difference $e = |Z - Z_n|$ linearly (or $(Z - Z_n)^2$ using the quadratic measure). Now calculate the average Z_m of all the values of Z_0 and the variance V of the set Z_0. V is the sum of the squares of the differences between an element Z_i and the average Z_m divided by N:

$$V = [(Z_1 - Z_m)^2 + (Z_2 - Z_m)^2 + \cdots + (Z_N - Z_m)^2]/N.$$

Let S be the standard deviation of the set, which is the square root of V: $S = SQRT(V)$. The linear relative difference will be $r = e/S$, where $e = |Z - Z_n|$.

The quadratic relative difference will be $r = e/V$, where $e = (Z - Z_n)^2$.

Note that the following notion of *distance from a set* can also be useful. It can be defined as the distance between the candidate value Z and the center of the set (its average value Z_m): $e = |Z - Z_m|$. The relative distance can then be defined as $r = e/S$, where S is the standard deviation of the set. These notions are also easily defined in the quadratic sense.

F. *Integers and reals.* We have just covered the notion of difference for the operator "belongs to a set." For candidates that are *integer* numbers, this notion is useless for the operator "does not belong to a set"; such a constraint can be strictly satisfied quite easily. However, for candidates that are *real* numbers, both "belongs to" and "does not belong to'' are interesting because of potential accuracy (precision) problems.

The comparison of two real numbers cannot be performed without allowing for their precision, which can be affected by binary representation, truncations, and round-offs during calculations. For real numbers, the first notion of relative distance between a candidate value and a set, covered in (E), is preferable to the second notion, mentioned in the note: if the number is "almost equal" to one of the elements of a set, this will become readily apparent. And this quasi-equality will be even easier to see with quadratic measures. However, relative differences will be more important than absolute differences because real numbers can be very small or very large.

G. *Differences of alphanumeric variables.* Names are frequently misspelled. The discussion here will make use of the theory we have just covered for numbers, applying it to string variables.

Usually strings are written using characters of a usual alphabet such as ASCII or EBCDIC, where each character is represented with one 8-bit byte. However, when dealing with misspellings, it is often more interesting to consider *phonemes,* or at least to check whether a string cannot be easily recognized using its *phonetic* representation, where each sound of the natural language is represented using a special character in an alphabet of phonemes. In the following discussion, we shall use the notion of alphabet, disregarding its ASCII, EBCDIC, or phonetic nature. Strings will be represented using the characters of this alphabet, and we shall try to evaluate how close the representation of a candidate string is to a given string.

There will be several difference evaluation techniques.

a. *Counting erroneous characters*   In this technique, the two strings to be compared are placed opposite to one another, and each erroneous character counts as 1.

Example:

G R I F F I T H
G R I F I T H
$0+0+0+0+1+1+1+1 = 4$ errors: $e = 4$.

The relative error is $r = e/N$, where N is the length of the string (8 in this case); $r = 4/8 = 0.5$. It is obvious that, using phonemes, the spelling would have been correct: $e = r = 0$.

b. *Inserting missing characters, removing extra characters* In the previous example, one of the Fs is missing or extra. In the following improved matching technique, the system will try to find what characters can be added (or removed) to make a perfect match. It will find that one will suffice and decide that $e = 1$, $r = 1/8$.

This technique must, however, be used after the procedure (a), applied with both letters and phonemes, has shown that the phonetic representation gives a closer match than the literal representation. If the phonetic representation is not known, an alternative technique for finding potential missing characters is trying to match substrings ("ITH" here) in areas where the two strings do not match naturally. If the matching is improved, then the addition of characters may be attempted. The subdivision of the string into substrings will be attempted using 2, then 3, etc., subdivisions. The process may be time consuming. The attempt to match must be a "sliding" match because substrings are not necessarily located opposite one another. The sliding distance, however, must not exceed one syllable, which has a maximum of three characters in general.

To evaluate the difference "e," the number of characters of each slide (displacement) counts, if no extra or missing characters are found, and if the remaining number of erroneous characters after the best substring matching has been obtained. The relative difference will still be e/N.

For example,

```
C H E   S T O K O W A
T C H ECH T O C O V A
⟨-------⟩ ⟨-----⟩ ⟨------------------⟩   subdivisions
    1        0          0              slides
    1        2          2              errors after slide
e = 5,     N = 10,     r = 5/10.
```

In this example, too, the phonetic representation would have given a closer match than the literal.

c. *Allowing for swapped characters* A frequent typing mistake substitutes the word "fi" for "if," and "mitsake" for "mistake": two consecutive characters are swapped. The system may try to locate such swaps, counting one error each time the swap gives a better match than considering both consecutive characters as wrong. This procedure must not be applied with phonetic representations and must be applied only after the previous matching techniques have been tried. The purpose is the same: trying to obtain a better match.

d. *Weighted errors*   Another frequent typing mistake is writing "yes" as "yees": duplicating characters. It can be covered by trying to find what characters can be added (or removed) to make a good match, but it can also be covered by a better technique: *weighting errors*. In this technique, frequent mistakes, such as swapping or duplicating characters, or typing a character on the keyboard adjacent to the one that should have been hit, are considered less serious than others. These errors are given a lesser weight—0.5, for example.

It is possible to count errors differently depending on their *position* within the candidate string; errors in the last characters are weighted less than errors in the first characters. This is useful when the string will be used as a key in an index-sequential access to a file. If the first characters are correct, the search can be considerably narrowed, and then completed by a keyboard conversation, during which the user will indicate which candidate (if any) is correct.

H. *Does a given string belong to a set?*   The distances "e" between the given string and all the other strings of the set can be evaluated using the techniques described above. The elements of the set that come closest make up a subset C of Z_0 and can then be submitted to the user, who will select the one that matches. It is also possible to evaluate "r" for the strings that match best by dividing their e by the average difference D of the couples of elements of subset C.

For example

Candidate string: MENDELSSON,

Subset C of best-matching elements: MENDELSOHN, MENDEL-SONN, ENDELSSON. The differences are

```
MENDELSSON  −  ENDELSSON   = 1    (closest element of subset: e = 1),
MENDELSSON  −  MENDELSOHN = 2    (second closest),
MENDELSSON  −  MENDELSONN = 2    (also second closest),
ENDELSSON   −  MENDELSOHN = 3,
ENDELSSON   −  MENDELSONN = 3,
MENDELSOHN −  MENDELSONN = 1,
```
average difference of subset C: $(3 + 3 + 1)/3 = 7/3$,
relative difference: $r = 1/(7/3) = 3/7$.

The candidate MENDELSSON is closer to ENDELSSON than the elements of C are to one another as an average. It is as close to

ENDELSSON as the next closest elements of the subset: MEN-
DELSONN and MENDELSOHN. If all three elements of C are displayed on a screen for the user to choose, they should be ranked by
increasing distance: ENDELSSON, then MENDELSOHN and
MENDELSONN.

I. *Overall distance function of a set of soft constraints.* When P soft
or semisoft constraints have been defined, each candidate is evaluated
for each constraint, and its relative distance r_i is calculated. We also
define a set of P weighting factors:
$a_1, a_2, \ldots, a_p$ such that $a_1 + a_2 + \cdots + a_p = 1$. These factors will give
the relative importance of the constraints within the overall function F,
which will be defined as $F = a_1*r_1 + a_2*r_2 + \cdots + a_p*r_p$. F will be zero
only when all constraints are strictly satisfied.

Example

CONSTRAINT	WEIGHT
Number of rooms = 3 (semisoft, <3 not accepted)	0.2
Rental price ≤ $500 (semisoft, >500 weighted)	0.3
Pleasantness	0.5

The first constraint rejects apartments with fewer than 3 rooms and
weighs units of 4 rooms and over. The second constraint accepts any
price but weighs prices over $500. The third constraint simply wants
beauty to be maximized: we shall express it as a difference with a
"maximum beauty" value of 20.

The following table summarizes the evaluation of F for 3 apartments:

Apt	Rooms	Rental price	Beauty	F
1	3	450	10	0.25
2	3	560	13	0.211
3	4	620	18	0.189

$F_1 = 0.2*0 + 0.3*0 + 0.5*[(20 - 10)/20] = 0.25,$
$F_2 = 0.2*0 + 0.3*[(560 - 500)/500] + 0.5*[(20 - 13)/20] = 0.211,$
$F_3 = 0.2*[(4 - 3)/3] + 0.3*[(620 - 500)/500] + 0.5*[(20 - 18)/20] = 0.189.$

J. *Selection with soft and strict constraints.* The following algorithm
is suitable for searching in a database with a combination of soft,
semisoft, and strict constraints.

1. Enter question; check if valid.

2. Chose how to navigate (in a navigational database) or to combine relations (in a relational database) to make up the set of candidates to be compared against the given constraints.

3. Read first candidate.

4. Evaluate with strict constraints. If rejected, go to step 6.

5. Evaluate with semisoft and soft constraints; calculate F. Store in a work file the output fields or attributes and the associated F.

6. Read next candidate. If there is one left, go to step 4; otherwise go to step 7.

7. Sort the work file by ascending value of F.

8. Write the work file in the sorted order.

The conclusion is that the soft constraint theory can be used in many applications:

- autocorrecting input software,
- intelligent search through a database,
- query or system operation using a natural language, and others.

More applications are discussed in other chapters of this book.

4.3.7 Minimum Difference Constraint

A "negative" soft constraint can be defined as follows: The difference ("e" or "r" or F) between the given constraint value(s) and a candidate must be greater than a minimum value. This definition is a way of *separating* elements.

Example

An input value is PIGOT, and the closest database value is BICOT. The "positive" soft constraint theory cannot reject PIGOT; it can only evaluate its distance from BICOT: $e = 2$, $r = 2/5$.

The negative soft constraint theory can recognize PIGOT as being definitely different from BICOT if their difference e is greater than a given minimum: 1, for example. Since $e > 1$, PIGOT is different from BICOT.

4.3.8 Alphanumeric Inclusion

This constraint is a strict one. The given database candidate Z must include a substring R:

• *At the beginning:* if R is L characters long, Z must be at least L characters long, and the first L characters of Z must be R. This is very useful when searching for a key with a sequential index.

• *Somewhere:* there must be a substring of Z equal to R. This is useful in syntax analysis software (compilers, for example).

• *At the end:* the last L characters of Z must be R. This is useful in examples such as: "I forgot his long name, but the last syllable was SKY" (Sikorsky, Malinovsky, etc.).

4.3.9 Alphanumeric Inclusion with "Wild Card Characters"

This case is an extension of the previous case: one or several of the characters of the substring R can be "*" or "?."

• ? represents an unknown character that definitely exists.

• * represents an unknown substring of characters that may have zero characters.

Example

The following list gives the results of the comparisons ("included" or "nonincluded") of Z = BALTHAZAR with various R strings.

Comparison of BALTHAZAR

with	result
LT??	included
?Z	included
?B	nonincluded
R??	nonincluded
B?L	included
BAL*	included
B*L	included
R*	included
K*	nonincluded
T	included
*ZAR	included
*	included
?	included

4.3.10 Constraints on Virtual Attributes

A candidate has one or several attributes $a_1, a_2, \ldots, a_n$. A virtual attribute is a function of these attributes. Examples using numeric attributes are $F = a_1 - a_2$; $F = 3*a_4$; $F = a_2 - 100$. Examples using string attributes are F is the length (number of characters) of a_1; F is the first character of a_3; F is the greatest in the collating sequence of a_1 and "K" (if a_1 = "IOWA," F = "K"; if a_1 = "TEXAS," F = "TEXAS").

Virtual attributes are not stored. They are recalculated each time a candidate must be evaluated.

4.3.11 Constraints on Integer Attributes

When an attribute is an integer, we can test

- if it is even or odd,
- if it can be divided by a given integer D,
- if its remainder in a division by D is R (or $<$R, or $>$R, etc.),
- if it is a prime number,
- if it is a power or an integer root of a given integer I,
- etc.

4.4 Vertical Constraints

In this section, the candidate is a set of individual records, tuples, or candidates in the horizontal sense. Each of these individual subcandidates can be compared using horizontal constraints.

Example from Order Entry

The candidate is a complete order, comprising one header record and N order lines.

The header record can be subject to horizontal constraints such as, "Order-date must be before May 31."

The individual order lines can be subject to such horizontal subdatabase level constraints as, "The item number must exist in the ITEM file."

The total order must satisfy a *vertical* constraint such as, "The order-value field of the header record must be equal to the sum of order-line values of all the individual lines multiplied by 1.08 (tax)."

The order may comprise items from 1, 2, or all 3 categories of existing items. But it must satisfy two other vertical constraints:

- Items must belong to more than one category.
- The order must be *balanced*. This means that no individual category may comprise more than 80% of the value of the order. (The value of a

category is the sum of the values of order lines belonging to that category.)

4.4.1 Vertical Functions

The previous example featured a vertical function: the sum of the values of a given real or virtual attribute throughout all the subcandidates of the candidate. Other elementary vertical functions are the average value, the minimum, the maximum, and the count.

Example

ITEM-NUMBER	QUANTITY	UNIT-PRICE	VALUE
2165-A	1	2.56	2.56
5410	12	0.30	3.60
8619/3	3	1.05	3.15

The sum of values is 2.56 + 3.60 + 3.15 = 9.31.
The minimum quantity is 1.
The maximum unit-price is 2.56.
The average unit-price is (2.56 + 0.30 + 1.05)/3 = 1.303.
The count (number of) tuples with a quantity > 1 is 2.

The vertical function can be used in a horizontal or vertical constraint, as in the following examples:

Example 1
Find an order header that has an order line with a value greater than 50% of the sum of the values of all the order lines of that order. The comparison involves a horizontal constraint on the value of an order line and a vertical function: 50% of the sum of the values of the lines belonging to that order.

Example 2
Find an order that has more than 20 lines. This is a vertical constraint using a cardinal: the vertical function "count."

Example 3
Find an order that has more than 20 lines and an average value per order line less than $2. The average value per order line is the sum of the values of the order lines divided by the number of lines (count).

4.4.2 Position Constraints

Assuming that a candidate has its subcandidates ordered by a certain attribute, the position of a subcandidate can be tested by a constraint, as in the following examples:

Example 1
The subcandidate that verifies a given horizontal constraint is the first or the ith.

Example 2
The first subcandidate that verifies a given horizontal constraint is the only one. In this case, an equivalent constraint is, "The number of subcandidates that verify a given horizontal constraint is one."

Example 3
The order line that has the maximum value of all the order lines of that order is the last line. In this case, the vertical function "maximum" is used together with a condition on the maximum function of a position.

Example 4
The order lines are *sorted in ascending order* by value. This is a difficult constraint by software development standards. It implies comparing vertically each order line value with the value of the next order line. It is a *total order* constraint. One way of testing it is to sort the order lines by value, and then compare each line of the sorted order with the line *in the same position* of the original order.

Example 5
The subcandidate that verifies a given horizontal constraint is located after the subcandidate that verifies another given constraint.

Example 6
When the subcandidate in position i verifies a constraint C, the subcandidate in position i + 1 verifies a constraint D. This type of constraint is also quite difficult to handle, particularly if the constraint D uses a vertical function of an attribute of the subcandidate in position i, or if the constraint C uses a function of an attribute of the subcandidate in position i + 1.

Example 7
The subcandidate that verifies a constraint C has a position that verifies a constraint D, where D uses a function of an attribute of that subcandidate. This example links a position with the contents of the subcandidate located in that position.

Example 8
Find a record of type 3, which has a successor of type 5, and a predecessor of type 1.

These eight examples demonstrate the considerable number of types of position constraints. The most difficult constraints are those that imply the verification of conditions between different subcandidates, groups of subcandidates, and positions: these are *pattern-recognition* constraints.

4.4.3   Soft Vertical Constraints

Soft vertical constraints can be defined like soft horizontal constraints. The "e" and "r" differences will apply to vertical functions. The position being an integer, soft position constraints will use integer values for "e."

Combining horizontal and vertical constraints within an "F" is also possible, and may be useful in pattern recognition, when the pattern data originate from electronic measuring devices that have a limited precision.

4.5   Selection Using Relational Algebra

Relational algebra features both horizontal and vertical functions and constraints. The text here does not attempt to describe all the possibilities of a relational language. Instead it gives three examples of selections using the SQL language (Structured Query Language) available on IBM systems (SQL/DS under DOS/VSE, and DB2 under MVS) and in the DBMSs ORACLE and INGRES, which run on many different micro, mini, and mainframe systems. The SQL vocabulary is introduced in chapter 5.

All three examples refer to the following database:

CUSTOMER (*cust-number*, cust-name, state, etc.),

ORDER (*order-number*, cust-number, etc.),

ORDER-LINE (*order-number*, *item-number*, quantity, value).

Example 1

Find the names of customers who have several orders, and list them in alphabetical order.

```
Select cust-name        *(find cust-name)*
From CUSTOMER           *(take cust-name in relation CUSTOMER)*
Order By cust-name      *(sort the names in alphabetical order)*
Where cust-number In    *(the cust-numbers must belong to the result of)*
   (Select cust-number*(this selection builds up a set of cust-number)*
   From ORDER          *(take cust-number in relation ORDER)*
   Group By Cust-number  *(group all orders of a given cust-number into
                           the same subset to count them)*
   Having Count (order-number) > 1)  *(count the order-number occur-
                                        rences and keep only a cust-num-
                                        ber with a count >1)*
```

The texts between *(and)* are comments. The SQL reserved words are underlined. The Select condition in parentheses is executed first. It builds up a set of cust-numbers; the first Select performs a join operation between this set and the CUSTOMER relation (which is also a set), based on the cust-number.

Example 2

Find the names of the customers who have no orders. Instead of solving this case like the previous case, we use the relational difference, with the SQL words *Not In*.

```
Select cust-name
From CUSTOMER
Order By cust-name
Where cust-number Not In
   (Select cust-number
   From ORDER)
```

Example 3

Find the California customers who have orders totaling over $1000.

```
Select cust-name
From CUSTOMER
Order By cust-name
```

Where state = "CALIFORNIA" *and* cust-number *In*
   (*Select* cust-number
   From ORDER
   Where order-number *In*
     (*Select* order-number
     From ORDER-LINE
     Group By order-number
     Having Sum (value) > 1000)
)

4.6   Pattern Recognition

4.6.1   Definition and Application Areas

A pattern is a structured collection of data elements. The elements can be numbers, character strings, or bit strings. They can represent business data, text, sounds, images, or knowledge frames from an artificial intelligence knowledge database. They are structured because of the sequence in which they were entered, or relationships that may exist among different elements. The purpose of pattern recognition is to retrieve elements or groups of elements, comparing them to a given element, and discover relationships among elements.

Pattern recognition applies to many areas:

In robotics, an electronic eye "sees" images. These images are converted into numeric data: digits and bits. The data are fed into a computer, which must recognize one or several shapes in the image. The shapes have a *definition* (number of different points per line, number of different lines per image) measured in pixels, due to the resolution of the equipment, which captures and converts the image. In addition to this error factor, the position of the image may not be accurate, another source of recognition difficulty. The various soft constraint definitions can help the recognition or dimension measuring processes.

In artificial intelligence, pattern recognition may be used to see whether a sequence of inference rules follows a certain type of thought, such as recurrence, syllogism, or analogy. It can help analyze data to find hidden relationships among knowledge elements.

In business data processing, pattern recognition is a powerful complement to statistics. It can be used to find sales trends and motivations or correlations between practice and results.

4.6.2   Extended Database Structures

When data represent such real-life information as images, text, or the results of scientific experiments, the data elements do not have a regular, repetitive structure. Unlike business records, these records do not have fixed contents. Fields are often missing. Redundant information can exist anywhere. The number of record types can be so great that each type cannot be stored in a file of its own. All this implies that *the databases considered for pattern recognition cannot follow the relational model,* which is far too restrictive. It is difficult to build and maintain a data dictionary because the data elements and relationships are not stable; new types of data elements can appear frequently, and others may disappear without advance notice.

This implies that we shall generally discuss *extended databases,* which do not satisfy the second and third definition criteria of databases: nonredundancy and structure.

The *types* of records stored in the files of such extended databases will be identified either by a *type field,* located at the beginning of a given record, or by *contents* of the record using structure rules and compilation techniques.

The *types of relationships* will be **explicit** and **implicit:**

Explicit relationships are physically implemented, using pointers, pointer arrays, pointers + lists, secondary indexes, and hashing. Each relationship has its own paths, running from record to record, easy to identify and follow.

Implicit relationships are not physically implemented. When the DBMS accesses an initial data element, composed of one or several records or fields, belonging to one or several files (what we previously called a ''candidate''), it tries to find another data element using search criteria, strict or soft. If it succeeds, it links the two elements with an implicit relationship.

The *extent* of each field or record will be identified using a dictionary entry only when the associated definitions are *stable* enough. When stability cannot be guaranteed, we shall have to use field and record *delimiters*, which are recognizable strings of bits or characters. For more details about unstructured databases, see chapter 5.

4.6.3 Search Constraints

All the types of search constraints covered previously will be used to retrieve information. The DBMS capabilities being limited in general, we shall have to use a DBMS-driving routine to make it powerful enough for such things as soft constraints and the use of implicit relationship paths as if they were explicit. Such a routine is seen by the DBMS as an application program. Its architecture is discussed in section 6.3.

In addition to complex search constraints, there may be another reason why the DBMS will be unable to process the database: there are no commercially available DBMSs designed to handle *unstructured* databases. Section 5.4 discusses the software architecture principles for open-content, unstructured, unstable databases.

4.6.4 Database Manipulation for Pattern Recognition

The classical database manipulation *primitives* (the standard operations from which other operations may be derived) are as follows:

· insertion, used to add data records to existing files;

· deletion, used to remove records from these files;

· modification, used to change the value of fields of retrieved records;

· selection, also used to retrieve records before they can be deleted or modified and before insertion, when the DBMS must verify a nonduplication condition: it will look for the key of the record to be added, and perform the insertion only if the key was not found.

These primitives implicitly assume that a data structure is defined before they are used. This assumption will generally not be true or even acceptable with unstructured, unstable databases. So we shall define primitives that make up a local, temporary data definition. When the data structure (consisting of the fields and relationships that exist) has been explored in part of the database, with the help of these new primitives, we shall know enough about the context to use the classical primitives.

The text will become clear as the concepts presented become more familiar. It uses four concepts, defined briefly and temporarily as follows:

· An *element* is a data element such as a field, a record, a group of adjacent fields, or records.

· A *link* is an explicit or implicit relationship between elements or structures.

· A *structure* is a logically meaningful combination of elements, links, and other (smaller, embedded) structures called substructures.

· A *rule* is a constraint that must be respected by elements or links.

The primitives we need to manipulate a database for pattern recognition and artificial intelligence are the following:

A. *Structure definition* primitives, to define the elements, links, rules, and structures to be stored, recognized, and manipulated.

B. *Structure analysis* primitives, which use the existing definitions to break down a structure into its components: substructures, elements, and links.

C. *Rule recognition* primitives, to find what predefined rules are actually used in the analyzed structure, and how well (in the soft-constraint sense) the rules are followed by the structure.

D. *Linking* primitives, which use explicit or implicit relationships, structures, and rules, to build new links or delete existing explicit links between two existing structures.

E. Usual *update* primitives: insertion, deletion, and modification.

These primitives will be grouped into a host software structure called *Structure Definition Language* (SDL).

This software will comprise a *dictionary of structures* containing elements, links, rules, and structures stored for future reference. Additions to this dictionary will be made

· manually, by writing descriptions in SDL,

· by a program that sends descriptions to the dictionary manager,

· by conversion of input data coming from instruments such as electronic eyes and graphic digitizers.

This software will also comprise a finite state machine that will

• analyze (compile) the SDL input descriptions, converting them into dictionary updates,

• drive the recognition and linking primitives to perform some of the database management tasks in association with user-written software.

4.6.5 Structure Definition Language (SDL) Concepts

4.6.5.1 Element

An element is an individual piece of conceptual information, represented in digital form inside the computer. It can be as small as one logical-type field represented by one bit, or as large as several records of a file (an element does not extend across several files). Examples are

• a number stored in a numeric field,
• one character or phoneme,
• a string of characters or bits representing an image,
• a logical record,
• a group of fields,
• a dimensioned field, such as a three-dimensional array of strings,
• a group of consecutive records,
• a complete relation or file.

The element can be analyzed for recognition purposes, but will not be broken down by any database manipulation primitive. It will always be considered and processed as one undivided piece of information.

SDL does not cover the physical storage aspect of data—only its conceptual aspect. The physical data manipulation will be performed by standard database management techniques.

Definition of an element in the dictionary of structures: The element is defined by its *name* (or *number*), its *definition domain* (4.6.5.2), an existence rule, and construction routine (5.4.10.2).

Extent of an element: When the element has a *fixed physical length* (examples: 1 bit; 1 single-precision floating-point number that takes up 4 bytes in FORTRAN 77), the extent of the element is known from the dictionary, in the description of the element's domain.

When the element has a *variable physical length* (examples: a string of characters in the BASIC language, a text describing a novel, a string of bytes describing the pixels of an image), the extent of the element is defined using a string prefix or a prefix + suffix combination. (The dictionary definition of the domain contains only the minimum and maximum lengths of an element, if defined.)

A prefix: This is a field (often 1 or 2 bytes long only) of fixed length and format, which gives the length of the element proper, which begins in the next byte. For example, a 17 character string will be represented using 18 bytes; the first byte contains the length, 17, represented as 11 in hexadecimal form. Since the prefix is only 1 byte long, a character string cannot comprise more than 255 characters (FF in hexadecimal).

A suffix: This is a small field of fixed length and content that is recognized and thus terminates the element. To be valid, the definition of a suffix must be a bit configuration that may not exist in valid data. Examples: hexadecimal 00 and FF for character strings.

4.6.5.2 Domain
A domain is the definition set of its elements. The notion has already been discussed in 2.2.2.2. The following discussion covers only the representation of a domain in the dictionary of structures.

Definition of a domain The definition stored in the dictionary of structures contains

· The identifying name (or number) of the domain.

· The physical representation of each element of this domain:

· *Numbers:* integer, long integer, real, etc.
· *Strings of bits, of characters with:* prefix/suffix, or fixed length minimum/maximum length.
· *Logical variables.*
· *Set variables:* cardinal, length of representation. (Example: if the set COLOR contains 5 elements—white, blue, red, green, black—its cardinal is 5, and the length of its representation is 3 bits for each element.) If the set is a table, stored in a disk file for example, the name/ access path of the table is required; the DBMS will access the table to verify the existence of an element when necessary.

· The dimension information, if an element is an array.

· A text that describes the domain for documentation purposes.

Depending on the application, some of the definition information may be optional.

A domain will be used to make the definition and manipulation rules of the elements more accurate, thus providing protection against programming or query errors. For example, a COLOR element may not be compared to a number but only to another color. Adding two colors may be defined for some colors but not others, depending on whether the result is another valid color. What can or cannot be done will be specified using rules, defined in 4.6.5.5.

4.6.5.3 Structure

Elements can be grouped using links to make up structures. Structures can be broken down (analyzed) into their components: elements and (some, but not all) links. Structures can also be grouped using links to make up bigger structures, the components of which are then called substructures. Grouping and analyzing follow rules.

4.6.5.4 Link

Linking can be defined between two elements, or an element and a structure, or two structures. A link is oriented from an *origin* to a *destination*. The origin of the link is always unique, but the destination can comprise several elements or structures: the link can implement a 1-to-1 or a 1-to-N *relationship,* or an ordered *list* of elements.

When a linking primitive establishes a link, it always starts from the origin and finds the destination. The destination retrieval process uses a structure analysis primitive designed for the retrieval of elements or structures that match given criteria. This process can be as simple as finding one record knowing its address, or as complex as recognizing a series of vertical substructures, each of which is made of several records that satisfy given soft and strict constraints.

When both the origin and destination are found, the linking primitive can establish physical structures to implement the link: pointers, pointer arrays, pointer + list, secondary index entries, and others. It can also leave the relationship implicit and communicate the destination parameters to the calling module, depending on what was requested.

Definition of a link in the dictionary of structures The definition comprises

· The link identifier: a name or a number.

· The name (or number) of the origin element or structure. If the origin is in the dictionary of structures, this will suffice to define the origin. But if it is not, and if it is not stable enough to be entered into the dictionary, an *origin "pointer"* must be physically stored with the origin. This pointer will comprise two fields: the link identifier (name or number) and a "pointer" to the *destination descriptor* (see below).

· The name (or number) of the destination element or structure. If the destination is in the dictionary, this definition will suffice. But if it is not, it will be described by the destination descriptor. This descriptor is a record that stores the list of all the elements or substructures of the destination, with sufficient information to retrieve the data physically. Examples: a pointer array, a secondary index.

· The name of the *existence rule* (5.4.10.5).

· The name of the *software module* used to retrieve the destination, or of the stored database view if that will suffice.

Physical implementation of a link   In the database, the link is implemented using its origin pointer and destination descriptor. In addition, the link can be accessible through a keyed-access file, the key being a combination of (link name + origin key, destination key).

4.6.5.5 Rule
A rule describes an existence condition, or an order in a structure.

· *Data rules* are an extended form of the data existence conditions that are implemented using co-routines. Data rules apply at element level and structure level.

Example 1: element level.   An element is a statement written in COBOL and terminated by a period followed by a space or a carriage return. The rule is that the statement must comprise at least 1 COBOL reserved word, such as MOVE or IF.

Example 2: structure level.   A structure is made of a CUSTOMER tuple linked by an implicit customer-HAS-orders relationship link to all its ORDER tuples. The rule is, The total value of all the orders of a customer may not exceed the customer's credit limit.

· *Link rules* are a form of existence constraints, implemented using co-routines. They describe permitted types of links.

For example, a CAD (computer-aided design) database contains the definitions of two elements: a line and a circle. The line is defined with the parameters (u, v, w) of its equation, $ux + vy + w = 0$, and the circle with the coordinates (a, b) of its center and its radius R. A rule specifies that the link "is tangent to" can be implemented between these elements if the distance between the line and the center falls between $R(1 - r)$ and $R(1 + r)$, where $r = 0.0001$.

When a link primitive has been called by a program, before the explicit or implicit result is accepted, the link rules will be verified. In fact, data and link rules cannot always be separated. In some cases, data rules may vary depending on existing links, explicit or implicit. So the expression of rules will not attempt to separate these two types of rules.

The same origin and destination can be linked by *several* links representing different relationships, as in the following example:

PART (*part-number,* part-name, . . .)
and

MACHINE-TOOL (tool-number, tool-name, function, . . .)
are linked with the following 1-to-N relationships:

1 part *IS MADE ON* N machine-tools,	(1)
1 machine-tool *IS USED IN THE MAKING OF* P parts,	(2)
1 part *IS A COMPONENT OF* C machine-tools.	(3)

In some cases some of these relationships may be mutually exclusive, and this obligation will be described by a rule. For example, type "X3" parts cannot be components of tools used to make them.

• *Order rules* describe a sequence that must be observed among the components of a structure. For example, the ORDERs of a CUSTOMER must be stored in the order "last in first out."

Unless otherwise specified, all the rules are in effect simultaneously: they are linked by an implicit "*and*" condition. If in some instances, there must be a choice between rules A, B, and C (one only would suffice), an "*alternative*" will be specified.

Definition of a rule in the dictionary of structures   A rule is identified by a name (or number), the name of its application domain, and the name of the software module or co-routine that implements it (5.4.10.7).

In the dictionary of structures, a rule must be retrieved knowing the element(s), structure(s), and link(s) to which it applies.

4.6.5.6 Law

A law is a group of rules, identified by their names or numbers. It has the same effect as its component rules except that the observance of the rules can be weighted.

The theory of soft constraints can be applied to certain types of rules. When a rule is not strictly followed, the difference between strict adherence and reality can be measured.

Example 1

When the total value of the orders of a customer exceeds the credit limit, the difference e = order total − credit limit and r = e/credit limit can be calculated: the rule is "soft."

Example 2

A rule requires the first machining operation of a sequence of operations performed on tools of class H to be "mount part." No compromise is possible; no "e" and "r" values may be defined. The operation is or is not "mount part." In this case, no weighting is possible: the rule is "strict."

Example 3

A database contains service centers and customers who may need service. A customer may be linked to a service center if the distance between his site and the center is less than 80 miles: this is a linking rule. To allow for exceptions, adherence to this rule can be measured ("e" is the distance in excees of 80 miles) and weighted.

When r values have been defined, a global F value can be defined, with coefficients applicable to the rs. The law can be more or less strictly enforced. A lower bound of F can be defined. Depending on the value of F, the "quality" of a structure can be high or low: if the rules are very closely observed, the structure will be called "tight"; if not, it will be "loose." Tight and loose are the structural equivalents of strict and soft.

4.6.6 Image Pattern Recognition

The following text is not a complete discussion of the image recognition problem. It is a collection of ideas that demonstrate how pattern recognition can be performed.

An electronic image, as seen by a video camera, is a series of lines. Each line can be digitized to represent all its pixels. A pixel will be described by a number of bits that represent its color and intensity (quantity of light). For example, if 8 colors are each seen at 8 levels of intensity, it takes $3 + 3 = 6$ bits to represent 1 pixel.

Assuming that each line is 800 pixels wide and that each image comprises 400 lines, one image has $800 \times 400 = 320,000$ pixels, or 1,920,000 bits (240,000 8-bit bytes).

4.6.6.1   Global Recognition

Can a given image be recognized as one of the known images stored in an image database?

Each stored image has a number of parameters, such as

• average intensity,

• color distribution: $X_1\%$ of color 1, $X_2\%$ of color 2, etc.

The computer will calculate these parameters for the candidate image and compare them with each stored image to find a match. This will be done in the soft constraint sense to allow for imprecision. The stored images will be accessed by key, using an index-sequential file on color distribution percentages.

The closest possible match will be located, the relative differences will be calculated between the candidate and the database image, and a global recognition decision will be made.

4.6.6.2   Detailed Recognition

The detailed recognition of an image that has been globally recognized can be performed by dividing the image into a number of rectangles of similar size, and then comparing each rectangle in turn in the same global manner. After a few such subdividing operations, a good level of accuracy can be obtained. For example, the first subdivision will divide the original image into 4 parts, the next subdivision into 16 parts, etc.

4.6.6.3   Light Gradient Technique

Simple technical images are often monochrome—that is, black and white, as opposed to colored. The issue then is to recognize (or measure distances in) simple shapes, which can be schematically represented with approximately a dozen lines. Each line is in fact a series of points where the light intensity changes very rapidly from dark to bright: the gradient of intensity is high. Then instead of storing 240,000 bytes to represent the image, it is sufficient to store a reasonable number of points of each of these lines. For example, 12 lines of 20 (average) points each, or 240 points, will suffice. In each point, the signed gradient (positive if the intensity increases from left to right) will be stored as a two-hexadecimal-digit precision number; there are 256 levels of gradient (128 decreasing and 128 increasing levels). The position of each point can also be represented in an x–y coordinate system, with a 256 × 256 resolution. Each point will therefore be represented using 3 bytes: 2 for the coordinates and 1 for the gradient. The total input image, as far as recognition is concerned, will contain 3 × 240 = 720 bytes, considerably fewer than the previous 240,000. The candidate database image will be read into memory, and then stored as a table of 256 rows and 256 columns, providing direct access to the gradient value of a given row × column combination.

In this case, 240 constraint comparisons will suffice for a complete analysis.

4.6.6.4 Pattern Recognition with Varying Positions

The previous examples assumed that the input image to be recognized always comes in a well-defined position, with respect to both x–y and angle; this is often the case in robotics, but not always. Sometimes the dozen or so high-gradient lines to be recognized are more or less randomly positioned. The recognition problem is then more difficult.

An initial recognition can be performed using a circular portion of the input image, compared to a circular portion of the same size of the database candidate. In this circular area, an evaluation of two types of gradient functions will be performed, and then compared.

For example, the two types of functions can be

• F1: the number of input gradient points in the circle,
• F2: the average intensity for each of 4 quarter circles, obtained in the slicing of the circular area by two perpendicular diameters.

The search for the best position to interpret the image will then be performed in two steps.

First, the best x–y position will be sought by comparing various values of F1, obtained when the circle is moved to various positions. The best match will be retained, if acceptable in the soft constraint sense. Then the best angular position will be sought by comparing various quadruplets of F2, obtained when the circle is rotated.

This technique works under some convergence conditions, which should not be studied in theory but experimented with in practice.

When the best position has been found using this circle approach, the recognition of some high-gradient lines will be attempted using the entire image.

1. The high-gradient points of the input image are examined, retaining only those relatively close to another point: a maximum of 3/256 of the image away, for example.

2. A program attempts to fit a series of line segments and circle arcs to these points using least-squares techniques. The objective is to obtain only a dozen lines or so, which fit the various points rather closely.

3. These lines are compared to database candidates, which have also been analyzed in a similar way.

When the image is simple, this technique yields good results. In some cases, it is even possible to measure distances between recognized image elements, thus evaluating manufacturing tolerances.

5 DBMS Techniques and Database Architectures

5.1 Features and Functions of a DBMS

This section describes the services provided by a DBMS from a user's standpoint. It does not describe the techniques used to manage the data files or to develop the DBMS software; the former are covered in the rest of this chapter, and the latter are outside the scope of this book.

From a license purchaser's standpoint, one major decision is important: Is the DBMS intended for a nonprogrammer, in all or some of its functions, or is it intended for a programmer? Some DBMSs, of course, are clearly intended for both user populations or have functions covering the wide spectrum of requirements of both user categories.

With such a simple classification in mind—programmer versus non-programmer—there is no fundamental difference between the DBMSs that run on a microcomputer, those that run on a mini, and the big professional software masterpieces that run on a mainframe; all provide the same types of service. The differences between them are of a quantitative rather than qualitative nature: the size files that can be processed, the throughput that can be expected, the number of users who can access the database simultaneously, and how much the license costs. Indeed some DBMSs, such as ORACLE, run identically (with no additions or restrictions except volumes and performance) on such machines as an IBM 3083 under MVS, on a DEC VAX under VMS, and on an IBM PC/XT under MS-DOS.

Therefore we shall describe functions without regard to the size of the supporting machine. Furthermore, there exists a database culture in the same manner as a computer science; it is a set of facts, properties, constraints, and problem areas common to all databases and supported applications. This culture is never propagated by DBMS vendors, who tend to teach what their software products do, and how to use them, instead of describing industry-wide truths.

Sometimes these vendors restrict their description of technological reality to the achievements of their more or less obsolete or restricted products. As a result, their users do not know what the state of the art can help them do with other products; they even restrict their vocabulary and their thinking to the mental patterns covered in the training supplied for their own DBMS.

The situation is similar to that of the novice who has just read his first

BASIC language manual, written his first five-line program, and now thinks he knows Computer Science.

The descriptions in this chapter attempt to convey some unbiased database culture, and their purpose is to

• explain the problem areas of database management,
• show what a DBMS does to solve the problems,
• help users determine what functions they need for their application, what they should be looking for when they purchase a DBMS, and what the technical consequences of some trade-offs are,
• prepare readers to understand the motivation behind each file architecture principle discussed in the subsequent sections of this chapter.

The following checklist specifies the functions discussed:

1. disk space management,
2. file access management,
3. file linking,
4. data dictionary management,
5. application program interface,
6. program/data independence through mapping,
7. program/structure independence through multilevel views,
8. access conflict and deadlock protection,
9. backup and recovery,
10. data restructuring capabilities,
11. security,
12. database administration,
13. application portability,
14. data query,
15. evolution capabilities.

5.1.1 Disk Space Management

The DBMS needs space for its data files. It obtains this space from the operating system through CALLs. It does not bypass the operating system for any disk operation.

• The DBMS requests and obtains space to create *new* database files that have just been described in the data dictionary, or to expand *existing* files when that becomes necessary.

• The DBMS inserts new data records into the database files, using space obtained from the operating system, or space recovered from previously deleted records. To manage the space of deleted records efficiently, making them available for new data, is not so easy:

The DBMS can link all available records, building up a *chain* or *list* structure of deleted records (these structures are discussed in this chapter). It can then store the address of only one such "hole," and retrieve all the others in turn because they are linked.

The DBMS can also maintain, in a special file area, 1 bit for each record, with a value that means "available" or "not available."

• The DBMS extends the operating system's capabilities in areas where they are not sufficient for database management. For example,

• *Multivolume files.* Sometimes a file is too big for the disk or diskette where it resides; it needs to spread over several disks at the same time. Unfortunately, many operating systems do not handle multivolume files, so the DBMS does the interface work, making it transparent to its user, who sees a file with a unique span.

• *Areas.* The DBMS can group the related records of several logical files into a single physical file, to boost performance (see chapter 1 for a definition of the Area concept). Within an area, it manages the disk space regardless of the notion of record. It provides users with as many different record sizes and layouts as they need while hiding this complexity from the operating system.

• *File groups.* Some operating systems, such as MS-DOS and XENIX, place severe restrictions on the number of files that can be open simultaneously: 16 for MS-DOS and 20 for each XENIX task. These restrictions are generally not acceptable for database management, so the DBMS can group several files to decrease the number of files open at the same time. The user will see separate files, and the operating system will see only one. Sometimes this grouping affects index files too.

5.1.2 File Access Management

Accessing a file means reaching a given record, to read it or write it. All operating systems feature at least two types of file access modes: *sequential* and *random*.

In sequential access, the program reads (or writes) the file from the beginning, accessing all records in succession. With random (also called "direct") access, the program can reach a record specified by its rank (the first, second, . . . , Nth) directly, without accessing previous records first.

In addition, sequential files are generally opened in Read *or* Write mode, thus refusing to rewrite any record, while random files can be opened in Read *and* Write mode. This is linked to the fact that sequential files often feature *variable-length* records while random files generally offer only fixed-length records.

The behavior of one operating system, UNIX, is significantly different from the classical description. But in UNIX, the very notion of a record is different. UNIX is a perfect operating system for use with a DBMS, which will manage file records for each task, and a difficult system to use without DBMS, because its file structures are not easy to use with application programs.

In general, an operating system does not have *all* the file access capabilities required by database management, and we shall have to rely on the DBMS to perform those file access operations that are not possible with the operating system alone. The most usual file access modes required by database management are

• *Primary and secondary indexing*   Using an index (structure described in this chapter) a program can retrieve the records that have a field matching a given key value. For example, accessing the Customer file by customer name using an index built on the customer-name field, a program can supply a key value and retrieve

• the records that have a customer-name field that matches a given name *exactly*,
• the records where the field value is *greater than or equal to* the given name (where the value *begins with* a given string: this is the search with *partial key*, a useful capability),
• the records where the field value is *greater than or equal to* the given the alpha order sense),
• the records where the field value is *less than* or *less than or equal to* the given string.

Primary indexes (only one per file) guarantee the uniqueness of the key field; each record has a *unique* key field value, which does not exist in any other record of that file. For example, an index by customer-number on the Customer file must be a primary index.

Secondary indexes (0, 1, or several per file) do not guarantee uniqueness. An index by customer-name is secondary because two customers may have the same name.

• *Hashing*   Hashed or hash-coded access is a form of random access where the access key value, unique or not unique, is converted into a record number by a mathematical transform and an algorithm. Hashing is described in this chapter. It seems to serve the same purpose as an index, but it does not. The main differences are

• *updates* are faster with hashed access than with indexed access,
• updating *large* files is even faster with hashing than it is with indexing,
• partial-key searches are impossible with hashing.

• *Hash-coded index*   This form of access uses hashing (record address calculation) to find a key + pointer record in an index file; then the program follows the pointer to find the actual data record in the data file. The structure and advantages of hash-coded indexes are discussed in this chapter.

• *Database-key*   This form of random access reaches a specific record with an address equal to the database-key. This is not an actual physical address (a record number in a given file) but a symbolic address, which must be converted by the DBMS into a record number.

This type of access is not *by key*; it assumes that the database-key is known.

• *Bit-vector inverted file, or bit index*   This type of access, described in this chapter, uses sequential access through a special index file with *very small* fields (each field has only one or a few bits), to find records in a large database file that match *several* search criteria at the same time.

For example, using bit indexing, a microcomputer can find an employee record that matches 8 given search criteria among 10,000 other employee records in about 12 seconds. Each employee record is 2000 bytes long, and the number of potential search fields is 25.

5.1.3   File Linking

A database comprises data elements and relationships. A relationship is a correspondence between data elements, implemented to help retrieve the ''destination'' element(s) associated with a given ''origin'' element. The following situations may arise and are handled by the DBMS.

5.1.3.1 One-to-One (1-TO-1) Relationships

This is a relationship that exists between a key and an attribute. The attribute is determined by the value of the key. Conversely the value of an attribute does not determine the value of the key, since several tuples may have the same attribute value.

1-to-1 relationships are implemented by storing the key and attribute in the same record; the DBMS then manipulates them together.

5.1.3.2 One-to-Many (1-TO-N) Relationships

(See 2.2.3.5 and 1.2.6.2.) This is a relationship that exists between 1 "origin" tuple and 0, 1, or many "destination" tuples. In general, the "destination" tuples are in a different relation (we used the example Customer *HAS* Orders many times). The DBMS implements this relationship *explicitly* or *implicitly*.

Explicitly implemented relationships are relationships for which a physical access path is implemented:

• *Pointer + List:* A pointer in the origin record of file A points to the *first* destination record of file B; this contains a pointer that points to the *next* destination record of B, etc. The last destination record has a pointer value of zero.

It may also have a pointer that points back to the origin record; the structure is then known as a *Ring*.

These structures are further described in this chapter. They are never used by relational DBMSs.

• *Secondary index:* The destination file has a field with the same value as a field of the origin file. For example, the Order file has a customer-number field in each order record.

A secondary index is implemented based on this matching field, and points to the destination file. For example, when the program has just accessed a customer record, it can use the index by customer-name on the Order file to find all the orders of that customer.

This structure is used by both relational and navigational DBMSs. The secondary index can be *based on one field* of the destination file or *on several* fields.

For example, the index that points to the Order file can be based on two fields: the customer-number (major) and the date (minor). Using partial-key search (described in section 5.1.2), the application program can retrieve the orders of a given customer without knowing their date, and then find the date as the second part of each index key. In addition, the orders may be retrieved in *ascending date sequence*; the relationship is implemented with a given sequence based on a field. It can also be implemented in the order of insertion of the destination records (FIFO—First In First Out) or in the opposite order (LIFO—Last In First Out).

• *Hash-coded link:* The origin record carries a bit that flags the existence of destination records. The DBMS stores them in the destination file as *synonyms* of the same given origin key.

For example, when the customer record flag bit is set to TRUE, the DBMS can search for the orders of that customer in the Order file. These orders are stored as synonyms using a hashing algorithm; all have the same key (the customer-number). Hashing is described in this chapter.

The implementation of a 1-to-N relationship *cannot guarantee the sequence* in which the destination records will be retrieved, because the storage mechanism (hashing) makes them all synonyms. But it is generally quite fast because all destination records of a given origin tend to be located in the same file block or area; they are retrieved together, in one disk access.

• *Pointer Array:* The keys of the destination records of each origin record are stored in a table called "pointer array." Each key is followed by the pointer that designates the corresponding destination record. This structure is described in this chapter. Whenever possible, the pointer array is stored in a single record, and this record is located in the same area as the origin record.

The advantage of this structure is that it combines good performance with ordered (collating sequence) maintenance of destination records.

CODASYL DBMSs, such as IDMS, IDS II, and MDBS III, use pointer arrays. They also feature all the other relationship structures described here. Other DBMSs use only some of these structures. For example, relational DBMSs use secondary indexes but not pointer arrays.

Implicitly implemented relationships are relationships that are only described in the data dictionary but not implemented with pointers, indexes, etc. These relationships are known to the DBMS but not managed by it.

The *relationship management operations* performed by a DBMS are

• definition of the relationship in the data dictionary,
• implementation and maintenance when updates occur of the explicit relationship links,
• protection of these physical links in case a power failure, a program abort, or other malfunction occurs,
• use of these linking paths to retrieve the destinations linked to a given origin.

Doing all this for an application program makes the programmer's work quicker, simpler and safer, and far less technical.

With some DBMSs (CODASYL, for example), the management of a relationship, after it has been defined in the data dictionary, can be *Automatic* or *Manual*.

Automatic management is performed by the DBMS alone whenever an update occurs. For example, when a new order is inserted in the Order file, the DBMS will

• Verify the existence of the customer record that has the same customer-number as the order.

• Link the new order to the customer, using the appropriate linking structure. For example, if the structure is a Pointer Array, the DBMS will find the array, determine where (in the array) it must store the *link key* (order-number or order-date, for example) depending on the FIFO, LIFO, etc., convention used, and then store the key and its pointer in the array.

Manual link management is performed by the DBMS when a program requests it and with link key values supplied by the program. This nonautomatic procedure is used when some records must be linked and others must not.

For example, two files, Cars and Options, are linked by the relationship "Car *HAS* Options." This relationship can be managed only manually, since no automatic decision can exist about which option is available on what car.

Another issue in relationship management pertains to the locations of the origin and destination. In all the above examples, the origin and destination were in *separate* files. However, this is not always the case. In manufacturing applications, for example, an "Item" can be an assembly, which can be broken down into subassemblies (which are also "Items"), etc. This process can continue twenty levels deep or even more. CODASYL DBMSs can handle such situations, and so can relational DBMSs, using secondary indexes and special-purpose relations.

Example
The Item relation is

ITEM (*item #*, item-name, weight, etc.).

The Contents relation is

CONTENTS (*assembly-item #, subassembly-item #*, number-of-subassemblies-in-assembly, etc.).

Assembly-item # and subassembly-item # are item #s (they belong to the same definition domain). The indexes are

• by item # on ITEM,
• by assembly-item # on CONTENTS,
• by subassembly-item # on CONTENTS.

We can then answer these questions:
1. What subassemblies make up an assembly?
2. In what assemblies is a subassembly used?

Yet another issue in relationship management is that an origin record and destination records may be linked by *more than one* relationship.

Example
A database contains two relations:

COURSE (*course #*, course-name, date, location, etc.),
PERSON (*person #*, name, address, etc.).

The 1-to-N relationships that link origin tuples in the COURSE relation to destination tuples in the PERSON relation are

COURSE *IS-ATTENDED-BY* PERSON   and   COURSE *CAN-BE-OF-INTEREST-TO* PERSON.

The DBMS will follow the path of only one relationship during a search, as instructed by the application program. When a new destination record is inserted, a link must be initiated manually because the DBMS does not know whether the new destination belongs to zero, one, or several relationships.

5.1.3.3 Many-to-Many (N-TO-P) Relationships
This type of relationship was covered in 1.3.5.2. An N-TO-P relationship consists of two 1-TO-N relationships in opposite directions. CODASYL DBMSs can handle such relationships automatically. Relational DBMSs can handle them using secondary indexes but only in manual mode.

5.1.4 Data Dictionary Management

The data dictionary provides some or all of the functions described below. The DBMS accesses the data dictionary continuously while it works for application programs.

1. Definition of fields and files, with all the information described in the MSD slips. Most commercially available dictionaries cannot handle all the information supplied in MSD. For example, the existence constraints of a field are limited to the description of an interval such as this: X may vary between -10 and 99.

2. Definition of relationships, with all the information described in the Access or Relationship Path (P) slip of MSD.

3. Definition of external schemas or subschemas. This subject was introduced in 1.3.2.5. The following information can be managed by the DBMS for each user:
· list of files that can be accessed,
· for each file: list of fields permitted, passwords required to access the file, operations permitted on that file—Read, Write, Append,
· list of relationships accessible to a given user, and access type: read (use to find the destination of an origin) and write (update).

4. Definition of views, with all the information described in the MSD access slip and in section 1.3.1. Even nonrelational DBMSs can some-

times feature multilevel views, and can catalog complex access operations. In addition, a view may be executed only with given passwords.

5. Definition of implementation parameters required for the physical schema of the database, such as volumes, data locations, and physical file structure options.

6. Definition of nondatabase entities, such as screen forms and printout contents and layouts.

7. Listing and cross-referencing of the various descriptions; the DBMS can print listings showing where a given element is used (in which other element, in which program module, in which external schemas, etc). It can, of course, print regular data dictionary listings describing each element: relation, attribute, relationship, screen form, etc.

In addition, some programmer workbench packages can keep track of the *history* of a data dictionary, storing the different versions of the dictionary contents.

8. Automatic generation of data definition (declaration) statements, as required in the Data Division of COBOL programs, for example. Similarly the data dictionary utility of a DBMS can supply the screen forms generator and report writer programs with the data definitions they need.

This saves programming time and helps maintain the software; a unique, centralized version of a data definition is easier to update and more consistent.

In CODASYL systems, the definition of new fields, files, and relationships always comprises two phases: a dictionary update phase, followed by a program creation/update phase. A third phase, used to define the physical file parameters, can then take place.

Static dictionaries, which were the only type available until a few years ago, required "recompiling" after each update of the data definitions. In spite of the program/data independence (described below in this section) programs had to be relinked. The entire database (or most of it) had to be unloaded and loaded once more. This evolution job required many hours, and was performed slowly and cautiously as infrequently as possible.

Nowadays, *dynamic* dictionaries can be updated with the required password during program execution, even in multitasking mode. Recompiling, relinking, unloading, and reloading are no longer required. This flexibility is achieved using an *interpreted mode* instead of a *compiled mode* of operation within the DBMS. Each time an access is requested, the DBMS checks the current description of the data in the dictionary and uses it. Access locking occurs only while the actual definitions are updated, which takes a few seconds. Previous versions of the database definition are maintained concurrently with the current version, to describe "old format" data, which can be stored and manipulated concurrently with "new format" data. Obsolete definitions are erased when they are no longer needed by currently stored data.

5.1.5 Application Program Interface

This section describes how an application progam can use the DBMS. It does not describe the query capabilities, featured in another section of this chapter, and it assumes that the reader has read chapter 4. Depending on the DBMS, some of the capabilities described may or may not exist. When they do not exist, it is generally possible, with some programming effort, to implement them using the functional interface technique described in chapter 6.

Two categories of services are available to an application program that uses a DBMS:

• *data definition* (conceptual and physical schemas): the program can obtain from—or insert into—the data dictionary the definitions of the fields and files it will use;

• *data manipulation*: the program can make the DBMS perform database accesses to get data from it or put data into it.

There is an important difference between the two types of DBMS:

• *Relational* DBMSs will let the user define new relations and new attributes in the application program while manipulating data. The two services, data definition and data manipulation, can be mixed. They can be obtained using the same relational language—SQL, for example.

• *Navigational* DBMSs separate data definition and manipulation. These are performed in succession using two different languages: the Data Definition Language (DDL) and the Data Manipulation Language (DML). CODASYL DBMSs also use a third language, to define the *physical* schema of a database: the Device Media Control Language (DMCL).

5.1.5.1 Application Development Language Interface
DBMSs interface with a user program in one of the following ways:

1. *CODASYL systems*

1.1. the *DDL* source statements define
- logical data characteristics,
- methods of storing the records,
- record contents,
- set relationships.

These definitions are compiled through the DDL processor to produce an Object DDL, stored in the data dictionary.

1.2. the physical schema of the database is then described using the *DMCL*: disk space allocation, page sizes, etc. The DMCL definitions are compiled through the DMCL Processor to produce a DMCL Object description. The DDL and DMCL objects together make up the Object Schema of the database.

1.3. the *DML* statements are embedded in a COBOL program. This source program is compiled through a preprocessor. This preprocessor also reads the object schema in the data dictionary and produces a source COBOL program, where the appropriate declarations have been inserted in the Data Division to describe the database, and the DML statements have been translated into DBMS calls. The COBOL source is then compiled and linked into executable code. See figure 5.1.

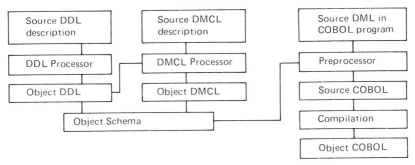

Figure 5.1
CODASYL application program interface.

The DDL, DMCL, and DML vocabularies comprise many words used in a COBOL-style syntax. The following syntax samples are extracted from an IDS II manual. The reserved words are in capitals; the nonoptional words are italicized.

DDL

SCHEMA NAME IS schema-name.
AREA NAME IS area-name.
RECORD NAME IS record-name-1

```
                              | DIRECT database-parameter-1
       LOCATION MODE IS       | CALC USING database-identifier-2
                              | VIA set-name-1 SET
             | ANY AREA          | [AREA-ID IS database-parameter-2]
     WITHIN  | area-name-1. . .  |
             | AREA OF OWNER
[level-number-1] database-data-name-1
                      PACKED
          | SIGNED                     DECIMAL integer-1 [.integer-2]
          |           UNPACKED
  TYPE IS | SIGNED BINARY | 15
          |               | 31
          | CHARACTER integer-3
[OCCURS integer-4 TIMES].
```
SET NAME IS set-name-1 *OWNER* IS record-name-1
ORDER IS *PERMANENT* INSERTION IS
```
     | FIRST
     | LAST
     | NEXT
     | PRIOR
     |          | WITHIN RECORD-TYPE
     | SORTED   | BY DEFINED KEYS
                  [RECORD-TYPE SEQUENCE IS record-name-2 . . .]
                                    | FIRST
                  DUPLICATES ARE    | LAST
                                    | NOT ALLOWED
```

MEMBER IS record-name-1
       INSERTION IS *AUTOMATIC RETENTION* IS *MANDATORY*
       INSERTION IS *MANUAL RETENTION* IS *OPTIONAL*
[*DUPLICATES* ARE *NOT* ALLOWED FOR database-identifier-1. . .]
```
        | ASCENDING  | | database-identifier-2 |
[KEY IS |            | | RECORD-TYPE           | ]
        | DESCENDING | | DATABASE-KEY          |
```
SET *SELECTION* [FOR set-name-1 IS]
       THRU set-name-2 OWNER IDENTIFIED BY

DMCL

SCHEMA NAME IS schema-name
    [*DATE* IS | yy mm dd | *TIME* IS hh mm]
               | yy ddd |
    [*SCHEMA* INTERNAL *FILE* NAME IS ifn]
    [*IDSOPT* INTERNAL *FILE* NAME IS ifn]
    [*IDSTRACE* INTERNAL *FILE* NAME IS ifn]
    [BUFFER *POOL* NAME IS name]
    [NUMBER OF *BUFFERS* IS integer]
    [EXTEND NUMBER OF *AREAS* TO integer]
    [EXTEND *GLOBAL* POINTERS TO integer BYTES]
    [*NO LOCAL* POINTERS].
AREA NAME IS area-name
    [*AREA* INTERNAL *FILE* NAME IS ifn]
    NUMBER-OF-PAGES IS integer
    NUMBER OF *LINES-PER-PAGE* IS integer
    PAGE-SIZE IS integer BYTES
    [*CALC-INTERVAL* IS integer PAGES]
    [EXTEND *LOCAL* POINTERS TO integer BYTES].
RECORD NAME IS record-name
        RANGE [*WITHIN* area-name] IS | integer *PAGES FROM* PAGE integer | . . .
                        | *PAGE* integer *THRU* integer |
SET NAME IS set-name *NO LOCAL* POINTERS.

DML (in Data Division)

DATA DIVISION.
SUB-SCHEMA SECTION.
DB schema-name.
    [*DB-DESCRIPTIONS* IN | *WORKING-STORAGE* | SECTION.]
                          | *LINKAGE* |

    | *RECORDS* ARE | *ALL* | |
                  | [*NOT*] record-name. . . | | .
    | *REALMS* ARE | *ALL* |
               | [*NOT*] realm-name. . . |
WORKING-STORAGE SECTION.
77 identifier *USAGE* IS *DB-KEY.*
LINKAGE SECTION.
77 identifier *USAGE* IS *DB-KEY.*

DML (in Procedure Division)

USE FOR *DB-EXCEPTION.*
ACCEPT ident-1 *FROM* | realm-name | *CURRENCY.*
                     | record-name |
                     | set-name |
CONNECT [record-name] *TO* set-name.
DISCONNECT [record-name] *FROM* set-name.

ERASE [record-name].

FIND record-selection-expression [*RETAINING* CURRENCY FOR | *MULTIPLE REALM RECORD SETS* name. . . |

Record-selection-expressions:
    [record-name] *DB-KEY* IS ident-1
    | *ANY* |
    | *DUPLICATE* | record-name
    | *NEXT*
    | *PRIOR*
    | *FIRST* | [record-name] *WITHIN* | set-name
    | *LAST* | realm-name
    | integer-1
    | identifier-1 |
    CURRENT [record-name] *WITHIN* | set-name
                                    | realm-name
    OWNER *WITHIN* set-name
    record-name *WITHIN* set-name [*CURRENT*] [*USING* identifier. . .]
GET [identifier]. . . .
IF [*NOT*] [set-name] (*OWNER* or *MEMBER* or *TENANT*)
MODIFY identifier [*INCLUDING* . . .]

The version of IDS II from which the above sample was extracted has 170 DDL reserved words, 18 DDL Processor directives, 518 DML/ COBOL reserved words, and about 120 miscellaneous reserved commands and options!

2. *Relational systems* The relations are flat tables in normal form (described in 1.3.3.3). Both definition and manipulation statements are integrated in a unique language and can be written within a program or independently.

• If written independently of a program, they can be compiled, stored, and then executed independently or within a program.

• If written within a program, they are either interpreted directly or precompiled, and then compiled using an approach similar to CODASYL, as the example in figure 5.2 shows.

The application language can be COBOL, PL/1, or Assembler. No DMCL (physical database description) is required; an overall space allocation is made at the beginning of the application development cycle.

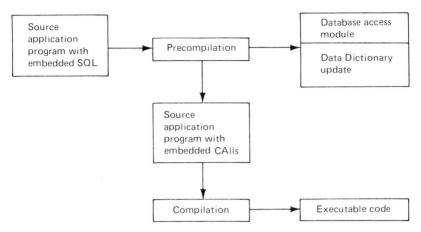

Figure 5.2
IBM's SQL/DS.

The syntax is extremely simple, unlike that of CODASYL systems. The following list contains the *complete* SQL data manipulation vocabulary, 27 reserved words:

SELECT data-name . . . *FROM* relation-name . . . *WHERE* condition
INSERT INTO relation-name (data-name . . .) *VALUES* (constant . . .)
DELETE FROM relation-name *WHERE* condition
UPDATE relation-name *SET* data-name = constant *WHERE* condition
Grouping: *GROUP BY, HAVING*
Sorting: *ORDER BY*
Qualifiers: *LIKE, DISTINCT, ANY, ALL, IN, BETWEEN, UNION, AND, OR, NOT*
Vertical functions: *MIN, MAX, SUM, AVG, COUNT*

3. *Other systems*   There are over two hundred DBMSs in existence, so I cannot describe them here. However, it is important to note here that there is a strong tendency nowadays for DBMS packages to include programmer workbench facilities: complete application development environments, with program generators, very high-level ("fourth generaton") languages, debugging and documentation tools, all built around the DBMS and its DD.

5.1.5.2 Standard DBMS Operations

The previous section contained examples of application interface languages, but the languages are shown rather than explained. Some explanations are available in the subsequent DBMS descriptions and case studies. In fact, readers who need accurate and detailed knowledge about a given language can easily find the manual supplied for that purpose by its vendor. Here we describe the underlying concepts, which exist behind all the DBMS languages and which, in spite of the (sometimes huge) vocabularies, are quite simple.

These concepts are the *standard operations* or *primitives* of a DBMS. They are divided into two categories:

· data definition and evolution,
· data manipulation

1. *Data definition and evolution* The user can *define* or *modify the definition* of

· fields or attributes,
· files or relations,
· relationships and access paths.

Of course, a definition can subsequently be *undefined* or deleted, provided that no actual data were implemented with it. To undefine a data element, the user must first delete all its occurrences.

2. *Data manipulation* Data manipulation is possible only after the necessary definitions have been made. The most important operation, called *search, selection,* or *retrieval,* was extensively discussed in chapter 4. It is the most important because all other operations need it.

The word "update" is vague, and should be avoided whenever a misunderstanding can occur. Update can mean insertion, modification, deletion, link creation or suppression.

5.1.5.3 Insertion: Also Called Record Creation or Record Addition

This operation adds a new record (or tuple) in the appropriate file (or relation). The stored record contains all the fields that were defined with actual values. The DBMS checks that all mandatory fields (the key and others) are supplied in the CALL that requests the insertion. Depending on the DBMS, the fields that were defined in the DD, but were not given values in the CALL, may or may not be stored.

The DBMS also performs the update of all access and relationship paths that must be maintained automatically (see the discussion of Automatic/Manual in 5.1.3.2)—indexes (primary and secondary), pointer arrays, list structures, etc.—so that the new record is correctly linked to all other related records.

Insertion requires selection; when a record must be *unique*, the DBMS must perform a selection to verify that no other record has the same key. When it must be stored *after* or *before* another record, it must also perform a selection to locate it.

5.1.5.4 Modification: Also Called Field Update

This operation changes the value of a field, which is part of a record just retrieved by a selection. It is defined by three elements:

• The selection that retrieves the record where a field is to be modified. This selection can be single-level or multilevel. If it is multilevel, the record to be modified is at the last level accessed (this is obvious: if it had been at a previous level, we would not have accessed subsequent levels).

• The identification of the field to be modified: name or number.

• The new value of that field.

In a multitasking (also called multiprogramming) environment, a modification involves three operations:

• selection, with locking of the record to be modified, to prevent access conflicts,

• calculation of the new value and assignment to the field,

• rewriting the modified record, updating links and indexes if necessary (if one or several are based on the modified field), and then unlocking the record.

Note

A field that is the key or part of the key of a record cannot be modified, because a change may affect the uniqueness of the record. To modify a key, the record must be deleted, and then reinserted with the new key. In turn, deleting a record may be subject to restrictions (see 5.1.5.5).

First extension of the notion of modification The mode of operation defined above implies that the new value of the modified field is calculated *by the application program*.

Example

An inventory management program wants to reduce the quantity in stock of item 4530 by 5 units, which have just been sold. It asks the DBMS to read and lock the record of item 4530 and pass back the Quantity field. It then subtracts 5, moves the new value to the Quantity field, and asks the DBMS to rewrite the record and unlock it. (Locking/unlocking is described in section 5.1.8.)

Using a Functional Interface (FI), described in chapter 6, we can *extend the notion of modification*, and make available to the program a *more powerful* and *faster* operation.

This can be done by replacing the new field value, in the definition of a modification, by two values A and B such that the new value Y of the field can be derived from the old value X by $Y = A * X + B$.

• If $A = 0$, X is replaced by B. This is the previous notion.

• If $B = 0$, X is multiplied by A. This is useful when, for example, a price must be increased by 3.5%, regardless of its current value. A is assigned the value 1.035 and $B = 0$.

• If $A = 1$, X is increased or decreased by B, depending on the sign of B. This is useful when the inventory management program wants to remove 5 items of 4530 from stock: $A = 1$, $B = -5$.

This extended modification operation is more powerful and faster because it can be performed as follows:

• The application program decides to remove 5 units of item 4530 from stock, and sends the request to the FI with $A = 1$, $B = -5$.

• The FI receives the request, asks the DBMS to read the Quantity in stock of item 4530, performs the subtraction, and asks the DBMS to rewrite the record with the updated quantity. It then passes back to the application program a "done" acknowledgment.

1. The DBMS is not asked to lock-unlock the record. The function is performed by *uninterruptibility*; the FI will not consider any other request before it has finished processing this one. It cannot be interrupted, and since it is the only program that can gain access to the Inventory subdatabase, no access conflict may occur. Uninterruptibility enhances performance, since locking-unlocking in the DBMS is a leading consumer of computer power. It will not cause bottlenecks if

the architecture constraints described in chapter 6 for the FI are respected.

2. The DBMS performs the read and rewrite operations in quick succession because the FI has a high priority. It is quite likely that the record of item 4530 remained in the DBMS buffer pool and does not have to be refetched from the disk.

3. The FI can add intelligence to the operation, such as verifying the respect of the existence constraints. For example, if an inventory update results in a negative quantity in stock, the FI will not perform it; instead it will return an error response to the application program. This verification is automatic for all modifications, so the program does not have to verify any data existence constraint.

4. If several modifications are requested horizontally (in the same record) or vertically (in different selected records), the FI can perform them as a small batch operation. For example, increase by 3.5% the prices of all items that contain copper.

5. The possibilities offered by the FI to one program are in fact available to all programs that can access the same subdatabase; this saves programming effort, and improves software quality through standardization.

Second extension of the notion of modification   Let us assume that the new field value, Y, is a function of the previous value, X, and also of other values of fields accessed with the same multilevel view that finds the record containing X.

Example
A multilevel view used for modification accesses

CUSTOMER (*cust-number*, name, discount-percentage . . .),
ORDER-HEADER (*order-number*, cust-number, . . .),
ORDER-LINE (*order-number, item-number,* quantity, item-unit-price, value).

The application wants to change the quantity of item-number 4530 in the last order of customer cust-number = 87684.

  CUSTOMER is accessed by cust-number; then ORDER-HEADER is accessed using a secondary index by *cust-number and order-date* sorted by decreasing date for a given cust-number; then ORDER-LINE is accessed by its key: order-number, item-number.

The application program requests that the old quantity be changed to 200. But the FI knows that the value field is a function of the quantity (200), and of the discount-percentage (10%). It calculates

(new) value = 200 * item-unit-price * (100% − 10%).

In this example, Y (the new value) is a function of X (the old value), of the quantity read in the same record, and of the discount percentage read from the customer-record.

We can now define Y as one of the two functions F_1 or F_2:

F_1: $Y = a_{1,1}X_{1,1} + a_{1,2}X_{1,2} + \cdots + a_{2,1}X_{2,1} + a_{2,2}X_{2,2} \cdots + a_{n,pn}X_{n,pn}$
          $+ AX + B$,

where

the $a_{i,j}$ are coefficients,
$X_{1,1}, X_{1,2}, \ldots, X_{1,pl}$ belong to the first record accessed in the view, R_1,
$X_{2,1}, \ldots, X_{2,p2}$ belong to the second record, R_2,
$X_{n,1}, \ldots, X_{n,pn}$ belong to the nth record, R_n,
A and B are given by the application program.

F_2: IF C_1 THEN A_1 ELSE
        IF C_2 THEN A_2 ELSE, etc.,

where C_1, C_2, etc., are groups of conditions to be satisfied by the records reached at the various levels R_1, R_2, etc., and A_1, A_2, etc., are functions of the same type as F_1.

If the conditions C_1 are satisfied, Y is calculated using A_1. If they are not satisfied, conditions C_2 are tested; if they are satisfied, Y is calculated using A_2, etc. This is similar to the extended assignment possibilities of ALGOL-type languages: Y: = IF C1 THEN A1 ELSE. . . .

It is easy to implement conditional modifications in the FI, and easy for the programmer to code them using a language that only understands IF. . .THEN. . .ELSE and arithmetic expression constructs. Such conditional modifications can also be read, written, and modified by non-DP users.

In figure 5.3, two input files, Formulas and Conditions, are used by

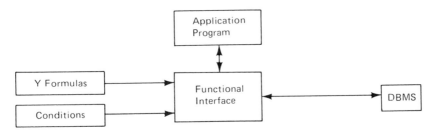

Figure 5.3
Modifications using a Functional Interface.

the FI to interpret program requests for modifications. The files can be created and updated directly by end users.

Important Note
When a multilevel view must be invoked for a modification, the locking process must lock all the records at all the levels accessed by the selection to preserve the consistency and integrity of the database. For example, to modify the quantity and value of an ORDER-LINE record, the CUSTOMER and ORDER-HEADER records must also be locked until the two modifications are finished. Otherwise, if a discount is changed or an ORDER-HEADER is deleted, there may exist a time when the database is inconsistent.

5.1.5.5 Deletion
This operation deletes (removes) one or several complete records from the database. It is defined by a selection that retrieves the record(s) to be deleted. Deletion is performed not by physically "erasing" a record, but by logically marking it. Marking uses a bit or byte that means "deleted." After the record-marking operation, the DBMS removes the access and relationship references of the record in indexes, pointer arrays, list structures, etc.

It then makes the deleted records available for future insertions, by including them in a "list of available records." This list can be physically represented by a file containing one bit for each record of the database, with a value 0 if the record is available and 1 if it is not. Alternatively it can be represented by a pointer in each available record, pointing to the next available record. The first of these records has its address in a special table.

After a deletion, a record is no longer linked (implicitly or explicitly) to other records of the database. This can be a problem because of existence constraints. For example, the record of a CUSTOMER who has ORDERS in the Order file cannot be deleted because the corresponding order records would then become inconsistent. Deletion is therefore restricted to those records where it can cause no problem.

However, the existence constraints can be rather complex. For example, deleting an ORDER may require updating the total-orders field of the customer record. This consistency constraint will be written on an MSD slip describing the customer + orders subdatabase co-routine.

If the DBMS is navigational and if the CUSTOMER *HAS* ORDERS relationship has been declared, the DBMS can verify automatically that the customer record is not deleted if it has orders. But the DBMS cannot protect the total-orders field automatically. As a result, navigational DBMSs can enforce some existence constraints but not others, causing confusion among programmers. It also encourages them to declare all relationships to the DBMS to obtain automatic protection; this causes poor performance, because many relationships do not deserve to be implemented physically. They are not used ("traversed," as the specialists say) often enough by selections, yet they are maintained up to date.

Relational DBMSs ignore relationships. They can define secondary indexes and multilevel views. Since no linking or existence verification is automatic, the co-routines must be implemented in the FI to provide full protection.

5.1.5.6 Link Creation and Suppression

This operation performs the linking as explained in section 5.1.3 or removes an existing link. A link connects an origin record with one or several destination records. When linking is performed, the DBMS "knows" the origin record and uses a selection to find the destination records. In general, DBMSs can link an origin record only with one destination record. To obtain automatic linking with all the records that can be retrieved by the same selection, the DBMS capabilities must be extended using an FI.

5.1.6   Program/Data Independence through Mapping

In the previous section, we saw how an application interfaces with a DBMS using standard operations, one or several DBMS languages, and perhaps a functional interface. This discussion covered initial programming only. Database evolution was briefly described as the process of creating, deleting, or modifying the definitions of fields, files, and relationships.

Database evolutions are caused by functional specification changes that affect the application. In general, new fields, files, and relationships are added as the scope of the application expands. Sometimes data elements become undefined; they no longer exist. Alternatively, field sizes may be changed.

When database management was invented, each file accessed by a program was completely described in the program; all its fields were known, with their relative positions and sizes within the record. Evolution required changing this description—adding new fields, for example. Since the compilation process assigns addresses to all data elements defined, the program had to be recompiled and relinked.

Recompiling one program is a small task. But recompiling and relinking all programs that access a given file may take many hours. And other tasks had to be performed for each evolution: unloading and reloading the database into the new reformatted files.

Recompiling was required because a program was not "independent" of the data. It knew the existence, size, and position of fields (new or old) that were not relevant for itself but only for other programs.

The solution to the program/data independence problem is called *mapping*. Mapping is a DBMS function that communicates with a program using only the fields of the program's external schema: the DBMS passes to the program and receives from it only the fields that the program actually uses. The other (irrelevant) fields are hidden from the program. If more fields are added to the file but remain unused by the program, the latter need not be recompiled. In addition, the order of the fields in the program's subset of the record is defined by the program, independently of their order in the file.

For an insertion, the program may pass to the DBMS only the key and mandatory fields. The DBMS will usually supply default values for the missing fields, compatible with the data dictionary. *Today, all real DBMSs feature mapping.*

5.1.7 Program/Structure Independence Using Multilevel Views

Mapping is only an elementary level of independence; the program still knows which files it accesses and which access and relationship paths it uses. The program logic reflects the structure of the database. If the structure changes, the program is affected.

Example
A navigational database has 3 files,

CUSTOMER (*cust-number,* name, . . .),
ORDER-HEADER (*order-number,* cust-number, . . .),
ORDER-LINE (*order-number, item-number,* quantity, item-unit-price, value),

and two relationships:

CUSTOMER *HAS* ORDERS   and   ORDER *HAS* LINES.

We assume that the relationships are implemented using pointer arrays and that the program needs the following access operation: "Find a given customer's last order and a specific item line in that order."

The selection will access the customer record in the Customer file first, follow the pointer in the pointer array to the last order header, and then follow the second pointer array's pointer to the order line. The program logic reflects the existence of all three files, the relationships, and the navigation.

If we now implement a secondary index by customer number directly to the order header, and if the program does not need to access the customer record, a shorter navigation can be used: access the order header through the new index by customer number, and then follow the pointer array path to the order line. To use this shortcut, the program must be modified, recompiled, and relinked; it is not independent of the database structure.

Program/structure independence can be achieved using single-level or multilevel views. This is straightforward using relational DBMSs, and has to be achieved using a functional interface with navigational DBMSs. Independence and simplicity are therefore another advantage of the FI technique.

Program/structure independence is useful because

1. *It makes evolutions easier.* If the program sees the database, each time it accesses it, as *a single flat file that contains only the required fields*, it is not affected by structure changes as long as its own data fields are not changed. In the above example, each record of the flat file, as seen by the program, will contain

ORDER-LINE (*cust-#*, *item-#*, quantity, item-unit-price, value).

2. The program logic flow reflects the existence of this apparent single-level database. It is much simpler. Programming is thus faster and safer.

5.1.8   Access Conflict and Deadlock Protection

Problem
When two or more programs modify the same record of the same file, this is what may happen:

1. Program A and program B both read the inventory of item 1432 and find a quantity of 5.

2. Program A, which is a fast batch program, removes 3 pieces from the inventory, calculates 5 − 3 ---⟩ 2, and writes a new quantity of 2 in the inventory field of item 1432.

3. In the meantime, program B, a slow interactive program that has to wait for user inputs, adds 10 pieces to the quantity it has read: 5 + 10 ---⟩ 15. It then writes the new quantity, 15, in the inventory field, which should contain 2 + 10 ---⟩ 12—*an access conflict has occurred*, erasing the modification performed by A.

5.1.8.1   Access Locking
Access conflicts can be avoided using a technique called *access locking*. When a program asks the operating system to lock a given record of a file, no other program can access that specific record. Depending on the system, the access restriction can apply to all types of access (read and write), or only to "read with the intent of deleting or modifying the record." It can also lock a single record, a complete block of records, or even the entire file. When the program finishes modifying the record, it asks the operating system to unlock it, thereby releasing it to other programs.

The DBMS has *exclusive access* to the files it manages; each file is locked for its own exclusive use as soon as the DBMS starts executing, and is unlocked only when DBMS execution ends. The following mechanism, which can be implemented without a DBMS, is managed by the DBMS when there is one.

1. Program A asks the DBMS to read the record and lock it.

2. A few milliseconds later, program B tries to read the record, intending to modify the quantity field, and is denied access; the DBMS does not answer the program's read request, and the program has to wait.

3. Program A completes its modification and asks the DBMS to rewrite the record and then unlock it.

4. The DBMS then remembers that B is waiting and reads the record for B, locking it again.

5. B performs its own modification and asks the DBMS to rewrite the record and then unlock it.

With this mechanism, the two modifications are performed in sequence, thus avoiding the access conflict; the DBMS provides access conflict protection at the record level.

Program B waits for program A to complete its modification, which is necessary only because both programs want to modify the same field. To improve performance, some mainframe DBMSs provide *field-level* locking: if two programs want to modify different fields of the same record, they can proceed without waiting.

The DBMS locking/unlocking mechanism is also useful in preventing a *record deletion* from being performed while a modification is in progress.

The mechanism is also necessary with multilevel views, when the modification of the record at the last level of the selection is a function of fields read at previous levels (see 5.1.5.4). All the records of the view must then be locked and unlocked *together* by the DBMS.

5.1.8.2 Deadlocks and Dynamic Backout

The previous paragraphs described an access conflict occurring with *one* file accessed by several programs intending to modify a field or delete a record. When several programs wish to update *several* files, this is what may happen:

1. Program A reads file F1 and locks its record number 43.
2. Program B reads file F2 and locks its record number 67.
3. Program A tries to read record number 67 of F2 and has to wait.
4. Program B tries to read record 43 of F1 and has to wait.

A and B can wait forever, as each one waits for the other to complete its update; this is a *deadlock* situation.

Deadlocks can occur with *and without* a DBMS, when locking/unlocking is used. They can be severe when more than two programs are locked together in a "cyclic" mode: A waits for B, which waits for C, which waits for D, which waits for A.

Real DBMSs have a *dynamic backout* capability (the expression *dynamic backout* was first used by IBM for its hierarchical DBMS DL/1). It breaks the deadlock in this way:

1. The DBMS detects the deadlock situation.

2. It finds which program has waited least in the deadlock and *undoes* its last transaction—*it restores the updated file to the status it had before the update*. The DBMS can do that because it keeps track of all file blocks before they are updated, by copying the not-yet-updated blocks to a journal file (or "LOG") of "before images."

3. The deadlock cycle is broken. If it is not because the remaining programs have formed another deadlock, the DBMS will undo another program's last transaction, and so on. All programs resume work.

4. The DBMS detects the end of the deadlock and restores the undone transactions, in the reverse order of their undoing—the first undone program transaction is restored last.

Dynamic backout is vital to all multiprogramming systems. Unfortunately many existing minicomputer DBMSs do not implement it correctly; the would-be user must be cautious, and test it if possible. When multilevel views are used, dynamic backout must affect the *entire* views, not only the last (updated) record, to preserve consistency.

5.1.8.3 Undoing Multiple Transactions: Committing

Problem

A computer works in multiprogramming mode with several CRTs doing order entry. Orders are processed in *real-time* mode: as soon as an order line is entered, the inventory is updated. Orders are received by telephone; each keyboard operator enters the customer's order while he is on the line.

After keying in the first 19 lines of an order, for which the computer has stored the lines in its database and modified the inventory quantities, the CRT operator finds an out-of-stock situation on the twentieth item. When he hears that no immediate delivery can be promised for the twentieth item, the customer becomes angry, tells the operator to cancel the *entire* order, and hangs up. The computer must now *undo* all its updates as if the order had never been taken.

Another operator also receives by telephone and keys in delivery transactions each time a new item is received from its supplier. The inventory is updated immediately, and order entry operators can start taking orders for the item received and promising immediate delivery to their customers. After keying in a number of delivery lines, an operator is told that a delivery described ten minutes ago is canceled; the item was found broken while unpacking and will be returned to the supplier. The computer must also undo the delivery transaction for this item. But what if, in the meantime, orders have been taken for this item and can no longer be satisfied? The goods have been promised to customers who are no longer on the phone! They will have to be called one by one. . . .

These two "undo" situations result in difficult problems, technically and from an organizational standpoint. Technically, it is necessary to undo multiple database updates: insertions and modifications. This is sometimes called "Transaction chain restart," because the best way to process each group of related updates is to *restart all* the updates concerning records affected by canceled transactions.

The computer notes in the journal file, for each transaction, the "before" image (see 5.1.8.2) and the transaction itself: insertion, modification, or deletion. To cancel a transaction, the computer restores the file with its "before" image, and then reprocesses all subsequent updates of the same record. If an update has become logically impossible (an item for which an order was taken has in fact become out of stock), the computer gives a warning, cancels that transaction too, and continues the reprocessing. Totals computed across several transactions will have to be recalculated too.

Note that this procedure requires the journal file to contain images of *records* (before update) and *transactions* (example: subtract 5 items from quantity in stock of item 1432).

Unfortunately, all except one or two DBMSs retain only record images, before *and after* an update. They do not keep transaction images; they are unable to reprocess and discover transactions that have become logically impossible—such as negative inventory levels—because applying before and after record images is always possible. So with all those DBMSs, it is necessary to

• use a functional interface to accept modifications in the form "subtract 5 from quantity in stock": this is the $Y = A*X + B$ form of modification discussed in 5.1.5.4;
• keep a journal of "before" and "transaction" images, using the FI;
• make note in this journal of variable values or screen contents that must be restored after a restart;
• make provision in the application programs or in the FI for restarts.

DBMSs do not retain the correct journal information because their designers failed to anticipate that undoing multiple transactions was logically necessary! The response they give when asked, now that most of them have heard of the problem, is that they offer "commit" capabilities.

Commit

One theory behind committing is, "Don't perform an update until you are sure." Accordingly, the transaction chain starts with a "begin of chain" transaction and ends with an "end of chain." All transactions performed before the "end of chain" mark are still uncertain. They can be undone without danger or difficulty. The "end of chain" transaction is called "commit" transaction; it confirms all updates. In practice, updating is performed in "small batch" mode after each commit. Committing also requires locking/unlocking to protect against access conflicts and dynamic backout (rollback) to protect against potential deadlocks.

This mode of operation is acceptable only if the time to execute a transaction chain is very short. This is a non-real-time approach; it is not satisfactory when large transaction throughputs and long transaction chains exist. The commit program refuses to "take chances," though the probability of having to undo transaction chains is small. A better way of handling large throughput situations is the one previously described, which only uses a small batch in the (infrequent) situations when undoing is necessary, and which detects the logical impossibilities using an FI: that is the only true real-time solution.

Another way of implementing the "commit" capability is to perform the updates as soon as they reach the DBMS, without waiting for the "end of chain" call. The DBMS retains all the "before update" and "after update" record or block images, and uses them to undo the updates if required. This is an improvement over the "small batch" implementation, but it still cannot guarantee the data consistency, as the "before + transaction image" approach can.

5.1.9   Backup and Recovery

When a hardware or software breakdown occurs, or a power failure suddenly stops the computer, adequate protection must be provided:

• The integrity and consistency of the data in the file must be protected; data must not be lost or become erroneous.

• The existence constraints must be satisfied, even if that implies not committing unfinished transactions or reprocessing transaction chains.

• Interactive users must see on their screen, at the end of the recovery process, the exact status of their work. The screen they were working on when the breakdown occurred may be lost, replaced with data representing the end of the last well-processed transaction.

• If a program was keeping a running total of amounts based on transaction data, the total must have a correct value, reflecting the exact finished transactions, when the recovery is over.

• At the end of the recovery, all programs must resume work as if nothing had happened, except wasted time.

All this is quite difficult to achieve, especially if it has to remain fairly transparent to the screen operators. And if the recovery process must be fast, the software and system operating procedures must be well adapted. The techniques used to achieve recovery are "cold restart" and "warm restart."

5.1.9.1   Cold Restart

A cold restart of a system uses the following procedure:

1. The origin of the system breakdown is analyzed to find the required corrective action: hardware or communication line repair, changes in operational procedures, software modifications, etc.

2. If the disk drives that store the database may have been damaged, they must be tested with disk packs or diskettes that do not contain a backup version of the database; otherwise a backup may be damaged by bad drives.

3. When the drives have proved good, a database backup copy is mounted. The database is restored to the state it was in at the time the backup was made—at the end of the previous day or week, for example.

4. All database updates since the backup copy was made are retrieved from the log or journal file(s) and reprocessed. The "after" images are applied to the updated records or blocks until the last committed transaction chain of each running program has been restored. The unfinished or noncommitted transaction chains are dropped. Better, if "before + transaction image" journaling strategy was used, the "before" images of all the finished transaction chains are applied, in the order in which they were initially performed, and then the corresponding transactions are reprocessed using the FI.

The cold restart procedure obviously applies to severe system breakdowns during which the database files have been damaged so greatly that the following "warm restart" recovery procedure cannot apply. The cold restart procedure takes time—often several hours, and sometimes more than one day. It is very harmful to the organization, which cannot continue processing until it is finished.

5.1.9.2   Warm Restart

When the database files have not been damaged—with the exception perhaps of the last updated block of each file—the following procedure can be used.

1. The DBMS is restarted, but not the application programs.

2. The DBMS undoes all the database updates, applying the "before" images in the reverse order until a "synchronization point" is reached;

at that point, the DBMS originally had all its files in good shape, and, of the transaction chains that were aborted when the breakdown occurred, none had started. (The DBMS makes note of such synchronization points in its log file from time to time, after it has stopped accepting transactions from programs that have just completed a transaction chain. It updates all data files, file headers, and internal tables. Ideally, when the DBMS is at a synchronization point, all programs are in an "end-of-transaction-chain" situation. In fact, the DBMS may decide to create a synchronization point even when some transaction chains are still unfinished. If a breakdown occurs shortly thereafter, it may have to back up to the *previous* synchronization point to find a situation where no active transaction was aborted.)

3. The DBMS applies the "after" images, in their initial order, to all the completed transaction chains that follow the synchronization point; then the application programs are restarted and informed of the exact data situation.

This strategy executes faster than the cold restart because it does not back up as far in the past, but the same data inconsistency problems may occur as above, if the "before + transaction image" strategy was not used.

5.1.10 Data Restructuring Capabilities

The data restructuring operation physically reorganizes the database to recover record space and improve performance. During real-time operation, records are created and deleted randomly; see 5.1.1 for details on disk space management.

Logically consecutive records, such as the lines of a given customer order or the movements of an item in stock, may be stored in noncontiguous records in different blocks. Empty records ("holes") may appear anywhere following inevitable deletions. After a while, the database files become badly disorganized.

Disorganization affects performance in two ways:

• The number of disk accesses required to retrieve logically consecutive records exceeds the number of blocks that would store the records if those were physically consecutive. For example, the 6 lines of an order may be spread over 4 blocks instead of being in the same block; retrieving them would require 4 disk accesses instead of one.

• The total disk space required by a file with many holes exceeds the space required by the nondeleted records. For example, a file contains 22,000 deleted records and 110,000 nondeleted records; it takes as much space as a file of 132,000 records, 20% more than the logical minimum. It may have to extend over 2 disks instead of one, or the lack of disk space may force physical fragmentation of other files.

Restructuring reorganizes a data file, eliminating unused records by grouping at the end of the file, and making logically consecutive records physically consecutive. Some DBMSs perform restructuring using a new file into which nondeleted records are copied in the logical order. Others manage to use the same file plus a work area, thus requiring less total disk space.

Restructuring is often combined with an evolution of the conceptual or physical schemas. The "new" records may allow space for additional fields, for example, or the hashing formula may be changed, or the block size may be modified, etc. Sometimes new access paths, such as secondary indexes, may be implemented.

The restructuring functions described above may be performed by the DBMS alone. However, if a functional interface is available, the restructuring operation may also perform a logical verification of the data to determine whether all existence constraints at field, record, or subdatabase level are respected. This may be quite useful.

To do such a verification + restructuring operation

1. Select ALL the records of a given file (retrieving them without constraints) and put them in a work file.

2. Sort the work file in the logical order of the records. For example, an order line file will be sorted on order-number + item-number.

3. Delete the database file and re-create it in an "empty" state.

4. Perform a batch insertion of all the records of the sorted work file, sending them to the FI for verification. The FI will perform all levels of existence checking, and then send each record to the DBMS for actual database file updating.

The operations described in steps 1 and 2 can be performed in one combined operation if the DBMS is relational.

5.1.11 Security

The issue of security has been discussed in
- subject overview: 1.1.3.5,
- subschemas: 1.3.2.5 and 5.1.4,
- encryption: 3.2.1,
- dynamic password: 3.2.2.

The important role played by the DBA is described in 5.1.12.

Security is relatively easy to achieve in personal computer applications. A good locked door to protect access to the microcomputer, encrypted data files, passwords, a well-protected telecommunication access if the micro can be dialed through a modem, and a well-hidden data dictionary will generally suffice.

Security becomes a problem when the computer is large, runs for many simultaneous users (some of whom are programmers), and can be accessed via telephone lines. The problem of security must then be addressed *globally*; every access protection must be considered:

- Physical access to the computer room.

- Remote access through telephone lines and dedicated lines:
Transmitted data must be encrypted.
Access passwords.
Program code protection in addition to data files protection.

- Knowledge of staff responsibilities. (Who is the DBA? Who works in the computer room? Who programmed this application?)

- Data file encryption.

- Protection of the data dictionary. If the list of available information cannot be found, it is more difficult to steal it or alter it.

- Monitoring program and data file access. Which user number accessed what program or data? When did he access it, and through which terminal?

- Limiting access volumes. A given terminal or program must not be permitted to access more than X records per run or per day. This restriction can be imposed using a functional interface.

- Testing the quality of the protection from time to time by deliberately trying to break it, to verify its quality and determine how well security precautions are enforced.

• Changing passwords and other security precautions from time to time.

• Making program *source* codes accessible only in small modules, so that it is difficult to obtain the entire listing of a program, and so that no programmer has a complete picture of an important program.

• Protecting the program *object* code against memory dumps and code translation by inserting useless code, and dynamically changing instruction addresses and contents at execution time.

• Protecting functional interfaces carefully, because they are the last guards encountered before the databases are reached.

Security value must be substantially greater than protection cost.

5.1.12 Database Administration

5.1.12.1 Job Description
The database administrator (DBA) performs the following tasks:

• He maintains the data dictionary and associated cross-references to programs and users, as specified in MSD.

• He executes daily verifications of the integrity, consistency, and timeliness of the database, using the procedures described in 5.1.12.3.

• He controls access permissions:

• statically, by using subschemas that allow a given user or program to access only some subdatabases, files, or fields;
• dynamically, by allowing only specific access types to specific users: read, modify, insert (append), delete;
• by allocating passwords (static or dynamic) to each user.

The DBA also monitors the access history, when one is available: who accessed what, when, with what volume.

• He gives advice to users and system analysts using his functional knowledge of the database. A modern computer database often comprises thousands of distinct fields. Knowing what information is available, where it originates in the organization, where it is used, and what programs process it is often very useful. Many people access the computer, but each person knows only a small part of the data. Organizers, if there are any in the organization, know the information flow in general terms but not in detail. Therefore it is the DBA's function to know the information flow, data files, and fields. Of course the DBA cannot be a specialist in the various applications—accounting, invoicing, production scheduling, etc. But he can know which department or user creates what field or file information, who uses that information, and when.

The DBA will use that knowledge to help a project leader or analyst find out the consequences of a technical decision. He will help a user query a part of the database he is not familiar with. He will predict the consequences of delayed program execution.

The DBA must keep abreast with this functional knowledge of the database; he must spend a little time every day communicating with users to learn the history of the data he manages.

The DBA is the custodian of the information warehouse—he is responsible for what is in the database and its quality. And he can help DP professionals and users find the information they need.

5.1.12.2   DBA Personal Profile

• The DBA must perform mostly routine tasks; therefore he must have an *administrative* profile.

• He should have a moderate education level, with minimal data processing training.

• He must be interested in accuracy of details to be able to sustain the accuracy of database information. This quality is similar to the quality of an accounting clerk, who will not tolerate an account to be wrong by a single penny, and will work to find out why it is wrong and how it can be corrected.

• The DBA must have a good ability to communicate, in order to help users and participate in MSD functional specification teams. He must be interested in other people's problems in order to maintain his knowledge of the information.

• His level in the hierarchy must not be too high. A high-ranking executive may frighten lower-level employees enough to hinder the necessary communication. In addition, a high-ranking DBA might be more tempted to use the power he has through his knowledge of the information system.

5.1.12.3 Installing the DBA

Ideally the DBA will participate, acting as project secretary, in the development of each new application from its start. He will then report to the project leader during development of the functional specification. He will learn to understand the data, start building the dictionary, and collect and verify the test data.

Later, when the application development cycle is finished and the operational life of the database begins, the DBA will get involved again. He will start maintaining the dictionary, assigning passwords, and verifying the quality of the data. This verification is a daily routine task including such actions as these:

· Verifying transaction counts: If 1234 invoices were printed today, 1234 accounting movements must have been posted to the customer accounting file; no transaction was duplicated, lost, or rejected.

· Verifying transaction totals: If 1234 invoices totaled $345,678, the corresponding accounting debit movements must total $345,678.

· Verifying timeliness information: 17 database update jobs were supposed to be run today, in a certain order. He must

· check that all were run, which proves that the update data were available,

· check that they were run in the correct order, using the time-of-day information in the job execution log and the time-and-date-of-last-update information in the database file headers.

· Verifying DBMS error reports: What problems were reported?

· Verifying functional interface error reports: Which transactions were functionally rejected? What corrective action is required?

All of these tasks—dictionary maintenance, access permission management, database queries, data quality verifications—are performed using *predefined procedures*. The process of creating, testing, and documenting these procedures and then training the DBA to follow them is the *DBA installation procedure*.

5.1.12.4 Administration Effort, Budget, and Reporting

Database administration takes time. A DBA cannot perform all those tasks correctly if the data volume is too big. As a first approximation, a DBA can manage a database of about 1000 fields in 8 hours daily. If the database size is greater, several DBAs are required. If the database size is smaller, a part-time DBA will suffice.

The administration budget issue must be discussed with a number of considerations in mind:

• Database administration is like insurance; without it, the quality of data degrades quickly, and good security cannot be achieved.

• The knowledge and usage assistance supplied by the DBA will save a lot of other people's time and make better information available throughout the organization.

• When several DBAs are required due to the number of fields, they will specialize by application area or by organization component:

• Specializing in specific application areas, one DBA will manage administrative information (accounting, sales, payroll), another will manage production scheduling and control, etc.

• Specializing in the information of a component of the organization, one DBA will represent the Aerospace Component Division, another the Services Industry Division, another the Mechanical Parts Group, etc.

Ideally the DBA should report to a fairly neutral component of the organization, one that will not be accused of using the DBA more to its own profit than to the general profit of the organization.

He may report to the DP department if that department has a good service reputation and is not suspected of some form of information tyranny. Or he may report to the Management Information Systems Department, or another functional department such as Human Resources.

If he represents the information of a specific component of the organization, he will of course report to that organization.

5.1.13 Application Portability

Database applications are generally more integrated, more important, bigger, and used by more people than applications that use ordinary files. Their development and daily use require bigger budgets. Therefore they have to be planned to last longer than other applications. In the ever-changing world of DP, this implies *portability*, a quality that lets you run a given application in a different environment with no (or very minor) changes to software or data.

It is not reasonable to hope that a database and all its associated application software can be run in an environment that differs significantly from its original environment. If the DBMS, the operating system, the data communications monitor, or the hardware are changed, it is almost certain that the applications will no longer run.

The conversion effort may be insurmountable because of the volume of work, but also because of the integrated nature of the database. Since the database is seen by many terminal users who access it daily, an environment change may have to be invisible to users and performed for all users at the same time—over one weekend, for example.

In practice, this constraint is so severe that 95% of large systems that start out with a given DBMS + operating system + datacomm monitor combination will keep it forever; portability is considered impossible. Commercially, the organizations that run such a system have to keep purchasing the hardware, system software, and perhaps DBMS from the same suppliers without any real negotiating power. Lack of competition may mean higher prices and lower service levels.

Portability can be achieved when the following conditions are met:

• The operating system will not change. This is why hardware manufacturers keep releasing old patched and repatched operating systems on new improved hardware; they want to protect their customers' existing software. This is why portable operating systems such as UNIX, MS-DOS, and CP/M have been and will continue to be so successful.

• The DBMS will not change. This is one reason why such systems as ORACLE, which runs on IBM PCs, minicomputers, and mainframes, are so successful.

• The application program languages will not change. Portability may exist in *core image* form, and the programs need not be recompiled or even relinked. Or it may exist in *object* form, and the programs will need to be relinked. Or it may exist in *source* form, and both recompiling and relinking will be required. Language portability is one of the reasons why "C" and MICROSOFT GW-BASIC are so widely used by software developers.

In practice, to ensure maximum portability, a program should use only the standard, universal features of a given language, and not all the manufacturer-specific additions that are so tempting. And the most unportable statements—the disk/DBMS input-output and keyboard/ screen management statements—should be restricted to a few specialized, easy-to-change modules.

One of the big advantages of the functional interface technique is that it provides DBMS independence; the application programs do not see the actual DBMS. They communicate with a standard, relational, multilevel, functionally intelligent DBMS, which is the FI. When the DBMS must be replaced with a new DBMS, the user's application programs are not affected. The FI must be changed; its lowest level, the DBMS interface, must be reprogrammed, but this is far less expensive than modifying the applications. Good portability is achieved using the FI.

Some DBMSs, such as CINCOM's TOTAL, provide excellent portability across different operating system + hardware combinations: this is one reason for their success.

The CODASYL network DBMS family, which includes IDMS, IDS II, DMS 1100 (UNIVAC), DMS II (BURROUGHS), and others, claims excellent portability among different members of the family. While this is reasonably true at the DBMS language level (DDL and DML), it is less true at the physical data level and quite false at the data query capability and programming utilities levels.

5.1.14 Data Query

In many instances, the user needs to retrieve information, display it on a screen, print it, or write it to a file *without programming*

• because the time and cost to write a program are not justified or
• because the user cannot program.

By definition, selecting without programming is called *querying*.
    DBMSs offer two basic ways to describe a question:

1. using a *nonprocedural language*, such as

• *SQL* (also called Sequel, or Structured Query Language, and used by IBM's SQL/DS and DB/2 DBMSs, by ORACLE, and others),
• *QUEL* (a Query Language, used by INGRES);

2. using a "fill-in-the-form" approach, such as

- *QBE* (Query By Example, of IBM),
- *QBF* (Query By Forms, of INGRES).

Example

SQL (nonprocedural)	Result	
SELECT WORKDEPT, COUNT(EMPNO)	WORKDEPT	COUNT
FROM TEMPL	FIN	27
GROUP BY WORKDEPT	MFG	1860
ORDER BY WORKDEPT	SAL	239

This question retrieves the attribute WORKDEPT in the TEMPL relation, looking at every tuple of the relation. It groups the tuples by WORKDEPT and counts the number of different EMPNO attributes in each group. It then displays the WORKDEPT and count for each group, ordering the groups by WORKDEPT, in ascending order. This simple question accesses a single relation, without selection criteria.

For more information on the SQL relational language, see 5.1.5.1.

Example

QUEL (nonprocedural): What floor does Malcolm work on?

RETRIEVE (EMP.NAME, DEPT.FLOOR)
WHERE EMP.DNAME = DEPT.DNAME AND EMP.NAME = "MALCOLM"

Result:

name	floor
Malcolm	6

Note that in QUEL, the name of the relation is followed by "." and then by the name of the attribute, whereas in SQL it can be specified in the FROM statement. In this example, the search constraint is EMP. NAME = "MALCOLM," and the search performs a JOIN operation automatically between the EMP and DEPT relations; matching tuples must have DNAME in common.

Example

dBASE II (nonprocedural for query): display the last name and hire date for all employees hired after August 1, 1978, and count them.

USE EMPL
DISPLAY ALL LASTNAME, HIREDATE FOR HIREDATE >
780801
COUNT FOR HIREDATE > 780801

Example

QBE (nonprocedural "fill-in-the-form"): find the women in the finance
department who earn more than $20,000

TEMPL	LASTNAME	WORKDEPT	SEX	SALARY
	P.	P. FIN	P. F	>20000

The system displays a form containing the attributes of the table of
employees TEMPL. The user types "P." for print (=output) to indicate the attributes he wants printed for each selected tuple. He types
the comparison criteria of the constraints using the value (FIN for
finance and F for women) or the value preceded by the comparison
operator (>20000).

A query system also lets the user describe the format of the output.
The output may be directed to the screen or a printer, and the user may
either let the DBMS decide the formatting, or "paint" it himself, describing such things as

page layout:

- header lines,
- page counter,
- regular "output tuple" lines,
- column or line totals,
- page footer,
- number of lines per page,
- data level breaks that occur when the value of an attribute that is part
of the sort key of the output changes (for example, suppose a sales
statistic is sorted by customer and by item and encompasses all the
invoice lines of a given item—each time an item code changes, the total
sales for that item to that customer are printed; each time the customer
changes, the total sales to that customer are printed, followed by two
blank lines),

column layout: each column can be described, with the name of the field displayed, the column title, the display format, etc.,

field attributes: colors, bold print, underline, reverse video, blinking.

Modern query systems such as Knowledgeman (IBM PC) and TIS/MANTIS (IBM 43xx) also integrate query output and graphic display capabilities or interfaces to word processing and spreadsheets. The data retrieved by a query can be moved to the word processing or spreadsheet environment automatically, to be displayed in bar chart or other graphic formats without having to be reentered.

The most powerful query environments associate a mainframe database and a microcomputer. The mainframe downloads into the micro the data resulting from the query typed by the micro user at the keyboard. The micro user can then process the downloaded data locally, using a relational DBMS and a graphics package, for example, and combine the data with text. When the user need data, the micro query system brings them from the mainframe, leaving the communications transparent to the user, except for a little delay. After the user has finished working, he can send back data to the mainframe to update the big database or to send messages to other users. Examples of such mainframe + micro DBMSs are

· CULLINET's GOLDENGATE on IBM mainframe + PC,
· CINCOM's TIS on the same hardware,
· INFORMATION BUILDERS' FOCUS + PC/FOCUS, also on the same hardware,
· DUN & BRADSTREET's NOMAD2, again on the same hardware.

5.1.15 Evolution Capabilities

This issue has been defined and discussed in 1.3.4.2, 5.1.6, and 5.1.7. Ease of evolution is one of the benefits that make a big difference between using and not using a DBMS and between a high-quality DBMS featuring dynamic dictionary management and a DBMS that offers only static dictionary capabilities. In applications such as research, where the contents and usage scenario of a database cannot be well defined in advance and change often, ease of evolution is the first criterion used to select a DBMS.

In one instance ease of evolution is achieved *without a DBMS*: the PICK operating system has a built-in dynamic data dictionary.

5.2 File Structures

This section describes classical file management techniques used to solve storage, accessing, and linking problems. These issues have been introduced in sections 5.1.1–5.1.4. With the exception of bit indexing, which is not widely known, the readers familiar with such techniques as indexing, hashing, and lists can skip this section.

5.2.1 Files, Records, and Fields

The operating system manages physical files. Disk file space can be allocated as one contiguous area (figure 5.4) or several *pages* (figure 5.5). Space allocation can be *static*, so that files have a fixed size defined when they are originally created, or *dynamic*, so that file pages are allocated as required; the successive pages then occupy noncontiguous disk areas: the last byte of page N is not physically followed, on the disk, by the first byte of page N + 1; however, the operating system makes the paging transparent to the application programs, making those two bytes appear consecutive. The disk contents are described in a disk directory (figure 5.6), managed by the operating system, which lists all the file pages available and their physical location. As far as the programs are concerned—and the DBMS is a program—each file behaves like a contiguous set of *records*.

(One exception to this situation is the UNIX operating system, which basically does not know the notion of records—only some recent versions of UNIX do. File accessing, to read or write, begins at a certain *byte or word* address, and ends after a certain number of contiguous bytes have been transferred. For example, an application program can read bytes 42,586–46,314 with one input operation. Business data processing in a UNIX environment almost always demands a DBMS, because the intrinsic operating system file management functions are not sufficient.)

A file contains an integer number of records. Each record occupies a number of consecutive bytes or words. The operating system transfers to and from the program one record at a time, because the record is the logical group of data described in the program code. The record can have a *fixed* length, so that it is impossible for two different records of the file to have different lengths. Alternatively it can have a *variable* length, so that different records can have different lengths. This is

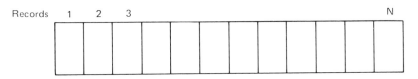

Figure 5.4
File in one contiguous area.

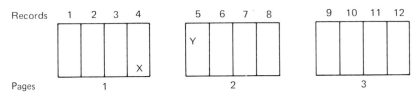

Figure 5.5
File in three pages. The last byte (X) of record 4 is followed by the first byte (Y) of record 5.

Figure 5.6
Page directory structure for one file.

particularly useful for files with large text fields, such as are produced by word processing applications: when texts have different lengths, each one can occupy a record space exactly as large as it needs, without wasted space (figure 5.7). If variable record lengths did not exist, the (fixed) record size would have to be quite large, to accommodate the largest conceivable occurrence of field data, thus wasting space for all other occurrences. Alternatively one logical record would have to be written over several consecutive smaller fixed-length records, thus placing a software complexity burden on the application programmer (figure 5.8), while still wasting space.

Field sizes can also be *fixed* (the same field has the same length in all records) or *variable*. Fixed-length records sometimes carry variable-length fields, but the most flexible structure features variable-length fields in variable-length records.

Variable field length is sometimes implemented with a "blank sup-

| B & W | 32 E 12th. New York NY 10010 |
| Jon Williams | 2530 South George Washington Ave Los Angeles CA 90055 |

Figure 5.7
Storage in two variable-length records.

1   B & W   32 E 12th. New York NY 10010
2   Jon Williams   2530 South George Washington Ave Los
0   Angeles CA 90055

Figure 5.8
Storage in three fixed-length records. Note the first field, which indicates the number of physical records used to store one logical record.

press" capability: when a text field reaches the operating system, with the actual contents left justified, there may be a number of blanks (space characters) that terminate the field on the right-hand side; the system then stores only the leftmost part of the field, suppressing the trailing blanks. Sometimes, when the operating system does not have that capability, it is implemented through the DBMS.

5.2.2   Segments, Blocks, Buffers, and Areas

In general, the minimum quantity of data that is written to the disk or read from the disk is not one record: it is one *segment*. The segment comprises a small number of adjacent disk bytes—128 or 512, for example. It is the manipulation unit of the disk hardware; the disk surface comprises an integer number of segments, and the disk controller transfers an integer number of consecutive segments during each access.

Records are usually grouped in *blocks*: one block often comprises several records. For example, a 4096 byte block comprises 64 records of 64 bytes each; the *blocking factor* is said to be 64. When the disk is accessed, 64 records are transferred each time. If the segment size is 512, one block extends over 8 segments. Grouping records in blocks decreases the number of disk accesses; this is important in sequential processing and also in random processing. In the example, reading a file of 6400 records, accessed sequentially from the first record to the last record, would require 6400 disk accesses if each access could only bring in 1 record; it requires only 100 disk accesses when each block contains 64 records.

Assume now that the file contains order lines, that an order comprises an average of 5 lines, and that we access the file randomly at the address of its first line and want to read all the lines of the order. Then a blocking factor of 64 will in general let us read the entire order in 1 disk access, or 2 in the worst case.

Depending on the operating system, a block may occupy an integer or noninteger number of segments. But since the hardware transfers an integer number of segments each time, the length of the area of memory that communicates with the disk generally has to be a multiple of the segment size. This area of memory is called a *file buffer*.

So, when an application program asks the operating system to read (randomly) record number 2751 of file A, this is what happens:

1. The operating system calculates the number of the block that contains record 2751. If the blocking factor is 64, it finds that the record is in the 43rd block.

2. The operating system asks itself if the 43rd block is not already in memory, in the buffer assigned to file A.

2.1. If it is, it extracts record 2751 from that block (the record is the 63rd record of the block) and passes it to the program.

2.2. If it is not, it fetches it from the disk, placing it in the buffer, and then extracts the 63rd record and passes it to the application program.

All this requires processor time. For example, on an IBM mainframe working under DOS/VSE, accessing a random record using the VSAM file manager requires the processing of about 2500 assembly language instructions, 2.5 milliseconds (msec) on a 1 million instructions per second (1 MIPS) machine. In fact the response time may be much longer, because it also comprises the physical disk access time (about 30 msec), the disk channel transfer time (about 2 msec), and some of the time spent by the processor working for other programs when ours loses its turn due to its request for I/O.

The concept of area was discussed in 1.2.6.3, 1.3.2.4, and 1.3.5.2. Physically the area is transferred as 1 block, in one I/O operation.

5.2.3 DBMS-to-Operating System File Interface

The discussion above described how the operating system works. But a DBMS does not use the file management capabilities like an ordinary program. It may, for example, bypass the operating system completely to perform physical I/O: this is quite dangerous, nonportable, and reserved to hardware manufacturers who sell their own DBMSs.

Example 1

The DEC CODASYL DBMS (called "DBMS") and relational DBMS (called "RDB") bypass the VMS operating system to achieve performance.

Example 2

IBM's SQL/DS file storage uses a *modified* VSAM ESDS technique, which makes it incompatible with other programs, and requires conversion utilities to import data from other VSAM or DL/1 files.

Alternatively, the DBMS may use only the block management facilities of the operating system and do its own record and area processing. This is often the case, in particular to provide such facilities as variable record size, hashing, area management, and record locking/unlocking. Large multitasking DBMSs also use their own buffer management strategies; the file buffers are part of a general *buffer-pool* area, managed as a virtual memory to optimize memory requirements and I/O.

The data written to a file can be written in *readable* or *binary* form. In readable form, they use an alphabet such as ASCII or EBCDIC, where each character or sign is represented by one 8 bit byte. In binary form, the memory words of each field or record are written to the disk as they are, without any special formatting. Thus the number 1234 is written as

· 31 32 33 34 (4 bytes in hexadecimal form) in ASCII,

· 0000010011010010 (the 16 bits of 2 bytes) in binary form.

The use of a binary representation for numbers generally requires less space and less processor time to convert to or from a computer-usable form than a readable representation. Good DBMSs use only binary representation for numbers, dates, and other nonalphabetic fields, and convert this representation to a format suitable to each supported programming language.

5.2.4 Sequential File

A sequential file is a file that can be accessed only beginning with its first record, proceeding with its second record, and so on. It behaves like a magnetic tape. When it resides on a disk, which is a direct ("random") access device, the operating system performs a direct access to each record in turn.

The disadvantage of a sequential file is that the Nth record can be accessed only after the $N-1$ previous records have been. This may slow down performance when the file has many records and when only a few of the records need to be accessed during a program run. This performance degradation is the case with all *master* files (see 1.3.4.7). It is not always the case with *event* (or history) files, especially when they are processed to obtain statistics.

Quasi-sequential processing can be defined as processing that requires access to the vast majority of the file's blocks. For example, when a bank processes the daily batch of check movements, there is a high probability that every block of the customer file will be accessed, if the blocking factor is 5 customer records per block or more. The best application design approach is then to sort the movements by customer and process them sequentially.

Sequential accessing generally requires less processor time per accessed record than random accessing (see section 5.2.5). It generally implies that records can be of variable length, and that a file can be open for reading or writing but not both (updating).

When a file is open for writing, the system places an *end-of-file mark* at the end of the last written record when it closes the file. This mark prevents subsequent reading from addresses beyond it. A file open for writing will contain, after it is closed, only the N records written in sequence during this run: any record stored during a previous run before or after the new end-of-file mark is lost.

Sequential files are not used for permanent data storage by a DBMS, because they cannot be updated and do not provide direct (random) access. However, modern database architectures do use them in combination with large memory. A small sequential file, less than 100K bytes long, for example, can be loaded from the disk in one (big!) sequential read, similar to the loading of a program, and then kept in memory, where it can even be updated. When the file is closed, the system writes it back to the disk (only if it has been updated) in one access.

Reading or writing 100K bytes on a 16 bit microcomputer with a 10MB hard disk takes only about 2 seconds. Updating it in memory, when it requires "pushing" 50K bytes to make room for a larger record, takes about the same time. The file is then kept sorted in memory to accelerate searching with *dichotomy* (also called *binary search*). It does not require indexing for quick data retrieval; retrieving a 100 byte record in a 1000 record file requires only 12 field comparisons and less than 1 msec. This approach is quite viable for master files, which undergo but few record insertions or deletions, because record retrieval in memory can be 100 to 1000 times faster than on disk or diskette, and processing a sorted file with dichotomy is much easier to program than indexed or hashed access.

5.2.5   Direct (Random) Access File

Direct (also called "random") accessing is a file access method that addresses a record defined by its number (or "rank") directly, without accessing other records.

Example
A small bank has a maximum of 80,000 customers. Each customer is given a 5-digit account number, between 00001 and 99999. (Numbers cannot be limited to 80,000 because when an account is closed, it cannot be assigned to a new customer before the following year.) The file structure used to store the customer records is a random file with 99999 records, where the record of customer number N is the Nth record of the file.

In general, operating systems limit random access files to fixed-size records, a disadvantage with respect to sequential file access. However, random files can always be open for reading, writing, or both. The possibility of updating is a big advantage over sequential file access.

Random files are used by all DBMSs for data storage. Often the DBMS uses a blocking factor of 1, and manages the records within each block to obtain variable record size regardless of the operating system's capabilities. Some DBMSs give direct access by record number to the application programs: dBASE II and III do that, and so do the CODASYL DBMSs using a record rank called the Database-Key (DB-KEY).

5.2.6 Index Structures

The first principle of quick record retrieval is to minimize the number of disk accesses. With that in mind, this section describes a quick retrieval method for records with a key field. The problem to be solved is: C being a constant (numeric, string, date, logical, . . .), find the records (if any) that have the value contained in their field K equal to C. K must of course belong to the same existence domain as C: if C is a date, K must be a date; if C is the name of a customer, K must be a customer name, etc. K is known as a *search key* field.

If the data file D is large and no special search-accelerating structure is used, the solution of the problem implies scanning the file sequentially, reading all of its N blocks. If N is large, this may be unacceptably slow. Accordingly the first idea behind indexing is to make N small. To achieve that, a second file, I, is built, with one record of D yielding one record of I using a projection: all the fields of D are dropped except the search key field, K (figure 5.9). Each record of I contains also a second field, besides K: the rank of the record of D that contains K. So each record of I is a couple (K, P), where the rank P is called *a pointer*, indicating the number of the data record of D that holds K.

Example

	Data file D	Index file I
Record size (bytes)	480 (Data)	10 (K + P)
Key field K size (bytes)	8	8
Pointer field P size (bytes)	—	2
Block size (segments of 256 bytes)	480	500
Records/block	1	50
Number of records	1000	1000
Number of blocks B	1000	20

To find a record of D where the key field has a given C value, scanning D would require an average of 500 disk accesses. If we first scan I, an average of 10 disk accesses will suffice to find a couple where K = C. Then, we also read the pointer P of the same record, access D directly at record P, and get the data: an average of 11 disk accesses are needed instead of 500. The economy originates in the blocking factor of I,

K	P
BURT	2
CHARLES	6
EARL	5
GARY	4
JOHN	1
MARTIN	7
PETER	3
ROGER	8

Index File

I

Rank	
1	JOHN. . .
2	BURT. . .
3	PETER. . .
4	GARY. . .
5	EARL. . .
6	CHARLES. . .
7	MARTIN. . .
8	ROGER. . .

Data File

D

Figure 5.9
Principle of indexing.

which can obviously be much greater than the blocking factor of D, since the couple (K, P) stored in each record of I takes much less space than one record of D.

The approach described can be considerably improved if we use the second principle of quick record retrieval, which applies to index files: A sorted file can be searched faster than an unsorted file.

In the previous example, our index file I is small: 1000 records of 10 bytes each. It is easy to read it into memory, sort it (that takes only a fraction of a second), and write it back to the disk in sorted form. We can now search through it using dichotomy (explained in 5.2.10). The number of disk (block) accesses to the index file I will be $x + 2$, where x is such that $2^x \geq B - 1$, B being the number of blocks. In the previous example, $B = 20$, so $x = 5$ ($2^5 = 32$ is the smallest power of 2 that is greater than or equal to 19). Since $x + 2 = 7$, we can find the index block that stores a given value C of the key K in a maximum of 7 disk accesses. In that block we will find the appropriate (K, P) couple, and one more disk access will take us to the actual data record in D.

Conclusions

1. So far, we have seen that a sorted index file can be used to accelerate the retrieval of a record for which a key value is given.

2. This technique works only when we have been able to plan for it, and build a sorted index based on the values of a key field. Retrieving a record with a field value for which there is no index will still require scanning the entire file.

3. This technique can also retrieve records based on the conditions K $\geq$ C or K $\leq$ C. One interesting case of K $\geq$ C is *partial key search*, where C is composed of the first few characters of K. For example, find customers whose names begin with "MA."

5.2.6.1   Primary and Secondary Indexes

The notions of key and uniqueness were discussed in 1.3.3 and 1.3.3.3. We simply need to repeat here the definitions:

• The primary index of a file is the index built on its uniqueness key field (a field that has different values in all records).

• A secondary index of a file is an index built on a field other than the primary key field.

A secondary index may have several records that contain the same key value K; however, all such records must contain different pointer values P; otherwise the index I will contain duplicate records. It will be redundant, which is contrary to the definition of a database (section 1.1.2). For example, an index by customer name on the Customer file is evidently a secondary index.

Obviously, a file may have several secondary indexes, but in general it has only one primary index, used to check nonredundancy when a new record is inserted. It may, of course, have no index at all or be an event file where redundancy is possible when two different events yield the same record contents.

Most DBMSs can maintain primary and secondary indexes on each file. This maintenance can be *automatic*, which implies that the index is updated by the DBMS each time keys are added, deleted, or altered. Alternatively, it can be *manual*, which implies that the index is updated when the application program requests it.

From a semantic standpoint, automatic index maintenance is not always possible. For example, two master files, called "autos" and "accessories," are linked by an N-to-P relationship: "auto *HAS* accessories" and "accessory *CAN BE MOUNTED ON* auto." This relationship is implemented using an auto-accessories relation (*auto#, accessory#,* quantity-of-accessories-mounted-on-auto). Two second-ary indexes point to this relation: an index I_1 by auto#, to retrieve all accessories that can be mounted on a given "auto," and an index I_2 by accessory#, to retrieve all "autos" that can receive a given accessory. These two indexes are updated automatically. A special index I_3 also points to the auto-accessories relation, indicating for each given "auto" the accessories *that are extra-cost options.* I_3 must be updated manually because the DBMS cannot automatically determine the com-mercial policy describing bundled and extra-cost accessories.

In fact what must be managed manually is not the index; it is the relationship implemented using the index. Manual management is re-quired each time there is no field value that can be used as a linking criterion.

5.2.6.2 Sequential Index: Implementation Issues
When an index is maintained in ascending order of its key, the data file it points to can have its own records in random order; that will not affect the speed of retrieval. However, a sorted index has another advantage: it can be used to scan the file in key sequence. Following the order of the index couples, the data file appears sorted in the same order, and the successor and predecessor of each record can be easily found. A file that has such a sorted index is called an *Index Sequential File.* Many structures can be used to implement an index sequential capability depending on the following parameters:

• An index may be *single-key* or *multikey.* A single-key index is what we have just discussed. A multikey index is a group of several indexes based on different keys but pointing to the same data file.

• The key field on which the index may be built is based on one actual field, a group of adjacent fields making up a global key, or a group of nonadjacent fields.

• The index file may be in the same physical file as the data file or in a separate file. The separate file approach has a drawback, especially if each file index is stored in a separate physical file: the DBMS may have to open so many files at the same time that it cannot be used correctly under the given operating system. For example, MS-DOS opens a maximum of 20 files at the same time, some of which cannot be disk files. A restriction that no more than 16 files can be open at the same time, counting both data files and index files, may severely limit many applications. This was the case for dBASE II.

5.2.6.3   Hierarchical Index: Optimizing Index Block Size

We can go one step further in our effort to minimize the number of disk accesses required to retrieve a couple (K, P) in an index. So far, we have

• packed many couple records into one index block,

• sorted the index file, I_1, by key value to be able to use dichotomy.

We shall now build an *index of the index blocks*, I_2 (figure 5.10). Each record of I_2 will contain only one field, K_2, which stores the value of the *last* key of a block of I_1:

• The first record of I_2 contains the last key of the first block of I_1.

• The second record of I_2 contains the last key of the second block of I_1, and so on.

This association "first to first," "second to second," and so on is such that no pointer is required in I_2; the number of the block of I_1 where a candidate key value C can be located is the number of the first record of I_2 that contains a value greater than or equal to C. This is very simple, and even more keys can be packed into a block of I_2 than into a block of I_1.

To find a record with a key value of C (or beginning with C, or $\geq$ C),

1. Search through I_2, using dichotomy, until you find the minimum value C_m such that $C_m \geq C$, in record number N.

2. Access block number N of I_1 directly.

3. Search through this block using dichotomy until you find the couple (K, P) such that K = C.

4. Access the data file D at record number P.

In the previous example, we had 20 blocks in I_1. I_2 therefore contains 20 records of 8 bytes each: I_2 is so small that it can easily reside in a memory table, and in one disk block. We will load it from disk when D is opened, and keep it in memory as long as we use D. So, if we do not count that initial I_2 disk access, performed when opening the file, we can now find any key of I_1 in 1 disk access (after finding its block

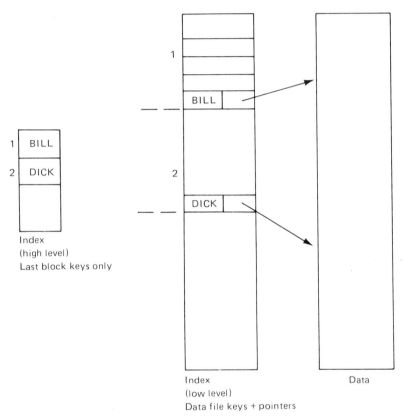

Figure 5.10
Index hierarchy.

number in I_2) and the associated D record in a second disk access; we have made big progress.

We can now consider building an index of the I_2 blocks, I_3; then an index of the I_3 blocks, I_4; etc. If we do that, I_3, I_4, etc. will have the same record structure as I_2: a key (the last one in a block) and no pointer. I_1, I_2, I_3, . . . make up a *hierarchy*.

But an obvious question is, How many levels of indexing do we need? The answer is provided by the third principle of quick searching, applied to hierarchical indexing: the last level of indexes must be smaller than one block so that it may be kept in memory.

In calculating the optimal index block size, assuming that the size, B, of an index block can be arbitrary, what is the optimal size? The answer depends on the number of levels of the index hierarchy, and on the amount of memory space we can allocate to B. Let

- K be the length of the key (in bytes, for example),
- P be the length of the pointer of I_1,
- M be the maximum number of keys (and records) in the data file.

A block of I_1 contains $B/(K+P)$ couples (actually the integer value of that expression). The number of blocks of I_1 must therefore be

$N_1 = M/(B/(K+P))$.

A block of I_2 contains B/K keys. The number of blocks required to store the last keys of N_1 blocks of I_1 is

$N_2 = N_1/(B/K) = MK(K+P)/(B^2)$.

Each time we change level, the number of blocks N_{n+1} will be derived from N_n by dividing by B/K:

$N_{n+1} = N_n/(B/K)$.

The process must stop when $N_x \leq 1$. For $x = 2$ we find $MK(K+P)/B^2 \leq 1$, so $B \geq (MK(K+P))^{1/2}$ (the square root of $MK(K+P)$), and for $x = 3$, $MK^2(K+P)/B^3 \leq 1$, so $B \geq (MK^2(K+P))^{1/3}$ (the cubic root of $MK^2(K+P)$).

Example 1
A customer file has $M = 12,000$ customer records. Therefore $P = 2$ (it takes a 2 byte binary integer to store a number as large as 12,000). The key is 4 bytes long: $K = 4$. A 2-level index requires a block size of at least $B = (MK(K+P))^{1/2}$, $B = (12,000 \times 4 (4 + 2))^{1/2} = 537$ bytes.

Example 2
An invoice line history file has $M = 800,000$ line records. Therefore $P = 4$ (it takes a 4 byte binary integer to store a number as large as 800,000). The key (invoice# + item#) is 6 bytes long: $K = 6$. A 2-level index requires a minimum block size of 6928 bytes. A 3-level index requires a minimum block size of 660 bytes.

Note 1

In fact the B formulas are not absolutely accurate because we have dropped the integer round-offs, and because B should be a multiple of both K and K + P. They should be used as an approximation, with which the various number-of-blocks calculations should be verified. In the first example, we could do this:

1. Take B = 540, which is a multiple of K = 4 and K + P = 6.
2. A block of I_1 contains 540/6 = 90 couples (exactly).
3. The number of blocks of I_1 is 12,000/90 = 133.3 rounded to 134.
4. A block of I_2 contains 540/4 = 135 keys (exactly).
5. The number of blocks required to store 134 keys is 1: the solution is acceptable.

Note 2

The B formulas use square, cubic, or fourth roots of an expression; they are *very stable* functions of these expressions. When the variables of a function vary considerably, the value of the function varies little. With a maximum acceptable block size of 3000 bytes, for example, we can build two-level indexes for quite large files, with long keys. M = 50,000, P = 2, K = 12 yields B = 2899 bytes. In almost every situation, a microcomputer indexed file, and in many situations a minicomputer file too, will need only two levels of indexing. In fact, master files are seldom a problem; only event files can become too big for a two-level index, because they may contain many events and because they may need multifield keys. Large event files are often history files, which do not require keyed access. They are processed sequentially and sorted whenever possible. And there are other record retrieval techniques: hashing and bit indexing.

5.2.6.4 Structure Consequences of Index Updating

So far, indexing has been discussed only as an aid to quick retrieval, but indexes also have to be updated.

Updating an index is necessary each time one of the following operations is performed on the associated data file:

• A new record has been inserted, and the index update is "automatic."
• A record has been deleted, and the index update is "automatic."
• The value of a field on which an index is built has changed in a record, and the index update is "automatic."

• An index is "manual," and the program wishes to add, delete, or modify a (K, P) couple.

An index update will

• add a couple,
• delete a couple,
• modify the pointer P of a couple (in the rare cases when the index is managed manually, and the program has requested it).

In addition, the various index levels must be updated to reflect a potential change in the value of the last key of a block. The key of a specific couple is never changed; instead, the existing couple is deleted, and a new couple is added. This implementation approach is linked to the fact that the primary key of a specific record is never changed; if necessary, the record will be deleted and re-created, which implies the associated index updates.

The biggest structure problem in the area of index updating is *block overflow*. When couples are added to the low-level index, I_1, of a hierarchy, index blocks will fill up. Since I_1 must remain sorted in order of ascending K value, couples that belong in a given block—because their key values are less than the first key value of the next block—will need more and more space. Unfortunately block lengths are fixed, so when a block overflows, the entire index must be reorganized. This is very time consuming and not acceptable in interactive or real-time environments.

The strategy used to solve the problem comprises the following (figure 5.11):

• *Hollow blocks*: The blocks are designed so that the average block is only X% full. For example, if the customer file in the first example of 5.2.6.3 had to store a maximum of 8000 customer records, the index could be artificially dimensioned to 12000 (50% more, so that the average block of I_1 is only 66% full). The blocks of I_2, I_3, etc. do not need to be hollow if the block overflow technique described below is used. The hollow block technique makes block overflow far less frequent.

• *Block overflow*: When a block A of I_1 is full and one more couple needs to be added, a new (empty) block B is taken at the end of the file or wherever one is available. This new block B becomes an overflow area of A. Half the couples of A are moved to B, so that both A and B

INDEX I₂

rec#	K
1	Adams
2	Dick
3	Kelvin
4	Laren
5	Roger
6	Urban

INDEX I₁

B#	rec#	K	DP	OP
1	1	Aaron	3	
	2	Adams	5	
	3	–	–	0
2	4	Basil	4	
	5	Boris	13	
	6	Brenda	15	11
3	7	Johnson	2	
	8	Kelvin	14	
	9	–	–	0
4	10	Laren	9	
	11	–	–	
	12	–	–	0
5	13	Maestro	16	
	14	Nichols	1	
	15	–	–	12
6	16	Sam	8	
	17	Tom	11	
	18	Urban	10	0
- -	- -	- - - -	- -	- -
11	31	Charles	6	
	32	Dick	7	
	33	–	–	0
12	34	Paul	12	
	35	Roger	17	
	36	–	–	0

DATA FILE

rec#	data
1	Nichols. . .
2	Johnson. . .
3	Aaron. . .
4	Basil. . .
5	Adams. . .
6	Charles. . .
7	Dick. . .
8	Sam. . .
9	Laren. . .
10	Urban. . .
11	Tom. . .
12	Paul. . .
13	Boris. . .
14	Kelvin. . .
15	Brenda. . .
16	Maestro. . .
17	Roger. . .

Figure 5.11
Hierarchical index with hollow blocks and overflows.

are now hollow and allow for new insertions. A pointer in A, called the *overflow pointer*, points to B.

If the last key of A has changed, the change is reflected in the associated record of I₂. If B also overflows, a new block, C, is chained to it and takes half its couples, etc. When massive record deletions cause many couple suppressions in I₁, blocks may become empty and available for future additions.

• *Index (and file) restructuring*: After some time, the number of blocks that overflow and the number of empty blocks in I₁ may reach 20% or so. Performance begins to degrade noticeably. The file and index are then restructured; the file is restructured as described in 5.1.10, and a new index is built, with all its blocks hollow and no overflows. Many DBMSs are also able to restructure an index without restructuring the data file.

Comments on Figure 5.11

1. Naming conventions:

· B# is the block number,
· rec# is the record number,
· K is the key,
· DP is the Data file Pointer,
· OP is the Overflow Pointer, which points to another block B of I_1 where a block A overflows.

2. Assumptions:

· The data file records are stored in the order in which they were created.
· I_1 has 3 records (couples) per block (which is an unusually low value, chosen only because this is an example).
· I_1 was created with blocks 2/3 full.

3. Description of index file I_1:

· Blocks 1, 3, and 4 are not full, and do not overflow.
· Block 2 is full, and overflows into block 11, which is not full and does not further overflow.
· Block 5 *was* full, and overflowed into block 12. But then, the couple in its record 15 was deleted. The system did not bring in a couple from block 12 to fill the gap in record 15, because it attempts to keep I_1 blocks 2/3 full.
· Block 6 is full, but has not yet overflowed.

4. Description of index file I_2: I_2 stores the last key of each block of I_1 in its corresponding record (the record that has the same rank as the block of I_1). Note how overflows are taken into account.

There are many other types of index structures besides the one described above. They will not be described in this book (with one exception) because they do not offer significant differences in terms of performance or file space. Only one other index structure, known as the binary tree (B-tree), will be described in this chapter.

5.2.6.5 Indexing Performance Problems

An indexed file is a high-performance structure for retrieval but not for updating. The technique described above demonstrates how much work is required to update an index. In practice, the poor performance of indexed files can become a serious problem in several circumstances:

• The indexed file has many records, so the index has more than two levels.

• The index key is long—for example, because it comprises several subkey fields, which tends to increase the number of index levels.

• The number of indexes for a given data file increases. Each data file update then requires several index file updates.

• There are many updates because the file is an event file, and thus less stable than a master file.

• The updates are performed in interactive mode while several programs execute concurrently. The index update time slows down all the programs. In addition, the necessary record locking used to prevent access conflicts locks indexes too, increasing the update times. To make things worse, the journaling mechanism used for backup, recovery, and transaction chain restart also has to make note of "before" and "after" images of index blocks.

Example

In 1980, one of my consulting customers had a PDP-11 minicomputer, which was used with only three VDTs and a slow printer, while such machines easily handled six or eight VDTs with acceptable response times. The three terminals were used in an order entry application, but each time an order line was typed (item number, quantity, delivery location code) the response time was 17 seconds! The origin of the poor response time was the inadequate architecture of the order line file. This file was updated by an index-sequential file management utility; no DBMS was involved. No fewer than *six* indexes were pointing to that file:

• the primary index, used to check the uniqueness of each record;

• a second index, based on the number of the shop where the delivery was to be made (but no access based on this index was ever made, so it was useless);

• four indexes were based on various data fields: origin of the order line (who had ordered), order date, inventory account number, and supplier number.

These indexes were used every evening in the program that printed the day's order lines to obtain the listing in a predefined sequence. No other use of these indexes existed or was planned. The developers did not even consider using a sort utility to sort the 3000 daily keyed-in records in the order required for the printouts. Actually it turned out that they did not even know a standard sort utility existed.

When a new order line was added, the number of disk accesses was considerable. In addition, the access conflict protection mechanism performed so many locks and unlocks that three concurrently updating terminals were enough to tie up the minicomputer completely. I removed the five useless indexes, and the response time dropped to about 1 second. The evening printing was preceded by sorts that required less than 1 minute. . . .

In addition to the performance problems due to the very nature of indexes, operations on indexed files sometimes suffer from poor performance due to poor implementation.

Table 5.1 was extracted from the system manual of a large manufacturer of 16 bit minicomputers. It gives the average number of disk accesses required to perform an index-sequential file operation.

This table shows that

• When the number of key fields (indexes) increases, the number of disk accesses required to perform a given operation first decreases, reaching an "optimum" with 3 indexes. This is quite good evidence of poor implementation.

Table 5.1
Average number of disk accesses by operation

Operation	NUMBER OF KEY FIELDS					
	1	2	3	4	5	6
READ BY KEY	8.85	6.55	5.3	5.3	5.3	5.3
READ NEXT	3.0	2.6	2.3	2.3	2.3	2.3
INSERT	17.0	17.5	13.8	42.1	70.6	98.9
REWRITE	3.6	3.4	3.2	3.2	3.2	3.2
DELETE BY KEY	20.25	17.95	14.6	42.9	71.4	99.4

• The number of disk accesses required for a record insertion or deletion when there are 6 indexes is close to 100. This is further evidence of poor implementation. In addition, it shows that updating an indexed file may require as long as 4 seconds when only one program is active, because a 16 bit machine can perform only a maximum of about 25 disk accesses per second. But when several programs run concurrently, it may take much longer.

After tens of thousands of minicomputers had been sold and many users had complained about the performance of the index-sequential file system, quoting the table above, the manufacturer finally decided to respond: the table was removed from the system manual!

Conclusions

• An index-sequential file system provides quick retrieval and slow updating.

• Even without a DBMS, performance can be bad.

• Poor software design has plagued the DP industry because many developers lack the qualifications.

• The use of indexes should be restricted to applications where there are many interactive queries and few updates (interactive or batch). In particular, retrieval with partial keys demands indexes.

• Database architecture cannot be designed independently of the planned usage, in spite of what many people think.

5.2.7   Hash-Coding

Hash-coding was invented to solve the performance problems of indexing. It is intended to decrease the number of disk accesses required to find or update a record.

5.2.7.1   Principle of Hash-Coding

A mathematical transform is used to convert a given key value into the address where the corresponding record should be stored.

Example

Assuming any key can be written using letters only, the transform algorithm replaces the various letters of the key with integer numbers, then adds the numbers to find the address: $A = 1$, $B = 2$, $C = 3$, . . . ,

$Z = 26$. A key such as "COMSAT" is transformed into $3 + 15 + 13 + 19 + 1 + 20 = 71$: the record of "COMSAT" should be at address 71.

In reality, the transform in the example is not a good transform. But it is sufficient to explain the principle of hash-coding and to show its drawbacks.

The principle of hash-coding rests on a key-conversion algorithm that attempts to disperse the addresses as much as possible. Many such algorithms exist, of which a few are discussed here. But there is no universally recognized "best" algorithm, because there are so many types of keys that no unique transform can scatter every type of key correctly. Hash-coding remains the best file access structure in many situations, but it has an intellectual defect: it is based on a pragmatic idea that "works well most of the time, and uses tricks to overcome the small problems that arise sometimes."

5.2.7.2 Synonyms

In the previous example, the record with key "SAMCOT" is also at address 71: this is a *collision*; COMSAT and SAMCOT are called *synonyms*.

Synonym problems happen with all hashing algorithms, in 2%–20% of the keys. For a given key, a good hashing transform minimizes the number of collisions, keeping their incidence to a few percent. In a population of keys, such as customer numbers, what counts is not the overall percentage of collisions; it is a *weighted percentage*, where the influence of each customer number is weighted with the number of times it is accessed. Customers with whom we do a lot of business, whose records are heavily accessed, count more than customers whose records are accessed once a year; the value of a hashing algorithm, measured in terms of number of collisions, is usually difficult to determine.

Let us show that collisions can be avoided at the expense of a lot of wasted space. In the previous example, assuming that the space character is coded 27, that a key has a maximum of 8 characters, and that a key with fewer than 8 characters will be left justified in an 8-character field padded with spaces on the right, the storage space required for a guaranteed absence of collisions would be

$$27^8 = 282,429,536,481 \text{ records!}$$

The transform would use the data representation and packing principle discussed in chapter 3. Our "record" (the key of 8 characters) has 8 "fields" of 1 character each. The base of each field (the cardinal of its set of values) is 27. The address of each record is a number N such that

$$N = L_1 * 27^7 + L_2 * 27^6 + L_3 * 27^5 + L_4 * 27^4$$
$$+ L_5 * 27^3 + L_6 * 27^2 + L_7 * 27 + L_8$$

where L_i is the value (0 to 26) of the ith character of the key.

Assuming that the characters of a key are independent, that each can be chosen arbitrarily, there are 27 choices for each of the first, second, . . . , eighth characters; the total number of choices is 27^8, the same as the number of Ns in the formula above. Other formulas exist that will avoid collisions, but all will require the same space.

This space is obviously unacceptably large: hash-coding transforms will have to entail some collisions and work with acceptable storage spaces.

However, all hashing strategies waste some space—20%–50%, for example. This is the price to pay to be able to reach the desired record with the first disk access for 90% of the accesses. For the remaining 10%, 2, 3, or more accesses will be required, so that, on the average, hashing claims to reach a record in 1.2 disk accesses.

5.2.7.3 Overcoming Collision Problems
There are many techniques used to overcome collision problems, including

1. choosing a better transform, to minimize the number of synonyms,

2. allocating more file space,

3. adding a MODULUS function with a PRIME NUMBER to the transform,

4. eliminating synonym-generating key structures,

5. addressing partially filled (hollow) blocks,

6. allowing for block overflow or using several hashing formulas in succession,

7. accessing a hash-coded index file first, and then the data file.

1. *Choosing a better transform to minimize the number of synonyms* The two previous examples demonstrated that a difference

exists between choosing an algorithm such as $N = L_1 * 27^7 + \cdots$ and an algorithm such as $A = L_1 + L_2 + \cdots$.

Some algorithms are better than others because the result they provide for a given key can be obtained for fewer other keys. Addition, of character values, for example, cannot be a good transform because the result of the addition of a group of letters can easily be obtained with the same letters occupying other positions in the key ("COMSAT" and "SAMCOT"), or with a letter that has a value equal to the sum of two others ($D = A + C$), etc.

Good algorithms use noncommutative operations on operands that are unique by nature. The data protection algorithm of section 3.4 is an example of such an algorithm, and we shall see here some more algorithm design guidelines and actual algorithms.

Some transforms can be excellent for some key structures and bad for others, so a conscientious designer will first test to find how many collisions are generated before accepting an algorithm. If we already have a file with all the key values, we can

• write a program than reads the file and calculates the hashed key values,
• write the keys and values in a second file, which is then sorted,
• read this sorted file with another program, count the synonyms, and produce a third file with the structure (key, number of synonyms),
• sort this ordered file by decreasing number of synonyms, and then print it,
• examine the printout to determine the proportion of collisions and the number of collisions affecting frequently used keys.

The good DBMSs that feature hashed access offer several transforms so that the user may choose.

2. *Allocating more file space*   When a set of R records is stored in a physical file of S>R records and gives X collisions, it is often beneficial to enlarge the physical file to T>S>R records; sometimes this generates Y<X collisions.

The hashing transform is not changed except to target a larger file space. However, this possibility is limited by the amount of file space we are willing to allocate to obtain fewer collisions. The method described below, which uses a MODULUS function and a prime number lends itself well to potential target space enlargements.

3. *Adding a MODULUS function with a PRIME NUMBER to the transform* This is one of the ways of reducing the number of collisions caused by the existence of address values in the target space that are the transforms of several keys in the source space.

• The key is first transformed using an algorithm that produces uniqueness, such as the one described in 5.2.7.2:

$$N = L_1 * 27^7 + \cdots, \text{ etc.}$$

• The resulting N is an address in a (huge) virtual space. It is then divided by a prime number, P, and the remainder R is used as the actual address. P is chosen to be only a little larger than the maximum number of keys that have to be stored in the data file. R lies in the range $0 \le R \le P - 1$. This operation is called "taking the modulus." The FORTRAN expression to calculate R is

$R = \text{MOD}(N, P)$.

Example

A file has a maximum of 800 records. Its key is a 6 character ASCII field. The initial transform is

$$N = C_6 + 256*C_5 + 256^2*C_4 + 256^3*C_3 + 256^4*C_2 + 256^5*C_1,$$

where $C_1, \ldots, C_6$ are the ASCII values of the 6 key characters.

We know that this transform yields no collisions. The modulus transform will assume that 25% extra space will suffice:

$P = 800 * 1.25 = 1000$.

In fact, since we want P to be a prime number, and since the smallest prime number greater than 1000 is 1009, we shall take $P = 1009$. The final address, ranging from 0 to 1008, will be

$R = \text{MOD}(N, 1009)$.

(R is the remainder in the integer division of N by 1009.)

The reason for using a modulus function is that this function maps the virtual space that contains N onto an acceptably small physical space. The reason for dividing by a prime number, P, is that by definition such a number has no divisor, so the number of source Ns that yield a given R value is minimal.

When a certain choice of the parameter P produces too many collisions, it is often sufficient to change it slightly to produce significant improvements. In the example, changing P to 1013 (the next prime number) could suffice. Sometimes, however, a greater change is required, such as enlarging the file by 35% instead of 25%.

Another initial transform formula that is sometimes used, though its results are less satisfactory because its virtual space does not guarantee uniqueness as the previous formula does, is

$$N = C_1 + 3 * C_2 + 5 * C_3 + 7 * C_4 + 11 * C_5, \text{ etc.,}$$

where the successive character values are multiplied by the successive prime numbers before they are added. However, this transform improves when the prime numbers are larger and spaced differently: 307, 409, 601, 863, 1039, 1511, etc.

4. *Eliminating synonym-generating key structures*   The notion of key structure and the technique required to eliminate collisions are shown in the following example.

Example
An item number is an 8 digit integer number, where

· The first two digits represent the item family, which can be only one of 10 values: 00, 10, 13, 14, 25, 38, 39, 40, 50, or 99.

· The next two digits represent the color, which can be any integer in the range 01 to 16.

· The last four digits are the item code:
· the first of these digits is always 1, except for one item: 00 01 0777;
· the last three digits belong to a set of 180 integers.

In this example, the fifth digit could be a cause of collisions if it were used in a transform formula, because its value is almost always 1: we shall drop it, assign a fixed address to 00 01 0777, and provide a formula for a 7 digit number with the structure nn nn nnn.

This method is general. When part of a key can take only a small number of values, V, we shall provide V transform formulas, one for each of these values. In the example, the first transform formula is

Assign a fixed address (0 perhaps) to 00 01 0777.

A second formula covers the rest of item numbers without their fifth digit. This second formula will take advantage of the data representation and packing principles described in chapter 3. We shall build three tables for the three parts of an item number. The first table will have a cardinal of 10, the second table a cardinal of 16, and the last table a cardinal of 180. Each element in one of these tables will be represented by a one-digit integer in base 10, 16, or 180, and the primary transform formula will be

$$N = X_1 + 180 * X_2 + 180 * 16 * X_3,$$

where X_1 is in base 180, X_2 is in base 16, and X_3 is in base 10.

This formula yields no collisions, but its target space contains $10 * 16 * 180 = 28,800$ records. If we have a maximum of 6000 real items, we shall try to use a space of $6000 * 1.25 = 7500$ records. Following the method described in technique 3, we shall choose a prime number value $P = 7507$ and $R = MOD(N, 7507)$. If the address 0 is reserved for 00 01 0777, we shall use $R = MOD(N, 7507) + 1$, and the file space will comprise $7507 + 1$ records.

Sometimes the space generated by the primary transform formula, before the MODULUS is applied, is acceptably small. We shall then use it directly because it makes up a *perfect* hash-coding transform. (A perfect hash-coding transform is a transform without collisions.)

5. *Addressing partially filled blocks*   So far, our hashing techniques have addressed records. There is another possibility, which eliminates the consequences of a small number of collisions: addressing blocks instead of records, and keeping those blocks only partially full on the average.

The same hashing transform formulas apply, but now they target a space of blocks. The blocks are hollow, just as the first-level blocks of indexes were in 5.2.6.4.

If two records now collide in the same block, there is a chance that the block has enough space to store them both; and when a retrieval operation reads the block, it finds the record without having to read another block.

6. *Allowing for block overflow or using several hashing formulas* Technique 5 cannot work if there are too many collisions because the size of a block is finite. It has to allow for block overflow. This can be done using additional blocks in 3 ways:

• An overflowing block can point to its first additional block, which in turn can point to a second additional block, and so on; the structure is the same as the one used for index block overflow in 5.2.6.4.

• Overflow pointers may require modification when an overflow block is suppressed because it has become empty, or when one more block is chained to the last block of a series. In addition, an empty overflow block must be found before records can be stored in it—at the end of the file, or in a list of empty available blocks—and this requires computing.

So instead of using pointers to find the overflow blocks, it is possible to use *overflow formulas*; if the initial transform has indicated an initial block that does not contain the required record, we can use a second formula to find a second candidate block; and if that new block still does not contain the required record, we can use a third formula; and so forth.

One way of deriving the series of overflow positions from the initial position is to multiply the initial block number by 2, then 3, etc. After a multiplication, use the MODULUS approach to come back into the physical address space, if required. To stop looking for blocks when the record with a given key just does not exist requires a *nonoverflow flag*, set in each block that does not overflow.

Naturally, with this technique, a block can belong to *several* transform results, because it can be reached directly by a transform value or indirectly by an overflow formula.

• An alternative to the overflow formula approach and to the nonoverflow flag consists of *overflowing in the next physical block*: the continuation blocks of block N are N + 1, N + 2, etc. The continuation of the last block of the file is the first block. In addition, each block carries two pointers (figure 5.12):

• The *overflow-start* pointer OS, which indicates how many blocks away the first overflow block of the current block is. If OS = 0, block N does not overflow. If OS = 1, it overflows into block N + 1, etc.

• The *overflow-end* pointer OE, which indicates how many blocks away the last overflow block of the current block is.

This approach tends to smooth out *accumulation points*, where many collisions have occurred. In some situations, a transform formula may be excellent, except at one or two accumulation points where hundreds

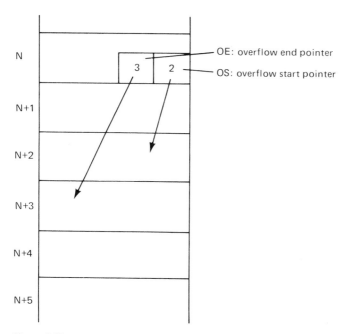

Figure 5.12
Hash-coding: maximum/minimum overflow.

or even thousands of keys have congregated. This is typical of a transform algorithm that is not suited to the key structure; but it happens
sometimes a year after the algorithm was successfully implemented,
because new key values were created.

   This approach also has another advantage: it tends to minimize disk
arm movements because it is likely that blocks $N+1$, $N+2$, etc., are
on the same disk cylinder as block N.

7. Accessing a hash-coded index file first, and then the data file   The
previous discussion assumed that the hashing formula produces the
address of data file records, as it very often does. However, there is an
alternative, which is necessary for large data files plagued by large
percentages of collisions.

   We can use all the hashing techniques described to indicate an *index
block*. The records of the block will be couples (key + pointer), as they
are in hierarchical low-level indexes. There will be no higher levels.
Each pointer points to a record of the data file.

This technique has several advantages:

• Instead of wasting data file space, where even a 20% waste can represent a lot of space, we waste index block space, where even 70% waste does not sacrifice very much space.

• This technique accommodates large blocking factors in the index file, thus tolerating severe collision situations, with accumulation points of 100 synonyms going almost unnoticed in terms of performance!

• Updating the index file takes less time than updating a hierarchical index, because there are no higher levels, and because the couples in one block do not have to be kept in sorted order.

• Locking-unlocking the index file is still necessary but less time consuming than with hierarchical indexes.

5.2.8 Bit-Inverted Files

Sample Problem

A scientific database has 5200-byte records containing 870 fields each. A query can use search criteria based on one or several of 30 fields. How can the database be structured and searched for records that satisfy several simultaneous criteria? The problem is that it is not reasonable to create and maintain 30 indexes for one file. Most DBMSs and file systems do not accept so many indexes per file. In addition, the update times would be very long. And one index could help narrow the search based on one criterion, but what if there are six in the query?

Solution

To make the search fast, we shall try to find what records *must surely be rejected* in a search. This will leave us with a (hopefully) small number of records to be examined one by one.

Since we try to reject records, and since many queries are expected to contain several simultaneous criteria, we build an *index of bit vectors* such that

• One index record consists of a group of bits called a bit vector.

• For each data file record we build one bit vector (figure 5.13).

• The relative position of a data record's bit vector is the same as that of the record itself. The Nth record yields the Nth vector: the data file and the bit vector index are called *parallel*.

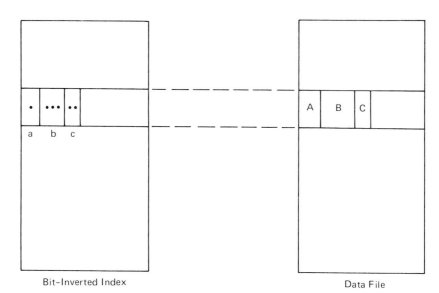

Figure 5.13
Bit-inverted index.

• Each data field on which search criteria can be expressed will be represented by a small number of adjacent bits (called the bit field) in the associated vector: 1, 2, or 3 bits in general.

• To convert the value in the data field to a value in the bit field, the set of values in the data field is divided into classes: 2 classes for a 1-bit field, 4 classes for a 2-bit field, 8 for a 3-bit field, etc. The number of classes is a compromise between the need for accuracy, which leads to selectivity, and the need for a concise representation, which leads to fast searching. Classes do not have to be of equal size. For example, to represent a date with 4 classes, we can decide that

0 means every date over one day old,
1 means yesterday,
2 means today,
3 means every date in the future.

A 30-field vector can thus be 64 bits long, or 8 bytes. Such records can be grouped 600 to a block, for example. Actually the block will contain a single physical record of 4800 bytes, which will be mapped onto a 600 element array in memory. The purpose of using array elements instead of records is that an array element is accessed more quickly than a record, with about 100 times fewer instructions executed.

To scan the file with the intent to eliminate records that do not meet the search criteria, we simply scan the index, block by block and bit vector by bit vector. The number of disk accesses to be performed will be 600 times fewer than the number needed to read the data file sequentially, assuming that 5200 byte records are stored one to a block. A file of 120,000 records can be scanned in 200 disk accesses, taking about 10 to 15 seconds on a minicomputer, including the processor time required to compare each bit vector with the criteria.

The processor time required to compare the bit fields with the given criteria will be very small because each comparison will involve

• a binary AND instruction, which extracts the bit field from its element word,

• a comparison with a predefined value.

Such bit-oriented instructions are among the fastest in existence on any computer. Suitable programming languages for such bit manipulations are Assembler, C, and some versions of FORTRAN. In some cases, it is even possible to scan a block that is already in memory while the next block is being fetched from the disk.

When a bit vector's fields contain acceptable values, the corresponding data file record must be accessed, and its fields must be compared.

This bit-inverted file approach requires minimal processing times for updates, since few operations are required to update the index. Updates are best performed in batch if data records must be added and deleted; the index file is then completely rewritten.

Note that a bit-vector index can also be used in conjunction with other file structures; a file accessed by hash-code and/or with secondary indexes can also have a parallel bit-vector index.

The disadvantage of this structure is that most DBMSs do not use it, so it must be programmed by the user. (That is quite easy to do if the address of each data record can be made available to the user: CODASYL DB-Key, etc.). This is a general problem: today, DBMSs are only intended and optimized for business applications that do not have unpredictable queries on many simultaneous criteria, and do not require the use of 30 criteria fields per file. Engineering and scientific application users must either write their own special DBMSs (for which many techniques are described in chapter 6), or use a functional interface (see chapter 6) as a DBMS—which is often a good solution—or add capabilities to an existing DBMS.

Other areas, such as personnel management, also need the bit-vector index approach to select employees using many criteria.

5.2.9   List Structures: One-Way, Two-Way Rings

Many applications need to store data in a certain collating sequence. For example, the manufacturing operations required to produce an item must be performed in a certain order; the user wants his manufacturing operations records stored in that same order.

The collating sequence is in general the ascending order of a certain field, such as an operation number. Unfortunately database records tend to be stored in the order in which they were created, and free records were allocated to them; this is a fairly random order, especially if hashed access is used. Therefore we need a structure that will at least make us retrieve the records in the predefined order of a field, even if they are stored in a different order.

Two types of structure are generally used for the purpose of maintaining a sequence: indexes and lists.

We discussed indexes in section 5.2.6 from the point of view of retrieval by key. Indexes are also used to implement a sequence.

The other type of structure used to implement a predefined sequence is the LIST structure (figure 5.14):

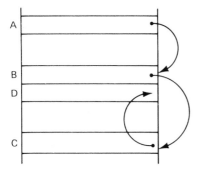

Figure 5.14
List A, B, C, D (forward).

• Each data record carries a pointer, P, which points to the next record in the sequence.

• The last record of the list carries a null pointer.

• Each record is accessed in turn, after its predecessor is accessed; if a list is long (if it links many records), finding a given record may require many disk accesses.

• The records of a given list belong to the same data file.

• A given data file can have records linked by *several* lists. For example, an inventory movements file can encompass several types of movement for each item: deliveries, returns from shop, returns to supplier, and others (see figure 5.15). All the movements of a given type may be linked to form a list in the reverse order of dates: today's deliveries are retrieved first, then yesterday's, etc. Each item has several lists of its own in the file.

• When each record of a file can belong to several lists, it has several pointers: one for each list (figure 5.17).

• Each list has its own semantics; the elements of the list make up an ordered set—they all share certain properties. For example, they all have the same movement type.

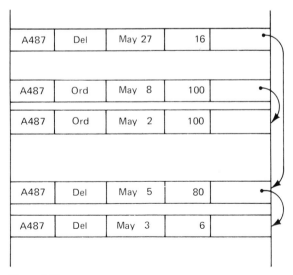

Figure 5.15
Lists of deliveries and orders for item A487 (backward).

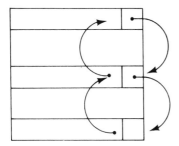

Figure 5.16
Two-way list.

Order#	Item#	Qty L1	Spec mounting seq L2
251	A487	6	2
251	A550	10	1
252	A106	1	
251	A605	3	3
252	A200	12	

Figure 5.17
Two lists running through an Order file: the list of an order's item lines (L1); the list that defines the mounting sequence of an order's special items (L2).

Figure 5.14 shows a *forward* list: each pointer points to the next record, where the value of the key field of the list, by which it is collated, increases from record to record. Figure 5.15 demonstrates a *backward* list: the records are linked in the reverse order of dates. Figure 5.16 shows a *two-way* list, which can be traversed in both directions.

A *ring* is a list whose last record is linked to its first record (figure 5.18). The advantage of such a closed structure is that if a traverse operation (one that accesses several records) enters a list at a record other than its first record, it can still run through *all* the records of the list. Such situations can occur in database structures where a traverse operation can jump from list to list at a "node" point. For example, the order records of a given customer make up a list L1; in addition, orders are also linked by due date, making up a list L2. A traverse operation may start at the first order of a customer, follow L1 until it finds an

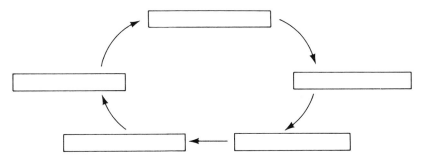

Figure 5.18
Ring (forward).

order that is already partially fulfilled, and then continue following L2 to find orders with due dates after the date of the current order.

Some DBMSs can maintain the pointers of a list *automatically* or *manually*, just as they do for index pointers (see 5.2.6.1).

Some DBMSs, such as DL/1, use list structures to implement 1-to-N relationships such as customer-HAS-orders: a pointer in the customer record points to the first order; then the orders of that customer are linked by a list structure. Others offer several alternative structures (see 5.3).

The disadvantages of list structures are

• When a list is long, traversing it to find a specific record may require many disk accesses.

• The list pointers are in the data file itself. If a record is accidentally damaged or erased, it may become impossible to retrieve the other elements of the list. This structure is more fragile and offers poorer performance than a structure with pointers external to data files, such as in the ADABAS DBMS.

When list structures are used, it is recommended that there be a field in each record that supplements the pointer and may be used by the database restructuring utility to reconstruct the pointer after an accident. For example, if two files, CUSTOMERS and ORDERS, are linked by the relationship customer-*HAS*-orders, which is implemented with the list of orders of a given customer in the ORDERS file, each order must carry a customer-number field, which is redundant, to allow for list pointer reconstruction.

Today list structures are avoided where the DBMS features indexes or *pointer arrays* (described in 5.3.3).

5.2.10   Dichotomy (Binary Search)

Dichotomy was briefly introduced in 5.2.4 and 5.2.5. This search technique is intended for use with elements sorted in ascending order of the search key. The elements can be file records or table elements. In the following algorithm, we shall assume that they belong to a table.

Algorithm

1. Compare search candidate with first and last table elements:
If found, end.

2. If candidate is less than the first element or greater than the last element, it is not in the table; end.

3. Let F be the position of the first element, and L the position of the last element. If $F = L$ or $F = L - 1$, the candidate is not in the table; end.

4. Compute $M = (F + L)/2$ (integer division).

5. Compare search candidate C with element in position M, T(M):
If found, end.
If $C < T(M)$ let $L = M$, go to 3.
If $C > T(M)$ let $F = M$, go to 3.

At each iteration, this algorithm divides its search interval [F, L] into two halves. Therefore if the number of elements in the table is $N + 1$ (or the number of intervals is N), the maximum number of candidate tests required is

$T = 2$ (for the first and last table elements) $+ X$,

where X is the smallest integer such that $2^X \geq N$. Since $N = L - 1$, where L is the initial number of elements, $T = 2 + X$, where $X = \text{MIN}(X \mid 2^X \geq L - 1)$.

Example
The table below gives the number of candidate tests for various table sizes:

Number of Elements in Table	Number of Iterations (maximum)
65	8
129	9
257	10
1025	12
4097	14
16385	16
65537	18
262145	20

This algorithm converges very rapidly. It is used more and more frequently today, in computers with large main memory, because more and more index files or even data files are kept sorted in memory for fast performance.

It is also used to search inside a block that has been read into memory.

5.2.10.1 Binary Tree (B-Tree)

A B-tree structure is a type of two-way list structure intended for fast storage and retrieval of elements. The elements can belong to a table, in memory, or on disk. Each element has a forward pointer, which points to its successor, and a backward pointer, which points to its predecessor.

Example

A set of 14 integer numbers is given in the following order: 21, 10, 5, 52, 24, 88, 41, 30, 67, 45, 16, 8, 95, 69. After storage in the database, the numbers and the pointers look like this:

Position	1	2	3	4	5	6	7	8	9	10	11	12	13	14
Number	21,	10,	5,	52,	24,	88,	41,	30,	67,	45,	16,	8,	95,	69
Predecessor	2	3		5		9	8							
Successor	4	11	12		6	7	13	10		14				

The first number, 21, is stored in position 1. The second number, 10, is compared with 21 and found to be less than 21. The first number's predecessor pointer being 0 (there is no predecessor when this comparison is made), 10 becomes the predecessor of 21, and its address, 2, is stored in 21's predecessor pointer. Then 5 is compared with 21 and found to be a predecessor. 21's predecessor being at address 2, 10 is compared with 5: 5 is a predecessor of 10, and its address, 3, is stored in 10's predecessor pointer. Then 52 is compared with 21, and found to be a successor: its address, 4, is stored in 21's successor pointer; and so on.

The graphic representation of this structure is a *tree*. 21 is the *root* of the tree; 10, 5, 52, etc., are *nodes* (see figure 5.19).

Comments on B-Trees

1. The tree graphic representation is not used for purposes other than explaining the structure. The data consist of three fields per node: a key, a predecessor pointer, and a successor pointer.

2. It is easy and fast to find where a new key element belongs in the tree, if it does not exist already. After the key is stored in the first available location, the pointers must be updated.

3. This structure is an alternative to a nonsequential index, provided that we also store a data record pointer at each node. It is not an alternative for a sequential index, unless a tree-following algorithm is implemented, to find the predecessor and successor of a given node.

4. The main difference with a nonsequential hierarchical index is the presence of the pointers at each node, which take up more room: this is a memory-voracious structure.

5. The top (root) of the tree and the first few levels under it can be stored in a block to make up a "high-level" index; the other nodes of the tree will also be stored in blocks, each block storing a "subtree,"

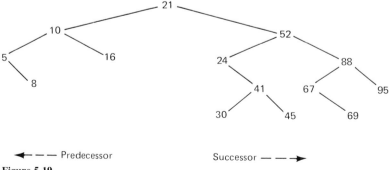

←— — Predecessor   Successor — — →

Figure 5.19
Binary tree.

the root of which is pointed to by a pointer of the level above. This minimizes the number of disk accesses.

6. Building a B-tree structure is one of the fastest sorting techniques in existence. It is well adapted to situations where memory size is not a problem. If the available memory is smaller, a slightly slower sorting technique, called *dichotomy insertion*, may be used. (Assuming that the beginning of a table to be sorted is already sorted—its first two elements being in the correct sequence will suffice—the third element is compared to the sorted part of the table using a binary search and inserted where it belongs, even if the elements to its right have to be pushed one place to the right; then the fourth element is also compared; and so on.)

7. This or another form of B-tree is used by some DBMSs for indexing.

8. In general a tree is not "balanced." In our example, there are more nodes on the right-hand side of the root than on the left-hand side. The number of comparisons required to reach a given node is not minimal on the average. It can be improved by balancing the tree, which means finding another root, and other relative positions for the keys, such that the average path length required to reach a node is minimal. In practice, this can be achieved by restructuring the tree:

· first the table is sorted;
· then the "middle" element of the table becomes the new root;
· its predecessor is the middle of the half-table made of the elements less than the root; its successor is the middle of the half-table made of the elements greater than the root;
· predecessors and successors are thus assigned, using the middles of the half-tables, until all the elements have been linked to a predecessor in the tree.

5.3 One-to-Many (1-TO-N) Relationships and Links

Relationships between data elements may exist for the following reasons:

· *Because of existence constraints or functional dependences.* For example, an order cannot exist if its customer does not exist. Such relationships are called *natural* relationships. They exist no matter what processing of orders and customers takes place.

• *Because of navigation requirements.* For example, if an MSD transaction demands that a quick direct path be implemented between a customer record and his order records, a customer ---⟩ orders linking path must be implemented.

In practice, the *second* reason is sufficient to implement a physical link, whether it corresponds to a natural relationship or not. In contrast, the *first* reason is not sufficient to implement the link, because the computer time required to create and maintain such links may not be offset by the time saved by the use of this "shortcut."

Therefore, after describing the record linking techniques in this section, we shall describe architecture-optimization techniques in chapter 6. This section contains only a few general qualitative tips for the implementation of links.

General Assumption

In all this section, we shall consider a record X, in file A, called "parent" or "owner" record, which must be linked to N records Y_x in file B, called "children" or "member" records.

5.3.1 Pointer + List

This technique stores a pointer in record X, which points to the first record Y_x in file B. Then each record Y_{xi} contains a pointer to its successor Y_{xi+1}: the Y_x records make up a list structure, and X points to the first element of the list (see figure 5.20). The last record Y_x has a null pointer; it is the end of the list.

Collating sequence   DBMSs can manage this linking structure like a list structure, involving a single file instead of two (see 5.2.9):

• With forward pointers only, it is a First In First Out (FIFO) list.
• With backward pointers only, it is a Last In First Out (LIFO) list.
• With two-way pointers, it is a two-way list.

The order of the member records, Y_x, can also be determined by the value of a given field; they can be stored in ascending or descending sequence or both, using two-way pointers.

Performance considerations   In the absence of a clustering effect that groups several Y_x member records of the same owner X into one block, this linking structure requires many disk accesses to retrieve a given

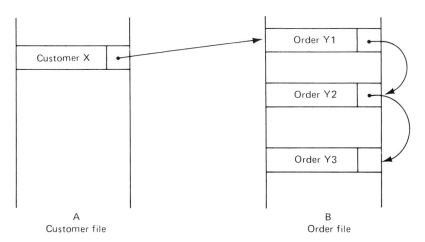

Figure 5.20
Pointer + List structure.

member when the number of members N is large. This can be a serious drawback. Some DBMSs have a restructuring utility (see 5.1.10) that must be used from time to time. Others feature clustering using blocks (CINCOM's TOTAL, for example) or areas (CULLINET's IDMS). Others provide more modern techniques, such as secondary indexes, hash-coded links, or pointer arrays, described in this section.

Recovery tip DBMSs may lose pointers when some combinations of hardware-software deficiencies occur. It is good practice to be able to recalculate pointers by storing the relevant information in addition to the pointers. For example, in a customer ---⟩ order structure, the customer record may store the number of the first order, and each order can store the number of the next order. This is redundant, but can be considered as the price to pay for safety.

Improved pointer + list structures To improve performance in such one-way list structures, the owner record can store *two* pointers—one to the *first* member record, and one to the *last* member record—to help find the last record fast.

Another possibility is the use of ring structures (5.2.9), where the last member record points to the owner (figure 5.21).

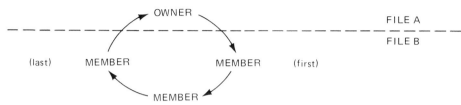

Figure 5.21
CODASYL ring structure.

5.3.2 Secondary Indexing

An owner record X can be linked with its member records Y_x using a secondary index on file B. This index is built on a key field of each Y_x record that stores the key K_x of X. To retrieve the Y_xs, B will be accessed using this secondary index, to find all records with a key value of K_x (figure 5.22).

Sometimes the key field on which the secondary index is built will include two or more fields. For example, to store the orders of a customer by date due, the index key will consist of the customer-number and date-due fields (figure 5.23). Alternatively, the date can be replaced with an arbitrary application program-assigned sequence number.

Many DBMSs feature secondary indexing as an implementation of 1-to-N relationships. For example, the relational DBMSs such as IBM's SQL/DS and DB/2, which keep relations in separate physical files and do not mix access paths with data, use secondary indexes to implement relationships. (The primary access, which guarantees tuple uniqueness, is implemented with primary indexes.) Secondary indexes do not guarantee or protect uniqueness, of course.

One secondary index block can store many key + pointer couples, thus requiring fewer disk accesses than a pointer + list structure to retrieve a key or to insert a key in a well-defined location in an ordered set of members. The existence of the higher levels of the index will also accelerate retrieval.

When a database, relational or navigational, contains many access and relationship paths, it may be difficult to find the optimal retrieval navigation automatically.

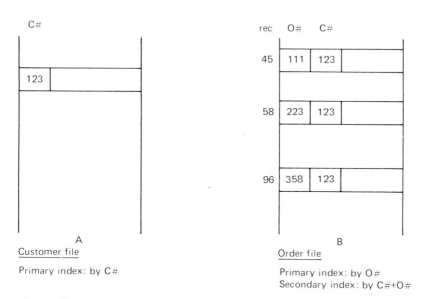

A
Customer file
Primary index: by C#

B
Order file
Primary index: by O#
Secondary index: by C#+O#

Figure 5.22
Secondary index. For C# 123, the secondary index key values and pointers are

```
    K          P
| 123  111 |   45 |
| 123  223 |   58 |
| 123  358 |   96 |
```

To find the orders of C# 123, access by partial key using the secondary index.

```
C#    Date      P
| 123   850123 |  45 |
| 123   850215 |  58 |
| 123   850604 |  96 |
```

Figure 5.23
Secondary index by C# and date-due. Index key values for 3 orders of C# 123: Jan. 23, 1985; Feb. 15, 1985; June 4, 1985.

Example

A database has a Customer file and an Order file linked by a 1-to-N relationship. The user wants to know which customers (name, address) have at least one order (number, date, value) worth over $1000.

Which is the better navigation of the following two?

1. Take one customer after the other by scanning the Customer file. For each customer, follow the 1-to-N relationship, whichever way it is implemented, and examine his orders one by one.

2. Take one order after the other by scanning the Order file. For each Order worth over $1000, access the Customer file by customer number and write the customer's name and address in a work file. Sort the work file and scan it to eliminate duplicate records.

In general, if the number of customers who will be selected is small, the second strategy is better. But there are many exceptions, such as the case when one customer record and all his order records share the same area. Automatic navigation optimization is not trivial.

5.3.3   Pointer Arrays

This linking technique is used mainly by CODASYL DBMSs (see figure 5.24).

Principle

To link an owner record X with member records Y_x, the (key + pointer) couples of the implementation are stored in an *array of pointers*. Each owner record X that has members has its own array. After accessing X, the DBMS accesses the pointer array and finds *all* the couples that represent the members of the owner ---⟩ member set.

Thus, within the same disk access, the entire set of member keys can be scanned. This is at least as fast as, and often faster than, a secondary index implementation. And updates are quite fast too. The couples of the array can be maintained in a certain collating sequence, thus providing an ordered link.

As to *physical implementation*, the pointer array is stored in the same area as the owner and member records of the set; it is transferred to memory when the owner and member records are. If the number of couples is too large to fit in the AREA, the general area-overflow

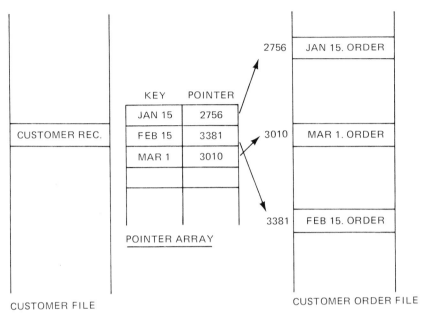

Figure 5.24
Pointer array.

mechanism is used. It is the same as the mechanism used for the data records.

5.3.4 Hash-Coded Links

Principle
The owner record, X, of file A carries a bit or a small field used as a flag that indicates if it has members. If members exist, they can be found at an address of file B given by a hashing transform of the key K_x of X.

Example
All the orders of a customer are synonyms stored in the same block of the ORDERS file. The address of the block is computed using a hashing transform of the customer-number.

Being synonyms may be an advantage in this case, as this creates a clustering effect similar to the area. As may be expected, a block-overflow mechanism will have to be implemented, as discussed in 5.2.6.4 and 5.2.7.3.

Disadvantages may exist: the synonyms may be unsorted, and the DBMS may be unable to maintain the member records in a given order. In addition, the general waste of file space associated with hashing may be a drawback.

5.4 Extended Databases: Unstructured, Open Content

This section is rather abstract and difficult because the concepts described are of a very general nature. It is intended for readers who are interested in new concepts about database management and have some background in the theory of languages and data structures.

Some preliminary information about the problem of *recognition* is discussed in sections 4.6.1–4.6.5. Here we examine the topics related to extended database description, storage, and structure.

5.4.1 Purpose of an Extended Database

Today the vast majority of databases are filled and used with business data, which are *stable* and *repetitive*.

• *Stability* means that the evolution operations (see 1.3.4.2, 5.1.6, and 5.1.7) are infrequent compared with other processing operations, such as data retrieval and update.

• *Repetitiveness* means that computerized business applications are primarily intended for the processing of relatively large volumes of data, where the number of distinct record layouts (relations) and relationships is small compared with the number of records. Typically a mainframe database contains about 300 relations and 1000 relationships, stored in about 10 million records, 90% of which are history records of event files.

New nonbusiness application areas such as knowledge (technical, scientific information, artificial intelligence), text (literature, law), images, and sounds, do not use databases today (though some people will refer to their data files as databases). They cannot use databases because their data do not follow the assumptions of nonredundancy and structure required by the definition of a database, and because no DBMSs are available to process their data.

The data of such new application areas are *unstable*. Consecutive records may have different contents; new fields, files, and relationship paths may be created frequently; etc. Also the very purpose of the database may be different: image recognition, language construct recognition in texts, use with an inference engine in an artificial intelligence machine, etc.

However, since complete departure from existing concepts and techniques is not always safe or practical, extended database capabilities will be presented as *extensions of known concepts*, and the corresponding software will use existing software design methods.

5.4.2 Definition of an Extended Database

The definition of an extended database (ED) does not follow the assumptions of nonredundancy and structure of a business database. We shall define an ED as "a collection of information elements stored and manipulated by a computer that makes it appear unstructured and open content."

Unstructured implies the following properties:

· *Variable-length* fields (called "elements").

· *Variable dimension* in repeated structures. If a field, an element as defined below, or a *structure*, which is a group of elements and links defined below, may exist N times in an encompassing higher-level structure, N may vary from structure to structure. For example, an ORDER is a structure that comprises an ORDER-HEADER element, and N ORDER-LINE elements linked by a relationship; N may vary from ORDER to ORDER.

· *Variable contents* in occurrences of a host structure (defined below with a set of elements and a set of links). This definition is a *maximum* definition; a specific occurrence of the structure may comprise only a subset of the maximum definition; it is still a valid occurrence if all its elements and links belong to those of the maximum definition. In other words, some elements or links may be missing.

For example, by definition a CUSTOMER structure consists of the substructures customer-id, customer-account, customer-orders, and some relationships. When another structure includes only customer-id, it is still a valid occurrence of a CUSTOMER structure.

However, we shall see that another condition must be fulfilled in order for a structure to be a valid occurrence of a given host structure: all the *rules* defined for the host structure must be respected by the occurrence.

• *Variable links* in occurrences of a host structure. A link is defined below as a generalized relationship. In a given occurrence of a structure, links may be missing without affecting the validity of this structure as an occurrence of the host structure. The same condition as above applies: the occurrence must abide by the rules defined for the host structure.

Open content implies ease of evolution of the unstructured database. It must be possible and practical to add, remove, or modify definitions of elements, structures, links, and rules.

5.4.3   Topics Discussed in This Section

This section describes mainly file architecture principles suitable for extended databases:

• physical storage of unstructured data, links and rules,
• data access by content and by structure,
• structure links and lists,
• rules: definition and access,
• SDL (Structure Definition Language) and the structure dictionary,
• principles of unstructured data recognition and manipulation.

5.4.4   Definition and Physical Storage of Data, Links, and Rules

Assumption
An operating system is available to perform the basic functions of disk access and file catalog management. Regarding file record management, the system must be able to perform either classical record management or UNIX-type random access to a string of bytes of a given length.

5.4.4.1   File Space Allocation
The easiest way to provide variable space allocation is to open a new file as often as possible. This technique is used in applications such as text processing but is suitable for many other areas. File retrieval, extension, and space recovery on deletion are then entirely managed by the operating system.

The limits are in two areas:

• The total number of files that can be defined or open at any one time is limited in some operating systems.

• Opening a file requires several disk accesses and a nonnegligible amount of processor time. For example, under the IBM DOS and MVS operating systems, opening a VSAM file requires a considerable amount of code and data manipulation: several hundred kilobytes have to be brought into memory, page by page, if they are not already there.

These limits are quite severe if we try to use entire files to obtain variable-length records.

We assume that the operating system can

• provide a file directory or cataloging facility for naming, creating, deleting, retrieving, and accessing files,

• provide copy and backup-restore utilities;

• allocate space to a file in such a way that file extension is transparent to the DBMS (we will call a *page* a contiguous disk area allocated to a file to extend its size).

Today even microcomputer operating systems provide these services, which can be used to implement levels 2, 3, and 4 of the file system to be described.

5.4.4.2 Record Management: File System Hierarchy

Within a file, we need the notion of record. But since a record can vary in length and content, it will be defined by a begin address and a length. And since we want each file to be open content, we need the ability to extend record lengths easily. A suitable storage structure can be as follows:

Level 0: system level. The system uses 3 file catalogs with fixed names, dedicated to system software, system data files, and applications. These catalogs store the roots of all file catalogs of level 1.

Level 1: catalog level. A hierarchical catalog is provided with directories and subdirectories and perhaps access security information such as passwords. At the lowest level of this hierarchy, a file directory lists the names and addresses of all the files in the catalog.

Level 2: file level. Each file begins with a header that contains

- type of file (system, application, program, data);
- number of records in the file;
- date and time of last update;
- host record structure: list of element numbers, as recorded in the dictionary;
- record key information (the notion of key is defined below);
- minimum lengths to allocate to a new record, a new page;
- number of pages in the file;
- directory of pages—each page has entries for
  page number,
  page address,
  page length,
  space available for new records or record extension,
  the numbers of the first and last records in the page.

Level 3: page level. Each page contains an integer number of disk segments and begins with a header that contains

- the owner file name and page number, for recovery purposes;
- the directory of the records in the page:
  record number or 0 (which means "hole" and designates space available for record extension or creation),
  address,
  length.

Level 4: record level. A record contains a header and data. The header comprises

- Pointers to the first and last extensions of the record (a variable-length record is a list of contiguous data areas linked by forward pointers).
- A field map. For nondimensioned fields (fields other than arrays) the map comprises *couples* (field number, actual length), where the number is the relative position of the field, in the host structure described in the file header. Dimensioned fields are described using their field number, the actual value of each dimension, and the total length. For example, a two-dimensional array of character strings that is "field" 35 in this record contains 6 rows and 41 columns, for a total of 4506 bytes; its description is: 35,6,41,4506. A field must be entirely included in one page, but a record may be split across several pages.

This file and record structure is used for all the information in the database: elements, structures, links, and rules. It is an underlying, transparent structure: the application program manipulates structures and elements that can comprise several fields or records, and are mapped into this physical structure by dictionary information described in SDL. This is an extension of the notion of view.

5.4.4.3 Definition and Representation of Links: Vector Function
A link is defined and represented by

• A name.

• An origin, which is an element or structure. The origin is defined by its name and the information required to find it: a *key* (defined below) or a pointer.

• A destination, which is another element or structure, also defined by a name and a key or pointer.

• An existence *rule* (defined below).

Before we define a key, we need to define a *Vector Function* (VF).

A VF is an algorithm applied to an element or a structure to calculate the values of its component fields. These fields can be numbers, alpha strings, logical values, or any other type defined below for SDL element fields. A VF is a multidimensional virtual attribute.

A VF is implemented in a software module whose input is an occurrence of the element or structure for which the VF was defined, and whose output is the set of vector component fields.

This notion will be used to define a key, *soft* structures, and *soft* rule observance.

The *key* is a vector function represented by a record. This record has fixed contents for each type of key: all occurrences of a given key will be stored in one file.

The notion of key can be used to identify an element or a structure when it is

• nonambiguous: 1 key vector defines 1 occurrence of the element or structure;

• practical: given the key vector, the structure can be retrieved, perhaps with the assistance of a rule to describe the navigation.

The *pointer* is a generalized database-key (DB-key). It can be

• A record address: file name + record number, as stored in the page directory; the record is then the first or root record (if there is one) of the element or structure.

• An address of a *destination descriptor*, a type of pointer array that stores all the pointers to the elements that make up the origin or destination structure. This allows handling list structures internal to one file, as well as 1-to-1, 1-to-N, and N-to-P relationships that link data stored in one or two files. Here the number of files is not limited: an origin structure is linked to a destination structure.

A link will be used as a bridge to find a destination structure or element by a direct path from the origin.

A link is stored in a link record that belongs to a link file: all links between comparable origins and destinations are stored in the same file. This file has a header that describes the host structure of the link occurrences and their rule of existence.

5.4.4.4 Definition and Representation of Rules and Laws

A rule is a generalized co-routine, used to define existence or validity conditions for an element, structure, link, or program module (see 4.6.5.5). Because of its general nature, the description of a rule needs a powerful language: we shall use suitable computer languages for the actual computer-usable description, plus English for the specification, just as we did in MSD.

A rule is represented by a record that contains

• a name;

• a type of action:

existence constraint of element, structure, or link,
processing specification or limitation: search, link, calculation, storage, etc.

• a target domain: which elements, structures, links, or program modules does the rule apply to?;

• a specification text (English);

• an implementation routine (co-routine).

Law

(See 4.6.5.6.) A law is a structure made of

- rules,
- special rule links called *logical connectors*,
- rule weight coefficients.

The logical connectors in a law are parentheses (. . .), *NOT, AND, OR* (nonexclusive OR), with priority of evaluation in that order, and from left to right. They are used to group rules into laws. The notion of law is recursive; one or several laws grouped with logical connectors make up a law.

Each rule or law within a law can be weighted, in the soft constraint sense described in chapter 4, so that *soft* (approximate, not-too-strict) rule observance is possible. In addition, the notion of *soft data structure* can be defined using vector functions and weight parameters for each structure: the VF is first evaluated using the data in the structure, and then compared to an ideal vector; then the weight coefficients are applied; and so on. Sample rule weight factors for artificial intelligence can be probabilities.

Physical storage of rules and laws uses two types of files:

- Type 1 contains rule and law records.
- Type 2 contains implementation routines (co-routines).

5.4.4.5 Storage of Structures

One element can belong to several structures. Therefore structures will not be stored as such. A structure is like an element: an abstract view of the data, provided on request to the application program by the DBMS. The only physical implementation of structures is in the storage of the links, rules, laws, and access structures defined below.

5.4.5 Access by Element Content

File access techniques are intended for record retrieval. In this case, the application program will pass to the DBMS the contents of an element or a field together with a request for retrieval of the records that match the given values. For example, the element contents are item-family and quantity-in-stock. The search criteria are

- item-family = 06,
- quantity-in-stock < 1.

The DBMS must find the item records that have the corresponding fields matching the given values with the given constraints.

Access by content contrasts with access *by address* (using a DB-key or pointer as defined in 5.4.4.3) and access *by structure*, where the DBMS must recognize a structure, not just field values.

The techniques for retrieving a record based on the contents of fields are the same as those used for retrieving from a classical database, but applied to unstructured files. However, they adhere to one important principle:

The data and access structure information (key, pointers) reside in separate files.

Thus scanning the data can be done primarily by scanning the structure (index, bit-inverted) files, which is faster. If the data are stable enough, indexes on field values can be built and maintained. Many structures describing different views of the data can be assembled and disassembled without writing to the actual data files.

If many simultaneous search criteria can be used, a bit-inverted index can be defined. In other situations, a hash-coded access (direct or indexed) can be the right solution: these are all classical techniques. The problem of access by content is not the most difficult problem in extended database management, and it can be solved using classical architectures.

5.4.6   Access by Structure (File Level, Database Level)

The purpose here is to show architecture principles that can be used to help a DBMS retrieve a structure—that is, retrieve an *initial* element of this structure; from this initial element, a recognition process can be conducted using syntax-analysis (compilation) type techniques introduced at the end of this section.

Example

In a library of source programs, find the programs that are written in BASIC. A program is a structure made of substructures that are statements. Statements are made of reserved words and user-defined words, connected with links specified in grammar rules. Program-level rules exist, too. Answering the question will involve two steps:

1. Find the beginning of each source program.
2. Try to recognize it as a BASIC program.

This subsection deals only with structures that help find the beginning of a structure. We shall be looking for records that contain the initial element of a structure that consists of elements, substructures, and links that respect certain rules. The search will use a hierarchical *index of structures*.

At *detail level*, the index contains one record per data file record where an *initial* element is stored. The index record is an *existence vector* that comprises

· an element name (the initial element),
· the number of links that start at this element,
· the list of these link names,
· a pointer or key of this element.

This existence vector is examined to verify the element name and the link names, to begin recognizing the structure. Note that element values are not stored in the index: the emphasis is on recognizing *a structure*. However, values will be combined with structure information, in the architecture discussed in 5.4.7: access by structure and content.

At higher levels the structure is similar, except that
· The "element" information is replaced with substructure information, where the substructure described consists of a rule and a number of elements and links; recognizing a bigger encompassing structure can accelerate the search for a detail of this structure. To describe this subset of the host structure, detailed in the lower-level index, the bit-inverted file technique can be considered. If necessary, it can even be used in the lower-level index to describe the fields of the host structure that actually exist in the initial element.
· The pointer or key fields are replaced with the numbers of the records of the lower-index level where the details of the substructure are described.

5.4.7 Access by Structure and Content

The structure index architecture does not contain element values. Such values can be added to accelerate retrieval of the initial element of a structure.

Whenever possible, we can add *key* values:

At higher index levels a structure key can help determine whether a given structure is the one we are looking for. For example, if we are looking for a BASIC program in a source library, a key element can be the following vector:

- the number of source lines,
- the object code size,
- the names of the input and output files.

Thus, if we are looking for a "small" program, a candidate with 2250 source lines will not do. If we want a program that calculates sales statistics, the names of the input files will help.

At lower index levels a key can be an accurate element acceptance criterion, as good as a pointer for retrieval purposes.

5.4.8 Access Structure for Links and Lists

Links constitute information, not just one dimension of structures; they must be stored with an access method designed for fast retrieval and scanning.

A *link file* is used for each type of link, identified by its name, origin, destination, and semantics or navigation rules. Each record contains a couple composed of an origin and a destination (each including one or more elements).

A *list* is a special type of link; it can be stored and processed like other links. The origin is unique (even if it is a structure), and there are N destinations (elements or structures) in a certain order. As an extension of the classical notion of list, the collating sequence of the elements can depend on the value of a function of the data in the elements and be automatically sequenced or be arbitrary and defined manually.

An *index by orgin* and/or an *index by destination* can be defined and maintained. Each lower-level record contains an origin key, a destination key, and the associated pointer to the link record. To accelerate retrieval and updating, the various techniques intended for index management described in 5.2.6, 5.2.7, 5.2.8, and 5.2.10 can be considered.

5.4.9 Access Structure for Rules

Rules and Laws also constitute information. A rule may be used in the definition of data or links. It may also be used to guide, protect, verify, or control execution of program modules (MSD calls these "program-protection co-routines" in 2.2.3.2).

So, rules are stored and manipulated like other types of information. The actual computer language text of a rule is stored in a special file. The page directory of this file holds the list of rules in the page by number. To accelerate retrieval of rules, two types of index can be implemented:

An index by target domain, to search for a rule that applies to a given group of elements, structures, links, or programs. Since this index is used to search for a domain, which is a structure, the types of indexing described in sections 5.4.6 and 5.4.7 can be employed.

An index by rule name, to search for a rule by the name it is given in a link, element, structure, or program. Each entry in this index is a couple: (name, pointer).

5.4.10   Structure Definition Language (SDL)

The purpose of SDL is to describe the elements, structure, links, and rules for dictionary storage. For each entity, the description includes

- type,
- name,
- semantics of the definition or target domain, described in English,
- existence constraints, rules, and laws,
- physical representation,
- physical-to-logical mapping logic,
- comments, in English.

As to *scope*, the SDL representations in this section do not constitute a real syntax: they are a first step toward a syntax, offered to show a direction of research. In addition, they are intended only for information description, not manipulation. The italicized words are reserved words, the texts between brackets [] are optional, and, if followed by ". . . ," can be repeated several times.

5.4.10.1   Preliminary Definitions

- The construct

⟨name⟩ [/*⟨comments and semantics⟩*/],

where ⟨name⟩ is a user-defined name, and [/*⟨comments and seman-
tics⟩*/] is an optional text, will be called an ⟨entity name⟩.

· The construct

⟨name of programming language routine⟩ [/*⟨human language rules⟩*/]
will be called ⟨co-routine⟩.

· The construct

⟨co-routine⟩ [, logical connector ⟨co-routine⟩] . . .
will be called a ⟨user rule⟩. (Logical connectors are (), *NOT, AND,
OR*.)

· The construct

(weight, co-routine) [,logical connector (weight , co-routine)]. . . ,
where the text between brackets is optional, will be called a ⟨law⟩.
The "weight" is a measure of importance or a probability.

5.4.10.2   Element

A element comprises fields and functions (horizontal and vertical) of
fields. It is a logical view of this information, which can originate in one
or several records. As far as the DBMS is concerned, an element is not
further subdivided; it is received or delivered in one call. A good analogy to an element is a relation, derived from a relational database,
using relational algebra operations and functions to calculate virtual
attributes. But this is only an analogy, because an element has no
reason to respect the Fourth Normal Form (or any other similar) restriction, and elements cannot be manipulated with relational algebra.
Another good analogy for an element is an Abstract Data Type (ADT),
an entity belonging to a set governed by algebraic rules. An element is
defined by

ELEMENT ⟨entity name⟩ (field description) [(field description)]. . . ,
[*DIM* integer constant [, integer constant]. . .],
RULE ⟨user rule⟩,
MAP ⟨routine name⟩.

A field description is limited to a field name in SDL. However, this
name gives access to an actual field description, stored in a classical
DBMS data dictionary. The field types considered for use with an
extended database are these:

• INTEGER*n, where the number n after the asterisk is the number of bytes used to store the field.

• DECIMAL*n.p, where n.p represents the number of digits before and after the decimal point.

• REAL*n, where the number n after the asterisk is the number of bytes used for this floating point representation.

• COMPLEX*2n, used for complex (real + imaginary) numbers stored in 2n bytes with the same precision.

• LOGICAL*2,4, which represents a TRUE or FALSE logical field stored in 2 or 4 bytes (FORTRAN standard), or LOGICAL*0 for a field stored in a single bit.

• [V]CHAR*n, which represents a character string. If the V option is used, the length is a maximum of n characters; if not, the length is fixed.

• [V]BIT*n, which represents a string of bits.

• FSET*n, which represents a finite set field n bits long. Such a field represents a variable with a maximum of 2^n values. For example, a color field representing a set of 6 colors (black, brown, blue, green, red, white) is a field of 3 bits declared as FSET*3.

All of these fields can be *dimensioned*, making up an array of N dimensions. Each array is declared by appending the list of *maximum* (host) dimensions to the field description, as described by the construct

[*DIM* integer constant [, integer constant]. . .].

An occurrence of such a field may have different (smaller) dimensions if required, defined in the field map of the record header.

The *RULE* ⟨user rule⟩ construct contains the name of the co-routine that verifies existence of the element data submitted for update. This implies that the DBMS will have to work as a back-end module of a front-end functional interface, described in chapter 6.

The *MAP* ⟨routine name⟩ construct contains the name of the program module that interfaces the application program (which sees an element) with the DBMS (which sees records and fields), both on retrieval and on update operations. This capability also requires an FI.

5.4.10.3   First Conclusions

It is now obvious that the notion of Element requires both physical data fields and software to put its descriptive power to work for the application program. This is how such a program will manipulate images, knowledge, and technical data elegantly.

It will prove easier to use and more powerful than an all-language approach, where such database notions are defined and manipulated with a complex all-purpose language. This is a simple, pragmatic approach, where each element can be defined, checked for validity, and manipulated using its own problem-oriented data structures and simple easy-to-learn languages.

It contrasts with the approach that tries to make one complex, abstract, general-purpose language suitable for description and manipulation of a wide variety of data structures. It is not as heavy and abstract; nor does it require complex compilers and gifted programmers.

It is implemented by the FI concept, which is simple and economical because of the learning curve phenomenon. Most verification coroutines look alike and have the same architecture, so they can be programmed "in series"; mapping routines are simple and similar too. If a complexity exists, it is in the FI, not in the application programs; a large number of application programs that depend on a single complex FI can be written using simple nonabstract languages.

The issue of having two separate software modules for *RULE* and *MAP* instead of one that integrates both functions is not very important. It simply means that physical mapping and verification are programmed separately. The advantage is proved by experience. The *RULE* software will, in general, require more maintenance than the *MAP* software; it will be specified by people oriented toward functional results rather than technical implementation. But if circumstances make it preferable to implement both as one integrated routine, it can be done without fearing unexpected theoretical consequences.

5.4.10.4   Structure

The notion of structure is derived from the notion of element, by adding links and recursion (a structure can comprise linked substructures, which in turn can comprise subsubstructures, etc.). It is defined by

STRUCTURE ⟨entity name⟩ ⟨element-or-link name⟩. . . ,
RULE ⟨law⟩,
MAP ⟨routine name⟩,

where ⟨element-or-link name⟩ is the name of an element, another (different) structure (called a *substructure*), or the name of a link, and ⟨law⟩ is the notion defined in 5.4.10.1.

A link defines its origin and destination, which do not need to be redeclared; they are implicitly part of the defined structure.

If structures or elements X_i are declared part of the defined structure S, without being linked to other substructures Y_i of this structure S, then S is *nonconnex*. (The words connex and nonconnex come from graph theory. A connex graph comprises only linked nodes, whereas a nonconnex graph comprises nonlinked subgraphs.)

This notion is important because it lets us create structures with unrelated substructures. For example, the structure FRUIT can comprise APPLES, PEARS, ORANGES, and other fruits. These unrelated notions become related by the structure.

The main differences between the notions of element and structure are that

• a structure also comprises links, not just data,
• a structure is not stored—it is an entirely abstract view, so it cannot be updated,
• a structure is a database-level entity, not a subset of a single file, like an element.

The notion of structure is powerful, too, considering that a structure can be *strict* or *soft*, as defined in 5.4.4.4.

Example
Source programs, written in different languages, can have defined substructures that include such notions as

• block or module substructures,
• declarations,
• assignments,
• arithmetic expressions,
• control statements,
• I/O statements,
• comments.

Each substructure comprises elements that are smaller substructures, reserved words, constants, user-defined words, and others. Substructures are linked by syntax rules. It is possible to define semantic structures that can subsequently be recognized, such as character string searches. It is also possible to define and recognize logical errors, such as a statement written after a branch statement to which no other statement ever branches; for example (in FORTRAN),

GOTO 1234,
X = X + 1.

5.4.10.5 Link
A link can be defined by

LINK ⟨entity name⟩ ⟨origin name⟩ ⟨linker⟩ ⟨destination name⟩,
⟨explicit-or-implicit⟩,
RULE ⟨law⟩,
MAP ⟨routine name⟩.

The origin and destination names are host structure names. Links can thus potentially be implemented between all occurrences of the origin and destination structures that satisfy the law.

The ⟨linker⟩ construct can be one of the following:

• an origin key name,
• an origin pointer name,
• *ALL* (to link automatically all possible origins and destinations that belong to the named host structures and satisfy the law),
• *SOME* (to declare the link in the data dictionary without actually attempting to establish the physical links; after such a declaration, *manual* on-request linking is possible).

The ⟨explicit-or-implicit⟩ qualifier (⟨EXPLICIT⟩ or ⟨IMPLICIT⟩) defines the physical nature of the link: explicitly stored, using a link record, or defined and verifiable but not stored.

The *MAP* ⟨routine name⟩ construct defines the routine that can physically implement or verify the link. Such a routine has to be protected against potential erroneous or impossible data situations; it is not always easy to separate it from the rules of the law.

5.4.10.6 Key
A key is defined by

KEY ⟨entity name⟩ *OF* ⟨element-or-structure-name⟩,
⟨key component name [(i)]⟩. . . ,
MAP ⟨routine name⟩.

Each key component name can be subscripted; it defines the components of the key and must be a field, element, or variable declared elsewhere. The *MAP* construct defines the vector function routine that calculates the key.

5.4.10.7 Rule

A rule can exist for processing reasons that are not linked with the existence of elements, structures, or links. It can be a program-protection co-routine, as defined in MSD, or even a routine created for some special purpose by an application program that wants to use DBMS services to store it. And it can be used for program module documentation purposes; the definition of the rule in the data dictionary is useful documentation:

RULE ⟨entity name⟩ ⟨data-or-process-where-it-applies⟩. . . ⟨co-routine⟩.

⟨data-or-process-where-it-applies⟩ is the name of an element, a structure, a link, a program module, or the word *CUSTOM*, which means that the programmer reserves the rule for yet-to-be-defined purposes.

Note that a rule can apply to many entities; in addition to the new application areas defined in 5.4.1, the concept of rule is one step in the direction of a new programming style. This style implies *nonprocedural* or *semiprocedural* programming. The action of the computer is described in terms of rules, which are the building blocks of a powerful language. This is the approach used by inference engines in artificial intelligence.

5.4.11 Principles of Unstructured Data Recognition and Manipulation

The recognition function will be performed by a structure analyzer. The analysis process can be *navigational*, which means application program driven, or *structural*, which means database structure driven.

During structural processing, the structure analyzer performs like the syntax analysis pass of a compiler. Its inputs are the database, the data dictionary, and parameters provided by the requesting program. Structures can be recognized in the strict or soft sense, using laws and vector functions. Data-driven recognition can be achieved; depending on what is already recognized, new recognition decisions can be made.

6 Optimal Database Implementation Techniques

6.1 Computer Load Evaluation

6.1.1 Purpose

Of all the programs that run in a computer, the DBMS is often the one that takes up the largest amount of resources: processor load, number of disk accesses, and disk channel load. Using a DBMS to perform file accessing is more costly than performing the same accesses through the operating system.

For example, on an IBM computer under DOS/VS, a random file access (RRDS) using the operating system's VSAM file manager requires the execution of 2500 assembly language instructions. In the same environment, a database file access using the DBMS DL/1 requires 9800 instructions, almost four times more. While some of the supplement is probably due to inefficient programming within DL/1, most of it results from the services provided only by a DBMS.

It is therefore important to estimate the load generated by a database application and predict the response times to be expected. In many instances, applications are developed and configurations are selected, only to discover unacceptable processing and response times. Ideally one should be able to predict resource drains and response times as early as possible. This section describes an approach that can minimize the risks.

6.1.2 Benchmarking DBMS Performance

Whatever the approach we use to evaluate the load and response times, we need to know the following DBMS performance parameters.

6.1.2.1 Average Path Length

This is the average number, A, of processor instructions required for one DBMS call.

For example, $A = 9800$ for DL/1. If the DBMS runs on a computer with a speed of S instructions per second, the average processor time, T, required to process one DBMS call is $T = A/S$ seconds. An IBM 4341 that runs at a speed of 1.2 MIPS (millions of instructions per second) can process a DL/1 call in

$T = 9800/1,200,000 = 8.16$ msec (milliseconds).

The average path length, A, is a convenient way of expressing the processor load. If the speed of the processor, S, changes, A remains the same on a given type of computer, so a new T can be easily calculated. However, A is not the DBMS response time, which also includes disk access times, channel speeds, operating system parameters, and DBMS tuning parameters. A is useful in determining whether the load of a project application is compatible with a given (DBMS + hardware + system) configuration.

6.1.2.2   Load of Each Type of DBMS Call

A DBMS can process many types of calls to retrieve, update, combine (relational algebra), link, restructure, restore, define, or redefine data or access paths. However, the number of calls we need to consider can basically be subdivided into four categories, which are by far the most frequent: insertion, deletion, modification, and selection. All four can be considered limited to one record or tuple at a time. Unfortunately, the number of parameters required to define the load of each type of DBMS call is still quite large.

In each call category, the file access structure must be considered: indexing, hash-coding, and other access types are not equivalent.

When Areas or Clusters (the equivalent of areas in the relational database world) exist, an access within an area already in memory costs less than an access to an area on disk.

Within a given type of file access, indexed, for example, accessing the first record with a given key value is more expensive than accessing the next record with the same value. With a hashed access, finding an initial synonym is more expensive than finding the next synonym.

In addition, a call can cost more when the DBMS works for many simultaneous users than it does when it works for only one. *Multithreading*, request-response queue management, and buffer-pool management take time. (Multithreading means that the DBMS works on several requests at the same time, thus following several simultaneous processing threads; this is the DBMS's internal version of time-sharing and multitasking.) Finally, the DBMS backup logging mechanism takes time.

The number of parameters involved in the evaluation of the load of a DBMS call must not discourage us from benchmarking the DBMS. All parameters do not have the same importance. After the first days of benchmarking, the important parameters will be known, and the others will be dropped. The precision required is about 10%–20%, since the benchmark tables subsequently will be used to predict the load of the DBMS calls as documented in the MSD view and access path slips. Since the phenomena that take place in a computer become more complex when its size increases, benchmarking small computers will be easier than benchmarking larger ones, and the results will be more accurate.

Some DBMS vendors—IBM, for example—provide benchmark information. Others do not, claiming that it is confidential and could be used against them in competition situations. And some simply lack such figures.

The results of the benchmark will be a table with four columns, one for each category of call, and as many rows as required to hold the various parameter values: access type, area, first/last record, and number of simultaneous users (see table 6.1).

Each row × column box of the table contains one or several of the following measures:

· path length in instructions,
· processor time in milliseconds,
· number of disk accesses,
· total DBMS response time (elapsed time).

The tests are performed using user-written programs and measures available both through the system's resource logging mechanism and an external clock. The processor load can also be evaluated using an auxiliary program running in lower priority and performing a number of loops; when this program runs alone, it performs N_{max} loops; when it runs while the DBMS is running, it performs N loops. The DBMS load is $N_{max} - N$, and can be expressed as a fraction of the total processor power.

6.1.2.3 Estimating the Average DBMS Call Execution Time

When the benchmarks have been run, it is useful to estimate the time required to run an "average DBMS call."

By definition, such a call is a weighted mix of the calls described in table 6.1. The weight coefficients used are arbitrary, of course, but they must reflect the activity expected to take place.

In business applications, the following mix of calls can be used:

Table 6.1
DBMS benchmark results[a]

| | Benchmark of DBMS . . . Number of simultaneous users. . . | | | |
	SELEC-TION	INSER-TION	MODIFI-CATION	DELE-TION
Index				
Unique or first		(1)	(2)	(2)
Nonunique or next		(3)	xxxx(4)xxxx	xxxx(5)xxxx
2 indexes	xxxx(6)xxxx		xxxxxxxxxxx	
3 indexes	xxxx(6)xxxx		xxxxxxxxxxx	
Updating 1 index	xxxxxxxxxxx	(7)	(8)	(9)
Hash-code				
Unique or first				
Nonunique or next			xxxxxxxxxxx	xxxxxxxxxxx
etc.				

a. (1) The cost of verifying that duplicates do not exist is included. (2) The cost of retrieving the record is included, but not the cost of updating an index based on that field. (3) The cost implies that a duplicate record was inserted previously and that no selection to find the slot where to insert the new record is required. (4) Same cost as modifying unique plus selection of "next." The cost of updating the index is not included. (5) Same cost as deleting unique plus selection of "next." Updating the index is included. (6) Selection can use only 1 index at a time. (7) This is the cost of inserting one entry in a secondary index. (8) This is the cost of updating a secondary index based on the modified field. (9) This is the cost of deleting one entry in a secondary index.

- 60% of DBMS calls are SELECTIONS.
- 20% of DBMS calls are MODIFICATIONS.
- 11% of DBMS calls are INSERTIONS.
- 9% of DBMS calls are DELETIONS.

In addition, when insertions and suppressions are involved, the following mix of numbers of indexes can be used:

- 40% of updates are performed with 1 index.
- 40% of updates are performed with 2 indexes.
- 10% of updates are performed with 3 indexes.
- 10% of updates are performed with over 3 indexes (assume 4).

In this approximation, a 1-to-N link can be counted as 1 index if it crosses an area border, or ignored if it does not; an N-to-P link can be counted as 2 indexes if it crosses an area border, or ignored if it does not.

Table 6.2
Average DBMS call times

CALL TYPE	SELECTION	MODIF	INSERTION	DELETION
MICRO (615)	400	600	1500	1000
MINI (85)	60	80	160	200
MAINFRAME (9)	5	12	17	20

The average time required to run a DBMS call, d, is defined as follows:

• If the system is a single-user computer, it is the total DBMS response time, including processor and disk access times.

• If the system is a multiuser computer, it is the processor time required to run a DBMS call when only one application program is running.

Orders of magnitude of the average DBMS call times, d, are as given in table 6.2. The numbers are expressed in milliseconds. The numbers for MICRO (615), MINI (85), and MAINFRAME (9) are computed by weighting the numbers on the corresponding lines using the coefficients 60, 20, 11, and 9. The micro has a hard disk. The assumed speed of the mainframe is 1 MIPS.

6.1.3   Evaluating Computer Load from Specifications

This is a first approximation of the load based on the detailed functional specifications. It uses the DBMS calls required by the transaction slips. It assumes that the application runs as specified, and that all DBMS calls are identical to the "average call." The transactions considered are restricted to those that must be executed at peak computer usage hours. The principle of this approximation is straightforward: we shall sum up the number of DBMS calls performed per second and compare it to the computer's throughput.

6.1.3.1   Number of DBMS Calls per File at Peak Usage Hour

From the access or relationship path slips described in 2.2.3.5, we derive the number of DBMS calls for each file or relation at peak usage hour. Table 6.3 is filled. Each access or relationship path that reaches the file for a given view is written on a separate line. The nature of the call (select, insert, delete, modify) yields an integer number of calls in

Table 6.3
Number of DBMS calls per file at peak usage hour[a]

FILE . . .

Path#	View#	View Name	Select (T_s)	Insert (T_i)	Delete (T_d)	Modify (T_m)	Key 1 (T_1)	Key 2 (T_2)	Key 3 (T_3)

a. T_s, T_i, T_d, T_m, T_1, T_2, and T_3 are totals: $T_a = T_s + T_i + T_d + T_m$; $T_b = T_1 + T_2 + T_3$.

the corresponding column and the same number in the column that indicates the access or link key. Each time a new key is found for that file, a new column is created.

The column totals are calculated; then $T_a = T_s + T_i + T_d + T_m$, which must be equal to $T_b = T_1 + T_2 + T_3 + \cdots$ (this is a verification). Note that in general T_i must be greater than or equal to T_d, except if more insertions than deletions are performed during non-peak hours.

The T_a values for the various files are added, making up a grand total T, which is the number of DBMS calls per hour at peak usage hour. In this approximation, we do not take into account the area concept, and we assume that all logically required access or relationship paths have been physically implemented. This approach is sufficiently accurate for our present purpose, and the tables above will be used to determine the optimal physical architecture at a later stage.

6.1.3.2 Total DBMS Load at Peak Usage Hour
The total number, T, of DBMS calls calculated above is now compared with the total DBMS throughput T_{max} derived from the average DBMS call time, d, described in 6.1.2.3:

$$T_{max} = 0.40/d.$$

The coefficient 0.40 is a safety factor: in practice, the usable throughput of a DBMS can be estimated as roughly 40% of the theoretical maximum $1/d$.

If $T < T_{max}$, the throughput is sufficient to handle the DBMS load, the remaining 60% capacity being available for other computations: the data communications monitor, the operating system, and the application programs.

Example

An IBM 4341 computer using DL/1 under DOS/VS features a processor speed of 1.2 MIPS. Each call to DL/1 takes up 9800 instructions, so d = 9,800/1,200,000 = 0.00817 second. Therefore T_{max} = 0.4/0.00817; T_{max} = 49 calls per second.

Assuming that the machine handles 30 VDTs and that each VDT sends every 15 seconds a transaction that requires 5 DBMS calls, in 15 seconds 30 × 5 = 150 calls must be processed. The DBMS load is T = 150/15 = 10 calls/second. Since $T < T_{max}$, the throughput is sufficient.

Assuming now that the remaining usable DBMS throughput is taken up by a batch program running in lower priority, and that 1 line is printed by this program after 2 DBMS calls, the printing speed is (49 − 10)/2 = 19.5 lines/second, or 1170 lines/minute.

Comments

In this case, one batch program takes up as much power as 39/10 × 30 = 117 VDTs, because its response time is much faster than a VDT user's response time. If the 4341 had nothing to do but run VDTs, it could support 49/10 × 30 = 147 VDTs.

This approach is only an initial approximation. It must be used with caution, and only to evaluate the overall feasibility of a proposed application in a given environment. Better evaluations can be obtained from some DBMS vendors, who use sophisticated simulation programs to estimate the loads and interactive response times.

6.1.3.3 Simulating the DBMS Response Times

If the previous approximation has shown that the total DBMS load at peak usage hour is acceptable, it may be interesting to evaluate the response time of the DBMS. This is the time required by the DBMS to process one call, between the moment when an application program issues the call and the moment when it receives the answer from the DBMS.

The response time may be a function of the database architecture and volume, the DBMS tuning parameters such as the buffer pool size, the characteristics of the computer and operating system, and the type and frequency distribution of calls. The influences of so many parameters are difficult to predict, particularly those that pertain to the

DBMS's tuning parameters and logical mechanisms, for which we shall use the benchmark results described in 6.1.2.2.

These parameters and results will be entered into a simulation program. This program will be run many times, simulating the various mechanisms used by a DBMS and operating system to process a DBMS call. The objective is to evaluate the response time of each DBMS call, as seen by each application program; more important, it is to perform a *sensitivity analysis* of these response times to the various parameters in order to discover which parameters are important.

Such simulation programs (for example, GPSS) are sold as standard packages that perform discrete numerical simulations of queuing systems. The parameters are entered in conversational mode or using a special simulation language. When many parameters affect the end result, a Monte Carlo sensitivity analysis may be performed to evaluate which parameters are most important.

Our purpose here is not to describe such packages, which are quite complex and powerful, and may be purchased at reasonable prices for execution on personal computers (about $1000). We shall simply describe the principle of such discrete simulators of queuing systems in a simple case, when the DBMS does not feature multithreading.

Principle of Discrete DBMS Response Time Simulation
Let us assume that a number of VDT users work interactively with a computer. After an image appears on his screen, each user thinks and types an input during a certain time T_u before he sends a transaction to the computer for processing. T_u is a random variable: the user's "response times" vary depending on the user, the application program, and chance. The distribution of these user response times is a random distribution; but its model being unknown, it is advisable to try several distribution models to test their influence: GAUSS, POISSON, and UNIFORM as a minimum.

After a transaction is sent to one of the computer's application programs, this program issues a series of DBMS calls. Each call is sent to the DBMS only after the program has received a response to its previous call. When a call reaches the DBMS, it enters a queue of incoming calls. If the queue is empty, the DBMS processes the call immediately, and delivers a response after its standard response time for that type of call. If the queue already contains one or several other calls waiting to be processed, the DBMS is currently processing the first call of the queue. The queue is managed as a First In First Out (FIFO) queue: the calls are processed in order of arrival. Since there is no multithreading, the DBMS is a unique server that processes only one call at a time. The simulation program makes note of the time t_1 when a call was initiated, and of the time t_2 when the answer was returned; the difference $d = t_1 - t_2$ is the response time.

The simulation runs for enough time to become a valid experiment. The response times are plotted against their frequency, yielding distributions like the one in figure 6.1. The time d_{90} such that 90% of response times d are less than d_{90} is of particular interest.

90% OF TRANSACTIONS ARE EXECUTED IN LESS THAN 3.2 SECONDS (d_{90}).
95% OF TRANSACTIONS ARE EXECUTED IN LESS THAN 3.5 SECONDS.

6.1.3.4   Simulation Using a Running Model of the Application
The best way to predict the future performance of a database application is also the most expensive: a benchmark running on the actual computer, with the actual DBMS.

The following programs must be developed, to emulate the functional specifications described in the MSD transaction slips, view slips, and access path slips.

1. *An interactive DBMS call emulator*   This emulator program is an *interpreter*, which sends to the DBMS the successions of calls specified in the MSD functional specs. It emulates the work of one VDT user, with his response times and exact usage scenarios.

The succession of calls to be performed (as specified by the view slips) is described in a file, which is loaded by the emulator at the beginning of execution. After it has received one DBMS response, the emulator waits during a time T_u (randomly distributed) before it initiates its next call. When a screen display is performed, it comprises a volume of characters transmitted equivalent to the exact screen formats specified in the MSD slips. Thus the load generated by screen displays is emulated. The load of keyboard inputs is considered too small to be significant, and the corresponding input data are made up artificially by the interpreter to emulate actual key-in.

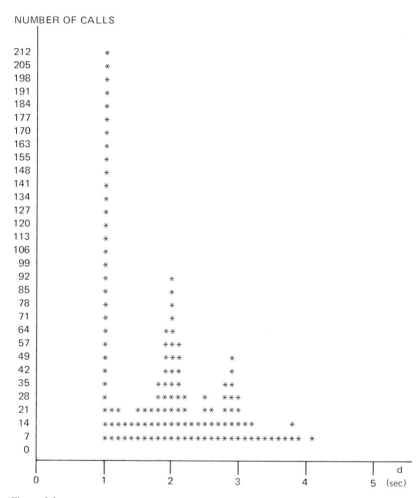

Figure 6.1
Response time distribution.

The benchmark runs a number of such emulator programs equal to the number of future interactive application programs. Program memory sizes simulate those of the future applications as best they can. However, the number of actual VDTs is not necessarily exactly equal to the number planned for the future application; if there are fewer VDTs in the benchmark, the frequency of their displays will have to be increased to represent the actual volume of displays accurately. This may prove to be a problem on some systems because of technical limitations, such as connecting several tasks to a single VDT, VDT line speed, etc.

2. *A monitor program* The various parameters of the benchmark, such as user response times T_u, number of simultaneous users, etc., are entered through a control program, which has its own VDT, and passed to the interactive call emulators. This program also monitors the response times of all the programs of the benchmark, making note of them in a journal file together with the originating parameters.

3. *A batch program emulator* A batch program emulator, similar to the interactive program emulator, is also required if batch programs are to be executed concurrently with the interactive programs. The batch programs send calls (views with dummy data) to the DBMS for processing, but they do not send data to VDTs for displays, and wait for $T_u = 0$ seconds between a DBMS response and the next view.

They are also driven by parameters supplied by the monitor, to which they also report their response times. If some batch programs of the future application will use nondatabase files, these must be included. All files, including the database, must have a size and structure similar to their future structure, but their data are "dummy."

4. *A processor load emulator* If required, the load of programs that require substantial CPU power may be simulated using a processor load emulator. This is a simple program, which loops N times each time it gets control. N may have to be adjusted to a suitable value. Varying N in successive powers of 10 will usually suffice: N = 10,000, or 100,000, for example.

The program is started and stopped by the monitor. On a general-purpose computer, used mainly for business applications, it runs in lower priority.

5. *A functional interface*   If the various database access calls will be verified and reformatted by a functional interface program that will relay the calls to the DBMS, it may be necessary to simulate it. As will be seen below in this chapter, the FI does not really take up power that would not be otherwise taken by standard application programs.

What the model must emulate is the communication mechanism that transmits data between the applications, the FI and the DBMS, and the associated program sleep-wake or start-stop mechanism: these may cause bottlenecks. If reentrance is not available, it may be necessary to test the effect of several FI programs, one per subdatabase, to eliminate the bottleneck. In general, the effect of the FI on performance will be minimal; the communication and sleep-wake mechanisms are quite fast on most computers. An order of magnitude of the CPU times required is 1 msec.

6. *A journal file analysis program*   The journal file will receive many entries from the monitor program: program mix and execution parameters, and response times. A small statistics program is required to calculate and print response time distribution parameters: average, mini, and maxi values, with their confidence and prediction intervals.

Running the simulation   The simulation must start with the conditions that represent the load at peak time and the best set of tuning parameters that have been suggested by the DBMS and operating system specialists.

First a general feasibility test will be conducted, to verify the order of magnitude of response times and general adequacy of the tuning parameters.

After some initial tuning, a sensitivity analysis will be performed to find the most influential parameters:

• hardware parameters, such as memory size,
• operating system parameters, such as the number of programs running concurrently, partition and virtual memory sizes, etc.,
• DBMS parameters, such as the buffer pool size,
• execution parameters, such as the average user response time T_u between calls, the number of batch programs, etc.

The purpose of this sensitivity analysis is to retain only the most important parameters for the subsequent tests.

The last part of the test is intended to find the best set of tuning parameters and the associated response times and maximum throughput. This will help determine the optimal economic hardware parameters and the maximum load acceptable before the response times become too slow.

This part of the test can be conducted as an *experimental optimization,* intended to find the maximum of an economic function of many parameters. The function must take into account hardware costs and the cost of the time when users wait for the DBMS to respond. The constraints belong to the following categories:

· budget limits,
· maximum user waiting time for 90% of the interactive transactions,
· ability to handle exceptional loads that exceed the normal load by a given percentage.

Hypotheses required for optimization   The usual hypothesis required for such an experimental optimization to converge toward a maximum of the economic function is *convexity.* While the mathematical definition of convexity is somewhat abstract, its practical implications are straightforward:

· There must exist a maximum of the function.
· The maximum must not be surrounded with "valleys": a continuous "ascending" procedure must be able to reach it.
· It must be possible to vary the parameter values continuously while the function remains defined.

These conditions are usually met. Note that it is not necessary for the function to be computable; it suffices that for each set of parameters its value can be determined experimentally.

Steepest ascent method   Starting from a known, acceptable set of parameters, the experiments are conducted following the method of *steepest ascent.* In theory this method is not the fastest method when the mathematical expression of the function is known. In fact, when the function is computable, there is no need for experiments, and the experimental error is zero. When experiments are used, there is an experimental error, and the steepest ascent technique is used with probabilities in mind. After the first series of N experiments, the parameters of the next experiment that are most likely to be favorable are those of a maximum gradient line.

The maximum gradient line is determined by a sensitivity analysis performed for each parameter around the current acceptable point. While it is possible, around this point, to vary the parameters one by one to determine their influence, that is not the most economical approach. The best approach uses statistical techniques such as *Latin Squares* and *Factorial Plans*. These techniques are intended for the conduct of agricultural and biological experiments, where the mathematical expression of the function (the yield of crop, for example) is unknown. They are described in books about the *Analysis of Variance* (the one by Scheffe, for example).

When the steepest ascent direction has been determined at one point, the next experiments are conducted at a point located at a short distance in the direction of the line. The experimental process converges toward the maximum as long as the experimental errors do not prevent the determination of the maximum gradient. Sometimes, as the maximum point draws near, some parameters lose their influence, and only the others must vary.

Series of tests   The simulation tests must be conducted in series that last a few hours. After test parameters have been entered via the monitor program, the other programs run until the response times are stable: this may require 5 or 10 minutes for a 50-task configuration, while the various transaction queues build up, and the DBMS and operating system have had enough time to optimize their memory and task management strategies. The parameters and results of the test are then written to the journal file, and new parameters are entered via the monitor; and so on.

After each series of tests, the analysis of the results requires a few more hours; then the next series of tests is prepared and conducted.

Results   The results of this simulation technique have been informative and accurate in a number of circumstances in which I participated in the tests. They proved the feasibility of the application with the suggested database architecture and computer hardware. Tuning and hardware configuration choices were optimized, and limitations were evaluated.

The subsequent implementation of the application will provide a means of computing corrective coefficients for the actual load and response times predicted by the model. Then when the application evolves, the model may be used again to predict the impact of the proposed changes.

6.2   Optimizing Access and Linking Structures

6.2.1   The Dynamic Schema (the Fourth Schema) of a Database

The first three schemas (*static* schemas) of a database were introduced in section 1.3.2. They describe the *logical and physical aspect of the data* of a database.

The fourth schema (*dynamic* schema) of a database describes the *access and relationship traversing volumes*. Each relation or file is represented with access and relationship arrows (figure 6.2):

• *Access* arrows indicate the nature and number of *direct accesses* to that file, as calculated in 6.1.3.1. One arrow is drawn, pointing to the file, for each separate access key of the access volume table. If the DBMS is relational, both direct accesses and relationships are implemented using direct access techniques (indexing in general); therefore the calculations performed in 6.1.3.1 at peak usage hour will suffice. If the DBMS is navigational, interfile relationship traversing volumes must also be calculated and represented as follows:

• *Relationship* arrows are drawn between each pair of files linked by a 1-to-N relationship, which indicate the nature and number of traverses of that relationship that go from the "1" file toward the "N" file.

6.2.2   Qualitative Architecture Decisions

The database architecture decisions comprise

• decisions about the *contents* of each physical file (list of fields) and its record and block *sizes,*

• decisions about the *grouping of files* into areas (navigational databases) or clusters (relational databases) and the appropriate area or page sizes,

• decisions about file *access* techniques: indexes, hashing, etc.,

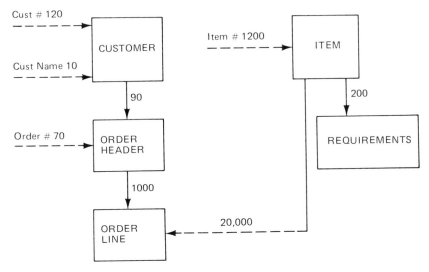

Figure 6.2
Sample dynamic schema of a business database: number of accesses and traverses per day (network database).

• decisions about file *linking* techniques: secondary indexes, hashing, pointer array, etc. (navigational DBMSs only).

These decisions are based on fairly simple rules described below.

6.2.2.1   Deriving Physical Files from Logical Files and Accesses

File contents   A physical file contains a single- or multiattribute key, and all of its associated attributes that are accessed together. Being accessed together means that many or most accesses to a record of that file will access the designated attributes.

In general, therefore, *one* static (stored) relation as defined in the MSD detailed functional specification (DFS) yields *one* physical file. The key of the physical file is the uniqueness key defined in the DFS.

In some cases, however, one or several groups of attributes within the relation are *optional*. This means that a given such group may exist in some case records and not in others.

Example

All customers have a billing address. In general, this is their shipping address too. But 10% of customers have both a billing address and a shipping address. The group of attributes that make up the shipping address are optional, and more frequently absent than present.

Some DBMSs handle optional fields automatically. In ORACLE, for example, the relation must be defined ("CREATEd") with all its attributes, optional or not. The DBMS will not reserve the physical space, in each tuple, for absent attributes; the absence of an attribute will thus not take up any (wasted) space. Such DBMSs are equipped to handle variable record contents, and the automatic verification of the presence of compulsory ("NOT NULL" in ORACLE) attributes. Defining NULL (optional) and NOT NULL (compulsory) attributes is the only decision required from the user.

Other DBMSs feature fixed record contents only; if a field is missing in a record, a space equal to its minimum length is wasted. This may become a problem when

• the percentage of existing occurrences of an optional group is small (10% in the example above),
• conserving disk space is important,
• grouping as many records to one block is important (heavy sequential batch processing).

In this case, optional groups may be stored in a different file, thus taking up space only when they exist. This secondary file must be linked to the primary file using a 1-TO-1 linking technique:

• a pointer from the primary record to the secondary record, if any;
• a uniqueness key of the secondary record identical to that of the primary record, with indexed or hashed access by that key; the primary record must then carry a field (minimum: one bit) that indicates the presence of a secondary record.

The second technique is safer than the first; if, by accident, the pointer of the first technique is lost, it is impossible to associate the primary and secondary records automatically; the presence of the key, in the second technique, makes that link destruction impossible.

Record and block sizes   Choosing *record size* is no user concern, in general: it is calculated by the DBMS. However, when the DBMS features variable record contents (therefore variable record size), predicting the total disk space required by a file is impossible. The user must make assumptions based on the percentage of absent information, or extrapolate the physical size of the complete file from that of a sample.

Choosing *block size* may be a user concern. In the majority of cases, interactive processing causes completely random access to files. In each master file (defined in 1.3.5.4), only one record is accessed at a time: the blocking factor may be 1. In an event file, all the events linked to a given master are accessed together: the block size must be large enough to accommodate the majority of event groups, so that only one disk access is required to access all the events of a given master.

When a large percentage of application runs are sequential, the block size must be as large as possible to minimize disk accessing. Some applications are *sequential by nature;* for example, when a program must run in batch mode (after the daily key-ins are over, for example), and each block has a high probability of being accessed (as is the case for the daily check processing in a bank: each customer's block has a high probability of having at least one movement), then the best processing strategy is sequential.

6.2.2.2   Areas and Clusters
Many DBMSs feature areas or clusters (discussed in 1.2.6.3, 1.3.2.4, and 1.3.5.2, and in 5.2.2). *Area* is a CODASYL term, whereas *cluster* is a relational term.

The decision to group relations into areas is based on the dynamic schema of the database (defined in 6.2.1).

When two relations are joined so often that many or most views that access the first relation also access the second relation, the two relations should be grouped in one area. The *area key* is the access key to the first relation of the view. Each tuple of this first relation is stored in the same physical block as the corresponding (joined) tuples of the second relation: they can all be accessed in one disk access.

An area may contain two or more linked relations. In the example of section 6.2.1, two area grouping strategies are possible:

1. (CUSTOMER + ORDER HEADER + ORDER LINE) and (ITEM + REQUIREMENTS) or

2. (ITEM + ORDER LINE + REQUIREMENTS) and (CUSTOMER + ORDER HEADER).

Assuming that all the access and join operations are executed at peak load hours in interactive mode, strategy 2 is obviously better than strategy 1, because the 20,000 accesses to ORDER LINE coming from ITEM add up to a maximum of 1200 accesses (as performed to access ITEM).

The size of the area must be chosen as a compromise between disk space and the number of disk accesses. Block (or page) size, area size, and buffer pool size are related; they must be chosen as a compromise between disk and memory space, and the number of disk accesses.

All DBMSs that feature areas or clusters have an area overflow mechanism transparent to the user except for the processing time it requires. The flexibility, safety, and performance of the area management software is one of the main differences between good and bad DBMSs; it takes several years to clean out the software errors in that area and document the possibilities and user alternatives correctly.

6.2.2.3 Situations Where a Sequential Index Is Required

This and 6.2.2.4–6.2.2.5 deal with qualitative file access and linking decisions. For both types of physical architecture decisions we shall first try to recognize a case when only one structure can be chosen, and then discuss alternatives, if any.

File accessing situations when a sequential index *must* be used meet conditions 1 and 2 or condition 3:

1. *The access key is selective enough.* This means that even if there are several selection criteria that must be met by the tuples we look for, *one* criterion uses a single- or multiattribute key in such a manner as to eliminate almost all (more than 99%, for example) of the records of the target file. We shall access the file using an index based on that key, and then browse through the target records to find those that match the other criteria, if any.

2. *The type of constraint* on the key is one of the following, where K is the key value found in the database tuples, and C a constant given in the selection constraint:

- $K \geq C$,
- $K > C$,
- $K \leq C$,
- $K < C$:

in short, all types of constraints except $K = C$ and K *not equal to* C. Finding tuples that match $K = C$ *can* be performed using a sequential index, but other techniques are also available. Hashing works too, in that case, but should be preferred because it is often faster.

Even constraints such as K *belongs to a given interval or a given set,* in the strict or soft sense as described in section 4.3, can benefit from the use of a sequential index.

A type of constraint that is frequent in business applications is a constraint on the *first few characters of K,* which must meet one of the above conditions. This can also benefit from the availability of a sequential index. For example, find customers whose names begin with "RO." Note that searching on a criterion of the form K∗ = C (or >C) can benefit from a sequential index, but not a criterion of the forms ∗K = C or ∗K∗ = C (where ∗ is a nonempty character string).

3. *The retrieved tuples must appear in collating sequence.* The sequence constraint is in general not the only constraint on that key. For example, to retrieve the orders of a given customer sorted by due data, a two-attribute key is required: customer-number + due-date. A sequential index on that key will point to the order file.

6.2.2.4 Situations Where Direct Access Is Possible
In some not-too-frequent instances, the numeric value of the search key can be equal to the relative address of the record in the file.

For example, an employee file holds 700 or 850 employee records; the employee number is a 3-digit integer. We shall use a 1000-record file accessed randomly: the record number of employee number X will be X. This simple and fast access method works with all DBMSs that feature the database-key (DB-KEY) concept: the application program can specify a DB-KEY value as a record address to be used by the DBMS.

6.2.2.5 Situations Where a Bit Index Is Required
When many searches use several constraints simultaneously, and each constraint is of the form $C_1 \leq K \leq C_2$, it is advantageous to use a bit index, as described in section 5.2.8.

6.2.2.6 Direct and Indirect Hashing
When the only constraint is of the form K = C, the best strategy is the use of hashing, as described in section 5.2.7. Direct hashing, where the address computed from the key value points to the data file, is the fastest technique.

However, it should not be used when there are too many synonyms, or when disk file space must be conserved. Indirect hashing, where the address points to an index file block, is the next best technique, because it is suitable for situations with many synonyms, yet still conserves disk space.

Note that the existence of synonyms may be an advantage when the hashing technique is used to implement 1-to-N relationships: the N "children" records may appear grouped in the same data block.

6.2.2.7 File Linking Decisions
File linking applies only to navigational DBMSs. The following is a summary of the discussion of section 5.3.

1. List structures must be avoided (poor performance, risk of losing pointers) except when the chained elements are in the same block, page, or area.

2. Whenever the collating sequence of the N children of one parent is not important, the best strategy is to store the children as synonyms in a file accessed by a hash-coded key built on the parent key. However, other access or linking structures must then use a different technique: indexing or pointer array.

3. When the collating sequence is important, or independent access (an access that does not follow an access to the parent file) is required, a sequential index may be used.

4. In all other cases, the only linking structure that combines performance with maintaining a collating sequence is the pointer array.

6.2.3 Quantitative Architecture Decisions

The issue here is choosing among various access and linking alternatives after the various simple qualitative decisions have been made.

6.2.3.1 Principles
Each time a structure decision is made (for example, file F will be accessed by key K using direct hashing), costs are involved. These costs may be expressed in terms of number of disk accesses and processor instructions (or milliseconds) required to perform the various access and linking operations implied by the DBMS calls. For a given file, the number of calls of each type is given (at peak usage hour) by

table 6.3. For a given DBMS, the cost of each type of operation is given by table 6.2. The costs implied by an alternative are obtained by multiplying numbers of calls by corresponding unit costs, and then summing up for the alternative.

Within an area, the cost of following pointers from a parent to its children, or from a child to another child, can be considered negligible because only a few processor instructions are involved.

The various alternatives are then compared. On processor-bound systems, the number of disk accesses is ignored, whereas on disk-bound systems the processor load is ignored; on large well-balanced configurations, a global load called *computer resource units* (CRUs) is calculated, using weighting factors:

- L being the load, measured in CRUs;
- P being the processor load, measured in seconds;
- D being the number of disk accesses;
- K_p and K_d being two weighting factors;

$L = K_p * P + K_d * D.$

Sometimes the L formula also includes disk I/O volumes. The best alternative is the one that minimizes the load.

6.2.3.2 Divide the Database into Subdatabases

Each area, access, or relationship implementation decision may have consequences on other decisions.

Example

An ORDER file must be accessed by order-number (primary key) and customer-number (secondary key). If one of the two accesses is implemented using direct hashing, then the other must use a secondary index.

Therefore the number of structure alternatives can, in theory, be very large! In practice, a database must not be so integrated by its architecture that any individual structure decision may affect many other decisions. Specifying and developing such highly integrated databases may take too long, and the subsequent implementation will probably not be flexible enough for evolutions.

So the first step of a qualitative design process is dividing the database into subdatabases. A subdatabase comprises a number of logically (and perhaps physically) linked files that contain data belonging to one application area, such as accounting, order processing, inventory control, or production scheduling. By definition, no physical link is implemented between data of different subdatabases: they all can be unloaded and reloaded separately. A program can access two different subdatabases at the same time (order key-in may need to access the order processing and inventory control subdatabases). Depending on how the functional interface is implemented (one FI for the entire database, or one FI per subdatabase), a specific multilevel view may access one or several subdatabases.

After the division into subdatabases has been completed (if it had not existed from the beginning), separate optimizations will be performed on each subdatabase.

6.2.3.3 Decide Which Access and Link Paths Are Explicit/Implicit

By definition, an access or a link path is *explicit* when it is physically implemented; otherwise it is called *implicit*. In a relational database, all relationships are implicit, unless a secondary index is implemented to join N children to 1 parent.

When a path is implicit, a view that follows it must traverse the corresponding file sequentially until it finds the records required.

The following procedure can be used to decide which paths may be implicit and which must be explicit.

1. All access paths required by interactive transactions must be explicit because a VDT user should not wait too long.

2. When a collating sequence is required only by batch programs, the associated access or linking structure may be left implicit, and sorting will be used on demand; otherwise an explicit structure must be implemented.

3. When an access or relationship path is required only by batch programs, the various alternatives are

· leave the path implicit and process sequentially,
· implement an explicit path using a known technique, such as indexing and indirect hashing.

Each alternative must be costed, and the various alternatives compared. The result is not obvious in general.

6.2.3.4 Calculate the Impact of Various Alternatives

After the qualitative architecture decisions have been made, the costs of the various alternatives of each separate subdatabase can be evaluated. All calculations are simple, but in some cases there may be a lot to perform. We shall use the example in 6.2.1.

In that example, we made clustering decisions in 6.2.2.2. The situation is now as shown in figure 6.3. There are two areas, the CUSTOMER AREA and the ITEM AREA, delimited by a line. We shall not quantify the structure decisions inside the areas (6.2.3.1), but shall decide what implementations (if any) are required to access the various areas from "the outside," and what physical links should be implemented (if any) between the two areas.

Assuming that all the accesses and links of the previous dynamic schema are performed at peak usage hour in interactive mode, all the arrow paths must be physically implemented. This leads to the dynamic schema of figure 6.4. We shall assume that the results of a benchmark of the DBMS have yielded the values below, where only the processor path lengths (in thousands of instructions per call) are represented, the system being CPU-bound.

Path Type	SELEC-TION	INSER-TION	MODIFI-CATION	DELE-TION
Index (unique/first)	3.5	4.5	3.8	4.0
Hashing (unique/1st)	2.4	2.7	2.7	2.7
Pointer array	0.5	5.7	0.8	0.9

Customer area

1. The access by Customer name must obviously be implemented using a *sequential index*, since access by partial key may be necessary if only the first few letters of a name are known.

2. Of the two remaining accesses, only one may be implemented using hashing, which is faster; the other must use index sequential. Assuming that the distribution of access operations is

Path Name	Total	SELEC-TION	INSER-TION	MODIFI-CATION	DELE-TION
Cust #	120	116	2	1	1
Order #	70	2	68	0	0

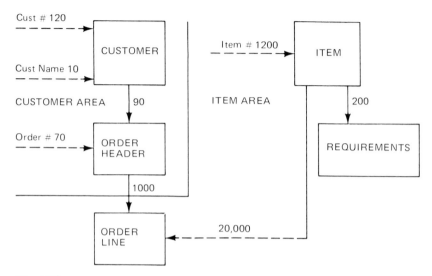

Figure 6.3
Use of Areas for subdatabases.

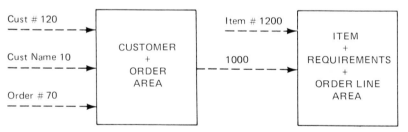

Figure 6.4
Dynamic schema using Areas.

The two alternatives are

A. Cust # is hashed, Order # is index sequential.

B. Cust # is index sequential, Order # is hashed.

The costs are

Alternative A: $116*2.4 + 2*2.7 + 1*2.7 + 1*2.7 = 289.2$
$+ 2*3.5 + 68*4.5 \qquad\qquad = \underline{313}$

      Total   602.2

Alternative B: $116*3.5 + 2*4.5 + 1*3.8 + 1*4 = 422.8$
$+ 2*2.4 + 68*2.7$ $= \underline{188.4}$

Total $= 611.2$

Alternative A costs less than alternative B (about 1.5% less).

Item area   There are 3 alternatives in this case:

C. The order header ---> Order line relationship is implemented using hashing on the order line by order number, and the access by item number on the item file is implemented using a sequential index.

D. The relationship is implemented using a pointer array physically located in the customer area and pointing to the lines of the orders of that customer, and the access by item number is implemented using hashing.

E. The relationship is implemented using a sequential index, and the access by item number using hashing.

The traverse volumes are

Path name	Total	SELEC-TION	INSER-TION	MODIFI-CATION	DELE-TION
Relationship	1000	100	900	0	0
Access by item #	1200	1200	0	0	0

The costs are

Alternative C: $100*2.4 + 900*2.7 =$ 2670
$+ 1200*0.5$ $= \underline{600}$

Total $=$ 3270

Alternative D: $100*.0.5 + 900*5.7 =$ 9180
$+ 1200*2.4$ $= \underline{2880}$

Total $=$ 12060

Alternative E: $100*3.5 + 900*4.5 =$ 4400
$+ 1200*2.4$ $= \underline{2880}$

Total $=$ 7280

Conclusion: Alternative C is by far the best choice.

This small example shows that finding the optimal architecture of a database is simple, but cannot be achieved by guessing.

6.3   The Functional Interface

6.3.1   Principle

The functional interface (FI) is a program inserted between the application programs (AP) and the DBMS. Through the FI, the APs see the DBMS as being relational (even if it is not) and functionally intelligent (which it never is).

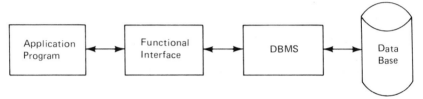

The FI receives from each AP a relational view (defined in section 1.3.1). It performs the functional verifications required before updates:

• tuple insertion or deletion,
• attribute value modification.

These verifications are performed using co-routines, defined in 2.2.3.2. A view received from an AP is transformed into CALLs acceptable to the DBMS. The DBMS executes the CALLs and returns the answers to the FI, which formats the final response to the view and passes it to the AP.

6.3.2   Architecture

The text below is a detailed description of the FI architecture, and of its interfaces with the AP and DBMS.

6.3.2.1   Modules of the FI

The FI contains the following modules (see figure 6.5):

1. The *application program interface* (API), which receives the view from the AP, checks its validity, formats the FI's response to the AP, and then passes it to the AP.

2. The *sequencer,* which defines and initiates

• the sequence of co-routine calls required to validate an update,
• the sequence of relational database operations required for execution by a virtual DBMS (VDBMS).

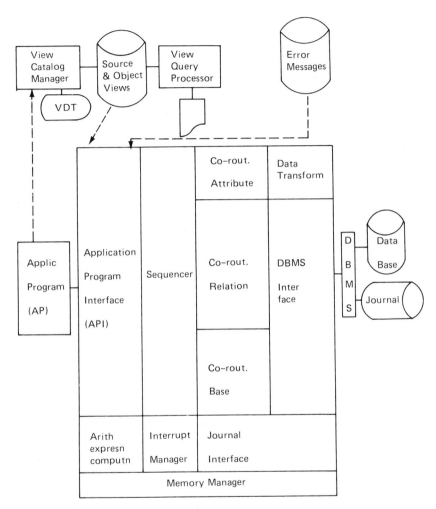

Figure 6.5
Functional Interface (FI).

3. The *data verification co-routines* at all three levels: attribute, relation, and database.

4. The DBMS interface, which converts the calls to the VDBMS into calls to the real DBMS.

5. The *data transformer*, which converts the incoming data described in user format into data sent to the DBMS in encrypted and/or packed format. It also converts the data received from the DBMS in encrypted and/or packed format into user-visible data.

6. The *journal interface*, which manages the view note-taking process required by the backup/recovery/transaction chain restart operations (sections 5.1.8 and 5.1.9).

7. The *interrupt manager*, which handles the uninterruptibility and reentrance processes defined in 6.3.2.10.

8. The *view catalog manager*, which receives the views from the AP or directly from a VDT, verifies them, and stores them in a catalog for future use.

9. The *view catalog query processor*, which displays on a screen or prints views extracted from the view catalog.

10. The *memory manager*, which manages a memory buffer area for the FI.

6.3.2.2   Application Program Interface (API)

The AP sends to the FI a group of data comprising a view number and the associated view execution parameters, such as a customer number, search criteria comparison values, etc. The FI reads the view from the view catalog and checks the validity of the parameters supplied by the AP. If the view cannot be executed, the FI retrieves the appropriate error message from the error message file and returns it to the AP. If the view can be executed, its address in the memory buffer is passed to the sequencer, along with its execution parameters and the identification of the AP.

The verifications performed by the API are

1. Existence of the view in its catalog.

2. User authorization to execute the view.

3. Existence and validity of the execution parameters required by the view in the AP call:

• *Execution flag* (the AP may set this flag for nonexecution when the view is an update operation; in that case the FI performs all the verifications required by the update—the co-routines, essentially—and returns an "executable" or "nonexecutable" answer).
• *List of attributes* (required except if the view is a deletion).

When the view is a *selection*, the list must be a subset of the list included in the view. If the AP does not supply this list, the FI assumes that all the attributes required in the view are requested by the AP.

When the view is a *modification*, the list includes the constants of the arithmetic expressions described in the view. These constants must be used by the FI in combination with the attribute values found in the selection (see 5.1.5.4 for important information).

When the view is an *insertion*, the attributes of the list are also constants required by the arithmetic expressions described in the view; they are also used in combination with attribute values coming from the tuple to be inserted. This tuple is unique, or it may belong to a relation when the AP has requested that all the tuples of the relation be inserted in the database. When the tuple is unique, all its attribute values are supplied by the AP; otherwise they come from the relation file.

As to the *contents of the view catalog,* the catalog contains 2 files, managed by the DBMS:

• the view "source" file, which stores views that are verified and ready for use by the API;
• the view "object" file, which stores the DBMS declaration and execution statements required by the DBMS for the execution of each view.

A: Contents of a Source View (see 2.2.3.5)

A *view number,* used as a primary access key to the view.

An *operation type:* insertion, modification, deletion, or selection.

A *selection hierarchy,* which contains three elements per level:

• the *access* or relationship path P. . . used to access the file by a key or relationship (join) path in a specified collating sequence,
• the *target file* accessed,
• the *search constraints* (attribute, operator, arithmetic expression

used to compute the comparison value or set identifier when the operator is "belongs to" or "does not belong to"), as described in chapter 4.

This selection hierarchy is used to retrieve the tuples that make up the result of a selection, or will be deleted or modified. When the view is an insertion, the selection is used to *verify the uniqueness* (when it must be guaranteed) and/or *find the location* where the new tuple will be inserted (when the collating sequence of the tuples must be maintained). The DBMS may or may not perform the appropriate selection automatically.

An attribute list (except for deletion).

• When the view is a *selection,* the list contains attribute numbers and arithmetic expressions that define virtual attributes.

• When the view is a *modification* or *insertion,* the list contains couples (attribute number, arithmetic expression). In such an arithmetic expression,

> • the attributes must come from the selection used to retrieve each tuple to be modified, or from a file of tuples to be inserted (the operation is then a UNION if no virtual attributes are used),
> • the additional parameters to be added, subtracted, multiplied, or divided with the attributes above may be constants supplied by the view or values of variables supplied by the AP.

The *name of a file,* which contains the input tuples to be used in the insertion or the output file to be used with a selection (import/export).

In addition to the number of the view, *the AP supplies the following parameters:*

A *user number,* to be compared with the set of numbers authorized to use the view.

An *execution flag,* which indicates whether the (update) view must be executed with its parameters or the FI must only verify if it could be executed. This validation capability is used by programs that want execution to be initiated only after the validity assurance and more computations on their part. The result returned by the FI is an integer: 0 if the view could be executed, or the number and text of an error message if it could not. A 0 result is meaningful only at the time the verification was performed, because a database evolution or update may change the data before an actual execution of the view takes place. Therefore if an actual execution is subsequently requested by the AP, the verifications are performed again.

The *constants* of the arithmetic expressions used to calculate the comparison values of criteria, to evaluate arithmetic expressions for virtual attributes used in modification or insertion. The arithmetic expressions proper are described in the view itself, but some of the constants can belong to the view, while others are supplied by the calling AP.

Generally, the only parameters included in the cataloged view that need to be fixed are the identifiers of the attributes (A. . .), relations (R. . .), and access/relationship paths (P. . .).

B: Contents of an Object View

An object view contains the DBMS statements required for the data definition and manipulation associated with each source view.

If the DBMS requires the precompilation of such statements within the calling program, these statements are inserted in the code of the FI and precompiled with it; the FI must then be recompiled each time a view is added, and its DBMS interface module contains many DBMS data definitions and call statements. This method is not very flexible, but its execution performance is good.

If the DBMS dynamically interprets the calls, no precompilation is necessary; the calls are sent by the FI to the DBMS as required, and the object view is not needed.

The *views of the catalog are created and updated* by the view catalog manager, from descriptions received from a VDT or an AP. It is therefore possible to create views dynamically during execution, for immediate or subsequent use.

6.3.2.3   The Sequencer

Principle
The sequencer receives from the API a view and also execution parameters.

If the execution flag is set to "noexecution," no locking is performed. If it is set to "execution," each verification or access operation that requires locking to prevent access conflicts or ensure consistency will lock the corresponding tuple, attribute, and/or the associated data dictionary definitions.

Locking is performed by the FI using its interrupt manager module. It is a *logical* locking mechanism; the FI will not start sequencing other potentially dangerous accesses to the locked data elements, and will not let evolutions alter data definitions in use before the end of the current view execution.

Note that even multilevel *selections* must be protected against the evolution or update of tuples it accesses, to prevent inconsistent results. So even selections may require locking if they reach several levels.

When the AP has requested an update, the sequencer determines the co-routines to be executed using the contents of the view, initiates their execution, makes note of any resulting errors, and passes them to the API. The API in turn will read the error message file to document the errors, and then pass them to the AP.

For a selection, and for the updates accepted by the co-routines, the sequencer will then determine the sequence of calls to the virtual DBMS that can perform the processing required by the view. The sequencer then passes this sequence to the DBMS interface for actual execution.

While execution is in progress, the data reached that need to be locked are locked. However, when a data element locked for another AP is reached, and the FI needs to access it also for the current AP, the FI first checks to see whether a deadlock situation could not result for 2, 3, or more programs. If the danger exists, the current view is dropped, and its previous (successful) locks are unlocked; the FI will try to reprocess the view later.

In addition, two multilevel update views can be prevented from intersecting by the FI. This preventive mechanism acts *before* an actual deadlock can happen or a data inconsistency can be created: an update is performed only when *all* the locks it requires have been performed successfully, since the update operation is always performed at the last level of the view hierarchy.

The locking technique is described in 6.3.2.10.

A: Co-Routine Verifications

When an insert, modify, or delete operation must be carried out, the FI performs the necessary verifications using the co-routines written separately and then included in its code.

At all three levels (attribute, relation, database), the routines to be called are defined using the identifiers of the attributes and relations of the view, and the data dictionary. Each attribute is associated in the data dictionary with a unique co-routine. Each relation is associated with two co-routines: a relation-level routine and a database-level routine.

The sequencer determines the list of checks to be performed, in order of increasing levels: attribute, then relation, then database.

• When the view is a *deletion,* the selection of tuples to be deleted is performed first; then each tuple undergoes the relation and database level verifications, before actual deletion takes place. The execution of these co-routines may automatically imply other database updates; for example, when an inventory is altered, the corresponding changes must be posted to some accounting file.

• When an *insertion* is performed, the FI first checks the attributes of the new tuple, one by one, using the attribute-level co-routines. Then the relation-level verifications are executed using the relation co-routine, and then the database-level verifications, before the tuple is inserted.

• When the view is a *modification,* the selection of each tuple to be modified comes first. Then comes the computation or direct replacement of each modified attribute, then the three levels of co-routine verifications, and then the actual update.

When a co-routine is executed, it returns an answer zero if none of its rules is violated, or one or several error message numbers otherwise. The sequencer passes the message numbers to the API, which retrieves the corresponding message texts from the error message file and passes everything to the AP.

At *attribute level* the verifications deal with the syntax and the value (which must belong to the specified domain).

At *relation level* the FI checks the presence of mandatory attributes, and the various horizontal and vertical constraints.

For the vertical constraints (such as sum of debit postings = sum of credit postings) it is necessary to wait until all the tuples of a given group that must verify a global vertical constraint have been supplied by the AP. As each tuple is supplied, it undergoes the attribute-level verifications and the horizontal relation-level verifications, and is returned to the AP if erroneous. If correct, it is stored in a work file managed by the memory manager module, and waits until all the vertical constraints have been checked.

At *database level* (and at other levels if required) the FI makes the DBMS calls needed by the verifications to be performed.

The rule about functional checks is simple: *the FI executes 100% of the work; the APs 0%*—their role is merely to implement the scenarios.

The sequencer builds up a table of the calls required for the verifications (co-routines and DBMS), with the names of variables to be verified. It then initiates the calls one by one and makes note of the results. If an attribute is virtual, it is calculated first, before it is included in the list of verifications.

B: Calls to the Virtual DBMS

When all the co-routine verifications are finished, the secondary updates generated by the current view are prepared in a work file. The sequencer now translates the view into a sequence of calls to a virtual DBMS. This VDBMS is relational and complete. It features the five single-level basic set operations: selection, join, project, union, and difference. It also features duplicate tuple suppression and the various vertical operations. It is independent of all real DBMSs, of all operating systems. It is used as a step in the standard translation of the operations of a multilevel view into real DBMS calls. The view is first translated into VDBMS operations; then each single-level VDBMS operation is translated into DBMS calls by the DBMS interface module. The VDBMS calls and their parameters are stored in a file managed by the memory manager module. All locked data elements are still locked, and will remain locked until the DBMS has physically completed the last physical operation of the view.

Translating the views into DBMS calls A view can be

• a *direct insertion* into a relation (union of two relations, of which the second relation may sometimes contain a single tuple);

• a *multilevel selection* where the various relations of the hierarchy are linked by joins using more or less simple access/relationship paths; the result is an output relation S that contains 0, 1, or N tuples;

• a multilevel selection (as described above) followed by *attribute modifications* in the selected tuples of S;

• a multilevel selection followed by the *deletion*, in the last level of the hierarchy, of the tuples of S.

The VDBMS features the following standard operations:

• Single-level selection, with several selection constraints and projection of the selected tuples. The selection constraints can be any of those described in chapter 4, including the set inclusion constraints: "belongs to" and "does not belong to."

• Join with project.

• Union of two relations, with projection of the resulting relation.

• Deletion of selected tuples from a relation, with projection of the resulting (remaining) relation.

Comments on the VDBMS

1. A projection is the last operation of each of the 5 operations above, because that is the implementation that turns out to be the most useful in practice. It includes the possibility of adding to any tuple one or several virtual attributes (this addition of virtual attributes is sometimes referred to as "antiprojection").

A stand-alone projection can be performed using a single-level selection without constraints.

2. Projective selection of a relation R yields a relation S. It includes the *modification* of attribute values by eliminating in the selected tuples the attributes to be modified using a projection, then replacing them with new virtual attributes calculated by the same projection.

Projective selection also includes *uniqueness* criteria (if any), which implies the deletion of duplicate tuples remaining after the projection.

It also includes the possibility of *calculating vertical functions* (sum, minimum, etc.) and using the result in the calculation of virtual attributes of S.

It further includes the possibility to *group* the tuples of S by a certain attribute. For example, if R(Customer #, Amount) can contain several tuples for a given customer, a vertical sum by customer can replace all the tuples of a given customer with a unique tuple, where the amount is the sum of the amounts of that customer. A vertical count can evaluate the number of tuples thus merged into one "total" tuple and add a virtual count attribute to each customer tuple:

(Customer #, total, count).

3. The join operation, required by the theory for completeness, is achieved by associating the current tuple of level N (reduced by projective selection to its useful attributes only) to all the tuples of level $N+1$ retrieved by a selection on that level with the matching criteria; at least one of the criteria involves a real or virtual attribute of level N in the description of the matching condition of the two relations. In the cataloged view, the join operation is described using an access to level $N+1$ based on

• a multiattribute key, where each attribute is real or virtual,
• a group of constraints on level $N+1$ involving at least one attribute of level N.

4. The union operation performs the insertion of one or several tuples in a relation R yielding a relation S. If necessary, S can be maintained in a predefined collating sequence (FIFO, LIFO, or by order of a multiattribute key) using an index. This index is specified in an access/relationship path slip, and used by at least one view, as required by MSD consistency rules. But the existence of that index is invisible to the VDBMS, as are all other indexes: the VDBMS is not concerned with fast access because it does not access any file.

5. The deletion operation also implies selection and projection. It performs deletion as well as the relational difference (the criterion is then "belongs to relation B"). After a selective deletion the remaining relation is projected if necessary. The initial relation R is unaltered, and a new relation S is built when the operation is a relational difference $S = R - B$; otherwise, tuples are deleted from R.

6.3.2.4 Attribute-Level Co-Routines
Each attribute must abide by existence constraints. Some constraints concern the syntax, others the definition interval or domain, etc. All the existence rules that apply to one attribute without involving other attributes or relations are coded in an attribute-level co-routine. This

co-routine is an integer function F(A), compiled independently of other co-routines. It is called with the value A of the attribute to be verified, and returns F.

F = 0 if no error was detected; otherwise, F is the number of the first error detected. A single number, F, will suffice for an attribute, because the potential number of errors is small: syntax error, value outside of existence domain, etc.

After an attribute-level error has been detected, the sequencer will pass to the API a couple (attribute number, error number). The verification of other attributes will continue, but not the relation- and database-level verifications.

6.3.2.5   Relation-Level Co-Routines

Since a single relation may be updated with a given view (when several levels are involved, only the last level is updated in that view), only one relation will have to be verified. This implies a single co-routine at relation level, and perhaps another at database level. However, relation-level and database-level verifications need be performed only if all attribute-level verifications were successfully completed.

At relation level all the horizontal and vertical verifications required by the existence constraints will be performed on the given relation. This will often require database read accesses using the DBMS.

The verification of vertical constraints may require the use of a work file to store (temporarily) the incoming tuples until all the vertical group is complete. The verification will accept or reject the incoming tuples one by one, store only the accepted ones in the work file, and then perform the vertical verifications when the last incoming tuple carries an "end-of-group" mark. The response returned by the FI to the AP after the last incoming tuple is either

• "tuple rejected (attribute or horizontal constraint violation), please send a corrected tuple or a ⟨⟨cancel group⟩⟩ request," or

• "last tuple is OK but group was rejected (vertical constraint violation), so group was canceled, or

• "entire group is OK," update is performed.

6.3.2.6   Database-Level Co-Routines

Each relation has a second co-routine at database level, to perform the verifications that involve other relations. This second co-routine can be

considered as "the watchdog of the subdatabase that contains the relation," which relates it to the subdatabase as the attribute-level co-
routine is related to the attribute; or it can be considered as related to
the relation and specialized in the verification of the external implications of an update.

At database level, an update often generates secondary updates,
which will have to be verified. In theory, this is a recursive process. In
practice, things are simple. The database-level co-routine performs all
the external duties of the existence verification process.

The database-level constraints can sometimes be verified attribute
by attribute after the attribute-level constraints. However, in practice
it is better to

• dedicate one database level co-routine to each relation,
• merge this co-routine with the relation-level co-routine,
• process the merged routines as one routine with internal (horizontal
and vertical) verifications, and external verifications and generated updates,
• send all error messages to the AP, not only the first detected error.

6.3.2.7 Interpretive Relational DBMS Interface

The calls to the VDBMS generated by the sequencer are independent
of the real DBMS. Depending on the features of the latter, the type of
the DBMS interface will be one of the following:

• interpretive relational DBMS interface, or
• interface to another, nonrelational and/or noninterpretive DBMS.

The second case covers the relational and navigational DBMSs with
precompiled definition and manipulation statements, and the navigational DBMSs that interact with the APs through CALLs.

We describe here the interface with an interpretive relational DBMS,
such as ORACLE, SQL/DS, and INGRES. All three also support a
precompiled mode of operation, but here we shall make use only of the
immediate interpretive mode: when the DBMS receives an SQL or
QUEL statement, it executes it immediately, whether it comes directly
from a keyboard or from an AP.

Translating the calls to the VDBMS into calls to such a DBMS is
fairly simple, because the VDBMS operations involve a single level or
a single join operation. Since a multilevel view may generate several

VDBMS calls, it may be necessary to create temporary work relations, and then delete them.

Requirements for uniqueness, collating sequence, and performance can also require the physical creation of appropriate indexes, as defined in the access paths associated with each view. Such indexes can be permanent, like the database relations they point to, or temporary when they point to work relations. In the latter case, it may be preferable to sort a relation quickly rather than build an index.

The answer of the DBMS is a couple (output relation, message of good/bad execution completion) that will be passed on to the API.

Comment on the Generation of Calls to the VDBMS
The one-view-at-a-time generation by the sequencer may be replaced by a preliminary generation by the view catalog manager, but the advantage of this approach is less important than one might think: the final execution by the DBMS takes so much more time that the performance gain would appear negligible.

It is also possible to create manually an object view even for an interpretive relational DBMS, to save the CALL generation times of the DBMS interface. But it is not obvious that the human time spent doing that would be offset by the execution time economies.

6.3.2.8   Interfacing with Nonrelational, Noninterpretive DBMSs
For such a DBMS, the DBMS interface code must contain data definition and manipulation instructions ready to use.

In the general case, the automatic generation of such instructions from the MSD views is too complex to be practical. The following approach may be recommended:

1. The view catalog manager can generate, in the object view, the sequence of VDBMS calls that the sequencer would have created at execution time.

2. A programmer or DBA sees those calls and manually translates them and enters them in the catalog via the catalog manager's VDT interface.

3. The definition and manipulation statements are incorporated to the source code of the DBMS interface and precompiled with it.

4. The DBMS interface provides a view of each database file, which is a flat relational table.

In this context, the generation of VDBMS calls by the sequencer is in fact limited to the supply of execution parameters to the manually generated calls. The sequencer still has to insert in the sequence of jobs to be performed the calculation of virtual attributes, and the definition and manipulation of temporary work relations. Views being relational manipulate one relation at a time, not one record, and the corresponding loops must be managed by the sequencer.

Each DBMS response is passed on to the sequencer by the DBMS interface. The sequencer thus builds, using projects, joins, and virtual attribute calculations, the tuples and relations required; it then returns control to the API.

6.3.2.9   The Views Catalog

The views catalog stores the source and object views originating in a direct terminal input or a generation by an AP.

The catalog manager program handles the input of source views, their verification and translation into VDBMS operations.

The verifications concern

• the existence in the data dictionary of the attributes and relations, and the verification that each attribute indeed belongs to the relation defined in the view,
• the existence of the access/relationship paths,
• the validity of the arithmetic expressions, the selection constraints and, generally, the syntax consistency and integrity of the view,
• the user access authorizations.

These verifications imply the access of the catalog manager program to the data dictionary. Unfortunately this is impossible for many DBMSs; their dictionaries are not intended for access by user-written programs. It is then necessary to develop a computerized MSD dictionary, which is relatively easy and requires only an index sequential file structure with (if possible) variable-length records.

The issue of deciding whether it is the DBMS that manages the views catalog, and perhaps the MSD dictionary, is not very important: the services of a DBMS are not indispensable for this kind of problem.

The only important advantage is the possibility of locking the evolutions on demand, as described in 6.3.2.3. In addition, the use of a specific DBMS makes the catalog and dictionary software nonportable.

Concerning the computerization of MSD, it is important not to expect to be able to use such a tool conveniently outside of a *multiple-window* environment. The specifier and developer who use MSD constantly need the ability to see several (at least 4) slips at the same time. This requires windows. If such an environment is not available, as is the case today on all personal computers, a paper slip system with an additional computerized index sequential cross-reference is preferable to a single-window screen.

The views catalog is also accessed by a query processor, which can selectively retrieve and display or print views and cross-references such as, "In what view(s) is attribute Ax used?"

6.3.2.10 Multitasking, Uninterruptibility
An FI must be able to satisfy two contradictory requirements:

1. function in transactional mode, with fast response times, and
2. manipulate entire relations with sometimes many tuples.

It is normal that a program that requests the processing of a batch of 10,000 tuples should wait a few minutes. But it is not acceptable that a program that needs only a few tuples should wait more than a few seconds. Since the same FI must serve these two types of request simultaneously, *it must share its time among requests.*

The first (and easy) solution to this time-sharing problem is the use of *several FI tasks* at the same time, sharing the processor's time under control of the operating system. This solution is viable under the condition that the FIs process *separate* databases, to avoid potential access conflicts and deadlocks. The help of the DBMS to solve these conflict problems is not sufficient; since the views processed by an FI are relational and multilevel, the number of tuples handled by each view transaction and the possibilities of trajectory intersection are intrinsic sources of conflicts.

So this initial solution is viable only for systems that do not perform updates while they process queries. For example, queries are processed during normal hours, and updates are performed in batch mode at night.

A better solution is available when the operating system features *reentrance*. Then the same FI code can work alternatively for several APs. The logic of the FI is the same for all the APs: it exists only once in memory. But each AP has its own data area in the FI: the data are not shared. The operating system manages the reentrance in transparent mode for the designer of the FI: at any time, the FI works for a given AP with the correct group of data; the system can interrupt the process and make the FI work for another AP with the corresponding group of data, and then resume the work for the initial AP. Time-sharing is thus obtained without wasting memory space.

The locking and nonintersection requirements of 6.3.2.3 require that the FI know, when it works for a given AP, what it has started to do for the other APs. This in turn requires the existence of a common non-reentrant area of memory, where the FI can make note of the various relations, tuples, and attributes it has logically locked for an AP, and must therefore be kept unavailable to the other APs.

This in turn requires the possibility for the FI of making and reading notes about locked data without being interrupted by the reentrance process: this is achieved through *uninterruptibility*. The FI that wants to make notes, read notes, or delete notes asks the operating system not to interrupt it until further notice. It keeps control of the processor during the (very few) instructions required to access a memory table, and then tells the system that it can again be interrupted. No I/O operation is involved during the uninterruptible phase.

This strategy is implemented using the interrupt manager. Its net effect is that the APs ignore the notions of locking, access conflict, and deadlock. In spite of the duration of multilevel, multituple operations, conflicts will be prevented before they can possibly happen. Note that, besides uninterruptibility, another necessary condition to prevent conflicts in a manner transparent to APs is that each view must be *self-contained:* it must define all the selections and calculations required. This is often possible, but not always. When it is impossible because the nature of the processing is procedural, and outside of the scope of the relational definition capabilities, a program may require the processing of several views to complete a single transaction. We have seen in 5.1.8.3 that the feature required when logical conflicts occur in that case is *transaction-chain restart,* with such possibilities as COMMIT + ROLLBACK and logging "before images *and* views," and that the FI also has an important role to play in that case.

Note that with an FI the DBMS no longer needs to lock data. This may be possible, and may turn out to be an advantage in terms of performance with some DBMSs.

6.3.2.11   Functional Journaling

The FI must use the DBMS to write and maintain its transaction journal, and recover it in case a breakdown occurs.

Besides the views and parameters transmitted to the FI, a good protection of the application programs also requires the safe storage of

• the screen image associated with each start of transaction chain where it might be necessary to return,

• the values of various variables at that time.

The AP therefore sends to the FI a special message that means "start of transaction chain" with the above data. By default such a message may terminate the previous chain, but upon program termination an "end" message is still necessary. The FI adds to this message a *time stamp* or a field intended to synchronize it with the before images managed by the DBMS, and sends it to the DBMS for safe storage in a logically sequential file.

When recovering from a breakdown, the DBMS sends to the FI the last "start of chain" message, and restores the files to the corresponding status using the "before" images. The programs are restarted, and send a "handshake" message to the FI requesting permission to work with it. The FI answers that there was a malfunction, and sends the screen and variable data that need to be restored; the APs then set the variables to the correct restart values and display the corresponding VDT images, and the effect of the breakdown is "forgotten."

To undo a transaction chain, an AP sends to the FI an appropriate message; the FI then has the DBMS perform the rollback using the before images. The FI then uses the DBMS to retrieve the views processed since the chain started, and reprocesses all those not canceled by the message of the AP. Each view is rechecked before execution in the new context, to trap functional impossibilities caused by the cancellation. The FI sends to the AP the list of errors generated by the undoing process, if any, so that the AP may take the appropriate action.

6.3.2.12   Data Representation, Packing, and Encryption

The definition of these transform operations is given in chapter 3. The FI can process them in a manner transparent to the AP. During an update, the transforms will be executed after the co-routine verifications. During a selection, the transforms will be executed before returning an answer to the AP: the DBMS will work with transformed data.

The use of transformed data is not transparent to the DBMS interface, which must adapt its DBMS calls to process the new formats. For example, the DBMS will perform the search operations comparing packed input values to packed database values. This will accelerate the search process, since packed data comparisons are faster, and only the elements passed to the AP will be unpacked.

6.3.2.13   Temporary Work Files

The memory manager module handles the work files required by the FI. These work files are memory resident as often as possible to avoid unnecessary disk or DBMS I/O. They are managed like *virtual memory arrays,* which are memory arrays that can reside on disk when memory space is not sufficient, but are swapped back and forth between disk and memory transparently for an accessing program. If the virtual storage mechanism is efficient, the use of arrays will cost fewer instructions to access than the READ or WRITE statements—as much as 100 times fewer.

This virtual memory capability can be obtained through the operating system or be managed by the FI. A mechanism such as the CALLOC and MALLOC routines of MICROSOFT's C language implementation (version 3) under MS-DOS and XENIX can make the development of virtual memory routines reasonably simple.

6.3.2.14   Virtual Attributes

Virtual attributes are calculated using arithmetic expressions, using the standard operators: $+$, $-$, $*$, $/$, $**$ (exponentiation), and parentheses. The evaluation of an arithmetic expression is performed using a memory stack where the operators and operands are stored in "Polish notation" form.

Since the values of the variables are known only at execution time, the FI must evaluate the expression. A special arithmetic expression calculation module will be included in the FI. The expressions will be prepared in Polish notation form when views are stored in the catalog; then the sequencer will prepare the variable assignments required before the actual calculation takes place in the special module.

6.3.2.15   The Functional Interface as a Package

A general FI program, usable for a wide variety of applications in a variety of environments, seems to be a good idea.

Unfortunately, developing such a standard software package implies finding solutions to a number of architecture issues, including

1. communication technique between the FI and the AP, which may vary with the operating system and language,
2. communication between the FI and the DBMS: same problem as issue 1,
3. co-routines, which are application specific,
4. memory management module, which may depend on the virtual memory capability,
5. formats of data (numbers, character strings, dates. . .) that are a function of the language and the hardware,
6. multitasking, reentrance, and interrupt management, which are operating system functions.

An FI package must therefore be specialized for an operating system and language environment. Each time a new application is implemented, or an evolution of a currently operational application is planned, the co-routines and perhaps the DBMS interface will have to be updated.

When the DBMS changes, most FI modules may remain unaffected. In all cases, the FI's main advantage—isolating APs from the DBMS—remains. In the worst case, 80% of the FI may need rewriting, but not the many APs.

6.3.3   Performance Issues

The services provided by the FI may seem impressive. But how much do they cost in terms of processor load and memory space?

• The cost of executing the co-routines is obviously the same with or without a FI, since the same verifications need to be performed.

• Storing the co-routines only once in the FI may save memory space in comparison with a possible duplication in separate programs.

• Calling the DBMS from an AP or from an FI implies the same calls.

• Handling access conflict prevention within the FI will often cost less than the locking-unlocking-backout mechanism of the DBMS.

• Executing self-contained multilevel relational views, each one equivalent to several navigational DBMS calls, decreases the number of messages exchanged with APs. The APs will be able to spend less time in memory because they have less to do, and they will be swapped in and out of memory faster since they are smaller.

• The cost of intertask communication between the APs and the FI is a supplement. In practice, however, it turns out to be quite small: about 1 msec on a minicomputer.

• The cost of retrieving a view from the catalog at each AP call can be dramatically decreased if the memory management module is used correctly; the most frequently used views will in fact be memory resident.

• The size of the technical modules of the FI in memory is small compared with the DBMS and its buffer pool.

All in all, the presence of the FI is reasonably neutral from a resource standpoint.

6.3.4   Conclusion: Pros and Cons of the FI Technique

The first disadvantage of the FI approach is that it is widely unknown! Few DP specialists have heard of it, and few computer sites use it, so no one ever writes about it, and no DP course teaches it. . . .

The second disadvantage is its technical level. The system concepts required frighten many DP professionals who are used only to trivial algorithms, simple architectures, and COBOL-type languages in business applications.

The third disadvantage is . . . portability! The FI isolates the APs from the DBMS, and this provides portability, which is why hardware manufacturers and DBMS vendors are against it.

The main advantages are

Centralized functional data verification using co-routines   The APs no longer have existence verifications to perform. When a data element in the database is erroneous, it is no longer necessary to find which AP is responsible; adding more and tighter controls to the co-routines will suffice. It is no longer necessary to check that programmers implement all necessary syntax, consistency, and integrity verifications, and that the implementations are the same from one programmer to the next.

Simpler programs Without all the data verification, with externally stored multilevel views, and without some calculations and data transforms, the programs are much shorter.

Faster application development and maintenance The development and debugging speeds vary like the square or the cube of the length of the program. Programs that use the FI are not only shorter, they are are fundamentally simpler; their architecture is the exact replica of the hierarchy of transactions, each module being the image of the scenario it supports.

When the database undergoes an evolution, the use of stored multilevel views protects the program better than direct DBMS interfacing. Program-to-data independence is enhanced to program-to-structure independence. During each access, the program always sees the database as a unique flat table; this makes its structure simpler, therefore saving development and maintenance time.

Distributed competence Programmers who use an FI no longer have to learn the DBMS language(s) and its operation procedures. Actually they no longer use disk I/O, or only for simple work files. They can easily benefit from transaction chain restart and full database + screen image + program variable protection in case of breakdown.

The developer of the FI must master its system-type techniques. But one specialist is easier to find and train than many, and he will love the challenge of developing the FI technical modules.

Independence from the DBMS, portability Being able to change DBMS is sometimes an advantage—for example, when the same program must run in different environments, or when the evolution and continued availability and maintenance of the DBMS are uncertain.

Security The FI separates data representation and structure from APs. It is easier to encrypt the data and conceal the existence of fields, files, relationships, and access paths from programs. The FI, being unique, is easier to protect than many programs and files. The distribution of competence can help prevent some programmers from knowing too much about the database.

The right way of implementing transaction chain restart We saw in sections 5.1.8 and 5.1.9 that the FI approach is the only one that guarantees correct, transparent backup/recovery and transaction chain restart capabilities.

Improving the performance of some DBMSs   Some DBMSs, such as ORACLE Version 4, feature data locking at table level only instead of page, tuple, or tuple attribute level. This implementation strategy has tragic consequences when the number of APs that can update the same table simultaneously increases, or when batch programs are executed concurrently with interactive programs: the number of access conflicts increases rapidly.

The FI can help improve the situation:

• Its multilevel views are executed faster in uninterruptible mode, without returning control to the AP, thus decreasing the probability of conflicts.

• The FI detects conflicts and deadlocks before they happen, not after, thus suppressing the need for time-consuming dynamic backouts and DBMS lock/unlocks.

• The FI can "lock" at tuple or even tuple attribute level.

6.3.5   Limited Functional Interfaces

The FI has many features, functions, and benefits. But in many situations the user does not need so many possibilities; the development of the FI is then simpler.

Example: FI without a DBMS

In many cases (single-tasking personal computers, systems where all updates are performed in batch mode without concurrent interactive query), there is no DBMS and no need to handle many concurrent database access requests. The FI is then much simpler:

• Multiple simultaneous queries are handled by as many FIs as required, in multitasking mode, with or without reentrance.

• The DBMS interface contains one specialized access module per physical database file. That module makes the file appear like a flat table to the outside world.

• There is no journaling, no uninterruptibility.

6.4 The Decision Machine

6.4.1 Purpose

The decision machine (DM) is to the programs what the FI is to the data. The DM manages program starting and stopping, in accordance with the MSD dynamic co-routines. It will start a program when the co-routines and environment conditions authorize execution.

When it is implemented with its execution rules, the DM simplifies the daily running of the programs:

• It will authorize program starting only when the conditions are met.
• It can automatically start a program on a certain date, at a given hour, or whenever predefined conditions exist.
• When a program stops, the DM automatically initiates the termination co-routine defined in the MSD specifications.
• Depending on the environment conditions (available resources: memory, peripherals, etc., or other tasks currently executing) and the historic context (previous task executions), a program may be started with different parameter sets.
• The DM can communicate with the APs to receive or supply information about the environment or historic context, and make note of program messages about the progress of its execution.

In short, the DM is an advanced form of job control system. It is intended to make running a multitasking computer simpler, and allow novice users to initiate immediate or deferred program execution safely.

6.4.2 Principle

In the following text the word "program" will be used without regard to the level of transaction (in the MSD sense). We shall talk about starting and stopping a program, whether this is a large, free-standing program, or a small task of a large program, or a sequence of chained tasks. We shall use the word "date" to designate a date, an hour, or a date + hour combination.

6.4.2.1 Parameters and Consequences of a Program Starting Decision
The conditions required to start a program belong to 3 categories:

1. The *historic* conditions take into account the program executions that happened previously and are now finished. Each condition (or program initiation rule) concerns itself with one or several past events, stored in a history file with the following information elements:

• *Name* of the program subject of the event.
• *Date* (year, month, day, hour, minute, second) of the event.
• Value of each *status variable* of the program at the time of the event. The number of these variables is not limited. Each variable describes an aspect of the execution: the number of transactions processed, the number of errors, correct termination, etc.

Each AP with an event of interest to communicate sends it to the DM using a message with the above contents.

2. The *context* decisions describe the hardware, software, executing program mix, and startup conditions at one point in time. For example, available disk space, system date and time, software version, files on-line, tasks running, user permission to run a given program.

3. The program *startup status:*

• 0—startup not planned,
• 1—startup requested, will be performed as soon as the conditions are met,
• 2—currently executing.

When a program is started, 3 additional events may take place:

a. The DM passes initial parameter values to the program.
b. The DM plans the startup of the program's successor (another program or an end co-routine module), which will start as soon as the current program has sent a message saying that it is stopping, assuming that no other condition prevents the successor from starting.
c. The DM evaluates the consequences of the program's startup to prepare future decisions.

6.4.2.2 Schematic Operation of a Decision Machine
The decision machine does not execute permanently (see figure 6.6). It wakes up when

• a message reaches it, coming from its direct VDT interface or its AP interface,

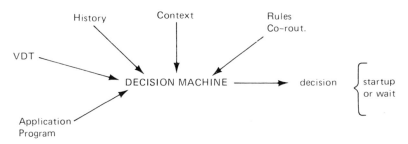

Figure 6.6
Schematic operation of a decision machine.

• a certain date (and hour) has arrived (the system wakes up the DM after a preset waiting time).

This is how the DM immediately makes note of new events, requests for program startup, or information. The DM can go to sleep after it has asked the operating system to wake it up after some time, or at a certain hour; it will then check to see whether the time to start a program has come. If an event, message, or request arrives before the scheduled wake-up time, the operating system wakes up the DM immediately to process it (see also figure 6.7).

6.4.3 Architecture

6.4.3.1 Processing History File
This file stores the event messages sent by the programs (or the operating system in case an abort occurs). Its contents have been described in 6.4.2.1. It has two index sequential access modes:

• by name of program and date of event,
• by date of event.

The operations on this history file are

Appending an event: When a program sends several messages during the same run, only the *last* value of each status variable is memorized in a unique message comprising all variables with the date of the last message sent. This is intended to decrease the volume of the history file.

Deleting obsolete events: When events have become too old, depending on the program name and the date, their corresponding final messages are deleted.

If one or several of the conditions below exist:							
Message request startup coming from VDT or AP	Message cancel[g] request[d] from VDT or AP	Rule that requests startup	Request in queue	Startup rule that applies	Rule that cancels immediate startup request	Inhibit rule that applies	Result Action of DM
yes no yes	no no no	no yes yes	no no no	does not matter	no no no	does not matter	Place request in queue
does not matter	yes no yes	does not matter	yes yes	does not matter	no yes yes	does not matter	Cancel request
does not matter	no	does not matter	yes	yes	no	no	Startup
yes	yes						Contra-diction
		yes			yes		
				yes		yes	
				yes	yes		

Figure 6.7
Actions of the decision machine resulting from the existence of messages, requests, and rules.

Retrieving events that match given selection criteria: name of program, date, and value of status variable. The answer can be provided

· on the requesting VDT or a printer,
· in the requesting AP's interprogram communication area, within the limit of the size of that area.

6.4.3.2   Authorization File
In addition to user authorizations associated with a view (6.3.2.2), the DM can handle authorizations associated with a program or to its own operations. These authorizations are stored in a file (user number, authorized program).

This file is indexed by two sequential indexes:
- by user number and program name,
- by program name.

Using the first index it is possible to know what programs are available to a given user.

The operations on this authorization file are

- *Granting* an authorization (ignored if it already exists).

- *Revoking* an authorization (ignored if it does not exist).

- *Retrieving* existing authorizations by user number and/or program name, the output being similar to the output of the history file.

These operations should be protected, for example, with the dynamic password described in 3.2.2.

6.4.3.3 Startup Queue

The startups requested but not yet executed are stored in a waiting queue. In this queue, a startup request comprises two attributes:

- the date after which a program may be started (called "earliest start-up date"),
- the name of the program to be started.

This file is kept sorted by order of increasing date.

Operations on the queue are

Inserting a startup request.

Dropping a given request, or all the requests that match given criteria.

Finding the Nth request, or the requests that meet some program and/ or date conditions. (Finding the Nth request is useful for the scanning process performed frequently by the DM.)

This queue is stored on disk as long as it contains at least one request.

6.4.3.4 Startup Rules File

This file stores the rules that govern startup and startup inhibition. It does not store *immediate* startup requests; to start a program at once, a request coming from the DM's VDT or an AP is necessary, and this request must have reached the DM (and have been placed in the start-up queue) before the DM examines its rules. The rules file can store *deferred* startup rules; when the conditions are met, the DM will first convert a deferred startup rule into an immediate startup request in the startup queue; then, the next time it goes through its queue, it may start the program if the rules, history, and context allow it.

The rules file is indexed by the three-attribute key (program name, rule number, rule line number). It comprises two parts:

Part 1. The program name is *. This part contains the general rules, processed first each time the queue contains at least one request.

Part 2. This part contains one group of rule lines for each program. The DM processes only the groups of the programs in the queue.

Operations on the rules file A full-screen editor program creates, displays, and updates rules. A new or modified rule is translated into object rules, and then stored in the rules file. The DM reads the rules file and interprets the rules.

6.4.3.5   Rules Language

Data types

Number (signed real, accuracy 14 digits).
Logical.
Date (accuracy 14 digits YYYYMMDDHHmnSS).
Program Name (maximum length 30 characters).

Constants

Numbers (rules to match variable, similar to BASIC).
Logical (T for TRUE, F for FALSE).
Date (YR. . . .   MH. .   DY. .   HR. .   MN. .   SD. .   or
          DE. . . . . -14 digits-).
Program Name (maximum length 30 characters).

Names of variables

Numeric: begin with an N.
Nn (where $0 < n < 1000$) is a general-purpose variable.
Nprog[j] (where prog is the name of a program and [j] the jth status variable).
NSYSname (where name is the name of an environment variable that

• cannot be assigned a value by a rule,
• obtains its value from the system each time the rule
  NSYSn = ? is executed,

• retains its previous value otherwise.

Logical: begin with an L.

Ln (where $0<n<1000$) is a general-purpose variable.

LSYSname (where name is arbitrary) is an environment variable that follows the same rules as above.

Date: begin with a D.

Dn (where $0<n<1000$) is a general-purpose variable. Its first 4 digits are the year, the next two are the month. . . , and the 13th and 14th are the second.

DSYSname (where name is arbitrary) is a system date (same rules as above).

Program name: begin with a P.

Pn (where $0<n<1000$) is a general-purpose variable.

PSYSn (where $0<n<1000$) is a program currently in execution (same rules as above).

Numeric expression   Similar to BASIC (arithmetic expression).

Logical expression

• Logical variables linked by the operators NON, AND, OR, ().

• Number, date, string and program comparisons of the form (X oper Y) where X and Y have the same type, and oper is one of the usual comparison operators $<$, $\leq$, $=$, $\geq$, $>$, and $<>$. The priority of operators is, as usual, first (), then NON, then AND, then OR from left to right.

Examples

L12.

N080 $<$ 10.

DSYS1 $<$ DE19860218 AND P1 $=$ CUSTINV02.

Date expression   A date expression comprises two dates linked by an operator. The first operand is a date variable Dn or constant YR. . . . MH. . , etc. If the second operand is similar, then the operator must be $+$ or $-$.

If it is a numeric expression, then the operator is $*$ or $/$.

This allows the calculation of the difference between dates (duration), and the product or the quotient of a duration by a numeric expression.

Statements   Each statement is written on one rule line, for one program, or for all programs (program name *). The format is

Program-name Rule-number Line-number Statement

(separated by spaces and terminated by a carriage return).

    There are two types of statements:

· the assignment,
· the conditional block.

The assignment statement   An assignment statement gives a value to a variable. The general form is

Variable = Value,

where Value is a constant, an expression of the same type, or another variable. When the type of the variable is SYS the Value must be ?.

Examples

N001 = 47.1*(N002 − N003).
N123 = NSYSNPROG − NCUST[2].
L010 = T.
D5 = YR1986 + MH02 + DY18 + D4.
DSYSDATE = ?.
P5 = CUSTINV05.

The conditional block   A conditional block is a sequence of statements terminated by a change in rule number, program name, or both, or the end of the rules file. It has the form

PRL   IF logical expression
PRL   START   (optional list of initial parameters in parentheses separated by commas), (optional successor name in parentheses), (optional earliest start date in parentheses)
            (START may be replaced with NOSTART or FORGET, with none of the options)
PRL   Assignment. . .
PRL   Assignment. . .
etc.

where

· The PRLs stand for Program-name Rule-number Line-number,
· START places the program in the startup queue,

· NOSTART prevents the program from starting,
· FORGET cancels any existing startup request, whether the program is or is not in the queue.

The initial parameters of the optional list, if any, will be passed to the program when it starts.

The successor name is the name of an end co-routine or the name of a program that must execute after the current program terminates.

The earliest startup date is the value of the special variable DMIN assigned somewhere in the same conditional block. It will remain associated with the program in the queue.

The list of optional assignments will be executed if the condition specified in the block header is true.

The rules to start a program are independent. The order in which they are written is immaterial. They must contain no contradiction. As soon as the rules processor that scans the rules file has found a condition that applies, it executes the START/NOSTART/FORGET and the assignments of the block, and then moves on to the next program.

6.4.3.6 Modules of the Decision Machine

· The DM has a module to manage each of the above files. One of them is the rules processor above.
· It also has a VDT interface and an AP interface for messages and queries.
· It has an environment query module, which can answer questions about SYS variables and what rules and rule lines were processed, with the corresponding decisions (TRACE function).
· It has a decision module, which works as follows:

Wake up
If queue is empty go to sleep
If queue is not empty:
    Process general rules (program *)
    For each program in the queue:
            For each conditional block until condition is met
                Process the decision and assignments.
Sleep.

The sleep time is specified when the DM is started.

7 Relational DBMS ORACLE
(Product Review of Version 4: April 1985)

New relational DBMSs become available each month. How reliable are they? How good is their performance? Are they professional tools? Are they suitable for applications comprising both interactive and batch programs? Do they feature a dependable protection against the various types of breakdowns, access conflicts, and aborts? And what about their memory and disk space requirements?

In order to answer some of these questions I embarked on a product review of ORACLE, advertised as being relational and portable from the IBM PC to the minis and mainframes.

To make the review more realistic, I became an ORACLE customer. I obtained a complete software license through Integrated Computer Systems (ICS), an educational institution for which I teach database management in the United States and Europe; I read the complete documentation, installed the product on an IBM PC-XT and on a (compatible) COMPAQ. I then developed a small test application featuring order entry and production requirements. Then I ported the application (database and programs) on a VAX 750, on which I developed three additional batch COBOL programs. In this process I had to obtain assistance from the vendor to answer questions and solve a few problems. The text below summarizes the experience.

7.1 Product Description

ORACLE is a relational DBMS, sold with a programmer workbench that generates interactive application programs, a user interface called User Friendly Interface (UFI), and a communication module called ORALINK. ORALINK can transmit and receive portions of a database between any two ORACLE sites.

Physically the customer of an IBM PC-XT license receives three small binders that include about 1200 pages of manuals and 6 diskettes, which contain the software and demonstration databases.

7.1.1 Relational Model

A relational DBMS is a DBMS that defines, queries, and manipulates its database using relational algebra concepts. In relational algebra, files are defined and manipulated as sets, in the mathematical sense. A file is a set called "relation." Its elements are records called "tuples."

A relation is generally represented as a flat rectangular table, whose rows are the tuples, and whose columns are the fields or "attributes." All tuples contain the same attributes: there is only one type of tuple in a relation; in addition, the theory requires that all attributes defined be present in each tuple. In practice, ORACLE allows nonkey attributes to be defined as optional ('NULL'): they will take up disk space in only those tuples where they actually exist.

ORACLE is really relational: it uses only relational concepts. Relational algebra operations are described using a language called SEQUEL (Structured Query Language, or SQL). SQL is also used by IBM for the mainframe DBMSs SQL/DS and DB2, and by so many recent relational DBMSs that it has become a de facto standard.

The relations are physically and logically independent. No pointer is ever used or defined to link the data in two files. Data access is by contents; the user describes the result he wishes to obtain, not the manner in which the data must be processed. This nonprocedural approach uses search criteria (WHERE . . .), grouping (GROUP BY . . .) for counting or totaling, but no such thing as IF . . . THEN . . . ELSE . . . .

7.1.2   The SEQUEL Language

SQL is straightforward, and easy to understand and learn. Two sample data retrieval statements (called SELECTIONS) follow.

"Find the attributes of item # 4870"
SELECT * FROM ITEM WHERE ITEM# = 4870;

The * after SELECT stands for "all" items.

"Find all the employees who live in Chicago and have the same job as Martin. List the names in alphabetical order."

The relations used are

EMP (E#, Name, Job, Dept#, Salary) and DEPT (Dept#, Deptname, Location)
SELECT Name, Location, Salary, Job
FROM   EMP, DEPT
WHERE   Location = 'Chicago'
    AND EMP.Dept# = DEPT.Dept#

AND Job IN
(SELECT Job from EMP WHERE Name = 'Martin')
ORDER BY Name;

The first AND indicates a JOIN operation on EMP and DEPT, which automatically associates each employee tuple with its matching department tuple where the Dept# is the same.

The second AND states that the value of the Job attribute of the tuples we are looking for must belong to the set of employees whose name is Martin. Belonging is specified with IN, and the set (of one employee in this case, Martin) is the result of the SELECT statement in parentheses.

This example shows that SQL describes the answer required, not the search algorithm: it is nonprocedural.

SQL is *simple*. There are about 30 reserved words in the definition/query/manipulation language (compared with several hundred in some CODASYL network systems!). The total number of reserved words of ORACLE is 105, including the system commands, the programmer workbench, the format commands, and the database administration.

7.1.3 Completeness

Some relational DBMSs are not "complete": some set operations cannot be performed without writing a procedural program. ORACLE is complete: it can perform the minimum set of six operations required for completeness: SELECTION, PROJECTION, JOIN, DIFFERENCE, DUPLICATE ELIMINATION, and UNION.

For a manager who intends to ask unexpected, unprepared questions, completeness implies the possibility of obtaining the answer to any question about the attributes of the database, so long as the question does not imply recognizing a data pattern. Fortunately pattern recognition is not necessary in business data processing, or in management decisionmaking. It implies such questions as, "Find a customer whose first invoice is greater than the sum of the next two invoices."

7.1.4 Physical Model

ORACLE handles relations stored in different files. When two relations are logically linked by a relationship that is frequently traversed, they can be stored together in a single "CLUSTER"; this is equivalent to the AREA concept of the CODASYL systems.

For example, in the database of this review, I tried grouping each CUSTOMER tuple with all its ORDER HEADER tuples and all their ORDER LINE tuples. The same disk access to a customer cluster could then also access all his order headers and lines. This is a good performance improvement over completely separated storage.

Access to the data is performed via indexes. A relation can be accessed by an unlimited number of indexes. ORACLE imposes no practical restriction on the order of the attributes that make up an index key. The indexes are stored with a balanced binary tree structure in files separated from the data files. The elementary index atom is a two-field couple, which contains a logical key and a database key; the latter yields an absolute address of the associated data tuple in the database after a hashing conversion.

From the operating system's point of view, ORACLE manages in fact a single physical file called "partition," in which it stores its relations, indexes, and dictionary. It can thus open and manage simultaneously an unlimited number of relations, attributes, and indexes under PC-DOS/MS-DOS, in spite of the limitation of this operating system to 16 disk files open at any one time.

ORACLE can also, if the database administrator instructs it to, manage several partitions residing on different disks. Emulating one such disk in memory, for small frequently accessed tables, greatly increases the speed of ORACLE.

7.1.5 Data Dictionary

The DBMS and all its utilities use a common data dictionary. This dictionary is a database in its own right. It is managed via the same SQL, so it is easy to query and update. It stores the definitions of relations, attributes, access permissions (subschemas), and views, which are predefined queries or other SQL sentences.

The dictionary can be updated while the database is being accessed: new attributes can then be defined without disturbing other users or restructuring the database. New indexes can also be created while the database is being used. The database will not require unloading and reloading, or recompiling or relinking a program that does not have altered attributes. This is an impressive flexibility feature, which considerably speeds up software development and maintenance.

7.1.6   Programmer Workbench

ORACLE features utilities to generate programs to manage the screen and print reports.

Interactive Application Facility (IAF) is used to define a screen form, with the associated input data verifications. It generates an interactive program that will input data to the database, retrieve them, update them, or delete them. One form can access several relations, and one interactive program can comprise several forms. The entire SQL language is available to perform data checking and calculate virtual attributes. (A virtual attribute is a nonstored attribute computed using an arithmetic expression from other attributes.) Multilevel views are, of course, available.

IAF is easy to use. It takes only a fraction of an hour to generate and customize an interactive application that manages relations defined in the data dictionary, including all the forms and data verifications.

RPT/RPF is a report writer that defines the extraction of data from the database, performs computations, and then prints a formatted report. The power of this utility is considerable, and makes it well suited for rather complex batch jobs, which can be developed in hours instead of days. For simpler tasks, UFI will often suffice.

7.1.7   Application Language Interface

IAF and RPT/RPF will suffice for not-too-complex applications, which make up the majority of minicomputer applications, and most microcomputer applications. For complex applications, database accessing can be performed from within an application program written in COBOL, BASIC, PASCAL, FORTRAN, PL/1, C, or Assembler. The programmer may use all SQL instructions, as he does under UFI, to access existing relations or define new relations. In some languages, SQL functions are accessed using a CALL statement. In others, SQL statements can be embedded directly in the program source code; programs are then precompiled to verify and translate SQL statements into CALLs, then compiled to produce object code. In spite of all the data dictionary accesses, a precompilation generally requires less than one minute on a VAX 750.

An interesting capability of ORACLE is defining and storing multilevel access views outside application programs, and then using them within the programs. When this happens, a given program no longer knows the structure of the database; it knows only the names of views and attributes. The database always appears as a content-addressable, single-file/single-record storage box; indexes or other access methods and relationship implementations have vanished. Not only does this make program logic simpler, it also protects programs from data structure changes, a better isolation than the classical program/data independence.

Unfortunately only the C and Assembler interfaces exist under PC-DOS/MS-DOS. This restriction is not a big problem, in practice, since microcomputer applications can almost always be completely developed using only the existing UFI, IAF, and RPT/RPF tools. In addition, it should be possible to write a small assembly language interface between a given application language and the DBMS processor: the only problems are data format conversion and passing CALL arguments.

7.1.8 Direct Keyboard Interface

User Friendly Interface (UFI) lets the user define, store, retrieve, and modify SQL statements without writing a program. UFI is easy to learn and very powerful: one SQL statement, written on a dozen lines, can define a multilevel database access, with the associated attribute values, vertical and horizontal output formats, etc. All data definition and manipulation capabilities exist, and can be predefined for future use, with or without variable call arguments.

7.1.9 Portability

An ORACLE database can be ported as is, including the data, SQL/IAF/RPT/RPF programs, and administrative information on personal computers of the IBM PC-XT family, running under PC-DOS/MS-DOS: DEC/RAINBOW, TI/PC, HP 150, etc.

It can also be ported without modification on minicomputers running under UNIX System V, DEC/PDP (RSX 11M+) and VAX (VMS and UNIX S V) families, PRIME, ATT 3B20, HP 9000, FORTUNE 32:16, DATA GENERAL (AOS/VS), HARRIS (VOS), CONVERGENT TECH, and others.

It can also be ported to IBM mainframes under VM/CMS and MVS. The tests I ran revealed no practical restriction when porting a database between an IBM PC and a VAX/VMS, in either direction. Volume limitations may exist, of course, on the PC, and the response times may differ significantly, but otherwise it is possible to define data and applications on one machine and run them on another a few minutes later.

7.1.10   Linking Two ORACLE Sites: IMPORT/EXPORT and ORALINK

Any two ORACLE sites—PC, mini, or mainframe—can be linked to exchange portions of a database. The data are "exported" by one site, and sent via a communication link or a magnetic storage medium to the other site, which "imports" it into its database. ORACLE features two ways of achieving this communication: ORALINK and IMPORT/EXPORT.

ORALINK can also emulate an unintelligent TTY to start jobs on the remote site. A manager can thus connect his PC to a mainframe, extract data from the mainframe's database, and load them into his PC's database. He can then process the data locally, and send back results for consolidation within the bigger database. I used a COMPAQ and a PC to define the database and its interactive applications, and then ported everything on a VAX 750 under VMS, where I loaded the database using three COBOL batch programs. I then initiated, from a PC connected to the VAX via ORALINK, some selections from the VAX database, exported them to the PC, loaded them into the local database, and used them under UFI. It all turned out to be straightforward, and as fast as a 2400 bit/second link can be.

7.1.11   Documentation and Learning

The manuals are well written. Understanding and using SQL, UFI, the application generators, and linking facilities appear easy even in a self-teaching mode. Each feature or rule is followed by an example. It took me one week to read, install, and experiment on a COMPAQ for most of the capabilities described. I believe I learned easily because I found no exceptions: all rules apply in all situations; there are no "special cases." The logic of SQL is the logic of set theory: it uses few concepts, and its mental processes are natural and familiar to most programmers.

7.2 The Case Study

The case study comprised

- a self-study of ORACLE and an installation on a COMPAQ,
- defining functional specifications of a test application,
- describing the database to the ORACLE data dictionary on a PC,
- generating interactive programs to manage the files,
- porting the application to a VAX using EXPORT/IMPORT,
- VAX/PC compatibility tests,
- developing COBOL batch programs on the VAX,
- measuring processing speed on the VAX,
- testing access conflicts, backup/recovery on the VAX,
- extracting part of the database and porting it back to the PC using ORALINK.

7.2.1 Functional Specifications of the Test Application

The test application features order entry, followed by the batch calculation of production requirements by date and by item. Each relation comprises a small number of attributes; ORACLE has no practical limitation on the number of attributes, so it was not necessary to describe many attributes per relation to obtain a meaningful test. On VAX, the CLUSTERING concept was tested; the first cluster comprised the CUSTOMER, ORDER HEADER, and ORDER LINE relations, so that all the headers and lines of a given customer were physically located in the same disk area; the second cluster comprised the ITEM and REQUIREMENTS relations, so that the quantities required for the various delivery dates for one given item were located together.

The intent was to emulate a daily batch computation of the requirements by item and by date resulting from the orders (attribute RQMTS.deliverydate), and then totaling these requirements by item to update the attribute "ITEM.qtyonorder." On the PC a few sample records of the files were entered manually, but on the VAX COBOL batch programs were used to fill in the ITEM, CUSTOMER, HEADER, and LINE relations (see figures 7.1 and 7.2).

7.2.2 Processing Times

On an IBM PC-XT, the response times are barely acceptable when inserting. The first database access is always slow, because the DBMS must open its files. Subsequent selections are fast: less than 1 second to retrieve a tuple with a given key; sometimes, however, it takes as long as 10 seconds to create a complete order that requires about 15 DBMS calls. Ideally the micro should be at least twice as fast as an IBM PC-XT: a PC-AT or a WANG PC would be fast enough.

On a VAX 750, the response times of interactive applications are generally negligible (I tested the applications on a machine running with only half a dozen active CRTs; I do not know what happens when 30 CRTs access the database concurrently). The batch processing times were

- loading 1120 items: 85 seconds, or 13 insertions/second;
- loading 5000 customers: 410 seconds, or 12 insertions/second;
- loading 18,000 orders totaling 100,000 lines, verifying the existence of each order's customer and of each line's item: 184 minutes for 236,000 database accesses, or 21 accesses/second;
- using secondary indexes in addition to primary indexes increases insertion times by 20% for the second index and 110% for the fifth index.

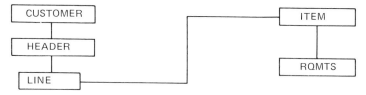

Figure 7.1
Conceptual schema.

Relations

CUSTOMER	(C#, name, st, city, zip, state)	Key: C# (Customer #)
HEADER	(O#, C#, deliverydate)	Key: O# (Order #)
LINE	(O#, item#, qty, value)	Key: O# + item#
ITEM	(item#, price, qtyonorder)	Key: item#
RQMTS	(item#, deliverydate, qty)	Key: item# + deliverydate

Index on	Primary/Secondary	Attribute
CUSTOMER	P	C#
CUSTOMER	S	name
HEADER	P	O#
LINE	S	item#
ITEM	P	item#

Figure 7.2
Physical schema.

Clusters
CUS (CUSTOMER, HEADER, LINE for a given customer)
ITM (ITEM, RQMTS for a given item)

Data volumes (VAX 750, 2MB)

Number of customers:	5,000	Number of items:	1,120
Number of order headers:	18,000	Number of order lines:	100,000

These batch processing times were measured with full recovery journaling. The performance is remarkable. It can be compared with the vendor claims about a navigational DBMS running on an HP 3000/44, a machine with a power comparable to the VAX 750: 5 insertions/second.

IT IS OBVIOUS TODAY THAT A RELATIONAL DBMS IS AS FAST AS A NAVIGATIONAL DBMS: the differences are no longer due to the data model, but to the quality of the DBMS software and database architecture.

7.2.3 Problem Areas

In this case study, the problems encountered were

• two lacks of protection against user errors, which are documentation interpretation problems:

• the definition of a cluster (which requires artificial attributes),

• the format of communication fields between a COBOL program and ORACLE;

• an error of the export/import utility, which does not transfer cluster definitions correctly from a PC to a VAX;

• when multilevel views are executed, ORACLE does not optimize its join operations—the execution is always correct, but it may be very slow if the user has not defined appropriate indexes.

This implies that ORACLE is like all other powerful DBMSs: it requires a good degree of user understanding to perform well. In this area, the vendor's assistance turned out to be immediate and excellent. Incidentally, I learned that the next version (Version 5) optimizes the management of joins since September 1985, and generally improves performance in a number of situations.

The problems above were all resolved, with the vendor's assistance, in a little over half an hour. With those exceptions, the software functioned as described in the documentation; debugging, executing, porting, and disaster recovery caused no trouble whatsoever. Neither did the protection against access conflicts and deadlocks.

7.2.4   Limitations

The relational approach of ORACLE results in some limitations:

• SQL does not allow the definition of attribute groups within a relation. A solution is defining a separate relation in the same cluster.

• SQL does not allow subscripted attributes. A solution is defining, in the same cluster, a separate relation where the subscript is an indexed attribute.

• It is impossible to define the value of an updated attribute as being the result of a selection. In our case study, the attribute ITEM.qtyonorder could not be updated using a selection on RQMTS. A solution is to re-create the relation ITEM, which can be done with insertions that result from a selection, but this may be more time-consuming than the ideal update capability.

• When it inserts tuples (records or table rows) into an existing relation (file or table), *ORACLE locks the entire table:* this is a serious drawback when the number of simultaneous users of that relation exceeds 3 or 4. The response times are then rather poor, and the probability of access conflicts rather high.

To solve this problem, the user should group as much as possible all the insert operations coming from a specific program in small batches, which is what happens with a functional interface (described in chapter 6). ORACLE does that to a certain extent in its COMMIT strategy, but it should lock at page level as all other good DBMSs do today, including ORACLE's major competitor, INGRES.

The technical limitations are negligible:

• number of relations open simultaneously in a database: no limit;
• maximum number of attributes per relation: 254;

• maximum length of a tuple: no limit;
• maximum number of B-tree indexes per relation: 254;
• variable-length tuples, with data compression for attributes and indexes.

The *data types* are these:

• Character: variable length, up to 240 characters.
• Text: variable length, up to 65,000 characters.
• Number (integer, real or decimal): maximum precision is 40 digits, including the exponent and decimal digits if any.
• Date: YYYY,MM,DD,hh,mn,s. Date arithmetic is possible to calculate such things as DATE + X DAYS ---⟩ DATE.

The minimum configuration (IBM PC-XT) is 512K memory, 10MB disk.

7.2.5   Program Development Speed

The total time required to develop, test, and run the programs of the case study was 2.5 days. The time required to understand the VAX and PC communication software (non-ORACLE) was the same; the actual export/import and ORALINK communication time was a matter of minutes. The overall program development performance using ORACLE and its programmer workbench is excellent.

7.3   Software License Policy and Prices

ORACLE prices vary considerably with the size of the computer, the number of licenses purchased, and the level of support committed. Orders of magnitude are $1,000 for an IBM PC-XT, $20,000–$50,000 for a VAX, $80,000 for an IBM 4341. The PC software is not copy protected.

7.4   Conclusion

ORACLE is an impressive, professional DBMS. It is relationally complete, portable, fast, and easy to use. After over 4 years in the marketplace, with over 2000 sites installed, it is reliable, well documented, and supported. The license prices are high, but the investment is quickly offset by the development speed and quality, and the ease of maintenance and evolution of the target applications.

Index

Access and linking structures
areas, 317–318
bit index and, 319
choosing, 320–325, *324*
clusters, 317–318
and derivation of physical files from logical files, 315–317
direct access and, 319
as dynamic schema of database, 314, *315*
explicit/implicit paths of, 322
hash-coding and, 319–320
principles of, 320–321
qualitative architecture decisions, 314–315
sequential index, 318–319
subdatabases, 321–322
Access by element content in extended databases, 289–290
ACCESS BY field, 119
Access by structure and content in extended databases, 291–292
Access by structure in extended databases, 290–291
Access locking, 217–218
Access structure for links and lists in extended databases, 292
Access structure for rules in extended databases, 292–293
Access/relationship path slip(s) in MSD design, *115*, 116–120
Alphanumeric inclusion, 171–172
with "wild card characters," 172
Application development language interface, 203–207
Application interface language(s) deletion, 213–214
Application interface language(s) features, 208–214
insertion, 208–209
modification, 209–*213*
Application interface language(s) linking, 214
Application language interface of ORACLE, 362–363
Application portability of DBMS, 230–232
Application program interface, 202–214
CODASYL, 202–206, *203*
functional interface and, 328–331
object view of, and functional interface, 331
relational systems, 206–*207*

source view of, and functional interface, 329–331
Area(s), 317–318
Attribute. *See also* Field(s)
defined, 38
Attribute level co-routine(s) of functional interface, 336–337
Attribute slip in MSD data dictionary, 91–95, *92, 95*
Attribute verifies a soft constraint, 162–163
Attribute verifies a strict comparison constraint, 161–162
Authorization file of decision machine, 352–353
Average path length for estimation of processor load, 300–301

B-tree (binary tree). *See* Binary tree
Backup, 222–224
Base(s)
for data packing, 130–137
2^n and reducing data packing costs, 142–143
Binary search (dichotomy), binary tree (B-tree), 273–275, *274*
Binary tree (B-tree), 273–275, *274*
Bit-inverted files, 265–268, *266*
Block, defined, 238
Block overflow in index updating, 251–252
Block size optimizing of in index, 247–250

CALCULATION METHOD field, 94
Call execution time, 302–*304*
Candidate, defined, 160
Cardinal, defined, 38
Cluster(s), 317–318
CODASYL, 61, 240
CODASYL application program interface, *203*–206
CODASYL network model of data, 61
CODASYL ring structure, *278*
Collisions in hash-coding, 257–265
overcoming problems with, 258–265
COMMENTS field, 95
Committing to undo multiple transactions, 219–222
Computer load evaluation
average path length, 300–301
call execution time, 302–*304*
types of DBMS calls and, 301–302

Computer load evaluation from specifications, 304–314, *305, 309*
calls per file at peak usage hour, 304–*305*
simulation of DBMS response times, 306–308
simulation of response time using running model, 308–314, *309*
total load at peak usage hour, 305–306
CONSTRAINTS field, 112
Constraints on integer attributes, 173
Constraints on virtual attributes, 172–173
CONSTRANTS:EXISTENCE field, 98
Continuous data streams, 143–144
COROUTINE field, 98
Co-routine slips in MSD, 104–108, *107*

Data
classical models of, 52–53
CODASYL network model of, 61
dynamic model of, 51–54
entity-relation model of, 62–64, *63, 68*
hierarchical model of, 56–58, *57, 58, 67*
master-event model of, 64–69, *65, 69*
network model of, 58–62, *60, 68*
operations of, 53–54
Data dictionary
computer-supported, 89–90
defined, 5
Data dictionary for MSD, 89–122
attribute slip in, 91–95, *92, 95*
relations and attributes in, 90–91
relationship in, 95–99, *96, 100*
Data dictionary management, 200–202
Data packing, 128–159
with compact codes, 132
reducing costs of, 142–143
usefulness of, 140–143
using multiple bases, 132–137
using multiple words, 137–140
Data protection, 128–159
dynamic password, 148–150
encryption, 147–148
keyboard input protection, 150–154
of stored data, 154–159
of transmitted data, 154–159
verification code, 154–159
Data query, methods of, 232–235
Data representation, 128–159
vocabulary (*see* Vocabulary for data representation)
Data representation for technical data, 143–147

coding by dictionary rank, 145
coding by exception, 145
continuous data streams, 143–44
functional interface (FI) technique, 146–147
slow-evolution processes, *144*–145
using functions, 145–146
Data restructuring capabilities, 224–225
Database
for answering questions, 1–2
conceptual schema of, 35
data existence constraints in, 33–35
data fields in, 33
data groups in, 33
defined, 5–7
exhaustivity of, 5
external schema of, 36
for horizontal integration, 2–3
nonredundancy of, 5–6
physical schema of, 35–36
purpose of, 1
schemas of, 33–36
selection in, 160–190
structuring of, 6–7
for vertical integration, 3–4
Database, extended, 282–299
access by element content in, 289–290
access by structure and content in, 291–292
access by structure in, 290–291
access structure for links and lists in, 292
access structure for rules in, 292–293
defined, 283–284
file space allocation in, 284–285
file system hierarchy in, 285–287
law(s) in, 289
links in, 287–288
purpose of, 282–283
record management in, 285–287
rule(s) in, 288
SDL (Structure Definition Language) in, 293–299
storage of structures in, 289
vector function (VF) in, 287–288
Database, needs for, 7–10
application development ease and speed, 7–8
application evolution ease, 8
multitasking, 9
security, 9–10
unpredictable queries, 8–9
Database, relational model of, 40–41
compared to nonrelational, 54–56

connection trap and, 50–51
evolution of, 45
physical implementation of, 44–45
relational algebra and, 45
tuple association in, 48–49
tuple modification in, 45–46
tuple selection in, 46–47
unwanted attributes in, *47*
Database administration, 227–230
Database administration administrator,
  job definition of, 227–228
Database fundamentals, 29–69
views on, 29–33
Database implementation techniques,
  300–357
access and linking structures, 314–325,
  315, 324
computer load evaluation, 300–314, *304,*
  305, 309
decision machine, 349–357, *351, 352*
functional interface, 326–348, *327*
Database-level co-routines of functional
  interface, 337–338
Database management system. *See*
  DBMS
Database project, key steps of, 13–29
cost documentation, 25–26
DBMS choice, 22–25
detailed functional specification, 19–22
file architecture design, 26–27
functional specifications group, 20–21
hardware choice, 22–25
preliminary functional specifications,
  13–18
program architecture design, 27–8
risk documentation, 25–26
sample information flow diagram, *18*
testing, 28–29
Database requirements by application
  area, 10–13
business DP, 10–11
industrial, 12–13
management information systems (MIS),
  11–12
personal, 12
scientific, 12–13
DBMS (database management system)
choice of, in database project, 22–25
and data processing (DP) department,
  4–5
overview of, 1–69
DBMS calls, types of, and computer load
  evaluation, 301–302
DBMS features, 191–299

access conflicts, 217–222
administration, 227–230
application portability, 230–232
application program interface, 202–214
backup, 222–224
data dictionary management, 200–202
data query, methods, 232–235
data restructuring capabilities, 224–225
deadlock protection, 217–222
disk space management, 192–193
extended databases, 282–299
file access management, 193–195
file linking, 195–200
file structures, 236–275
index structures, 243–268, *244*
LIST structures, *268–272, 269, 270, 271*
mapping, 215
multilevel views, 216–217
record linking techniques, 275–282, *277,*
  278, 279
recovery, 222–224
security, 226–227
DDL vocabulary, 204
Deadlocks, 218–219
Decision machine
architecture of, 351–357
authorization file of, 352–353
modules of, 357
and parameters of program starting decision, 349–350
principles of, 349–*351*
processing history file of, 351–*352*
rules language of, 354–357
schematic operation of, 350–*351*
startup queue of, 353
startup rules file of, 353–354
DEF. DOMAIN AND INTERVAL field,
  93–94
Deletion, 213–214
Detailed functional specification (DFS)
documentation produced by, 77–78
need for relational model, 76–77
organization prerequisites for, 81–82
requirements for, 70–79
scenarios in, 74–76, 82–83
sufficient detail in, 70–72
user-oriented approach to, 73–76
DFS. *See* Detailed functional
  specification
Dichotomy (binary search), binary tree
  (B-tree), 273–275, *274*
Dictionary rank, coding by, for technical
  data representation, 145
Dimension, defined, 38

Direct (random) access file, 242
Disk space management, 192–193
DMCL vocabulary, 205
DML (in Data Division) vocabulary, 205
DML (in Procedure Division) vocabulary,
    205–206
Domains in SDL (Structure Definition
    Language), 183–184
Dynamic backout, 218–219
Dynamic password for data protection,
    148–150
Dynamic schema of database, 314, *315*

Element(s) in SDL (Structure Definition
    Language), 182–183
Encryption for data protection, 147–148
Event file, defined, 50
Exception, coding by, for technical data
    representation, 145
Existence constraints, 160–161
Existence constraints, data, in database,
    33–35
EXISTENCE CONSTRAINTS field, 94
Existence in a discrete set, 161

Field(s), 237–*238*
  attribute, 36
  data, in database, 33
  defined, 38
  key, 36
Field update (modification), 209–*213*
File(s)
  defined, 236–238, *237*
  event, 38
File access management, 193–195
  indexing in, 194–195
File buffer, defined, 239
File hierarchy in extended databases,
    285–287
File interface, DBMS-to-Operating Sys-
    tem, 239–240
File linking, 195–200
  automatic, 198
  manual, 198–199
  N-TO-P relationships, 200
  1-TO-N relationships, 196–200
File space allocation in extended data-
    bases, 284–285
File structure(s), 236–275
  binary search (dichotomy), 272–275, *274*
  block defined, 238–239
  DBMS-to-Operating System File Inter-
    face, 239–240
  dichotomy (binary search), 272–275, *274*

direct (random) access file, 242
fields, 237–*238*
file buffer defined, 239
files defined, 236–238, *237*
index structures (*see* Index structures)
LIST structures, *268–272, 269, 270, 271*
random (direct) access file, 242
records, 236–237
segment defined, 238
sequential file, 240–242
FOLLOWED BY field, 112
Functional interface
  and application program interface, 328–
    331
  architecture of, 326–345, *327*
  attribute-level co-routines of, 336–337
  co-routine verifications by sequencer of,
    333–334
  database-level co-routines of, 337–338
  encryption of data by, 343–344
  functional journaling by, 343
  interpretive relational DBMS interface
    and, 338–339
  modules of, 326–328, *327*
  multitasking ability of, 341–342
  nonrelational, noninterpretive DBMSs
    and, 339–340
  object view of application program inter-
    face and, 331
  packing by, 343–344
  performance issues of, 345–348
  relation-level co-routines of, 337
  sequencer of, 331–336
  source view of application program in-
    terface and, 329–331
  temporary work files of, 344
  uninterruptibility of, 341–342
  views catalog and, 340–341
  virtual attributes and, 344
  virtual DBMS call by sequencer of, 334–
    336
Functional interface (FI) technique for
  technical data representation, 146–147
FUNCTIONAL PURPOSE field, 110
Functions for technical data representation, 145–146

Groups, data, in database, 33

Hardware, choice of, in database project,
    22–25
Hash-coded link technique for linking rec-
    ords, 281–282
Hash-coding, 256–265, 319–320

and access and linking structures, 319–320
collision(s) in, 257–265
and index structures, 256–265
synonym(s) in, 257–258
Hierarchical index, 247–250, *248*
Hierarchy, defined, 83
Hollow blocks in index updating, 251–*252*
Horizontal integration, database for, 2–3

IMPORT/EXPORT, and ORACLE, 364
Index Sequential File, 246–247
Index structures, 243–268, *244*
  bit-inverted files, 265–268, *266*
  block overflow and, 251–*252*
  block size optimization, 247–250
  consequences of updating, 250–253
  hash-coding and, 256–265
  hierarchical index, 247–250, *248*
  hollow blocks and, 251–*252*
  performance problems of, 254–256
  pointer, 243
  primary index, 245–246
  search key field, 243
  secondary index, 245–246
  sequential file, 246–247
Information systems, 123–127
  DP database and, 125–127
Insertion, 208–209
Interpretive relational DBMS interface, and functional interface, 338–339

Key(s), in SDL (Structure Definition Language), 298–299
KEY ATTRIBUTES field, 119
Keyboard input protection, 150–154

Law(s)
  in extended databases, 289
  in SDL (Structure Definition Language), 187
Link(s)
  in extended databases, 287–288
  in SDL (Structure Definition Language), 184–185, 298
Linking, 214
LIST OF ATTRIBUTES field, 98
LIST structures, *269, 270, 271*
  backward, 270
  disadvantages of, 271
  forward, 270
  ring, 270–*271*
  two-way, *270*

Management information systems (MIS), database requirements for, 11–12
Mapping for program/data independence, 215
Master file, defined, 50
MEANING field, 93
Minimum difference constraint, 171
MIS (management information systems), database requirements for, 11–12
Modification (field update), 209–*213*
MSD (management system design)
  access/relationship path slips in, *115,* 116–120
  attribute slip in, 91–95, *92, 95*
  co-routine slips in, 104–108, *107*
  data dictionary for, 89–122
  database design phase of, 78–79
  DFS phase of, 70–78 (*see also* DFS)
  objections to DFS approach to, 80–81
  program module design phase of, 79–80
  report layout slip in, 99, 101, 104
  screen form in, 99, 101, *102,* 104
  transaction slips in, 109–114, 116, *111, 113, 114*
  view slip in, 120–122
Multilevel views for program/structure independence, 216–217
Multitasking and database, 9

NAME field, 91, 98, 109–110
Nonexistence constraints, 161
Nonexistence in a discrete set, 161
Nonrelational, noninterpretive DBMS and functional interface, 339–340

1-TO-N relationship, record linking techniques in, 275–282, *277, 278, 279*
  CODASYL ring structure, *278*
  hash-coded links, 281–282
  pointer arrays, 280–*281*
  pointer + list, 276–*277*
  secondary indexing, 278–280, *279*
ORACLE, 358–369, *366*
  application language interface of, 362–363
  case study of, 365–369
  completeness of, 360
  conceptual schema of, *366*
  data dictionary of, 361–362
  documentation for, 364–365
  functional specifications of, 365–366
  IMPORT/EXPORT and, 364
  limitations of, 368–369
  ORALINK and, 364

ORACLE (cont.)
physical model of, 360–361
portability of, 363–364
problem areas of, 367–368
processing times of, 366–367
product description, 358–365
programmer workbench of, 362
relational DBMS model of, 358–359
use of SEQUEL (SQL) in, 359–360
user friendly interface of, 363
ORALINK, and ORACLE, 364

Pattern recognition
database manipulation for, 180–182
detailed, 188
in extended database structures, 179–180
global, 188
image, 187–190
light gradient technique, 188–189
search constraints in, 180
and selection criteria, 178–190
with varying positions, 189–190
Pointer, in indexing, 243
Pointer array technique for linking records, 280–281
Pointer + list technique of linking records, 276–277
Position constraints, 175–176
Primary index, 245–246
Processing history file of decision machine, 351–352
PROMPT TEXT field, 91, 93

Random (direct) access file, 242
Record management in extended databases, 285–287
Records, 236–237
Recovery, 222–224
cold restart, 223
warm restart, 223–224
Relation(s)
defined, 36–45
dynamic, 36–38
N-to-P, 39–40
normal forms of, 41–44
normal forms of, fourth, 41–44
1-to-N, 39–40
1-to-1, 39–40
static, 36–38
RELATION VERB field, 119
Relation-level co-routines of functional interface, 337
Relational DBMS, defined, 358

Relational DBMS ORACLE. See ORACLE
Relational techniques, 70–127
Relationship in MSD data dictionary, 95–99, 96, 100
Report layout slip in MSD, 99, 101, 104
Response time(s), simulation of, 306–308
using running model, 308–314, 309
Rule(s)
in extended databases, 288
in SDL (Structure Definition Language), 185–187, 299
Rules language of decision machine, 354–357

Scenario(s). See also DFS
defined, 74
description rules for, 83–86
sample, 86–89
SCENARIO field, 110
Screen forms in MSD, 99, 101, 102, 104
SDL (Structure Definition Language), 181–187, 293–299
domains in, 183–184
element(s) in, 182–183, 294–295
in extended database, 293–299
key(s) in, 298–299
laws in, 187
link(s) in, 184–185, 298
preliminary definitions in, 293–294
rule(s) in, 185–187, 299
structure(s) in, 184, 296–298
unstructured data recognition in, 199
Search key field in indexing, 243
Secondary index, 245–246
Secondary indexing technique of linking records, 278–280, 279
Security of DBMS, 9–10, 226–227
Segment, defined, 238
Selected, defined, 160
Selection
pattern recognition and, 178–190
using relational algebra, 176–178
Selection constraints
defined, 160
horizontal, 160–173
vertical, 173–176
Selection criteria, defined, 160
SELECTION field, 120
SEQUEL (SQL), 207
use of, in ORACLE, 359–360
SEQUEL/DS (SQL/DS), 240
Sequencer
co-routine verifications of functional interface by, 333–334

of functional interface, 331–336
  virtual DBMS calls by, 334–336
Sequential file, 240–242
Sequential index, 318–319
Slow-evolution process(es) for technical
  data representation, *144*–145
Soft constraint(s), 164–171, *170, 176*
SQL (SEQUEL), *207*
  use of, in ORACLE, 359–360
SQL/DS, 240
Startup queue of decision machine, 353
Startup rules file of decision machine,
  353–354
Storage of data
  with codes, 128
  full-length, 128
Strict constraint, 164
Structure(s), in SDL (Structure Definition
  Language), 184, 296–298
Structure Definition Language. *See* SDL
Synonym(s), in hash-coding, 257–258

Transaction slips, in MSD design, 109–
  114, 116, *111, 113, 114*
Tuple, defined, 38
TYPE SM ± field, 120–122

UNIQUE Y/N field, 119
USED IN RELATIONS field, 94

VARIABLE NAME field, 93
Vector function (VF), in extended databases, 287–288
Verification code, 154–159
  design specifications of, 155–156
  implementation of, 158–159
Vertical constraints, 173–176
Vertical integration, database for, 3–4
View(s)
  in database, 29–33
  defined, 30
  multilevel, 31–33
  single-level, 31
View slip(s), in MSD, 120–122
Views catalog, and functional interface,
  340–341
VIEWS WHERE USED field, 119
Vocabulary for data representation, 129–
  132
  alphabet for, 130
  base of, 130–132
VOLUME field, 98, 110
VOLUME (KEYS) field, 119

The MIT Press, with Peter Denning as consulting editor, publishes computer science books in the following series:

Artificial Intelligence, Patrick Winston and Michael Brady, editors

Computer Systems, Herb Schwetman, editor

Foundations of Computing, Michael Garey, editor

Information Systems, Michael Lesk, editor

Logic Programming, Ehud Shapiro, editor

Scientific Computation, Dennis Gannon, editor